JASHER
INSIGHTs

Book 1

This book is dedicated
to my dear son-in-law
Arturo Londoni and our
precious daughter Clare
Best Wishes   13.08.19

S.N.Strutt

ISBN 978-1-78222-689-5
Book design, layout and production management by Into Print
www.intoprint.net
+44 (0)1604 832149

CONTENTS

INTRODUCTION   10

Chapter 1   6th DAY OF CREATION   16

Chapter 2   SETH: THE IMAGE OF ADAM   29

Chapter 3   ENOCH   40

Chapter 4   ENOCH TRANSLATED   50

Chapter 5   THE RIGHTEOUS DIE   61

Chapter 6   NOAH'S ARK   67

Chapter 7   JAPHETH, HAM & SHEM   74

Chapter 8   NIMROD   82

Chapter 9   THE TOWER OF BABEL   89

Chapter 10   PELEG & THE DIVISION   98

Chapter 11   ABRAHAM DESTROYS THE IDOLS   104

Chapter 12   THE FURNACE   115

Chapter 13   CALL OF ABRAHAM   117

Chapter 14   RIKAYON: NAME OF PHARAOH   133

Chapter 15   FAMINE IN CANAAN   139

Chapter 16   MELCHISADEK   146

Chapter 17   COVENANT OF CIRCUMCISION   152

Chapter 18   CRUELTY OF SODOM   155

Chapter 19   SODOM & GOMORRAH   162

Chapter 20   SARAH & ABIMELEC   173

Chapter 21   ISAAC IS BORN   178

Chapter 22   ISHMAEL   185

Chapter 23	SACRIFICE OF ISAAC	192
Chapter 24	DEATH OF SARAH	207
Chapter 25	ABRAHAM & KETURAH	214
Chapter 26	REBEKKA, ESAU & JACOB	218
Chapter 27	ESAU SLAYS NIMROD	228
Chapter 28	ISAAC, REBEKKA & FAMINE	232
Chapter 29	JACOB DECEIVES ISAAC	237
Chapter 30	BETHEL & STAIRS TO HEAVEN	245
Chapter 31	LABAN	250
Chapter 32	CONFLICT: JACOB & ESAU	259
Chapter 33	SHECHEM	269
Chapter 34	SIMEON & LEVI DESTROY SHECHEM	277
Chapter 35	WAR WITH THE AMORITIES	289
Chapter 36	CHIMERAS	293
Chapter 37	WAR AT SHECHEM	298
Chapter 38	SLAUGHTER OF THE KINGS	305
Chapter 39	SUPER-HUMAN SONS OF JACOB	312
Chapter 40	SUPERNATURAL VICTORY	321
APPENDICES		330

BOOK II (Not included in this book)

Chapter 41   ARROGANT JOSEPH

Chapter 42   JOSEPH IN THE PIT

Chapter 43   JOSEPH SOLD INTO SLAVERY

Chapter 44   POTIPHAR

Chapter 45   WIVES FOR THE SONS OF JACOB

Chapter 46   BUTLER & BAKER'S DREAMS

Chapter 47   ISAAC DIES

Chapter 48   PHARAOH DREAMS 2 DREAMS

Chapter 49   JOSEPH LEARNS 70 LANGUAGES

Chapter 50   JOSEPH THE WARRIOR

Chapter 51   JACOBS SONS GO TO EGYPT

Chapter 52   GOLD FOUND IN THEIR SACKS

Chapter 53   BENJAMIN GOES TO EYGPT

Chapter 54   JUDAH THREATENS PHARAOH

Chapter 55   JACOB HEARS THAT JOSEPH IS ALIVE

Chapter 56   JACOB DIES AT 147 YEARS OLD

Chapter 57   WAR BETWEEN SONS OF JACOB & ESAU

Chapter 58   JOSEPH BECOMES PHARAOH

Chapter 59   LIST OF THOSE WHO WENT TO EGYPT

Chapter 60   DEATH OF JOSEPH

Chapter 61   ZEPHO SLAYS HUMAN-ANIMAL CHIMERA

Chapter 62   MORE OF JACOBS SONS DIE

Chapter 63   A PHAROAH WHICH KNEW NOT JOSEPH

Chapter 64   BALAAM

Chapter 65   PHARAOH AFFLICTS CHILDREN OF ISRAEL

Chapter 66   ISRAELITES MULTIPY IN EGYPT

Chapter 67   AMRAN & JOCABED, MIRIAM & AARON

Chapter 68   MOSES

Chapter 69   LEVITES: NOT FORCED TO LABOUR

Chapter 70   BABY MOSES LIFTS THE CROWN

Chapter 71   MOSES SLAYS THE EGYPTIAN

Chapter 72   KIKIANUS & BALAAM

Chapter 73   MOSES MADE KING OVER CUSH

Chapter 74   MOSES RULES FOR 40 YEARS

Chapter 75   EPHRAIM SLAIN

Chapter 76   ADONIAH THE QUEEN

Chapter 77   THE CUBIT & A SPAN-SIZED PHARAOH

Chapter 78   MOSES MARRIES ZIPORRAH

Chapter 79   MOSES & THE BURNING BUSH

Chapter 80   THE TEN PLAGUES

Chapter 81   MOSES LEADS ISRAEL OUT OF EGYPT

Chapter 82   THE TEN COMMANDMENTS

Chapter 83   AARON THE HIGH PRIEST

Chapter 84   THE EARTH DEVOURES KORAH

Chapter 85   KING ARAD & CANAANITES DEFEATED

Chapter 86   MOSES NUMBERS THE PEOPLE

Chapter 87   JOSHUA

Chapter 88   DEATH OF MOSES

Chapter 89   JOSHUA DESTROYS THE AMORITIES

Chapter 90   JOSHUA DIVIDES THE LAND TO ISRAEL

Chapter 91   DEATH OF JOSHUA

SALVATION

APPENDICES

JASHER INSIGHTS
BOOK I

The Book of Jasher

Referred to in

Joshua and Second Samuel

Faithfully Translated

FROM THE ORIGINAL HEBREW INTO ENGLISH

"Is not this written in the Book of Jasher?"--*Joshua, x. 13.*
"Behold it is written in the Book of Jasher."--*II. Samuel, i. 18*

SALT LAKE CITY:
PUBLISHED BY J.H. PARRY & COMPANY
1887.

This is the Apocryphal *Book of Jasher*. This is a translation of a Hebrew book printed in 1613. Sepir Ha Yasher, the Hebrew title of this book, means the 'Book of the Upright', or 'the Upright or Correct Record'. This text covers much of the same ground as the traditional Mosaic books of the Bible, from the creation of the world to the death of Moses, albeit with several minor variations.

Well, that is what is normally written above the **BOOK OF JASHER**. It is very important to state that the above-mentioned original Hebrew copy of the Book of Jasher was actually written in pre-Christian times, and eventually was translated into English in the early 1600's and printed in 1613. From what I have studied, the original Book of Jasher, which is a history book, was originally assembled and written in the time of Joshua - 3500 years ago. (**SOURCE**: http://biblefacts.org/pdf/Jasher_intro.pdf) **Unfortunately, the above traditional description does not do justice to the amazing Book of Jasher.**

First of all, I would like to state that I personally, from much study of the book, certainly believe that this book is an inspired writing, although I think that in parts of the book, the stories have been somewhat *embellished*, and some of the *dates are different* than either the Bible or the Septuagint version of the Old Testament. It is likely that the original Book of Jasher, as clearly mentioned in the Old Testament of the Bible has been either altered or tampered with. Nevertheless, it is *still* an excellent book to read. See a lot more about this in the **APPENDIX**.

2PE.1:21 For the prophecy came not in old time by the will of man: but holy men of God spake as they were moved by the Holy Ghost.

Secondly, the above statement *'This text covers much of the same ground as the traditional Mosaic books of the Bible, from the creation of the world to the death of Moses, albeit with several minor variations'* This is somewhat understated. The Book of Jasher in fact, gives a lot more background information to many of the biblical stories than even the Bible itself does.

The Book of Jasher also brings out the supernatural powers of God much more than the Bible does, for example as manifested through the sons of Israel, or Jacob's sons and their constant wars to rid the 'lands of Shem' of the Canaanites and other enemies.

In comparing with the Bible, the Book of Jasher describes in great detail about the Garden of Eden, Adam and Eve, Cain and Abel & the 'Origins of Evil'. It also talks about Cainan as the first person to write things down; and later his great grandson Enoch from before the Great Flood also writes things down on tablets of stone.

We will read the infamous **GEN 6** episode in greater detail in this book of Jasher.

GEN.6:2 That the sons of God saw the daughters of men that they were fair; and they took them wives of all which they chose.

GEN.6:4 There were giants in the earth in those days; and also after that, when the sons of God came in unto the daughters of men, and they bare children to them, the same became mighty men which were of old, men of renown.

In the time of Jared - the father of Enoch, **200 of the Watcher class of angels** descended to earth on Mount Hermon in rebellion against God. What was so special about these Watcher class of angels? In this book I will explain about it in detail. One of the reasons for the fall of the Watchers was that they said that they wanted to have their own wives and children. Well that is what most writers of GEN 6 say, but was that the real reason? Find out in this book. The Fallen angels made love to the beautiful women on earth but who was seducing whom? Read all about it in this book. You can also read much more about his topic in my book **ENOCH INSIGHTS**.

In this book gruesome and grisly giants are born from the offspring of the disobedient Fallen angels and human woman. There were many types of giants which were also of different heights. All incredibly dangerous. What are the possibilities of these same monstrous giants returning one day? You can find a possible answer to that question in this book.

How big were these giants? Read on to find out. Why did the giants become grotesque grisly cannibals who were terrorizing the inhabitants of the earth in Pre-Flood times?

This Book of Jasher portrays Enoch as a sort of King of kings for 243 years; it also talks a lot about Nimrod and Babel in the early times after the Great Flood.

This book describes the Tower of Babel as being at least 9000 feet high and gives many more details of the Tower's structure. It tells us that Nimrod was *'not fully human'*, but that he had the *'blood of the Nephilim'* and was 'becoming one of them'.

The Book of Jasher helps us to have a much better grip on the time sequence concerning the life of Abraham and his father, where they came from, and what life was really like back then. It shows Abraham as a mighty Warrior King, who was a real Idol Smasher & who totally obliterated all of his enemies.

Abraham is shown to be alive at the same time as Nimrod, and even at the same time as the great Patriarchs Shem and his father Noah. Quite remarkable, when one considers that Abraham was the 10th generation after Noah. Abraham apparently got his spiritual training at the houses of both Noah and Shem, whilst fleeing Nimrod.

Abraham was probably studying and learning from the Book of Noah and the Book of Enoch, which Noah had brought with him on the Ark at the time of the Great Flood.

Concerning Life - right after the Great Flood
There are lots of interesting details in this Book of Jasher that are not given in any other books about Noah and the Great Flood and his life after that; as well as those who were descendants of Noah and what happened to them.

You will read about *Rikayon* who allegedly brought the name of Pharaoh to Egypt. You will also encounter the nasty character of *Satan* himself who is also called *Mastema* in the Book of Jubilees (See my book 'Jubilees Insights'), & who is always lurking around in the background, trying to cause trouble for Abraham and his descendants.

CREDITS: COVER STORY
(**Artwork:** by Suzanne Strutt: www.instagram.com/suzannestruttartist & www.facebook.com/suzannestruttartist)

The cover story describes in great detail, - spread over many chapters in this book, the amazing story of Shechem, to which the cover of this book is dedicated. Just two of Jacob's sons totally destroyed an entire city of the Canaanites called Shechem, because the prince of the city had forcibly taken their only sister and forced himself on her. Later Jacob and all his sons came to live outside of *Shechem*, only to have the whole race of the Canaanites come out to fight against them, numbering in the tens of thousands, against a mere handful. Read what happens! It is exciting stuff!

Shechem was where Abraham, grandfather of Jacob was resting under a tree, when the angel of the Lord came to speak with him, and God promised to Abraham that all the lands that he could see to the North and South and East and West his descendants would inherit.

There is a strange story of some of the herdsmen of the descendants of Esau being terrified by hundreds of animal–human chimeras with the top part of their bodies being as a beast and bottom part as a human. These creatures simply rode off with all of their animals. It scared the living daylights out of the men, who then refused to go back to that location.

The following **'INTRODUCTION'** is to **Book II** for your interest only - so that you can be familiar with my book JASHER INSIGHTS II and what it contains.

JASHER INSIGHTS BOOK II
(Not included in this book)

The Story of Joseph and his brethren is even better than the good story in the Bible. It gives amazing details about what exactly happened to poor Joseph when he was sold as a slave into Egypt by his brethren and what happened along the way. There is a very seductive beautiful woman called Zelicah the wife of Potiphar, who is always trying to force Joseph to go to bed with her, when he was only 18 and was her slave. Hardly surprising, as her husband was a eunuch, according to this Book of Jasher. Read what happens. It is an absolutely fascinating story.

This Book of Jasher shows Joseph becoming a 'Warrior King' after getting out of prison, and who led his brethren to fight against all the enemies of Pharaoh and who won time and time again against greatly superior odds.

There are many details about Moses and his calling, that are not mentioned in the Bible and many details of what he did when he was first exiled from Egypt by Pharaoh - for 40 years.

13

There is also a dubious story about 'Moses being in jail', before being released and having become a king for a long time in the days after he had left Egypt. What did actually happen to Moses in the 40 years that he was away from Egypt? Find out by reading this book. This story is probably the most questionable in the whole Book of Jasher, but interesting anyway.

There is a fascinating description of Moses & the 10 Plagues of Egypt in this book, that is even more descriptive than the story in the Bible, where God calls a Sulanuth, or octopus-like sea creature from the sea, to bring some of His judgments. Quite a fascinating story that children would also like.

Joshua conquers the Promised land overthrowing many cities in the process: It shows how God fulfils His promise to Abraham to drive out all of the Canaanites from the lands of Shem.

There is a good description of other wars that were fought by Angeas, an African king with Zepho the grandson of Esau as his commander in chief. There are many ensuing wars described in detail.

There is a fascinating story of Zepho the grandson of Esau who fought against a large *human - animal chimera* which was described has having 'the top half of a man' and the 'bottom half of a beast'. Zepho killed this monster that was hiding in a cave, because it had decimated the herds and flocks of the local peoples. As a result, Zepho was made king of the land of Chittim (Cyprus).

There is a strange story, a bit similar to Balaam's ass in the Bible, where God opens the mouth of the donkey to actually speak to Balaam; only in this case it is a wolf talking with Jacob concerning his lost son Joseph. Joseph's brothers had told their father Jacob that a wild animal had killed Joseph. See what the wolf had to say about that!

I believe from having studied this book many times, that this book is very valuable, although some of the stories could be *somewhat embellished,* but then who's to say? Some of the miraculous stories in this book may seem far out to us in modern sceptical times, but then I could also argue: Who am I to question God's miraculous ways?

JAM.1:5 If any of you lack wisdom, let him ask of God, that giveth to all men liberally, and upbraideth not; and it shall be given him.

MAT.18:3 And said, Verily I say unto you, 'Except ye be converted, and become as little children, ye shall not enter into (or see and understand) the kingdom of heaven.'

In other words, we must think as a believing little child about things of Faith, and not be of a doubting sceptical & analytical mind, lest the spiritual things of God escape us and sadly pass us by through our unbelief, especially when it comes to outright miracles of God.

1CO.2:14 But the natural man receives not the things of the Spirit of God: for they are foolishness unto him: neither can he know them, because they are spiritually discerned.

You will also find an **APPENDIX** in the back of this book giving many more details and web refs.

THE FORMAT OF THIS BOOK

i) I have decided to divide this book of **JASHER INSIGHTS** into **BOOK I** and **BOOK II** to make for easy reading and for greater portability of both books.

ii) I have typed a chapter of the **Book of Jasher**, and included in each chapter my commentaries, which are just that: my opinions, speculations and theories, which are gleaned from much study of the subject matter. Most, if not all of which, could prove to be true, and are written with the express intention to motivate the reader to do a more thorough investigation for him or herself, to prove whether correct or not, as I am sure that some of the ideas, speculations and conjecture will be quite far out there, to some people.

iii) I have also put cross-references to the Bible, and other Apocryphal books where appropriate.

iv) **Details:**

The first '**comment**' in each chapter, will be noted as being '**Comment 1**' & then **C.2, C.3**, etc. The original Text from the Book of Enoch is in slightly larger text than either the 'comments' or 'Bible verses'. Three different types of writing are used. One for the original text, and another type of writing for my comments, and yet another for the Bible verses.

iv) The longest commentaries and conclusions are in the '**APPENDICES**' of this book of which there are around 20

Stephen Nigel Strutt (May 2019)

Chapter 1

Typed and re-written by S N Strutt – May 2019

Comment:1: In comparing this Book of Jasher with the Bible, it is immediately noticeable that most of the story of Creation of the world is missing. The first 5 days of creation are missing including the creation of all of the animals. This story of Jasher starts on the 6th day of Creation. Why did Jasher miss the first 5 days of Creation? This is still a mystery.

> 1 And God said, 'Let us make man in our image, after our likeness, and God created man in his own image.'

GEN.1:26 And God said, Let us make man in our image, after our likeness: and let them have dominion over the fish of the sea, and over the fowl of the air, and over the cattle, and over all the earth, and over every creeping thing that creepeth upon the earth.

GEN.1:27 So God created man in his own image, in the image of God created he him; male and female created he them.

C.2 Who was God speaking to here when He stated, 'Let us make man in 'Our Image'. This is especially interesting when God went on to create both a man and a woman. See the Appendix to see more about God's Holy Spirit being Female and part of the Trinity.

> 2 And God formed man from the ground, and he blew into his nostrils the breath of life, and man became a living soul endowed with speech.

C.3 Note here how Jasher mentions an extra detail which is not mentioned in the Bible 'endowed with speech' Why does Jasher mention this detail? It is obviously an important detail, but why? It would seem to indicate that 'endowed with speech' was a new concept at the time of the Creation, and perhaps it refers to the fact that other heavenly beings prior to creation, talked to each other in a much more efficient manner than human speech, and that from different observations of angelic behaviour, was probably telepathy.

> 3 And the Lord said, 'It is not good for man to be alone; I will make unto him a helpmeet.'

C.4 From much study it becomes self-evident that the Holy Spirit is very much female in nature. The Holy Spirit being female and the Mother of the Trinity, she probably had a lot to do with the creating of Eve. It all makes perfect sense. The Holy Spirit is the wife of God and His constant companion and Jesus is their Son. Jesus and the Holy Spirit apparently had a lot to do with the original creation. God knew from personal experience that He

Himself had a wonderful companion in His wife the Holy Spirit, and He also realized that Adam needed a beautiful companion as well.

4 And the Lord caused a deep sleep to fall upon Adam, and he slept, and he took away one of his ribs, and he built flesh upon it, and formed it and brought it to Adam, and Adam awoke from his sleep, and behold a woman was standing before him.

5 And he said, 'This is a bone of my bones and it shall be called woman, for this has been taken from man; and Adam called her name Eve, for she was the mother of all living.'

6 And God blessed them and called their names Adam and Eve in the day that he created them, and the Lord God said, 'Be fruitful and multiply and fill the earth.'

GEN.1:28 And God blessed them, and God said unto them, Be fruitful, and multiply, and replenish the earth, and subdue it: and have dominion over the fish of the sea, and over the fowl of the air, and over every living thing that moves upon the earth.

C.5 Notice that God's very first commandment to Adam and Eve was to make love and multiply. In our western culture today, many people are refusing to both marry or to have children and see children as just an inconvenience and annoyance to people's lives. As a direct result our western culture is dying out as I write this. In fact, this was one of the signs as to when a formerly Great Cultures disintegrated into the dusts of History that people no longer valued both marriage and the family. **COLLAPSE OF WESTERN CIVILIZATION:** https://youtu.be/v9ohrBhhN4k?t=136 >

7 And the Lord God took Adam and his wife, and he placed them in the garden of Eden to dress it and to keep it; and he commanded them and said unto them, 'From every tree of the garden you may eat, but from the tree of the knowledge of good and evil you shall not eat, for in the day that you eat thereof you shall surely die.'

C.6 From doing extensive research - it would appear that Adam and Eve could see fully and clearly into the positive spirit world or other dimensions - when they were first created. This means that they could see God's angels, spirit helpers and possibly even God's throne, as well as the inner workings of the spirit world and how it controlled the physical creation from behind the scenes. (See my other book '**Enoch Insights**', as Enoch could also see the *'inner workings'* of this physical world in a way that is very difficult to describe to those unfamiliar with the spirit world.)

17

C.7 Sadly, Adam and Eve lost the treasure of being so connected directly to the positive spirit world when they sinned. This might explain why in the book 'The Lost Book of Adam and Eve' it would show Adam and Eve to be so remorseful and sorrowful knowing that they had indeed lost Paradise and their connection with the Spirit world.

C.8 It was at this time that apparently God Himself *separated the physical realm from the spiritual realm.* One day when humanity have finally learned God's ways, and the New Heaven and New earth have finally come to rest upon the surface of the earth itself, then God will *reconnect the physical and spiritual realm* and *make them as one* as it used to be at the beginning of Creation.

---

8 And when God had blessed and commanded them, he went from them, and Adam and his wife dwelt in the garden according to the command which the Lord had commanded them.

9 And the serpent, which God had created with them in the earth, came to them to incite them to transgress the command of God which he had commanded them.

10 And the serpent enticed and persuaded the woman to eat from the tree of knowledge, and the woman hearkened to the voice of the serpent, and she transgressed the word of God, and took from the tree of the knowledge of good and evil, and she ate, and she took from it and gave also to her husband and he ate.

C.9 Let's look at this scenario for a minute. Adam is given this very beautiful companion called Eve, but then his companion disobeys God by eating the 'Forbidden Fruit' and he is left wondering what is he supposed to do now? He certainly does not want to end up lonely again as in the time before God had created this beautiful woman Eve, so, he instantly decided if she had eaten 'the forbidden fruit' than he had better do it also, so as not to lose her. Women themselves can be very enticing and luring and persuasive, just as Satan the snake in the Garden had been with Eve in persuading her to eat of the forbidden fruit in the first place.

C.10 Obedience minimized: Adam and Eve behaved more like very innocent or even naïve older teenagers, who made light of God's commandments. They simply did not see the importance of direct obedience to God. Mankind has generally been just the same ever since. 'Do your own thing' and 'don't believe in' or' listen to God'- is Satan's message for people today.

---

11 And Adam and his wife transgressed the commandment of God which he commanded them, and God knew it, and his anger was kindled against them and he cursed them.

C.11 What is important here, is to realize that in the biblical version of Adam and Eve, when God confronted Adam and Eve with their sin of disobedience that they just *made excuses*. Probably due to inexperience, Adam blamed God, & that it was the woman whom He had created that gave the 'forbidden fruit' to him. Eve on the other hand blamed the serpent. Neither one took responsibility for their wayward actions. Neither one apologized nor asked God to forgive them right away. If they had done, maybe the outcome of their 1st sin and mistake could have ended up differently. Of course, the truth is, as they had never known what sin was before, they also didn't fully understand yet, what real disobedience to God meant, and therefore the subsequent consequences. Perhaps this is why they didn't initially seem very moved about their initial sin and disobedience. Later however, they learned and found forgiveness when they were outside the Garden of Eden.

GEN.3:12 And the man said, 'The woman whom thou gave to be with me, she gave me of the tree, and I did eat.'

GEN.3:13 And the LORD God said unto the woman, 'What is this that thou hast done? And the woman said, 'The serpent beguiled me, and I did eat.'

C.12 In order to be 'beguiled' by someone or an entity like Satan, one has to 'put oneself' in the position of 'being willing' to be 'beguiled', so who is really to blame when one is tempted? In the case of the Creation story was is it Eve or Satan that was to blame? It would seem that both were to blame, and God rightly caught them out.

GEN.3:14 And the LORD God said unto the serpent, 'Because thou hast done this, thou art cursed above all cattle, and above every beast of the field; upon thy belly shalt thou go, and dust shalt thou eat all the days of thy life':

GEN.3:15 'And I will put enmity between thee and the woman, and between thy seed and her seed; it shall bruise thy head, and thou shalt bruise his heel.'

GEN.3:16 Unto the woman he said, 'I will greatly multiply thy sorrow and thy conception; in sorrow thou shalt bring forth children; and thy desire shall be to thy husband, and he shall rule over thee'.

GEN.3:17 And unto Adam he said, 'Because thou hast hearkened unto the voice of thy wife, and hast eaten of the tree, of which I commanded thee, saying, 'Thou shalt not eat of it: cursed is the ground for thy sake; in sorrow shalt thou eat of it all the days of thy life';

GEN.3:18 'Thorns also and thistles shall it bring forth to thee; and thou shalt eat the herb of the field';

GEN.3:19 'In the sweat of thy face shalt thou eat bread, till thou return unto the ground; for out of it wast thou taken: for dust thou art, and unto dust shalt thou return'.

> 12 And the Lord God drove them that day from the garden of Eden, to till the ground from which they were taken, and they went and dwelt at the east of the garden of Eden; and Adam knew his wife Eve and she bore two sons and three daughters.

GEN.3:24 So he drove out the man; and he placed at the east of the garden of Eden Cherubims, and a flaming sword which turned every way, to keep the way of the tree of life.

> 13 And she called the name of the first-born Cain, saying, I have obtained a man from the Lord, and the name of the other she called Abel, for she said, 'In vanity we came into the earth, and in vanity we shall be taken from it.'

GEN.4:1 And Adam knew Eve his wife; and she conceived, and bare Cain, and said, I have gotten a man from the LORD.

GEN.4:2 And she again bare his brother Abel. And Abel was a keeper of sheep, but Cain was a tiller of the ground.

C.13 In both the books of Jasher and the Bible apparently Eve stated, 'I have gotten a man from God', because that is what she *believed to be the case*. Is that really what happened or there is more to this story? Let's face it, Satan is the prince of this world, the prince of the air, and the greatest liar and deceiver of all time.

C.14 Look around you at this world, how that Satan has managed to deceive most people one way of the other. It is important for people to realize that angels of God have the power to change their form. They are in fact *shape-shifters* amongst other things. It wouldn't have been so difficult for Satan, the greatest of the Fallen angels to deceive Eve, after she had already fallen and disobeyed God into eating the forbidden fruit.

C.15 I believe that it is very likely that Satan disguised himself as Adam and thus fathered the first human being, unbeknownst to Eve. The only problem with that argument is that Eve would still have been still somewhat innocent if she had mistaken' Satan in disguise' for Adam.

C.16 Some people argue that if Eve had sex with the Fallen angel Satan, then he must have appeared to her in his original *most beautiful form* in the same way that the Fallen angels enticed the women on earth centuries later in Enoch's time.

C.17 I would even go so far as to hypothesize that it is unlikely that God would kick Adam and Eve out of the Garden just for eating a forbidden fruit. But if Eve had *deliberately* had sex with the Fallen angel Satan then yes that would be crime enough to get kicked out of the Garden of Eden.

IDOLATORY, demon worship, & giving women to Fallen angels:

C.18 Sadly, throughout history there is ample evidence that people tend to worship these Fallen angels and entities, just because they are more powerful than human-beings. There is also evidence that in many cultures of the past and especially in Pre-Flood times people gave their women to the angels freely in ritual sexual sacrifice. A practice known today in witchcraft. Maybe these people who participated in such practices thought that they would get a blessing from the Fallen angels. This is one of the ways that idol worshipping started. Remember the Idolatry of the Golden Calf from the time of Moses. Think of all the ancient gods and how they have been worshipped by mankind throughout millennia from India to Rome to Greece to Egypt to China. Idol worship equals demon worship!

C.19 From the above arguments we can all see why Eve would be kicked out of the Garden of Eden but what about Adam? He seemed to be a reluctant participant to the real crime whether eating a 'Forbidden Fruit' or allowing Eve to make love with a Fallen angel. Did Adam know about what Eve did if indeed that is what she did? Anyway, whatever happened, God considered *both Adam and Eve* to be guilty. What do *you* think really happened in that Garden of Eden?

C.20 CONCLUSION Here is what I think happened in the Garden of Eden. Satan the tempter first of all tempted Eve to eat of the 'Forbidden fruit'. She did that and then gave some to Adam. Then in their disobedient 'fallen state' the Devil came along in his most beautiful form and somehow enticed them to do something even worse and something considered to be Idolatry. Satan is very good at enticing people to commit sins and iniquities and then when they have committed those sins he loves to come and condemn them in their minds and accuse them. Perhaps in this particular case Satan came along and said to Adam and Eve, 'I told you that your eyes would be opened if you ate the 'Forbidden fruit' and now you are as gods knowing 'Good and Evil'. Satan knew that according to God's word **GEN 3.5** that a Messiah would eventually be born through the 'seed of the woman'. His plan was to mess that up by adulterating the 'seed of the woman'. If Satan could father a child through Eve, he thought then perhaps he could totally destroy the DNA of mankind and replace it is the Serpent's Seed. He thought that if enough people had the seed of Satan then the Messiah could not come through the corrupted seed of humans. Well, that was his argument. It didn't work fortunately for us as the Messiah was born through Mary. Somehow Satan managed to persuade Eve to have sex with him and Adam probably knew about it, but felt powerless to do anything about it, as Satan was the god who had helped them 'open their eyes to both Good and Evil- that is how Adam felt now in his 'fallen state'. This would also explain why when God finally catches them out, that they accuse each other and the serpent but are *not repentant* but 'fallen in their state of mind' before God, and therefore they are judged and kicked out of the Garden of Eden.

---

14 And the boys grew up, and their father gave them a possession in the land; and Cain was a tiller of the ground, and Abel a keeper of sheep.

15 And it was at the expiration of a few years, that they brought an approximating offering to the Lord, and Cain brought from the fruit of the ground, and Abel brought from the firstlings of his flock from the fat thereof, and God turned and inclined to Abel and his offering, and a fire came down from the Lord from heaven and consumed it.

16 And unto Cain and his offering the Lord did not turn, and he did not incline to it, for he had brought from the inferior fruit of the ground before the Lord, and Cain was jealous against his brother Abel on account of this, and he sought a pretext to slay him.

GEN.4:5 But unto Cain and to his offering he had not respect. And Cain was very wroth, and his countenance fell.

---

17 And in some time after, Cain and Abel his brother, went one day into the field to do their work; and they were both in the field, Cain tilling and ploughing his ground, and Abel feeding his flock; and the flock passed that part which Cain had ploughed in the ground, and it sorely grieved Cain on this account.

C.21 Why did Abel pass 'that part of the land which Cain had ploughed? Presumably there was plenty of land and only a handful of people around, so why didn't Abel explore some other new ground for his sheep to pasture on? Abel already knew the evil nature of his brother Cain from the last encounter at the vegetable sacrifice offering before God upon an altar, which didn't go well for Cain and in fact God had refused Cain's offering. So, why now deliberately provoke Cain by feeding his sheep on the very ground that Cain had so painstakingly just ploughed? Well, as they say 'brothers will be brothers', and they were but teenagers. It reminds me of Jacob's younger son Joseph with all of his older brothers. Joseph kept provoking his brothers by indicating that he was superior to all of them, and he ended up getting sold as a slave for his trouble. But again, he was only 17, and very inexperienced about life. (See Chapter 42 in this book about Joseph) Could it also be the case that Abel was inadvertently provoking his brother or goading him on, by taking his sheep right over the very field that Cain had just ploughed. No wonder Cain got very angry, but it wasn't a crime that deserved to be paid with death!

> 18 And Cain approached his brother Abel in anger, and he said unto him, 'What is there between me and thee, that you come to dwell and bring thy flock to feed in my land?
>
> 19 And Abel answered his brother Cain and said unto him, 'What is there between me and thee, that thou shalt eat the flesh of my flock and clothe thyself with their wool?'
>
> 20 And now therefore, put off the wool of my sheep with which thou hast clothed thyself, and recompense me for their fruit and flesh which thou hast eaten, and when thou shalt have done this, I will then go from thy land as thou hast said?

C.22 'It takes two to tango', as they say. Why didn't Abel just back away and humble himself realizing the evil-bent of his brother and so apologized for going through his field and then kept himself quiet? There is a very important verse in the Proverbs concerning behaviour which states:

PRO.16:7 When a man's ways please the LORD, he makes even his enemies to be at peace with him

> 21 And Cain said to his brother Abel, 'Surely if I slay thee this day, who will require thy blood from me?'

C.23 What was wrong with Cain? Why was he a homicidal psychopath? What was the need for him to kill his brother? Cain was Adam and Eve's first-born. If he was really born of God, why was he of such a seriously evil nature?

1JN.3:12 Not as Cain, who was *of that wicked one*, and slew his brother. And wherefore slew he him? Because his own works were evil, and his brother's righteous.

1JN.3:8 He that commits sin *is of the Devil*; for the devil sinned from the beginning. For this purpose the Son of God was manifested, that he might destroy the works of the Devil.

C.24 When talking about 'sin', it is talking about a deliberate negative action, whilst blinding oneself to the truth, and imagining that God doesn't even notice, or worse yet, not even caring if God noticed. In the case of Cain, I would use a much stronger word than 'sin', as in modern times the word doesn't convey much, as it is too ambiguous. *Iniquity* would be a better word than sin, in the case of Cain, and conveys his evil 'bent' much better.

C.25 There are many people who believe that Cain was the first of *Satan's seed* upon the earth.

C.26 Jesus made it crystal clear in the New Testament:

MAT.7:17 Even so every good tree bringeth forth good fruit; but a corrupt tree bringeth forth evil fruit.

MAT.7:18 A good tree cannot bring forth evil fruit, neither can a corrupt tree bring forth good fruit.

MAT.7:19 Every tree that bringeth not forth good fruit is hewn down and cast into the fire.

MAT.7:20 Wherefore by their fruits ye shall know them.

> 22 And Abel answered Cain, saying, 'Surely God who has made us in the earth, he will avenge my cause, and he will require my blood from thee should thou slay me, for the Lord is the judge and arbiter, and it is he who will requite man according to his evil, and the wicked man according to the wickedness that he may do upon earth.'
>
> 23 And now, if thou should slay me here, surely God knows thy secret views, and will judge thee for the evil which thou didst declare to do unto me this day.
>
> 24 And when Cain heard the words which Abel his brother had spoken, behold the anger of Cain was kindled against his brother Abel for declaring this thing.

C.27 Ever since Abel's sacrifice on the altar had been accepted by God, and his own rejected, Cain had sought an occasion or excuse, to kill his brother. Jealousy led to anger which festered hatred for his brother and final murder.

C.28 Jesus said to the Pharisees in the book of John:

JOHN.8:44 '*Ye are of your father the Devil*, and the *lusts of your father ye will do*. He was a *murderer* from the beginning, and abode not in the truth, because there is *no truth in him*. When he speaks a lie, he speaks of his own: for he is a *liar*, and the *father of it*.

C.29 Who was the first human-being that Satan murdered, which is referred to in this Bible verse of **John 8.44**, unless it is indeed referring to Abel being slain by his older brother Cain, who in turn was inspired by Satan himself to enact the murder. Satan tries to deliberately alter the truth, block the truth, and in the worst cases simply bury the truth so that future generations won't know what the truth is. Satan is such a Loser! Satan could not stand hearing that Abel was the righteous one, made righteous only by his simply obedience to God, instead of Satan's first seed upon the earth Cain, so he inspired Cain to murder Abel. It is almost inconceivable that the first human-being ever born

24

on this planet was a murderer! It sure proves that Satan was around at the beginning of the Creation and even before the Creation.

C.30 Here is a list of the lusts of the flesh, of which, one of them is *murder:*

GAL.5:21 Envyings, *murders*, drunkenness, revellings, and such like: of the which I tell you before, as I have also told you in time past, that they which do such things shall not inherit the kingdom of God.

---

25 And Cain hastened and rose up, and took the iron part of his ploughing instrument, with which he suddenly smote his brother and he slew him, and Cain spilt the blood of his brother Abel upon the earth, and the blood of Abel streamed upon the earth before the flock.

26 And after this Cain repented having slain his brother, and he was sadly grieved, and he wept over him and it vexed him exceedingly.

27 And Cain rose up and dug a hole in the field, wherein he put his brother's body, and he turned the dust over it.

28 And the Lord knew what Cain had done to his brother, and the Lord appeared to Cain and said unto him, 'Where is Abel thy brother that was with thee?'

29 And Cain dissembled, and said, I do not know, am I my brother's keeper? And the Lord said unto him, 'What hast thou done?' The voice of thy brother's blood cries unto me from the ground where thou hast slain him.

GEN.4:9 And the LORD said unto Cain, 'Where is Abel thy brother?' And he said, 'I know not: Am I my brother's keeper?'

GEN.4:10 And he said, 'What hast thou done?' 'the voice of thy brother's blood crieth unto me from the ground'.

C.31 Total defiance and total rebellion just like Satan. It would appear that Satan himself possessed Cain long enough to use him to murder Abel who was God's man.

JOHN.8:44b Concerning Satan: 'He was a *murderer* from the beginning, and abode not in the truth, because there is *no truth in him*. When he speaks a lie, he speaks of his own: for he is a *liar,* and the *father of it.*'

---

30 For thou hast slain thy brother and hast dissembled before me, and didst imagine in thy heart that I saw thee not, nor knew all thy actions.

25

> 31 But thou didst this thing and didst slay thy brother for naught and because he spoke rightly to thee, and now, therefore, cursed be thou from the ground which opened its mouth to receive thy brother's blood from thy hand, and wherein thou didst bury him.

C.32 Satan does not like to be accused of a crime even if it is true, and he also doesn't like to be told what to do. He hates anyone quoting the 'Truth of the Word of God' to him. He also tends to react violently when he has possessed some human and throws big tantrums when confronted. This is also how the demons behave as well as their human victims. Satan is the Father of all the children of Pride and is thus hyper-sensitive!

JOB.41:34 He beholdeth all high things: he is a king over all the children of pride

> 32 And it shall be when thou shalt till it, it shall no more give thee its strength as in the beginning, for thorns and thistles shall the ground produce, and thou shalt be moving and wandering in the earth until the day of thy death.

C.33 Cain seems to repent in this verse, but only because he was caught out by God Himself and judged and punished. God put a mark on him and had him banished from the land. Later, we find that he continued to be evil for the rest of his life. Cain reminds me of King Saul in the Old Testament, who appeared to be repentant before the prophet Samuel, but in fact he was just sad to have his iniquities exposed.

1SA.15:23 For rebellion is as the sin of witchcraft, and stubbornness is as iniquity and idolatry. Because thou hast rejected the word of the LORD, he hath also rejected thee from being king.

> 33 And at that time Cain went out from the presence of the Lord, from the place where he was, and he went moving and wandering in the land toward the east of Eden, he and all belonging to him.

GEN.4:14 Behold, thou hast driven me out this day from the face of the earth; and from thy face shall I be hid; and I shall be a fugitive and a vagabond in the earth; and it shall come to pass, that every one that finds me shall slay me.

GEN.4:15 And the LORD said unto him, 'Therefore, whosoever slays Cain, vengeance shall be taken on him sevenfold.' And the LORD set a mark upon Cain, lest any finding him should kill him.

GEN.4:16 And Cain went out from the presence of the LORD, and dwelt in the land of Nod, on the east of Eden.

C.34 The land of Nod is a big topic, but for here I will keep it short. 'Nod' is the Hebrew root of the verb to 'wander'. In the Septuagint LXX 4.12 'Thou shalt be 'groaning and trembling' on the earth. Nod also means 'to be moved', 'to be agitated', 'reed shaken by the wind'- **1Ki.14:15**

Nod also relates to 'resting' and 'sleeping'. Even in modern English we still have the expression 'To nod off to sleep.'

C.35 SPIRITUAL SLEEP Could the land of Nod be the 'original land' where Cain and his descendants started to live in the *'spiritual sleep'* of *'disobedience to God',* & where they accepted the lies of Satan such as 'there is no God' and 'Might is Right', and 'Do your own' and 'murder, rape & pillage others for gain, & 'to get rich quick: 'trick others out of their belongings'. It would seem that Cain was the first merchant and like unto those unscrupulous merchants of the earth described so well in the Book of Revelations:

REV.18:23 For thy merchants were the great men of the earth; for by thy sorceries were all nations deceived.

C.36 PARADISE & HELL The following story by Jesus Himself is very revealing. He is stating that down inside the earth are 'Hollow Places', where in one Hollow place is Hell and flames of fire & next to it Paradise. There is a big gulf between the two of them so that people cannot traverse from one to the other. In the Jewish book the Zohar, it is stated that the *Garden of Eden* was inside a *hollow earth*.

LUK.16:22 And it came to pass, that the beggar died, and was carried by the angels into Abraham's bosom (Paradise): the rich man also died, and was buried;

LUK.16:23 And in hell he lifted up his eyes, being in torments, and sees Abraham afar off, and Lazarus in his bosom.

LUK.16:26 And beside all this, between us and you there is a great gulf fixed: so that they which would pass from hence to you cannot; neither can they pass to us, that would come from thence.

ENOCH 22.2 Then Raphael (Archangel) answered, one of the holy angels who was with me, and said unto me, "These *hollow places* have been created for this very purpose, that the *spirits of the souls of the dead should assemble therein,* yea that *all the souls of the children of men should assemble here."*

C.37 If Paradise was indeed inside the earth then the Land of Nod being to the East of the Garden of Eden must have also been inside the earth.

---

34 And Cain knew his wife in those days, and she conceived and bare a son, and he called his name Enoch, saying, in that time the Lord began to give him rest and quiet in the earth.

35 And at that time Cain also began to build a city: and he built the city and he called the name of the city Enoch, according to the name of his son; for in those days the Lord had given him rest upon the earth, and

---

> he did not move about and wander as in the beginning.

(See **APPENDIX IV & V** for a fuller explanation on this subject of Cain & the Land of Nod)

> 36 And Irad was born to Enoch, and Irad begat Mechuyael and Mechuyael begat Methusael.

C.38 In conclusion describing this first chapter. The Book of Jasher does follow the Bible most of the time, although it does leave out some important verses. At other times though, it actually gives many more interesting details, that are not mentioned in the Bible.

Chapter 2

> 1 And it was in the hundred and thirtieth year of the life of Adam upon the earth, that he again knew Eve his wife, and she conceived and bare a son in his likeness and in his image, and she called his name Seth, saying, 'Because God has appointed me another seed in the place of Abel, for Cain has slain him'.

Comment:1: It is very important that we don't read the above verse in the wrong way: 'in the hundred and thirtieth year of the life of Adam upon the earth, that he *again knew Eve* his wife.'

This verse is *not* stating that Adam and Eve 'refrained from having sex for over 100 years', between having one child and the next. It is just mentioning the times when they 'came together' and the fruit thereof was a child.

Here is what it states in the New Testament of the Bible about Marriage:

1CO.7:3 Let the husband render unto the wife due benevolence: and likewise, also the wife unto the husband.

1CO.7:4 The wife hath not power of her own body, but the husband: and likewise, also the husband hath not power of his own body, but the wife.

1CO.7:5 Defraud ye not one the other, except it be with consent for a time, that ye may give yourselves to fasting and prayer; and come together again, that Satan tempt you not for your incontinency.

C.2 Why does this verse specifically mention 'bare a son in '*his likeness* and in his (Adam's) *image*'? Is it just possible, that God was trying to encourage Adam and Eve; so that they both knew that *this son* was indeed *fathered by Adam*, and not by Satan? As I have mentioned before, there are many people who believe that when Adam and Eve were in their '*fallen state*', having eaten the fruit from the Tree of the Knowledge of Good and Evil, that Satan took advantage of the woman, and disguised himself as Adam. As happened later with the Fallen angels taking the women on earth by force, is it just possible, that Satan was the father of Cain? This would explain why Cain was such a psychopath and was the first murderer on the planet earth. Satan was obviously determined to put his seed (Seed of Satan) into humanity. This would also explain why humanity became evil so quickly after creation. Cain's descendants were a lot like him, in attacking others and murdering them for gain. The following is taken from my book 'Enoch Insights' explaining how that Lamech was afraid that he was not the father of his son Noah, but that Noah was fathered by a Fallen angel. Fortunately, in Lamech's case he was proven to be wrong about his fear:

Book of Enoch Chapter 106: Verse 3-4 And he said unto him; "I have begotten a strange son, diverse from and unlike man, and *resembling the sons of God of heaven*; and his nature is different and he is not like us, and his eyes are as the rays of the sun, and his countenance is glorious. And it seems to me that *he is not sprung from me but from the angels,* and I fear that in his days a wonder will be wrought on the earth. And now my father I am here to petition thee and implore thee that thou mayest go to Enoch, our father, and learn from him the truth for his dwelling-place is amongst the angels."

2 And Seth lived one hundred and five years, and he begat a son; and Seth called the name of his son Enosh, saying, 'Because in that time the sons of men began to multiply, and to afflict their souls and hearts by transgressing and rebelling against God.'

C.3 Here in the Book of Jasher, it makes it very clear that mankind went astray very early on in time. In fact, only a few hundred years after the creation. This was largely due to the 'seed of Satan' as manifested in the children of Cain, who were murderers and robbers.

3 And it was in the days of Enosh that the sons of men continued to rebel and transgress against God, to increase the anger of the Lord against the sons of men.

4 And the sons of men went and they served other gods, and they forgot the Lord who had created them in the earth: and in those days the sons of men made images of brass and iron, wood and stone, and they bowed down and served them.

C.4 What 'other gods' is it talking about? It would seem that man had a hard time believing in a God that he couldn't see and had to believe in by faith alone. In his wickedness he wanted to create his own gods that he could actually see with his physical eyes, and thus started believing in the idols that his own hands did make. It is said that if you give any object too much attention then it becomes an idol. It also can become a form of worship of the Idol which in turn attracts bad spirits to that Idol.

MAT.12:45 Then goes he, and taketh with himself seven other spirits more wicked than himself, and they enter in and dwell there: and the last state of that man is worse than the first. Even so shall it be also unto this wicked generation.

5 And every man made his god and they bowed down to them, and the sons of men forsook the Lord all the days of Enosh and his children; and the anger of the Lord was kindled on account of their works and abominations which they did in the earth.

ISA.2:8 Their land also is full of idols; they worship the work of their own hands, that which their own fingers have made:

JER.1:16 And I will utter my judgments against them touching all their wickedness, who have forsaken Me, and have burned incense unto other gods, and worshipped the works of their own hands.

C.5 This is interesting, as it shows mankind worshipping idols very early after creation. Only some 200+ years After the Creation of the earth by God. By definition, idol-worshipping is normally linked to Fallen angels and their offspring the giants, who when they died became the demons, otherwise known as the 'disembodied spirits' of the giants. How is it even possible for mankind to have worshipped idols at so early a period in time? We know that the Fallen angels story happened circa 500-600 AC, according to Genesis 6.

What evil entities could mankind have actually worshipped back then in 230 AC? Well if I was to take a guess, I would say that they were worshipping Satan, who had already appeared at the beginning of creation in the Garden of Eden. That early on in time, mankind could not have worshipped some famous individuals who had died, because people lived to be well over 500 years old back then. So, it is a mystery as to who these idols represented, so early on in time after the original creation. It must have been Satan and some of the very first of the Fallen angels.

GEN.6:4 There were giants in the earth in those days; *and also after that*, when the sons of God came in unto the daughters of men, and they bare children to them, the same became mighty men which were of old, men of renown.

C.6 Now I have heard famous Bible scholars stating, that this verse means that the giants only came into existence around the time of Enoch in circa 550-650 AC (After Creation). These writers say that the giants came into existence because of Fallen angels making love with human women. They then state that, where above it states '*and also after that...*' is talking about after the Flood. However, the verse does not specifically say that. In reading the Book of Enoch, we found that Enoch was the first person to write things down, so that he was the first to write about the giants and their origin, as coming from the Fallen angels.

Let's consider the following. Satan is also a Fallen angel, and he was present in the original creation in Garden of Eden. Most Christian writers claim that all things were created at the beginning of the physical creation, including the angels, however this simply does not make any sense. Why? For Satan to appear at the very beginning of the Creation in the garden of Eden, then he must have already 'Fallen' before the creation of the physical universe by God Himself. By deduction, it is clear that also many other angels had already Fallen before creation, and were looking for another realm to go to, in order to avoid direct contact with God Himself.

If, for sake of argument, what I have just stated is true, then what if some

31

'Fallen angels' had also taken advantage of some of the women earlier than the time of Enoch, and that some giants had been created earlier than Enoch's time, but that no one had recorded it as having happened, as Enoch was the first to write things down.

C.7 Of course this Book of Jasher states something slightly different, and that Cainan, Enoch's great-grandfather, also wrote things on tablets of stone. Cainan was the son of Seth. Enoch and Cainan knew each other some centuries later, so it could have been Enoch that taught Cainan how to read and record things on tablets of stone. Just a thought! Most people really lived a very long time before the Flood. Seth, Enos, Cainan, & Enoch all knew each other. Imagine having 10 generations of your family all alive at one time. Such was the case before the Great Flood.

C.8 There is a sexual aspect to idol worshipping, which is still something that is very common in witchcraft today. We know that Cain was very evil, and was probably fathered by Satan himself, thus putting 'Satan's Seed' into the original Creation. Later, Cain's offspring were also very evil and robbed and pillaged others and raped the women. This type of people could easily have started the Idol worshipping, and in so doing they attracted very evil spirits such as 'Fallen angels', who could have come into this physical plane, seduced the women, and fathered the very first Giants somewhere around 350-400 BCE.

C.9 I do also think that these things did also happen after the Great Flood, and ever since, but that such actions are somewhat contained by the Angels of God, as one does not generally today see Giants walking around, at least not yet, although a few have been spotted upon occasion. (**For Giants today see: www.stevequayle.com**)

C.10 It is prophesied in the Septuagint version of the Book of Isaiah, that the 'giants will return to fulfil God's Wrath'.

ISAIAH 13.3 (Septuagint) 'I give command, and I bring them: *giants are coming to fulfil my wrath, rejoicing at the same time and insulting.* 4 A voice of many nations on the mountains, *even like to that* of many nations; a voice of kings and nations gathered together: The Lord of hosts has given command to a war-like nation, 5 to come from a land afar off, from the utmost foundation of heaven; the Lord and his warriors *are coming* to destroy all the world.

JOEL.2:2 A day of darkness and of gloominess, a day of clouds and of thick darkness, as the morning spread upon the mountains: a great people and a strong; there hath not been ever the like, neither shall be any more after it, even to the years of many generations.

JOE.2:3 A fire devoureth before them; and behind them a flame burns: the land is as the garden of Eden before them, and behind them a desolate wilderness; yea, and nothing shall escape them.

REV.19:11 And I saw heaven opened and behold a white horse; and he that sat upon him was called Faithful and True, and in righteousness he doth judge and make war.

REV.19:14 And the armies which were in heaven followed him upon white horses, clothed in fine linen, white and clean.

REV.19:15 And out of his mouth goes a sharp sword, that with it he should smite the nations: and he shall rule them with a rod of iron: and he treads the winepress of the fierceness and wrath of Almighty God.

C.11 A very scary thought! Fortunately, God's saved children will not be on this planet when the Wrath of God occurs, but they will have already gone home to heaven.

> 6 And the Lord caused the waters of the river Gihon to overwhelm them, and he destroyed and consumed them, and he destroyed the third part of the earth, and notwithstanding this, the sons of men did not turn from their evil ways, and their hands were yet extended to do evil in the sight of the Lord.

C.12 Here we see that many of the first Idols-worshippers were destroyed in a Flood that destroyed one third part of the earth, and probably destroyed those very first giants.

C.13 This 1/3 part of men being destroyed is similar to the Book of Revelations where in Chapter 8 during the period of time called 'The Great Tribulation', 1/3 of mankind is killed, 1/3 of everything is destroyed.

REV.8:7 The first angel sounded, and there followed hail and fire mingled with blood, and they were cast upon the earth: and the third part of trees was burnt up, and all green grass was burnt up.

REV.8:9 And the third part of the creatures which were in the sea, and had life, died; and the third part of the ships were destroyed.

REV.8:10 And the third angel sounded, and there fell a great star from heaven, burning as it were a lamp, and it fell upon the third part of the rivers, and upon the fountains of waters;

REV.8:12 And the fourth angel sounded, and the third part of the sun was smitten, and the third part of the moon, and the third part of the stars; so as the third part of them was darkened, and the day shone not for a third part of it, and the night likewise.

C.14 However later on in Revelation 16 at the actual Wrath of God everything is destroyed, just as in the story of Noah's Ark & the Flood – everything was destroyed.

REV.16:3 And the second angel poured out his vial upon the sea; and it became as the blood of a dead man: and every living soul died in the sea.

REV.16:19 And the great city (Jerusalem) was divided into three parts, and the cities of the nations fell: and great Babylon (Anti-Christ's cities worldwide) came in remembrance before God, to give unto her the cup of the wine of the fierceness of his wrath.

> 7 And in those days there was neither sowing nor reaping in the earth; and there was no food for the sons of men and the famine was very great in those days.
>
> 8 And the seed which they sowed in those days in the ground became thorns, thistles and briers; for from the days of Adam was this declaration concerning the earth, of the curse of God, which he cursed the earth, on account of the sin which Adam sinned before the Lord.
>
> 9 And it was when men continued to rebel and transgress against God, and to corrupt their ways, that the earth also became corrupt.

C.15 Here it states that the earth itself became corrupt because of man's continual rebellion against God. Corrupt in what ways exactly?

GEN.6:11 The earth also was corrupt before God, and the earth was filled with violence.

GEN.6:12 And God looked upon the earth, and, behold, it was corrupt; for all flesh had corrupted his way upon the earth

> 10 And Enosh lived ninety years and he begat Cainan;
>
> 11 And Cainan grew up and he was forty years old, and he became wise and had knowledge and skill in all wisdom, and he reigned over all the sons of men, and he led the sons of men to wisdom and knowledge; for Cainan was a very wise man and had understanding in all wisdom, and with his wisdom he ruled over spirits and demons;
>
> 12 And Cainan knew by his wisdom that God would destroy the sons of men for having sinned upon earth, and that the Lord would in the latter days bring upon them the waters of the flood.
>
> 13 And in those days Cainan wrote upon tablets of stone, what was to take place in time to come, and he put them in his treasures.
>
> 14 And Cainan reigned over the whole earth, and he turned some of the sons of men to the service of God.

C.16 In this book it states that Cainan was the first wise man of God on earth. Whilst both the Books of Enoch and of the Bible stated that it was Enoch, the son of Jared, and 7th from Adam who was the first wise man and prophet of God. It also mentions that Cainan wrote on tablets of stone. The tablets of stone are also mentioned in the Book of Enoch as well as the Book of Jubilees.

> 15 And when Cainan was seventy years old, he begat three sons and two daughters.
>
> 16 And these are the names of the children of Cainan; the name of the first born Mahlallel, the second Enan, and the third Mered, and their sisters were Adah and Zillah; these are the five children of Cainan that were born to him.
>
> 17 And Lamech, the son of Methusael, became related to Cainan by marriage, and he took his two daughters for his wives, and Adah conceived and bare a son to Lamech, and she called his name Jabal.
>
> 18 And she again conceived and bare a son, and called his name Jubal; and Zillah, her sister, was barren in those days and had no offspring.

GEN.4:21 And his brother's name was Jubal: he was the father of all such as handle the harp and organ.

> 19 For in those days the sons of men began to trespass against God, and to transgress the commandments which he had commanded to Adam, to be fruitful and multiply in the earth.

C.17 Disobedience to the First Commandment that God ever gave to mankind: *'to be fruitful and multiply in the earth'*, has resulted in much sorrow upon the earth. In modern times since around 1960 there have been over 1 billion abortions on the earth. It is said that most women upon the earth today will have at least one abortion in their lifetime. Many have testified their sorrow of not having children when they could have done so. Certain white races in particular seem to be dying out today, because of lack of having children, such as the Europeans and Americans. Most of the women who have had abortions, later on, have seriously regretted it, and many said they felt tormented by the memory of it.

> 20 And some of the sons of men caused their wives to drink a draught that would render them barren, in order that they might retain their figures and whereby their beautiful appearance might not fade.

35

> 21 And when the sons of men caused some of their wives to drink, Zillah drank with them.
>
> 22 And the child-bearing women appeared abominable in the sight of their husbands as widows, whilst their husbands lived, for to the barren ones only they were attached.

C.18 This is again also happening today, where so many of the earth's population are more interested in the beautiful appearance of women, and for them to stay beautiful for as long as possible, that they forget that women are supposed to be mothers of future generations. At the rate things are currently going, mankind is going to die out anyway, by his own hand of not having families anymore. So many are 'distracted' by modern devices, and simply don't see the importance of both marriage and having children. This is the modern trend in the West, as most young people are very busy working and motherhood is not emphasized in this generation. Very sad to see!

C.19 Modern pharmaceutical companies are largely to blame for birth control, and indeed *eugenics*, and making it so easy to avoid having children for convenience. Those who rule the planet today are determined to keep the earth's population down, and for this reason, they don't promote families and motherhood. Total disobedience to God's first commandment to men and women, as originally given to Adam and Eve in the beginning of Creation.

C.20 Tragically it looks like except for God's direct intervention, the human race is very shortly coming to an end - due to many factors. According to scientific reports, the sperm-count of men is 50% lower than it was just 30 years ago. Many women are also now infertile. In the 1960's the worldwide average was 6 children/couple. Today it is just over 2.4. In most of the Western countries it is as low as 1.2 – 1.4 which is not enough to maintain indigenous races. I was just reading how the Millennials don't intend to have children, as they say they simply can't afford to have them. In just another 20 years, the races of the West will diminish considerably through lack of having children. There are many factors, including chemicals in the water and in the air, and the food being contaminated especially processed foods. Many modern people don't do enough exercise and have become obese, which is now an epidemic. Sex drive is somewhat diminished in our modern society. People have become obsessed with electronic devices and other distractions instead. (SOURCE: https://www.theguardian.com/lifeandstyle/2017/jul/25/sperm-counts-among-western-men-have-halved-in-last-40-years-study)

> 23 And in the end of days and years, when Zillah became old, the Lord opened her womb.

> 24 And she conceived and bare a son and she called his name Tubal Cain, saying, After I had withered away have I obtained him from the Almighty God.

GEN.4:22 And Zillah, she also bare Tubal Cain, an instructor of every artificer in brass and iron: and the sister of Tubal Cain was Naamah.

> 25 And she conceived again and bare a daughter, and she called her name Naamah, for she said, After I had withered away have I obtained pleasure and delight.
>
> 26 And Lamech was old and advanced in years, and his eyes were dim that he could not see, and Tubal Cain, his son, was leading him and it was one day that Lamech went into the field and Tubal Cain his son was with him, and whilst they were walking in the field, Cain the son of Adam advanced towards them; for Lamech was very old and could not see much, and Tubal Cain his son was very young.
>
> 27 And Tubal Cain told his father to draw his bow, and with the arrows he smote Cain, who was yet far off, and he slew him, for he appeared to them to be an animal.
>
> 28 And the arrows entered Cain's body although he was distant from them, and he fell to the ground and died.
>
> 29 And the Lord requited Cain's evil according to his wickedness, which he had done to his brother Abel, according to the word of the Lord which he had spoken.

GAL.6:7 Be not deceived; God is not mocked: for whatsoever a man soweth, that shall he also reap.

GAL.6:8 For he that soweth to his flesh shall of the flesh reap corruption.

> 30 And it came to pass when Cain had died, that Lamech and Tubal went to see the animal which they had slain, and they saw, and behold Cain their grandfather was fallen dead upon the earth.
>
> 31 And Lamech was very much grieved at having done this, and in clapping his hands together he struck his son and caused his death.

> 32 And the wives of Lamech heard what Lamech had done, and they sought to kill him.
>
> 33 And the wives of Lamech hated him from that day, because he slew Cain and Tubal Cain, and the wives of Lamech separated from him, and would not hearken to him in those days.

GEN.4:15 And the LORD said unto him, 'Therefore whosoever slays Cain, vengeance shall be taken on him sevenfold. And the LORD set a mark upon Cain, lest any finding him should kill him.'

C.21 As can be clearly seen, Lamech received curses for slaying Cain. It stated in the above Bible verse that 'whosoever slays Cain, vengeance shall be taken on him sevenfold'. How was vengeance taken on Lamech or how was he actually cursed?

1) He was very sorrowful for having killed his great- great-grand-father Cain. 2) Because of his anger and grief, he inadvertently hit his own young son, resulting in a mortal blow which killed his son. 3) Both of his wives wanted to kill them 4) They both left him, at least for a season. 5) Eventually he got his wives back, but they bare him no more children. 6) It states also that he was going blind & 7) He was old for his age, and in fact older looking than his great-great grandfather Cain.

GEN.4:17 And Cain knew his wife; and she conceived, and bare Enoch: and he builded a city, and called the name of the city, after the name of his son, Enoch.

GEN.4:18 And unto Enoch was born Irad: and Irad begat Mehujael: and Mehujael begat Methusael: and Methusael begat Lamech.

C.22 Being a descendant of Cain and of Cain's bloodline, he could also have had the *biggest curse of being of Satan's Seed*, thus explaining his very *erratic behaviour* in accidentally killing both Cain and his own son. It does sound like a very strange story, doesn't it? Maybe there were other curses, to complete the 7 as mentioned in **Genesis 4.15**.?

Noteworthy to know is that after Lamech, no other descendants of Cain are mentioned in the Bible or other books. *Was Lamech the end of Cain's bloodline?* Or were there many descendants of Cain, who like him were murderers and plunderers as other writers claim and were the true 'Seed of Satan'.

> 34 And Lamech came to his wives, and he pressed them to listen to him about this matter.
>
> 35 And he said to his wives Adah and Zillah, Hear my voice O wives of Lamech, attend to my words, for now you have imagined and said that I slew a man with my wounds, and a child with my stripes for their having

done no violence, but surely know that I am old and grey-headed, and that my eyes are heavy through age, and I did this thing unknowingly.

36 And the wives of Lamech listened to him in this matter, and they returned to him with the advice of their father Adam, but they bore no children to him from that time, knowing that God's anger was increasing in those days against the sons of men, to destroy them with the waters of the flood for their evil doings.

GEN.4:23 And Lamech said unto his wives, Adah and Zillah, 'Hear my voice; ye wives of Lamech, hearken unto my speech: for I have slain a man to my wounding, and a young man to my hurt'.

GEN.4:24 If Cain shall be avenged sevenfold, truly Lamech seventy and sevenfold.

37 And Mahlallel the son of Cainan lived sixty-five years and he begat Jared; and Jared lived sixty-two years and he begat Enoch.

C.23 In looking at the K.J.V of the Bible it states that Jared was 162 years old when Enoch was born and not 62 as is stated in this Book of Jasher. (See the **APPENDIX VIII** for the **TIME-FRAMES**)

Chapter 3

1 And Enoch lived sixty-five years and he begat Methuselah; and Enoch walked with God after having begot Methuselah, and he served the Lord, and despised the evil ways of men.

2 And the soul of Enoch was wrapped up in the instruction of the Lord, in knowledge and in understanding; and he wisely retired from the sons of men and secreted himself from them for many days.

Comment:1: Here it states '*he wisely retired from the sons of men and secreted himself from them for many days*. Here it clearly shows that those who really love God should take frequent times to get all quite before Him and learn directly from God Himself. The problem with modern life is that most people allow themselves to be so rushed off their feet most of the time, and they are also so distracted by devices, amusements and the lusts of this physical life, that they don't make any time for God. Well Enoch apparently was the exact opposite. He really valued his 'Quite Time' with God, so that he could learn directly from the source of eternal Life. This is ultimately why God could use him so mightily.

C.2 Chapter 3 and 4 of this Book of Jasher tell us many details concerning the life of Enoch himself, and many more details are added concerning Enoch's life than we find in either the Bible or even the Book of Enoch itself.

3 And it was at the expiration of many years, whilst he was serving the Lord, and praying before him in his house, that an angel of the Lord called to him from Heaven, and he said, 'Here am I'.

4 And he said, 'Rise, go forth from thy house and from the place where thou dost hide thyself, and appear to the sons of men, in order that thou mayest teach them the way in which they should go and the work which they must accomplish to enter in the ways of God.'

5 And Enoch rose up according to the word of the Lord, and went forth from his house, from his place and from the chamber in which he was concealed; and he went to the sons of men and taught them the ways of the Lord, and at that time assembled the sons of men and acquainted them with the instruction of the Lord.

C.3 Jesus the Messiah described perfectly what the '*instruction of the Lord' was*, & said it perfectly in the Gospel of Matthew:

MAT.22:37 Jesus said unto him, 'Thou shalt love the Lord thy God with all thy heart, and with all thy soul, and with all thy mind.

MAT.22:38 This is the first and great commandment'.

MAT.22:39 And the second is like unto it, 'Thou shalt love thy neighbour as thyself.'

MAT.22:40 On these two commandments hang all the law and the prophets.

C.4 Here are some other brilliant verses from the New Testament:

2TI.2:15 Study to shew thyself approved unto God, a workman that needeth not to be ashamed, rightly dividing the word of truth.

1TI.4:15 Meditate upon these things; give thyself wholly to them; that thy profiting may appear to all.

C.5 Solomon also talked about '*instruction of the Lord* 'and he put it so well at the end of his book of Ecclesiastes in the Old Testament:

ECC.12:13 Let us hear the conclusion of the whole matter: Fear God and keep his commandments: for this is the whole duty of man.

---

6 And he ordered it to be proclaimed in all places where the sons of men dwelt, saying, 'Where is the man who wishes to know the ways of the Lord and good works? Let him come to Enoch.'

C.6 *'all who desired this thing'* Here it is clear to see that not everyone went to see Enoch to hear his instructions as to 'how to follow God' and to 'obey His commands'. Obviously, all those who were the 'Seed of Satan' would not have followed.

---

8 And the spirit of God was upon Enoch, and he taught all his men the wisdom of God and his ways, and the sons of men served the Lord all the days of Enoch, and they came to hear his wisdom.

9 And all the kings of the sons of men, both first and last, together with their princes and judges, came to Enoch when they heard of his wisdom, and they bowed down to him, and they also required of Enoch to reign over them, to which he consented.

10 And they assembled in all, one hundred and thirty kings and princes, and they made Enoch king over them and they were all under his power and command.

11 And Enoch taught them wisdom, knowledge, and the ways of the Lord; and he made peace amongst them, and peace was throughout the earth during the life of Enoch.

> 12 And Enoch reigned over the sons of men two hundred and forty-three years, and he did justice and righteousness with all his people, and he led them in the ways of the Lord.

C.7 This is a very important statement as Enoch reigned over mankind for 243 years and since he lived for 365 years altogether then he must have been 122 years old when he started to reign. Enoch was born in the year 622 *(A.C) so that would mean that he ruled over the kings on earth from around 744 A.C until his translation in 987 A.C *A.C= After Creation

> 13 And these are the generations of Enoch, Methuselah, Elisha, and Elimelech, three sons; and their sisters were Melca and Nahmah, and Methuselah lived eighty-seven years and he begat Lamech.

C.8 In this Book of Jasher it states that Methuselah was only 87 years old when he begat Lamech. In the King James Bible, it states that he was 187 years old - or exactly 100 years older. It would seem, that for whatever reason, there has been some tampering with the 'Time Charts' whether one reads the K.J.V of the Bible or the Septuagint version of the Old Testament or the Books of both Jasher and Jubilees, there are often time discrepancies. Why? Now that is a very good question that we would all like to have an answer for.

> 14 And it was in the fifty-sixth year of the life of Lamech when Adam died; nine hundred and thirty years old was he at his death, and his two sons, with Enoch and Methuselah his son, buried him with great pomp, as at the burial of kings, in the cave which God had told him.
>
> 15 And in that place all the sons of men made a great mourning and weeping on account of Adam; it has therefore become a custom among the sons of men to this day.
>
> 16 And Adam died because he ate of the tree of knowledge; he and his children after him, as the Lord God had spoken.

C.9 Adam died because he ate of the 'Tree of Knowledge of Good and Evil'. God warned him that if he ate of that particular tree that he would die. Well, he didn't actually physically die until he was 930 years old, but he certainly didn't live forever as was God's original plan for mankind. Because of Adam and Eve's disobedience they both died spiritually the very day they ate the fruit of the 'Tree of Knowledge of Good and Evil'. After that they could only maintain their spiritual lives by staying closer to God and in obeying Him more. Adam and Eve actually got much closer to God after they had made a serious mistake, because they now knew what disobedience was; and for the rest of their lives they tried their best to obey God. However, all those who have succeeded them have had to pay the price of physical death. Wonderfully, Jesus Christ came 2000 years ago and died for the sins of all mankind so that now we can all live forever through faith in Jesus. We will still suffer physical death as part of the original curse, but we can have eternal life if we simply choose Jesus Christ as our Saviour.

JOH.11:25 Jesus said unto her, 'I am the resurrection, and the life: he that believeth in me, though he were dead, yet shall he live.'

---

17 And it was in the year of Adam's death which was the two hundred and forty-third year of the reign of Enoch, in that time Enoch resolved to separate himself from the sons of men and to secret himself as at first in order to serve the Lord.

C.10 Now this verse seems to say something different as regarding the timeframe? We know that Adam died in circa the year 930 and that Enoch died in the year 987. It just stated that the year that Adam died was the 243th year of the reign of Enoch. This cannot be right. It would mean that Enoch started being the King of Kings in the year 687. Since Enoch was born in 622, this also means that he was 65 when he consented to rule over mankind and become a sort of King of Kings rather than 122 years old as I stated before. The numbers don't seem to add up, as Enoch only reigned over mankind for 243 years and died in the year 987, so there is some discrepancy here of some 57 years or 987-930? As you can see there is a discrepancy of 57 years between comments **C.2 & C.3**. We know that **Enoch** did not die the same year as Adam in 930, but that he actually died in 987. The year 987 would have been the real 243nd year of the reign of Enoch which would mean that as I stated originally in (**C.2**) he must have started being King of Kings in 987 -243 = 744 or when Enoch was 122 years old. Why this apparent discrepancy of 57 years? Now that is a good question! We don't really know why. The above verse, in order to be completely accurate, should have read '*And it was in the year of Adam's death which was the one hundred and eighty-sixth of the reign of Enoch*'

---

18 And Enoch did so, but did not entirely secret himself from them, but kept away from the sons of men three days and then went to them for one day.

19 And during the three days that he was in his chamber, he prayed to, and praised the Lord his God, and the day on which he went and appeared to his subjects he taught them the ways of the Lord, and all they asked him about the Lord he told them.

---

20 And he did in this manner for many years, and he afterward concealed himself for six days, and appeared to his people one day in seven; and after that once in a month, and then once in a year, until all the kings, princes and sons of men sought for him, and desired again to see the face of Enoch, and to hear his word; but they could not, as all the sons of men were greatly afraid of Enoch, and they feared to approach him on account of the Godlike awe that was seated upon his countenance; therefore no man could look at him, fearing he might be punished and die.

C.11 *'they feared to approach him on account of the Godlike awe that was seated upon his countenance'.* This is similar to the description of Moses when he came down from Mount Sinai with the 10 Commandments:

EXO.34:29 And it came to pass, when Moses came down from mount Sinai with the two tables of testimony in Moses' hand, when he came down from the mount, that Moses wist not that the skin of his face shone while he talked with him.

EXO.34:30 And when Aaron and all the children of Israel saw Moses, behold, the skin of his face shone; and they were afraid to come nigh him.

C.12 This verse above only makes sense if it is all happening within the 243 years of the reign of Enoch which apparently ended at his translation in 987 A.C

21 And all the kings and princes resolved to assemble the sons of men, and to come to Enoch, thinking that they might all speak to him at the time when he should come forth amongst them, and they did so.

22 And the day came when Enoch went forth and they all assembled and came to him, and Enoch spoke to them the words of the Lord and he taught them wisdom and knowledge, and they bowed down before him and they said, May the king live! May the king live!

23 And in some time after, when the kings and princes and the sons of men were speaking to Enoch, and Enoch was teaching them the ways of God, behold an angel of the Lord then called unto Enoch from heaven, and wished to bring him up to heaven to make him reign there over the sons of God, as he had reigned over the sons of men upon earth.

C.13 Now this is a very powerful statement. This event has only happened to a very few people as far as we know that they were taken up to heaven. Enoch's case is unique as he was taken up to heaven specifically to instruct the Sons of God or in other words the Angels of God in Heaven. Elijah comes to mind in the Old Testament.

C.14 How could a man, you may well ask, instruct and teach the angels of God? Don't the angels of God learn directly from God Himself by some sort of osmosis? Apparently, that is not how the angels learn.

C.15 Well let's think of this for a moment. The angels had suffered 1/3 of their fellow angels having fallen from Grace or they soon would do, that is, in the next 1000 years leading up to the Great Flood.

C.16 God needed Enoch to come to Heaven to instruct the angels in such a way, that they might be less likely to rebel against God Himself, and not fall into disobedience as had their former brethren Lucifer (Satan) & the Fallen Angels or the Nephilim.

C.17 Was Enoch successful in instructing the angels of God in heaven or was he not? That is a good question that I for one would like to know the answer for. I would think that many of the angels did listen to Enoch as he himself had been instrumental in reproving the Evil watchers down on earth.

C.18 The angels of God in observing the excellent example of Enoch could think, 'Well if a man can dedicate himself to God freely and willingly and be such a great example, then why can't we?

C.19 This reminds me of a verse in the Book of Enoch when the angels of God were so shocked to see the very severe judgement that God finally passed on the first Fallen angels:

BOOK OF ENOCH 68.2 And on that day Michael answered Raphael and said: 'The power of the spirit transports and makes me to tremble because of the severity of the judgement of the secrets, the judgement of the angels,: who can endure the severe judgement which has been executed and before which they melt away?

BOOK OF ENOCH 68.4 'And it came to pass when he stood before the Lord of spirits., Michael said to Raphael: ' I will not take their part under the eye of the Lord; for the Lord of spirits has been angry with them because they do as if they were the Lord. Therefore, all that is hidden shall come upon them forever and ever.

BOOK OF ENOCH 65.6 A commandment hath gone forth from the presence of the Lord concerning those who dwell on the earth that their ruin is accomplished because they have learned the secrets of the angels and all the violence of the Satan's, and all their powers - the most secret ones - and all the power of those who practice sorcery, and the power of witchcraft, and the power of those who make molten images for the whole earth.

---

24 When at that time Enoch heard this he went and assembled all the inhabitants of the earth, and taught them wisdom and knowledge and gave them divine instructions, and he said to them, I have been required to ascend into heaven, I therefore do not know the day of my going.

45

C.20 According to the Book of Enoch, Enoch not only instructed the kings of the earth, but also reprimanded the Watchers of heaven, or the Fallen angels:

Book of Enoch 12.2 'Enoch scribe of righteousness, go declare unto the Watchers of the heaven who have left the high heaven, and holy eternal place, and have defiled themselves with women, and have done as the children of earth do, and have taken unto themselves wives', "Ye have wrought great destruction on the earth".

JUD.1:6 And the angels which kept not their first estate, but left their own habitation, he hath reserved in everlasting chains under darkness unto the judgment of the great day. darkness for ever.

JUD.1:14 And Enoch also, the seventh from Adam, prophesied of these, saying, Behold, the Lord cometh with ten thousand of his saints.

---

25 And now therefore I will teach you wisdom and knowledge and will give you instruction before I leave you, how to act upon earth whereby you may live; and he did so.

26 And he taught them wisdom and knowledge, and gave them instruction, and he reproved them, and he placed before them statutes and judgments to do upon earth, and he made peace amongst them, and he taught them everlasting life, and dwelt with them some time teaching them all these things.

27 And at that time the sons of men were with Enoch, and Enoch was speaking to them, and they lifted up their eyes and the likeness of a great horse descended from heaven, and the horse paced in the air;

28 And they told Enoch what they had seen, and Enoch said to them, 'On my account does this horse descend upon earth; the time is come when I must go from you and I shall no more be seen by you'.

29 And the horse descended at that time and stood before Enoch, and all the sons of men that were with Enoch saw him.

C.21 Just as in the Bible a fiery horse came to take Elijah up to heaven, so God also originally sent a fiery horse to take Enoch up to heaven so that he could teach the Sons of God in heaven in the same way that he had taught the sons of men.

2KI.2:11 And it came to pass, as they still went on, and talked, that, behold, there appeared a chariot of fire, and horses of fire, and parted them both asunder; and Elijah went up by a whirlwind into heaven.

30 And Enoch then again ordered a voice to be proclaimed, saying, 'Where is the man who delights to know the ways of the Lord his God, let him come this day to Enoch before he is taken from us'.

31 And all the sons of men assembled and came to Enoch that day; and all the kings of the earth with their princes and counsellors remained with him that day; and Enoch then taught the sons of men wisdom and knowledge, and gave them divine instruction; and he bade them serve the Lord and walk in his ways all the days of their lives, and he continued to make peace amongst them.

32 And it was after this that he rose up and rode upon the horse; and he went forth and all the sons of men went after him, about eight hundred thousand men; and they went with him one day's journey.

33 And the second day he said to them, Return home to your tents, why will you go? perhaps you may die; and some of them went from him, and those that remained went with him six day's journey; and Enoch said to them every day, Return to your tents, lest you may die; but they were not willing to return, and they went with him.

34 And on the sixth day some of the men remained and clung to him, and they said to him, We will go with thee to the place where thou go; as the Lord lives, death only shall separate us.

35 And they urged so much to go with him, that he ceased speaking to them; and they went after him and would not return;

36 And when the kings returned, they caused a census to be taken, in order to know the number of remaining men that went with Enoch; and it was upon the seventh day that Enoch ascended into heaven in a whirlwind, with horses and chariots of fire.

C.22 Notice that 7 is Enoch's heavenly number. Born the 7th from Adam. Born at the beginning of the 7th century after Creation. Translated to heaven on the 7th Day. The 7th day is the Rest Day of the week, when God rested, after having created the Creation for 6 days. So, 7 is indeed a heavenly number and is the summation of the number of Creation = 4 and the number of the Trinity = 3 In simply mathematical terms: 7 (God's Number) = 4 (Creation) + 3 (Trinity).

37 And on the eighth day all the kings that had been with Enoch sent to bring back the number of men that were with Enoch, in that place from which he ascended into heaven.

38 And all those kings went to the place and they found the earth there filled with snow, and upon the snow were large stones of snow, and one said to the other, Come, let us break through the snow and see, perhaps the men that remained with Enoch are dead, and are now under the stones of snow, and they searched but could not find him, for he had ascended into heaven.

C.23 This is a very strange description. Why were large stones of snow produced at the translation of Enoch up to heaven? The snow was obviously very thick and deep, but the kings wanted to break through the snow in the hope of finding Enoch and the men that travelled together with him, but they didn't find him, as he had ascended to heaven. What happened to the men that refused to leave Enoch? Were they also translated to heaven as they had been the faithful ones? This sounds like it could have been an early Rapture of the pre-Flood Faithful. Maybe so?

C.24 After Enoch's time the whole world went completely astray. God has often sent His prophet or leader to warn the people for a generation. Then God waits to see if the people will stick with the sayings of the prophet or if they will go astray. As was clearly seen that in spite of Enoch being a King of Kings over much of mankind, that as soon as he was out the picture, the whole earth started following 'Satan and the Fallen angels', which ended up in their total destruction. For these above reasons I think it very likely that a whole host of people that travelled together with Enoch were also translated at the same time as Enoch, but that is just speculation on my part.

C.25 SUMMARY of CHAPTER 3: Even if there is a slight time discrepancy in the story above, does it really matter? I personally am just very thankful that such stories have been written down so faithfully, and yet so long ago, such as this valuable Book of Jasher.

C.26 SUCH A MIRACLE Just think how difficult it would have been to have accurate records of 'exact time sequences' or 'exact dates' thousands of years ago.

C.27 Many people would have had to be very diligent with the books in re-copying them at least every 200 years or so, as all books fade into dust within that time period if left open to the air.

C.28 Exact dates and date setting seem to be unimportant in the depth of Time itself, and something which even God Himself seems to 'blow on'. Many people have predicted 'exact times' of events that will happen and most of the time they are proven wrong, so perhaps exact 'date-setting' as in regard to 'end-time events' is not so important. God's Word we can be sure, will be fulfilled in His perfect time and not before!

C.29 What is really important about a book like this, is the wonderful memory of the spectacular and often supernatural events that have been portrayed by such excellent books as this Book of Jasher.

C.30 Warning to perfectionists: Nit-pickers and perfectionists probably won't like this book. One thing to know is that God Himself is not a perfectionist when it comes to us His creation. It is always best to leave oneself open and not to be immediately 'close up' as soon as some detail comes up that we can't account for.

C.31 Modern times are very sceptical times. In modern times it is much worse. We can't even trust modern History books, as they get re-written and altered time and time again according to the dictates of Science (falsely so-called) just as predicted in the book 1984 by George Orwell. The modern attitude of so many of those running society is not one of believing in God and His prophets and writings, but one of arrogance: 'The truth is whatever we say it is'.

C.32 What we were taught in school 50 years ago has been altered to something different. I am so happy to have the scriptures written by just people who wanted to keep as accurate records as humanly possible for future generations to read.

C.33 This Book of Jasher has on the other hand lasted thousands of years, due to the diligence of Jewish Scribes, who often had to be very secretive about what they were doing, as the 'Powers under which they served', often didn't appreciate the scriptures, and could have easily had them killed. Many times, they made extra copies of books and buried them in caves for the benefit of future generations such as ourselves! As evidenced by the Dead Sea Scrolls found in 1947, which have shed so much light on the Truth. Such diligence and love for the scriptures!

Chapter 4

1 And all the days that Enoch lived upon earth, were three hundred and sixty-five years.

2 And when Enoch had ascended into heaven, all the kings of the earth rose and took Methuselah his son and anointed him, and they caused him to reign over them in the place of his father.

Comment:1: Here are some excellent verses that back up the story of Enoch's translation into heaven and showing that he did not die.

Heb. 11:5 By faith Enoch was translated that he should not see death; and was not found, because God had translated him: for before his translation he had this testimony, that he pleased God.

Enoch 12.1 'Before these things Enoch was hidden, and no one of the children of men knew where he was hidden, and where he abode, and what had become of him; and his activities had to do with the Watchers (Good angels in Heaven), and his days were with the holy ones.

Enoch 39.3 "And in those days a whirlwind carried me off from the earth and set me down at the end of the heavens".

Enoch 71.1 'And it came to pass after this, that my spirit was translated, and it ascended into the heavens'.

Book of Jubilees 4.23 'And he (Enoch) was taken from amongst the children of men, and we (The angels of God), conducted him into the Garden of Eden in majesty and honour, and behold there he writes down the condemnation and judgement of the world, and all the wickedness of the children of men.

3 And Methuselah acted uprightly in the sight of God, as his father Enoch had taught him, and he likewise during the whole of his life taught the sons of men wisdom, knowledge and the fear of God, and he did not turn from the good way either to the right or to the left.

4 But in the latter days of Methuselah, the sons of men turned from the Lord, they corrupted the earth, they robbed and plundered each other, and they rebelled against God and they transgressed, and they corrupted their ways, and would not hearken to the voice of Methuselah, but rebelled against him.

C.2 Methuselah lived to be 969 years old and was the oldest person who ever lived. It states here, in the 'latter days of Methuselah'. Presumably this would mean, after he was circa 500 years old. His father Enoch died around 970 AC (After Creation) and was 365 years old when he died. His son was 300 years old when Enoch died. So, the above verse is stating that within 200 years of the death of Enoch, in around 1170 AC, mankind would no longer listen to Methuselah and the teachings of Enoch his father. The Great Flood came in 1656 AC, so around the last 500 years before the Great Flood the Pre-Diluvian world descended into chaos, anarchy and total depravity.

C.3 This gradual descent into madness, darkness, violence and depravity was caused by the influence of the 'Fallen Watchers' or 'Fallen angels'. Once God had removed Enoch from the earth, who was a great spiritual influence over the peoples of the earth to remain loyal to God, then gradually the Fallen angels were able to influence mankind more and more until the point that within 200 years of the death of Enoch, mankind had totally rejected the ways of the Lord.

C.4 The big question is: Why did God take Enoch to heaven at a mere 365 years old, when he could have lived to the ripe old age of his son Methuselah and lived to 969 years old? Wouldn't that have caused the peoples on the earth to have stayed loyal to God and then they wouldn't have been so easily led astray by the Fallen Angels and their offspring the giants? Then maybe the Great Flood wouldn't have been necessary, if humanity had remained tuned into both Enoch and God? Well of course the answer is in one word: CHOICE.

C.5 God lets people see the good example, but then he also lets mankind be tempted by the evil in order to give him the majesty of choice to decide between Himself God and Satan. That is how it has always been ever since, for all of mankind.

C.6 This is very parallel to the coming Golden Age of the Millennium where Jesus rules for 1000 years on the earth together with His Saints, and yet not all obey God in their hearts, even when for a season Satan and all of his evil devils and demons and entities have all been locked up in the Bottomless Pit for 1000 years. Mankind can't blame Satan for them being tempted to do evil and they can't blame God either, because the peoples of the Millennium could have seen God in the form of His Son Jesus ruling and reigning on earth together with His angels and angelized Saints.

ISA.26:10 Let favour be shewed to the wicked, yet will he not learn righteousness: in the land of uprightness will he deal unjustly and will not behold the majesty of the LORD.

C.7 THE MILLENNIUM: There will be a 1000-years of the 'Righteous Rule' of Christ Himself, with His Saints. When finally, the Golden Age has come to an end, millions of people will be again led astray by Satan himself when he is released from 'the Bottomless Pit'.

REV.20:7 And when the thousand years are expired, Satan shall be loosed out of his prison,

REV.20:8 And shall go out to deceive the nations which are in the four quarters of the earth, Gog, and Magog, to gather them together to battle: the number of whom is as the sand of the sea.

REV.20:9 And they went up on the breadth of the earth, and compassed the camp of the saints about, and the beloved city: and fire came down from God out of heaven and devoured them.

REV.20:10 And the devil that deceived them was cast into the lake of fire and brimstone, where the beast and the false prophet are, and shall be tormented day and night for ever and ever.

---

5 And the Lord was exceedingly wroth against them, and the Lord continued to destroy the seed in those days, so that there was neither sowing nor reaping in the earth.

6 For when they sowed the ground in order that they might obtain food for their support, behold, thorns and thistles were produced which they did not sow.

7 And still the sons of men did not turn from their evil ways, and their hands were still extended to do evil in the sight of God, and they provoked the Lord with their evil ways, and the Lord was very wroth, and repented that he had made man.

C.8 'repented that he had made man.'

GEN.6:6 And it repented the LORD that he had made man on the earth, and it grieved him at his heart.

---

8 And he thought to destroy and annihilate them, and he did so.

GEN.6:7 And the LORD said, I will destroy man whom I have created from the face of the earth; both man, and beast, and the creeping thing, and the fowls of the air; for it repents me that I have made them.

---

9 In those days when Lamech the son of Methuselah was one hundred and sixty years old, Seth the son of Adam died.

10 And all the days that Seth lived, were nine hundred and twelve years, and he died.

11 And Lamech was one hundred and eighty years old when he took

---

Ashmua, the daughter of Elishaa the son of Enoch his uncle, and she conceived.

12 And at that time the sons of men sowed the ground, and a little food was produced, yet the sons of men did not turn from their evil ways, and they trespassed and rebelled against God.

13 And the wife of Lamech conceived and bare him a son at that time, at the revolution of the year.

14 And Methuselah called his name Noah, saying, 'The earth was in his days at rest and free from corruption', and Lamech his father called his name Menachem, saying, 'This one shall comfort us in our works and miserable toil in the earth, which God had cursed'.

15 And the child grew up and was weaned, and he went in the ways of his father Methuselah, perfect and upright with God.

16 And all the sons of men departed from the ways of the Lord in those days as they multiplied upon the face of the earth with sons and daughters, and they taught one another their evil practices and they continued sinning against the Lord.

C.8 Within 200 years of the death of Enoch mankind led by the Fallen angels and their offspring the Giants got into ever increasing perversions copulating with animals and other creatures and projecting Nephilim DNA into animals and birds and reptiles to create all kinds of giants, hybrids, chimeras & monsters:

BOOK OF GIANTS: https://youtu.be/zEW1k0qU8Sg?t=256

17 And every man made unto himself a god, and they robbed and plundered every man his neighbour as well as his relative, and they corrupted the earth, and the earth was filled with violence.

C.9 This last verse is a perfect description of Cain: '*every man made unto himself a god, and they robbed and plundered every man his neighbour as well as his relative, and they corrupted the earth, and the earth was filled with violence.*' Cain was the first human-being born on the earth to a woman, and who probably was the very *first* 'seed of Satan' on the earth. The violence sown by Satan into the very first murderer Cain was then continued by the influence of the Fallen angels or Watchers in the days of Jared, Enoch's father in circa 500-600 A.C. God through the influence of Enoch for

243 years and Methuselah for another 200 years were able to keep at bay the negative influence of the Fallen Angels and their sons the Giants. Finally, it was as if all the good disappeared for a season or was hidden away, whilst Evil went on the rampage for around the next 500 years, as there were no longer any restraints against the Evil, until God's great Judgement of the Flood of Noah.

1JN.3:12 Not as Cain, who was of that wicked one, and slew his brother. And wherefore slew he him? Because his own works were evil, and his brother's righteous

JOHN.8:44 Ye are of your father the devil, and the lusts of your father ye will do. He was a murderer from the beginning, and abode not in the truth, because there is no truth in him. When he speaks a lie, he speaks of his own: for he is a liar, and the father of it.

C.10 As I have mentioned before, it is so clear that just as the Fallen angels started having sexual intercourse with the beautiful women on the earth, so Satan most likely deceived Eve by disguising himself as Adam and thus he fathered the first human being Cain. I think that this is very likely to be true as there is nothing ever good said about Cain, according to the Jewish historian Josephus writing about Cain in the 1st century A.D. (**SEE APPENDIX**)

---

18 And their judges and rulers went to the daughters of men and took their wives by force from their husbands according to their choice, and the sons of men in those days took from the cattle of the earth, the beasts of the field and the fowls of the air, and taught the mixture of animals of one species with the other, in order therewith to provoke the Lord; and God saw the whole earth and it was corrupt, for all flesh had corrupted its ways upon earth, all men and all animals.

C.11 'judges and rulers'. According to the Bible these 'judges and rulers' were the 'Fallen angels' of God known as the 'sons of God'. Interesting detail though, as it shows that the fallen angels subjugated mankind to be subservient to themselves and their progeny the Giants. The Fallen angels took the beautiful women of the earth by force from their husbands it states in the above verse.

C.12 Where it says the 'sons of men' it should read 'sons of God' according to other writings such as the Bible and both the books of Jubilees and the Book of Enoch. *'and the sons of men in those days took from the cattle of the earth, the beasts of the field and the fowls of the air, and taught the mixture of animals of one species with the other, in order therewith to provoke the Lord'*

C.13 Now here is an interesting point: Only the angels of God and in this particular case the 'Fallen angels', had the 'know how' to do what is mentioned in this verse i.e. *'took from the cattle of the earth, the beasts of the*

54

field and the fowls of the air, and taught the mixture of animals of one species with the other'. Normal human beings did *not* have the ability to do these things!

FALLEN ANGELS: http://www.outofthebottomlesspit.co.uk/419028514

GEN.6:1 And it came to pass, when men began to multiply on the face of the earth, and daughters were born unto them,

GEN.6:2 That the *sons of God* saw the daughters of men that they were fair; and they took them wives of all which they chose.

C.14 The Fallen angels started to also corrupt the DNA of animals, birds and fish, by somehow projecting their angelic DNA into these animals. We don't know exactly how they did that? However, when we consider that the angels are shapeshifters, perhaps they took on the form of different animals, beasts, birds and reptiles and some say even insects, in order to insert their DNA into them, and create the hybrid beasts such as the chimeras. The results of their hellish deeds were that monsters, giants and chimeras were created and started roaming the earth. It became a very dangerous place to live on the earth during the last 500 years before the Great Flood. No-one was safe, as anarchy totally took over as well as a *spirit of un-rest*. There is evidence from all over the world that many civilizations in pre-Flood times were very afraid of something and they started building their cities underground. What were they so scared of? Man-eating giants and reptilian carnivorous creatures, as well monsters, beasts, and chimeras, which had been originally created by the fallen angels' interference in God's original creation. (See my book 'Enoch Insights' for many more details on the subject of the 'Fallen angels' and their 'sons the giants' and the resultant monsters and chimeras.)

CHIMERAS: http://www.outofthebottomlesspit.co.uk/420942516

C.15 In the Book of Jubilees it describes many different types of giants each one much taller than the other class. The biggest ones devour the ones somewhat less tall than themselves. They in turn devour the giants smaller than themselves and the smallest giants devour mankind.

> 19 And the Lord said, I will blot out man that I created from the face of the earth, yea from man to the birds of the air, together with cattle and beasts that are in the field for I repent that I made them.

C.16 The women who made love with the Fallen angels started having children who became giants and were of old-time men of renown. Later in time after the Great Flood, the same thing started happening again and the offspring of women and fallen angels were known to us as the demi-gods in ancient mythology.

GEN.6:4 There were giants in the earth in those days; and also after that, when the sons of God came in unto the daughters of men, and they bare children to them, the same became mighty men which were of old, men of renown.

C.17 The Book of Enoch Chapter 10.9 explains how that God told his angels to provoke the races of Giants to fight 'the one against the other', and the end result was a terrible super-war well before the Great Flood followed eventually by the worldwide judgement of God in the Great Flood of Noah's time. What is very important to note is that because the Giants were very intelligent & malignant, and indeed had an intelligence inherited from the Fallen angels, then in the time period from the death of Enoch in around 1000 A.C (After Creation) until the Great Flood in circa 1656 A.C there was plenty of time for the Giants to build a *very advanced technology*. Think how far modern man has advanced in the past 150 years only. Imagine how the descendants of Fallen angels could have advanced in 500 years before being destroyed either by civil wars or by the final Great Flood. For more on this topic:

ADVANCED TECHNOLOGY-TESLA: http://www.outofthebottomlesspit. co.uk/413536147)

MASSIVE CYCLOPIAN BUILDINGS FROM PRE-FLOOD TIMES: http://www. outofthebottomlesspit.co.uk/421401449

> 20 And all men who walked in the ways of the Lord, died in those days, before the Lord brought the evil upon man which he had declared, for this was from the Lord, that they should not see the evil which the Lord spoke of concerning the sons of men.
>
> 21 And Noah found grace in the sight of the Lord, and the Lord chose him and his children to raise up seed from them upon the face of the whole earth.

C.18 I think that the Book of Jubilees gives the secret away by stating that there were 3 different levels of giants. That description by the way was talking about after the Great Flood. So, you can be sure that the giants before the Great Flood were much bigger and taller than those described after the Great Flood.

JUBILEES 7.22 'And they begat sons the Nephilim, and they were all unalike, and they devoured one another; the giants slew the Naphil, and the Naphil slew the Eljo and the Eljo mankind and one man another. These giants were of distinct different heights. Why?

C.19 Why have archaeologists found human skeletons from 9 feet to 12 feet, some of 24 feet and some of 35 feet and some of 45 feet high? I even read of one that was 75 feet high. According to the Book of Enoch before the Great Flood there were some giants much taller and up to an incredible 450 feet high. They surely must have been the **TITANS**. Apart from the different classes of giants there were also intelligent monsters which were hybrid creatures. See: **Book of the Giants**: http://www.bahaistudies.net/asma/book_of_giants.pdf>

FALLEN ANGELS AND HYBRID GIANTS

C.20 One of the weaknesses of human-beings as far as the Fallen angels could ascertain was that they stopped growing normally at around 18 years of age. Of course, before the Great Flood people didn't live to be only 70-80 years old but up to 900 plus! So, before the Great Flood people kept growing for perhaps 100-years. There is evidence that Noah and his wife who were born before the Great Flood were 12 feet tall. This information was devised from the size of the tombs of Noah and his wife.

GIANTS AND ELONGATED SKULLS: http://www.outofthebottomlesspit.co.uk/413325017

C.21 We know from the scriptures from what we have about events back then, that the Fallen angels increasingly in later generations, closer to the Great Flood, starting mixing their DNA not only with human women, but also with animals, birds, beasts and reptiles.

C.22 We know that 200 angels fell initially, but later after the death of Enoch in 987 AC that within a few hundred years of Enoch's death until the Great Flood in 1656 that millions more angels fell & this time seduced by willing beautiful women. These fallen angels and their sons the giants became more and more perverse in their behaviour. God had told his angels to provoke the giants to fight against each other until an end was made of them. It is also stated that the Fallen angels delighted in their sons the Giants or otherwise in later times or Post Flood times known as demi-gods.

C.23 REPTILIAN RACES Most of us have heard of the Reptilian races some-where or other - right? We have heard about them living deep down inside the earth in caverns or much deeper down inside a hollow earth. Are they real, and if so, what was their origin?

HOLLOW EARTH: http://www.outofthebottomlesspit.co.uk/421040248

C.24 HOW DID 'REPTILIAN RACES' COME INTO BEING? I believe it very likely that the reptilian race came into being because the Fallen angels who fell closer to the Great Flood wanted to have sons that were even bigger Giants than the first incursion of giants in the hope that they wouldn't get anni-hilated in battles with other giants. Perhaps this is how the exceptional and infamous TITANS came into being?

WHAT IS UNIQUE ABOUT REPTILES?

C.25 Well they never stop *growing*! This made the reptiles a perfect candidate for making bigger hybrids if the Fallen angels could splice their DNA into a human embryo. I believe that the fallen angels did somehow manage to mix the DNA of reptiles with human foetuses and thus created a hybrid that simply didn't stop growing! Even as it is at the age of puberty in humans, when the growth hormone really starts to kick-in, and boys suddenly shoot up in height at around 13-14 years of age.

C.26 DID GIANTS GROW HIGHER IN STAGES? Hypothesis: what if after every so many years the giants, (because they had some reptilian blood), started growing higher for a season. After many more years the reptilian growth hormone would kick in again and they would sprout even higher. This could explain how many different classes of giants are mentioned with each type distinctly much higher than the next type. This phenomenon is unique as normally it only happens in reptiles, but in the case of reptiles the growth is uniform. In human-reptilian hybrids it is very likely that the growth would have been in spirts every so many years. In pre-Flood times it could have been every 50-100 years or so. Basically, the longer the giant lived the taller and bigger he grew. That is what it would appear the case to be if the Fallen angels had managed to cross human DNA with reptilian DNA.

JUBILEES 10.5 For these are malignant, and created to destroy.

2 PETER 2.12 But these, as natural brute beasts, made to be taken and destroyed.

JUBILEES 10.2 And the sons of Noah came to Noah and told him concerning the demons (disembodied spirits of the slain Giants) which were leading astray and blinding and slaying his sons' sons.

ENOCH 15.8 And these spirits shall rise up against the children of men and women because they have proceeded from them

C.27 If the above hypothesis is correct then that could also explain why the giants developed strange eating disorders. When the giants body started growing higher, he would have needed a lot of food and quickly. The normal food of mankind was insufficient, so the giants started eating the humans and other giants to satiate their extreme hunger and growth. How awful! Carnivorous monstrous Giants!

CARNIVOROUS DINOSAURS. HOW WERE THEY CREATED?

C.28 Another very important question is how did ferocious meat-eating dinosaurs come into existence in a time when God Himself had only created animals to be herbivores and humans to be vegetarians at least in the time before the Great Flood? I think it very likely that the Fallen angels in their complete rebellion against God descended into complete madness and insanity and ended just as wacko as Satan. Satan inspired the Fallen angels to create hybrids from reptiles that would grow much bigger than lizards and crocodiles and mutate them into creatures like **T-REX** and heinous creatures such as **velociraptors** and flying dinosaurs such as **pterodactyls**, not to mention sea monsters.

DRAGONS AND DINOSAURS: http://www.outofthebottomlesspit.co.uk/413522871

DRAGON AND PHOENIX SEEN IN THE SKY OVER ICELAND: http://www.
outofthebottomlesspit.co.uk/413325062>

C.29 Now here is a very scary thought: In the Book of Revelation it talks about the final bloody battle of Armageddon in chapter 19. We are told that an angel talks to the fowls of the heavens and invites them to come to a grisly feast:

REV.19:17 And I saw an angel standing in the sun; and he cried with a loud voice, saying to all the fowls that fly in the midst of heaven, Come and gather yourselves together unto the supper of the great God;

REV.19:18 That ye may eat the flesh of kings, and the flesh of captains, and the flesh of mighty men, and the flesh of horses, and of them that sit on them, and the flesh of all men, both free and bond, both small and great.

C.30 Let's examine this situation for a minute. We have perhaps 200,000,000 soldiers slaughtered at the battle of Armageddon. Would it actually be conceivable that normal birds in the heavens could possibly do the job of devouring 200,000,000 human bodies? I think that here it is talking about the return of much bigger creatures such as *pterodactyls*. According to Revelations, many strange hybrid creatures are released from the Bottomless Pit during the Great Tribulation. In Revelations chapter 6 it states the following:

REV.6:7 And when he had opened the fourth seal, I heard the voice of the fourth beast say, Come and see.

REV.6:8 And I looked, and behold a pale horse: and his name that sat on him was Death, and Hell followed with him. And power was given unto them over the fourth part of the earth, to kill with sword, and with hunger, and with death, and with the beasts of the earth.

C.31 Why does it state that ¼ of the earth's population are *killed by the beasts of the earth*? What beasts? There are no beasts, at least not to my knowledge, that are going around devouring millions of people at least *not yet*. So, what is this important verse concerning the last days of mankind on the earth actually talking about?

C.32 COULD THE GIANTS AND MONSTERS COME BACK?

TRANSHUMANISM. Because of the Transhumanism movement there are many people out there tinkering with trying to create hybrids in modern times. Probably, and so far, most of the hybrids have died in the early stages of life, and in fact on the cellular level. What if genetic engineering becomes even more advanced and eventually monsters are created? You probably wonder why would any scientist or rational person even think to try to create such things? I asked that question to a politician and he said, 'If they can do it, then someone will!' It is just a matter of time until the door is opened one way or the other for the hybrid creatures to return. God help us all when that day arrives!

TRANSHUMANISM I: http://www.outofthebottomlesspit.co.uk/412370179

TRANSHUMANISM II: http://www.outofthebottomlesspit.co.uk/413033606

C.33 CERN PARTICLE COLLIDER. Another possible way for the Giants to return is to create a portal through which they could come - as at present the demons are known as the disembodied spirits of the giants and they are trapped in a lower dimension Those crazy scientists at Cern with all of their 'atom smashing' are actually trying to do what we certainly don't want to happen, and that is to open up portals for these Giants and other hybrids of the past including monsters to return to the surface of the earth. This is not fantasy. Look up CERN and what their insane intentions are.

CERN: (My comments to a video which has since been removed): **GOD'S WARNING TO CERN**:

http://www.outofthebottomlesspit.co.uk/421019283

Chapter 5

1 And it was in the eighty-fourth year of the life of Noah, that Enosh the son of Seth died, he was nine hundred and five years old at his death.

2 And in the one hundred and seventy ninth year of the life of Noah, Cainan the son of Enosh died, and all the days of Cainan were nine hundred and ten years, and he died.

3 And in the two hundred and thirty fourth year of the life of Noah, Mahlallel the son of Cainan died, and the days of Mahlallel were eight hundred and ninety-five years, and he died.

4 And Jared the son of Mahlallel died in those days, in the three hundred and thirty-sixth year of the life of Noah; and all the days of Jared were nine hundred and sixty-two years, and he died.

Comment:1: The dates mentioned here concerning the '*deaths of Seth, Cainan, Mahlallel and Jared*' are almost exactly the same as the Time-Chart in the K.J.V. of the Bible. The Bible states that Noah was born in the year 1056 years A.C. [A.C. = **A**fter **C**reation] (**See APPENDIX for more info**)

5 And all who followed the Lord died in those days, before they saw the evil which God declared to do upon earth.

C.2 It is interesting how that '*all who followed the Lord died in those days*'. In other Words, God was merciful upon His own people, who diligently followed Him, so He took them out of the picture before His 'great judgement' of the Great Flood came upon the earth.' As in the beginning of the story, so also at the end of the story of man's rule upon the earth. Just before God's pours out His Wrath at the End of the world, His own faithful children are Raptured up to heaven to eternally be with Him.

1TH.4:16 For the Lord himself shall descend from heaven with a shout, with the voice of the archangel, and with the trump of God: and the *dead* in Christ shall rise first:

1TH.4:17 Then we which are *alive and remain* shall be caught up together with them in the clouds, to meet the Lord in the air: and so shall we ever be with the Lord.

C.3 For the disobedient and rebellious, a totally different story will unfold:

2TH.1:8 In *flaming fire* taking *vengeance* on them that know not God, and that *obey not* the *gospel* of our Lord Jesus Christ. (In other words, they refused to accept

God's pardon and Salvation through His only begotten Son Jesus, who gave His life as a ransom for our sins.)

2TH.1:9 Who shall *be punished* with *everlasting destruction* from the *presence of the Lord*, and from the glory of his power;

2TH.1:10 When He shall come to be glorified in his saints, and to be admired in all them that believe (because our testimony among you was believed) in that day.

> 6 And after the lapse of many years, in the four hundred and eightieth year of the life of Noah, when all those men, who followed the Lord had died away from amongst the sons of men, and only Methuselah was then left, God said unto Noah and Methuselah, saying,

C.4 God instructs Noah to warn mankind for a period of 120 years about the coming Great Flood if mankind do not turn from their wicked ways:

> 7 Speak ye, and proclaim to the sons of men, saying, 'Thus says the Lord, return from your evil ways and forsake your works, and the Lord will repent of the evil that he declared to do to you, so that it shall not come to pass.'
>
> 8 For thus says the Lord, 'Behold I give you a period of one hundred and twenty years; if you will turn to me and forsake your evil ways, then will I also turn away from the evil which I told you, and it shall not exist, says the Lord.'
>
> 9 And Noah and Methuselah spoke all the words of the Lord to the sons of men, day after day, constantly speaking to them.
>
> 10 But the sons of men would not hearken to them, nor incline their ears to their words, and they were stiff-necked.
>
> 11 And the Lord granted them a period of one hundred and twenty years, saying, ''If they will return, then will God repent of the evil, so as not to destroy the earth.'
>
> 12 Noah the son of Lamech refrained from taking a wife in those days, to beget children, for he said, Surely, now God will destroy the earth, wherefore then shall I beget children?

13 And Noah was a just man, he was perfect in his generation, and the Lord chose him to raise up seed from his seed upon the face of the earth.

14 And the Lord said unto Noah, 'Take unto thee a wife, and beget children, for I have seen thee righteous before me in this generation.'

15 And thou shalt raise up seed, and thy children with thee, in the midst of the earth; and Noah went and took a wife, and he chose Naamah the daughter of Enoch, and she was five hundred and eighty years old.

C.5 Why does the text state '*in the midst of the earth*'. This would seem to indicate that at the time Noah and his family were still living on the inside of the planet or better known as Inner Earth. I could be wrong, but it sounds like the writer is making a point here as to the exact location of Noah at the times before the Great Flood.

C.6 This verse I find very funny. To state that Noah took a woman to wife when she was 580 years old in today's terms her age seems dangerously old, and yet she had 3 children. Amazing to think that Noah lived to be 950 years old and his wife something similar. In the beginning God intended mankind to live to be around 1000 years old. Then because of the sins of Adam and Eve, man didn't quite reach a 1000 but 930 in the case of Adam. In other words, mankind came up short compared to what God would have given him, if Adam and Eve had obeyed.

16 And Noah was four hundred and ninety-eight years old, when he took Naamah for a wife.

17 And Naamah conceived and bare a son, and he called his name Japheth, saying, God has enlarged me in the earth; and she conceived again and bare a son, and he called his name Shem, saying, God has made me a remnant, to raise up seed in the midst of the earth.

18 And Noah was five hundred and two years old when Naamah bare Shem, and the boys grew up and went in the ways of the Lord, in all that Methuselah and Noah their father taught them.

19 And Lamech the father of Noah, died in those days; yet verily he did not go with all his heart in the ways of his father, and he died in the hundred and ninety-fifth year of the life of Noah.

C.7 It states: *'He died in the hundred and ninety-fifth year of the life of Noah'.* It should actually state 'five hundred and ninety-fifth year of the life of Noah'. How do we know? Because the Great Flood came exactly 5 years later, when Noah was exactly 600 years old.

> 20 And all the days of Lamech were seven hundred and seventy years, and he died.

C.8 The Bible states that Lamech was actually seven hundred and *seventy-seven* when he died

> 21 And all the sons of men who knew the Lord, died in that year before the Lord brought evil upon them; for the Lord willed them to die, so as not to behold the evil that God would bring upon their brothers and relatives, as he had so declared to do.
>
> 22 In that time, the Lord said to Noah and Methuselah, 'Stand forth and proclaim to the sons of men all the words that I spoke to you in those days, peradventure they may turn from their evil ways, and I will then repent of the evil and will not bring it'.
>
> 23 And Noah and Methuselah stood forth and said in the ears of the sons of men, all that God had spoken concerning them.
>
> 24 But the sons of men would not hearken, neither would they incline their ears to all their declarations.
>
> 25 And it was after this that the Lord said to Noah, 'The end of all flesh is come before me, on account of their evil deeds, and behold I will destroy the earth'.

GEN.6:13 And God said unto Noah, 'The end of all flesh is come before me; for the earth is filled with violence through them; and, behold, I will destroy them with the earth'.

> 26 And do thou take unto thee gopher wood and go to a certain place and make a large ark and place it in that spot.
>
> 27 And thus shalt thou make it; three hundred cubits its length, fifty cubits broad and thirty cubits high.

> 28 And thou shalt make unto thee a door, open at its side, and to a cubit thou shalt finish above, and cover it within and without with pitch.

GEN.6:14 Make thee an ark of gopher wood; rooms shalt thou make in the ark, and shalt pitch it within and without with pitch.

GEN.6:15 And this is the fashion which thou shalt make it of: The length of the ark shall be three hundred cubits, the breadth of it fifty cubits, and the height of it thirty cubits.

GEN.6:16 A window shalt thou make to the ark, and in a cubit shalt thou finish it above; and the door of the ark shalt thou set in the side thereof; with lower, second, and third stories shalt thou make it.

> 29 And behold I will bring the flood of waters upon the earth, and all flesh be destroyed, from under the heavens all that is upon earth shall perish.

GEN.6:17 And, behold, I, even I, do bring a flood of waters upon the earth, to destroy all flesh, wherein is the breath of life, from under heaven; and everything that is in the earth shall die.

> 30 And thou and thy household shall go and gather two couple of all living things, male and female, and shall bring them to the ark, to raise up seed from them upon earth.

GEN.6:19 And of every living thing of all flesh, two of every sort shalt thou bring into the ark, to keep them alive with thee; they shall be male and female.

GEN.6:20 Of fowls after their kind, and of cattle after their kind, of every creeping thing of the earth after his kind, two of every sort shall come unto thee, to keep them alive.

> 31 And gather unto thee all food that is eaten by all the animals, that there may be food for thee and for them.

GEN.6:21 And take thou unto thee of all food that is eaten, and thou shalt gather it to thee; and it shall be for food for thee, and for them.

GEN.6:18 But with thee will I establish my covenant; and thou shalt come into the ark, thou, and thy sons, and thy wife, and thy sons' wives with thee.

> 32 And thou shalt choose for thy sons three maidens, from the daughters of men, and they shall be wives to thy sons.

33 And Noah rose up, and he made the ark, in the place where God had commanded him, and Noah did as God had ordered him.

34 In his five hundred and ninety-fifth year Noah commenced to make the ark, and he made the ark in five years, as the Lord had commanded.

35 Then Noah took the three daughters of Eliakim, son of Methuselah, for wives for his sons, as the Lord had commanded Noah.

36 And it was at that time Methuselah the son of Enoch died, nine hundred and sixty years old was he, at his death

C.9 The Bible states that Methuselah was actually nine hundred and sixty-nine when he died

Chapter 6

1 At that time, after the death of Methuselah, the Lord said to Noah, 'Go with thy household into the ark; behold I will gather to thee all the animals of the earth, the beasts of the field and the fowls of the air, and they shall all come and surround the ark.'

GEN.7:1 And the LORD said unto Noah, 'Come thou and all thy house into the ark; for thee have I seen righteous before me in this generation'.

2 And thou shalt go and seat thyself by the doors of the ark, and all the beasts, the animals, and the fowls, shall assemble and place themselves before thee, and such of them as shall come and crouch before thee, shalt thou take and deliver into the hands of thy sons, who shall bring them to the ark, and all that will stand before thee thou shalt leave.

3 And the Lord brought this about on the next day, and animals, beasts and fowls came in great multitudes and surrounded the ark.

4 And Noah went and seated himself by the door of the ark, and of all flesh that crouched before him, he brought into the ark, and all that stood before him he left upon earth.

5 And a lioness came, with her two whelps, male and female, and the three crouched before Noah, and the two whelps rose up against the lioness and smote her, and made her flee from her place, and she went away, and they returned to their places, and crouched upon the earth before Noah.

Comment:1: This is really quite amazing, as it goes totally *against the normal nature of animals*, so it had to be supernatural that two lion cubs would smite their own mother and drive her away!

C.2 This reminds me of a story in the Bible where the Philistines had captured the Ark of God, but that in every town of the Philistines, it caused terrible plagues and sores. So, the lords of the Philistines decided to send it back to Israel and they took two cows who were still milking their calves and hitched them up to a wagon and put the ark on it and the cows miraculous forsook their crying calves and plodded off over the hills all the way to Israel. A miracle in itself as the mother cows would not willingly leave their weaning calves, and yet under God's supernatural anointing they did exactly that and took the Ark back to Israel. (**1 Samuel Chapters 4-6**)

6 And the lioness ran away and stood in the place of the lions.

7 And Noah saw this, and wondered greatly, and he rose and took the two whelps, and brought them into the ark.

C.3 Why did Noah 'wonder greatly'? Because this action by the young lions was totally against nature and had to be by Divine guidance. In other words, God Himself was speaking to the lions and telling them exactly what to do!

8 And Noah brought into the ark from all living creatures that were upon earth, so that there was none left but which Noah brought into the ark.

9 Two and two came to Noah into the ark, but from the clean animals, and clean fowls, he brought seven couples, as God had commanded him.

GEN.7:2 Of every clean beast thou shalt take to thee by sevens, the male and his female: and of beasts that are not clean by two, the male and his female

10 And all the animals, and beasts, and fowls, were still there, and they surrounded the ark at every place, and the rain had not descended till seven days after.

11 And on that day, the Lord caused the whole earth to shake, and the sun darkened, and the foundations of the world raged, and the whole earth was moved violently, and the lightning flashed, and the thunder roared, and all the fountains in the earth were broken up, such as was not known to the inhabitants before; and God did this mighty act, in order to terrify the sons of men, that there might be no more evil upon earth.

12 And still the sons of men would not return from their evil ways, and they increased the anger of the Lord at that time and did not even direct their hearts to all this.

13 And at the end of seven days, in the six hundredth year of the life of Noah, the waters of the flood were upon the earth.

GEN.7:10 And it came to pass after seven days, that the waters of the flood were upon the earth.

> 14 And all the fountains of the deep were broken up, and the windows of heaven were opened, and the rain was upon the earth forty days and forty nights.

GEN.7:11 In the six hundredth year of Noah's life, in the second month, the seventeenth day of the month, the same day were all the fountains of the great deep broken up, and the windows of heaven were opened.

> 15 And Noah and his household, and all the living creatures that were with him, came into the ark on account of the waters of the flood, and the Lord shut him in.

GEN.7:13 In the self-same day entered Noah, and Shem, and Ham, and Japheth, the sons of Noah, and Noah's wife, and the three wives of his sons with them, into the ark;

> 16 And all the sons of men that were left upon the earth, became exhausted through evil on account of the rain, for the waters were coming more violently upon the earth, and the animals and beasts were still surrounding the ark.
>
> 17 And the sons of men assembled together, about seven hundred thousand men and women, and they came unto Noah to the ark.
>
> 18 And they called to Noah, saying, 'Open for us that we may come to thee in the ark--and wherefore shall we die?'
>
> 19 And Noah, with a loud voice, answered them from the ark, saying, 'Have you not all rebelled against the Lord, and said that he does not exist? And therefore, the Lord brought upon you this evil, to destroy and cut you off from the face of the earth.'

C.4 *Have you not all rebelled against the Lord, and said that he does not exist*? My goodness that is exactly how the world is today with its 'dog eat dog' mentality and 'Might is Right' and the 'Survival of the Fittest'. Apparently more than 50% of the 70,000,000 people living in the UK state that 'God does not exist!' According to the Bible it is only a very unobservant person who would state that there is no God

PSA.14:1 The fool hath said in his heart, 'There is no God'. They are corrupt, they have done abominable works, there is none that doeth good.

ROM.1:20 For the invisible things of Him (God) from the creation of the world are clearly seen, being understood by the things that are made, even His eternal power and Godhead; so that they are without excuse (for not believing in Him):

ROM.1:21 Because that, when they knew God, they glorified him not as God, neither were thankful; but became vain in their imaginations, and their foolish heart was darkened.

ROM.1:22 Professing themselves to be wise, they became fools.

---

20 Is not this the thing that I spoke to you of one hundred and twenty years back, and you would not hearken to the voice of the Lord, and now do you desire to live upon earth?

21 And they said to Noah, 'We are ready to return to the Lord; only open for us that we may live and not die.'

22 And Noah answered them, saying, 'Behold now that you see the trouble of your souls, you wish to return to the Lord; why did you not return during these hundred and twenty years, which the Lord granted you as the determined period?'

23 But now you come and tell me this on account of the troubles of your souls, now also the Lord will not listen to you, neither will he give ear to you on this day, so that you will not now succeed in your wishes.

24 And the sons of men approached in order to break into the ark, to come in on account of the rain, for they could not bear the rain upon them.

25 And the Lord sent all the beasts and animals that stood round the ark. And the beasts overpowered them and drove them from that place, and every man went his way and they again scattered themselves upon the face of the earth.

C.5 Here is a very unusual occurrence, where God commanded the animals to *attack* man and to *drive him away as he had become very wicked and disobedient.*

C.6 This is also how it is possible that in the end of Days in the time of the Devil-Incarnate ruling on earth as the infamous Anti-Christ that *God will allow 'Giants to ascent from the bowels of the earth to fulfil His Wrath'.* (**Isaiah 13- Septuagint**.)

C.7 I recently read about how historians have discovered that the Mayans and Incas who were cannibals, were themselves *devoured by Giants* that seemed to come out of nowhere. According to history, a large civilization (6.000,000) of Azteks and Incas were destroyed relatively quickly. Sounds like man is cursed if he becomes a cannibal, and will himself be destroyed, or even devoured! 'whatsoever a man soweth that shall he also reap'.

GAL.6:7-8 'For whatsoever a man soweth, that shall he also reap. For he that soweth to his flesh shall of the flesh reap corruption.' (See **APPENDIX** for more on this topic)

---

26 And the rain was still descending upon the earth, and it descended forty days and forty nights, and the waters prevailed greatly upon the earth; and all flesh that was upon the earth or in the waters died, whether men, animals, beasts, creeping things or birds of the air, and there only remained Noah and those that were with him in the ark.

27 And the waters prevailed, and they greatly increased upon the earth, and they lifted up the ark and it was raised from the earth.

GEN.7:18 And the waters prevailed and were increased greatly upon the earth; and the ark went upon the face of the waters.

---

28 And the ark floated upon the face of the waters, and it was tossed upon the waters so that all the living creatures within were turned about like pottage in a cauldron.

29 And great anxiety seized all the living creatures that were in the ark, and the ark was like to be broken.

30 And all the living creatures that were in the ark were terrified, and the lions roared, and the oxen lowed, and the wolves howled, and every living creature in the ark spoke and lamented in its own language, so that their voices reached to a great distance, and Noah and his sons cried and wept in their troubles; they were greatly afraid that they had reached the gates of death.

31 And Noah prayed unto the Lord, and cried unto him on account of this, and he said, O Lord help us, for we have no strength to bear this evil that has encompassed us, for the waves of the waters have surrounded us, mischievous torrents have terrified us, the snares of death have come before us; answer us, O Lord, answer us, light up thy

---

countenance toward us and be gracious to us, redeem us and deliver us.

32 And the Lord hearkened to the voice of Noah, and the Lord remembered him.

33 And a wind passed over the earth, and the waters were still and the ark rested.

GEN.8:1 And God remembered Noah, and every living thing, and all the cattle that was with him in the ark: and God made a wind to pass over the earth, and the waters assuaged;

34 And the fountains of the deep and the windows of heaven were stopped, and the rain from heaven was restrained.

GEN.8:2 The fountains also of the deep and the windows of heaven were stopped, and the rain from heaven was restrained;

35 And the waters decreased in those days, and the ark rested upon the mountains of Ararat.

GEN.8:4 And the ark rested in the seventh month, on the seventeenth day of the month, upon the mountains of Ararat.

36 And Noah then opened the windows of the ark, and Noah still called out to the Lord at that time and he said, O Lord, who didst form the earth and the heavens and all that are therein, bring forth our souls from this confinement, and from the prison wherein thou hast placed us, for I am much wearied with sighing.

GEN.8:6 And it came to pass at the end of forty days, that Noah opened the window of the ark which he had made:

37 And the Lord hearkened to the voice of Noah, and said to him, 'When thou shalt have completed a full year thou shalt then go forth.'

38 And at the revolution of the year, when a full year was completed to Noah's dwelling in the ark, the waters were dried from off the earth, and Noah put off the covering of the ark.

39 At that time, on the twenty-seventh day of the second month, the

> earth was dry, but Noah and his sons, and those that were with him, did not go out from the ark until the Lord told them.

GEN.8:14 And in the second month, on the seven and twentieth day of the month, was the earth dried

> 40 And the day came that the Lord told them to go out, and they all went out from the ark.

GEN.8:16 Go forth of the ark, thou, and thy wife, and thy sons, and thy sons' wives with thee.

> 41 And they went and returned everyone to his way and to his place, and Noah and his sons dwelt in the land that God had told them, and they served the Lord all their days, and the Lord blessed Noah and his sons on their going out from the ark.
>
> 42 And he said to them, 'Be fruitful and fill all the earth; become strong and increase abundantly in the earth and multiply therein.'

GEN.8:17 Bring forth with thee every living thing that is with thee, of all flesh, both of fowl, and of cattle, and of every creeping thing that creepeth upon the earth; that they may breed abundantly in the earth, and be fruitful, and multiply upon the earth

Chapter 7

1 And these are the names of the sons of Noah: Japheth, Ham and Shem; and children were born to them after the flood, for they had taken wives before the flood.

Comment:1: There is a very similar list in Genesis Chapter 10

2 These are the sons of Japheth; Gomer, Magog, Madai, Javan, Tubal, Meshech, and Tiras, seven sons.

C.2 Here is a LINK to show where the lands of Gomer, Magog, Meshech were located:

http://christinprophecy.org/wp-content/uploads/invaders_map.jpg

3 And the sons of **Gomer** were **Askinaz,** Rephath and **Tegarmah.**

4 And the sons of **Magog** were Elichanaf and Lubal.

5 And the children of Madai were Achon, Zeelo, Chazoni and Lot.

6 And the sons of **Javan** were **Elisha, Tarshish, Chittim** and Dudonim.

7 And the sons of **Tubal** were Ariphi, Kesed and Taari.

8 And the sons of **Meshech** were Dedon, Zaron and Shebashni.

9 And the sons of Tiras were Benib, Gera, Lupirion and Gilak; these are the sons of Japheth according to their families, and their numbers in those days were about four hundred and sixty men.

10 And these are the sons of Ham; **Cush**, Mitzraim, **Phut** and **Canaan**, four sons; and the sons of Cush were Seba, Havilah, Sabta, Raama and Satecha, and the sons of Raama were **Sheba and Dedan.**

C.3 You can find all these places on ancient maps. What is important to realize is that initially the sons of Noah all lived fairly close together but with time they spread out their lands further and further away from each other. http://www.marketing-und-vertrieb-international.com/images/gog-magog.jpg

11 And the sons of Mitzraim were Lud, Anom and Pathros, Chasloth and Chaphtor.

12 And the sons of Phut were Gebul, Hadan, Benah and Adan.

13 And the sons of Canaan were Zidon, Heth, Amori, Gergashi, Hivi, Arkee, Seni, Arodi, Zimodi and Chamothi.

14 These are the sons of Ham, according to their families, and their numbers in those days were about seven hundred and thirty men.

15 And these are the sons of Shem; Elam, Ashur, Arpachshad, Lud and Aram, five sons; and the sons of Elam were Shushan, Machul and Harmon.

16 And the sons of Ashar were Mirus and Mokil, and the sons of Arpachshad were Shelach, Anar and Ashcol.

C.4 The following map shows where the sons of Noah and their descendants were in the early days after the Great Flood: http://2.bp.blogspot.com/-VT4fduQsDng/VMkVcTcSfrl/AAAAAAAAQTI/NS0ARvhhPOs/w1200-h630-p-k-nu/026A-Image%2BSpread%2Bof%2BNoah's%2BGrandson.jpg

17 And the sons of Lud were Pethor and Bizayon, and the sons of Aram were Uz, Chul, Gather and Mash.

18 These are the sons of Shem, according to their families; and their numbers in those days were about three hundred men.

19 These are the generations of Shem; Shem begat Arpachshad and Arpachshad begat Shelach, and Shelach begat Eber and to Eber were born two children, the name of one was Peleg, for in his days the sons of men were divided, and in the latter days, the earth was divided.

C.5 Peleg, for in his days the sons of men were divided, and in the latter days, the earth was divided. What is this verse saying? It is stating that in the time that Peleg lived those gathered to together as one nation at the Tower of Babel (See Chapter 9 of this book) were scattered by God Himself to the 4 Winds, after God Himself had confused their languages.

C.6 In the later life of Peleg, then the continents moved apart. See Chapter 10 for more on this.

> 20 And the name of the second was Yoktan, meaning that in his day the lives of the sons of men were diminished and lessened.

C.7 Here it is stating that Yoktan, the brother of Peleg, got his name because in *his day* the *lifespan* of mankind became considerably *diminished*.

If we have a Bible Time-Chart on the wall, and glance at it, we will see that in the days of Peleg, who was born only 100 years after the Great Flood that he was himself the 5th generation from Noah.

We see for example that Peleg's & Yoktan's father was Eber who lived to be 464 years old. But how long did his sons Peleg and Yoktan live to be? The Bible Chart on my wall shows that Peleg lived to be 239 years old. So, verse 20 above is correct as the lifespan of mankind was literally halved in the very short time of one generation.

> 21 These are the sons of Yoktan; Almodad, Shelaf, Chazarmoveth, Yerach, Hadurom, Ozel, Diklah, Obal, Abimael, **Sheba**, Ophir, **Havilah** and **Jobab**; all these are the sons of Yoktan.
>
> 22 And Peleg his brother begat Yen, and Yen begat Serug, and Serug begat Nahor and Nahor begat Terah, and Terah was thirty-eight years old, and he begat Haran and Nahor.

C.8 It states in the last verse that Peleg had a son called *Yen*. In the Bible it states that his name was *Reu*.

C.9 All the names of people, that I have put in **bold** above, have had countries named after them. This is very useful, as we can trace the migration of mankind from the early days after the Great Flood from one central location around Mount Ararat in Turkey (Togarmah), and see where each nation originally came from, and where they eventually emigrated to. If you study the Links to the Maps given above, I am sure that you will find many of the other names listed above as Cities, Capitals or Countries somewhere. It is a very interesting study in itself to see the migration of peoples over the past 4500 years since the Great Food.

> 23 And Cush the son of Ham, the son of Noah, took a wife in those days in his old age, and she bare a son, and they called his name Nimrod, saying, At that time the sons of men again began to rebel and transgress against God, and the child grew up, and his father loved him exceedingly, for he was the son of his old age.
>
> 24 And the garments of skin which God made for Adam and his wife, when they went out of the garden, were given to Cush.

C.10 Here is another remarkable statement that a *former garment* used by Adam had supernatural powers. Is it just possible that Adam still had some powers given to him in the Garden of Eden which were also *transmitted to his clothing**1? It is certainly an interesting mystery! When we consider that originally God intended for mankind to live forever and to have eternal life and to have a strong connection with the spirit world, whilst in the Garden of Eden, which man lost when Eve disobeyed and ate the forbidden fruit. This reminds me of the great biblical movie: The Robe. In that movie anyone who put on Jesus's robes after his Resurrection would feel *greatly comforted and forgiven.*

C.11 See the book **'Corrupting the Image'** by Douglas Hemp).

The author claims that unlike what most people assume in reading the Bible, which states that Adam and Eve were originally created in *adult form* and *stark naked*; the author disputes that assumption, stating that Adam and Eve originally were *'clothed in light'* and garments of light very similar to the garments afforded to the Righteous when they go home to heaven. (**Revelations 19:8** And to her was granted that she should be arrayed in fine linen, clean and white: for the fine linen is the righteousness of saints.) These are apparently garments of light.

C.12 According to the author of **'Corrupting the Image'** Adam and Eve were created with a Triple Helix in their DNA. Incredibly one of the characteristics of the 3rd DNA strand was to create luminescence or garments of light for Adam and Eve.' (Source: http://www.outofthebottomlesspit.co.uk/413536147)

---

25 For after the death of Adam and his wife, the garments were given to Enoch, the son of Jared, and when Enoch was taken up to God, he gave them to Methuselah, his son.

26 And at the death of Methuselah, Noah took them and brought them to the ark, and they were with him until he went out of the ark.

27 And in their going out, Ham stole those garments from Noah his father, and he took them and hid them from his brothers.

28 And when Ham begat his first-born Cush, he gave him the garments in secret, and they were with Cush many days.

29 And Cush also concealed them from his sons and brothers, and when Cush had begotten Nimrod, he gave him those garments through his love for him, and Nimrod grew up, and when he was twenty years old, he put on those garments.

> 30 And Nimrod became strong when he put on the garments, and God gave him might and strength, and he was a mighty hunter in the earth, yea, he was a mighty hunter in the field, and he hunted the animals and he built altars, and he offered upon them the animals before the Lord.

C.13 Note how Nimrod put on the garment of Adam and it gave him wisdom. It is important to see, that some people use wisdom for a good purpose, whilst others use it for evil just like Satan.

Let's look deeper into how Nimrod is actually described in the Septuagint LXX:

Genesis LXX 10.8-10 And Cush begot Nimrod: he began to be a Giant upon the earth. 9. He was a giant hunter before the Lord. This contrast greatly with what is written in the King James version of the Bible which simply says:

GEN.10:8 And Cush begat Nimrod: he began to be a mighty one in the earth.

GEN.10:9 He was a mighty hunter before the LORD: wherefore it is said, Even as Nimrod the mighty hunter before the LORD.

C.14 The version of Genesis in the Septuagint says something totally different than the Bible. The Bible merely describes Nimrod as a 'mighty hunter' whilst the Septuagint describes Nimrod as a Nephilim Giant. A very big important difference in meaning!

C.15 Why did those who put the King James Bible together alter the original text? The best text that we have apparently, and the most reliable text, was the Septuagint version of the Old Testament from around 200-300 B.C.E. which was written in Greek. Sadly, the King James Version of the Old Testament has been corrupted in a few places, by following the Masoretic Text which came out around 500 years after the Septuagint. (See the **APPENDIX** for more details).

C.16 Why would anyone want to corrupt the original text, one may ask? Simple! Certain religionists did not want the public to know about the true nature of the 'Origins of Mankind', and especially about the evil influence of both the Fallen angels and their offspring – the Giants or their Nephilim descent from Fallen Angels.

C.17 THE BOOK OF ENOCH WAS BANNED FOR 1000 YEARS! WHY? It was banned by the Catholic church for over 1000 years, because it mentions in detail the Fallen Angels/ Watchers and their sons the Giants, and how they totally wrecked the planet and perhaps even other planets? We know that they built diverse super empires such as Atlantis, Lemuria and Mu before the Great Flood, and that they had very advanced technology based on anti-gravity and crystal power, what we would today call UFO's and laser technology today. There is so much evidence of this. (SEE: **TESLA TECHNOLOGY:** https://www.history.com/topics/inventions/nikola-tesla)

C.18 Apparently according to the Book of Enoch God's angels were told by God Himself to provoke one super-race to fight against another and that is when continents such as Atlantis sank into the sea. There were other empires around the world which were also wiped out in terrible wars in ancient times because of very advanced technology.

C.19 You will find the *best evidence* of this in the books of Ancient History from India. These books give amazing descriptions of what sounds like atomic war 5000 years ago. If you know your biblical Timeline, then you would realize that 5000 years ago was 500 years before the Great Flood. http://www.baha-istudies.net/asma/nuclear_war_ancient_india.pdf

C.20 According to this Book of Jasher and the Bible as well as other Apocryphal books, this was the exact same time when the world was descending into total anarchy and chaos as mankind totally forsook the ways of God (that had been previously taught to them by Enoch who died in 987 A.C = After Creation) in the post-Enochian period of the 500 years leading up to the Great Flood which occurred in 1656. (SEE my other book '**ENOCH INSIGHTS**' for a lot more information/Time Charts on this topic.)

---

31 And Nimrod strengthened himself, and he rose up from amongst his brethren, and he fought the battles of his brethren against all their enemies round about.

32 And the Lord delivered all the enemies of his brethren in his hands, and God prospered him from time to time in his battles, and he reigned upon earth.

33 Therefore it became current in those days, when a man ushered forth those that he had trained up for battle, he would say to them, Like God did to Nimrod, who was a mighty hunter in the earth, and who succeeded in the battles that prevailed against his brethren, that he delivered them from the hands of their enemies, so may God strengthen us and deliver us this day.

34 And when Nimrod was forty years old, at that time there was a war between his brethren and the children of Japheth, so that they were in the power of their enemies.

35 And Nimrod went forth at that time, and he assembled all the sons of Cush and their families, about four hundred and sixty men, and he hired also from some of his friends and acquaintances about eighty men, and be gave them their hire, and he went with them to battle, and

---

when he was on the road, Nimrod strengthened the hearts of the people that went with him.

36 And he said to them, 'Do not fear, neither be alarmed, for all our enemies will be delivered into our hands, and you may do with them as you please.'

37 And all the men that went were about five hundred, and they fought against their enemies, and they destroyed them, and subdued them, and Nimrod placed standing officers over them in their respective places.

38 And he took some of their children as security, and they were all servants to Nimrod and to his brethren, and Nimrod and all the people that were with him turned homeward.

39 And when Nimrod had joyfully returned from battle, after having conquered his enemies, all his brethren, together with those who knew him before, assembled to make him king over them, and they placed the regal crown upon his head.

40 And he set over his subjects and people, princes, judges, and rulers, as is the custom amongst kings.

41 And he placed Terah the son of Nahor the prince of his host, and he dignified him and elevated him above all his princes.

42 And whilst he was reigning according to his heart's desire, after having conquered all his enemies around, he advised with his counsellors to build a city for his palace, and they did so.

43 And they found a large valley opposite to the east, and they built him a large and extensive city, and Nimrod called the name of the city that he built Shinar, for the Lord had vehemently shaken his enemies and destroyed them.

44 And Nimrod dwelt in Shinar, and he reigned securely, and he fought with his enemies and he subdued them, and he prospered in all his battles, and his kingdom became very great.

45 And all nations and tongues heard of his fame, and they gathered themselves to him, and they bowed down to the earth, and they brought him offerings, and he became their lord and king, and they all dwelt with him in the city at Shinar, and Nimrod reigned in the earth over all the sons of Noah, and they were all under his power and counsel.

46 And all the earth was of one tongue and words of union, but Nimrod did not go in the ways of the Lord, and he was more wicked than all the men that were before him, from the days of the flood until those days.

C.21 Here we see that although according to this book of Jasher Nimrod had been given the 'stolen garments of Adam', and was also called 'A mighty hunter before the Lord', that he turned evil due to Nephilim blood in his veins.

47 And he made gods of wood and stone, and he bowed down to them, and he rebelled against the Lord, and taught all his subjects and the people of the earth his wicked ways; and Mardon his son was more wicked than his father.

48 And every one that heard of the acts of Mardon the son of Nimrod would say, concerning him, From the wicked goes forth wickedness; therefore, it became a proverb in the whole earth, saying, From the wicked goes forth wickedness, and it was current in the words of men from that time to this.

49 And Terah the son of Nahor, prince of Nimrod's host, was in those days very great in the sight of the king and his subjects, and the king and princes loved him, and they elevated him very high.

50 And Terah took a wife and her name was Amthelo the daughter of Cornebo; and the wife of Terah conceived and bare him a son in those days.

51 Terah was seventy years old when he begat him, and Terah called the name of his son that was born to him Abram, because the king had raised him in those days, and dignified him above all his princes that were with him.

Chapter 8

C.1 THE BIRTH OF ABRAHAM IS DESCRIBED AS A VERY PROPHETIC TIME

> 1 And it was in the night that Abram was born, that all the servants of Terah, and all the wise men of Nimrod, and his conjurors came and ate and drank in the house of Terah, and they rejoiced with him on that night.
>
> 2 And when all the wise men and conjurors went out from the house of Terah, they lifted up their eyes toward heaven that night to look at the stars, and they saw, and behold one very large star came from the east and ran in the heavens, and he swallowed up the four stars from the four sides of the heavens.

C.2 Imagine that Abraham's birth is heralded with a massive star coming from the East and then subsequently swallowing up 4 other stars. A very unusual vision to say the least.

C.3 Where have we heard of things like this before? Well to herald the birth of the Messiah Jesus 3 Wise-men or Kings who followed a star also from the East all the way to Bethlehem from Mesopotamia.

MAT.2:1 Now when Jesus was born in Bethlehem of Judaea in the days of Herod the king, behold, there came wise men from the east to Jerusalem,

MAT.2:2 Saying, 'Where is he that is born King of the Jews? for we have seen his star in the east and are come to worship him'.

C.4 'Moving Stars' in the sky can represent kings as in the case of both Christ and Abraham

C.5 We also heard about the Egyptian Pharoah complaining that 'A Deliverer' had been foreseen by a 'Falling Star for several generations.
Well the Deliverer Moses did come upon the scene and Egypt was indeed destroyed by the 10 Plagues of Egypt. A great movie showing this is the Ten Commandments: https://youtu.be/_s96r8YyRik?t=65

C.6 Falling stars often denote the 'fall of a nation', empire or a prominent king. They also signify the falling of the 'Powers' of the Air such as Satan himself. The Fallen Angels are also referred to as 'wayward stars'.

LUK.10:18 And he said unto them, I beheld Satan as lightning fall from heaven.

REV.12:4 And his (The Dragon = Satan)'s tail drew the third part of the stars of heaven, and did cast them to the earth: and the dragon stood before the woman which was ready to be delivered, for to devour her child as soon as it was born.

REV.12:9 And the great dragon was cast out, that old serpent, called the Devil, and Satan, which deceives the whole world: he was cast out into the earth, and his angels were cast out with him.

> 3 And all the wise men of the king and his conjurors were astonished at the sight, and the sages understood this matter, and they knew its import.

C.7 The following is a beautiful verse about a *star*. Amazingly, the following prophecy in **Numbers 24.17** was given to Balaam, who was a conjuror or Dark Arts magician, at the time when Balak the king of Moab ordered Balaam to curse the emerging nation of Israel when they were travelling by his land on the way to the promised Land. Balaam exclaimed to the king that he could not curse Israel as God wanted to bless them!

NUM.24:17 I shall see him, but not now: I shall behold him, but not nigh: there shall come a Star out of Jacob, and a Sceptre shall rise out of Israel, and shall smite the corners of Moab, and destroy all the children of Seth

> 4 And they said to each other, This only betokens the child that has been born to Terah this night, who will grow up and be fruitful, and multiply, and possess all the earth, he and his children for ever, and he and his seed will slay great kings, and inherit their lands.
>
> 5 And the wise men and conjurors went home that night, and in the morning all these wise men and conjurors rose up early and assembled in an appointed house.
>
> 6 And they spoke and said to each other, 'Behold the sight that we saw last night is hidden from the king, it has not been made known to him.'
>
> 7 And should this thing get known to the king in the latter days, he will say to us, 'Why have you concealed this matter from me, and then we shall all suffer death; therefore, now let us go and tell the king the sight which we saw, and the interpretation thereof, and we shall then remain clear.'
>
> 8 And they did so, and they all went to the king and bowed down to him to the ground, and they said, May the king live, may the king live.
>
> 9 We heard that a son was born to Terah the son of Nahor, the prince

of thy host, and we yesternight came to his house, and we ate and drank and rejoiced with him that night.

10 And when thy servants went out from the house of Terah, to go to our respective homes to abide there for the night, we lifted up our eyes to heaven, and we saw a great star coming from the east, and the same star ran with great speed, and swallowed up four great stars, from the four sides of the heavens.

C.8 This vision of the one bright star of Abraham destroying the four stars is fulfilled in this Book of Jasher Chapter 16 verse 7. When Abraham fought with the 4 kings who came to destroy Sodom and Gomorrah and 3 other cities of the plain who had rebelled against the new high king Charledomer to whom Nimrod becomes subservient for a season. Abraham fights the 4 kings to recover his nephew Lot whom they had taken captive. (See Jasher Chapter 16)

11 And thy servants were astonished at the sight which we saw, and were greatly terrified, and we made our judgment upon the sight, and knew by our wisdom the proper interpretation thereof, that this thing applies to the child that is born to Terah, who will grow up and multiply greatly, and become powerful, and kill all the kings of the earth, and inherit all their lands, he and his seed forever.

12 And now our lord and king, behold we have truly acquainted thee with what we have seen concerning this child.

13 If it seemeth good to the king to give his father value for this child, we will slay him before he shall grow up and increase in the land, and his evil increase against us, that we and our children perish through his evil.

14 And the king heard their words and they seemed good in his sight, and he sent and called for Terah, and Terah came before the king.

15 And the king said to Terah, I have been told that a son was yesternight born to thee, and after this manner was observed in the heavens at his birth.

16 And now therefore give me the child, that we may slay him before

> his evil springs up against us, and I will give thee for his value, thy house full of silver and gold.

C.9 It is strange indeed that both king Nimrod and his conjurers were so full of fear as to what this *star* would do to them all in the future. Did it actually come to pass? Yes, it did indeed as you will soon read about in chapter 17. It just goes to show that it doesn't matter how much power and wealth and control the wealthy leaders of the world have, they also feel insecure and are afraid of losing their power and their positions with all of their evil-begotten riches often gained at the price of the sacrifice of the lives of many others. It is as though the Bible old adage 'You reap what you sow' is completely true. Those who know God personally have nothing to fear, but the violent and wicked and perverse such as the leaders of countries tend to be and have a lot to fear concerning' impending judgement on themselves as every man shall give account of not only his deeds but of every idle word.

MAT.12:36 But I say unto you, 'That every idle word that men shall speak, they shall give account thereof in the day of judgment.'

MAT.12:37 'For by thy words thou shalt be justified, and by thy words thou shalt be condemned'.

JAMES.2:19 'Thou believe that there is one God; thou do well: the devils also believe, and tremble'.

---

17 And Terah answered the king and said to him: My Lord and king, I have heard thy words, and thy servant shall do all that his king desireth.

18 But my lord and king, I will tell thee what happened to me yesternight, that I may see what advice the king will give his servant, and then I will answer the king upon what he has just spoken; and the king said, Speak.

19 And Terah said to the king, Ayon, son of Mored, came to me yesternight, saying,

20 Give unto me the great and beautiful horse that the king gave thee, and I will give thee silver and gold, and straw and provender for its value; and I said to him, Wait till I see the king concerning thy words, and behold whatever the king saith, that will I do.

21 And now my lord and king, behold I have made this thing known to thee, and the advice which my king will give unto his servant, that will I follow.

---

22 And the king heard the words of Terah, and his anger was kindled and he considered him in the light of a fool.

23 And the king answered Terah, and he said to him, Art thou so silly, ignorant, or deficient in understanding, to do this thing, to give thy beautiful horse for silver and gold or even for straw and provender?

24 Art thou so short of silver and gold, that thou shouldst do this thing, because thou canst not obtain straw and provender to feed thy horse? and what is silver and gold to thee, or straw and provender, that thou shouldst give away that fine horse which I gave thee, like which there is none to be had on the whole earth?

25 And the king left off speaking, and Terah answered the king, saying, Like unto this has the king spoken to his servant;

26 I beseech thee, my lord and king, what is this which thou didst say unto me, saying, Give thy son that we may slay him, and I will give thee silver and gold for his value; what shall I do with silver and gold after the death of my son? who shall inherit me? surely then at my death, the silver and gold will return to my king who gave it.

27 And when the king heard the words of Terah, and the parable which he brought concerning the king, it grieved him greatly and he was vexed at this thing, and his anger burned within him.

28 And Terah saw that the anger of the king was kindled against him, and he answered the king, saying, All that I have is in the king's power; whatever the king desireth to do to his servant, that let him do, yea, even my son, he is in the king's power, without value in exchange, he and his two brothers that are older than he.

29 And the king said to Terah, No, but I will purchase thy younger son for a price.

30 And Terah answered the king, saying, I beseech thee my lord and king to let thy servant speak a word before thee, and let the king hear the word of his servant, and Terah said, Let my king give me three days'

time till I consider this matter within myself, and consult with my family concerning the words of my king; and he pressed the king greatly to agree to this.

31 And the king hearkened to Terah, and he did so and he gave him three days' time, and Terah went out from the king's presence, and he came home to his family and spoke to them all the words of the king; and the people were greatly afraid.

32 And it was in the third day that the king sent to Terah, saying, Send me thy son for a price as I spoke to thee; and should thou not do this, I will send and slay all thou hast in thy house, so that thou shalt not even have a dog remaining.

33 And Terah hastened, (as the thing was urgent from the king), and he took a child from one of his servants, which his handmaid had born to him that day, and Terah brought the child to the king and received value for him.

34 And the Lord was with Terah in this matter, that Nimrod might not cause Abram's death, and the king took the child from Terah and with all his might dashed his head to the ground, for he thought it had been Abram; and this was concealed from him from that day, and it was forgotten by the king, as it was the will of Providence not to suffer Abram's death.

PSA.37:12 The wicked plots against the just, and gnashes upon him with his teeth.

C.10 It is incredible to see how totally insane many of the leaders of the world have been. The more powerful that they become the more insane they act - just like Satan himself, as monsters who destroy, torture, maim and kill to get want they want. 'The ends justify the means' is their satanic slogan. How could any human being smash a baby's head in and kill it as described above, unless they were possessed by a demon. This above verse proves that Nimrod was indeed a devil or was demon-possessed Nephalim. Only a complete monster would smash a baby's head in.

PSA.9:17 The wicked shall be turned into hell, and all the nations that forget God.

35 And Terah took Abram his son secretly, together with his mother and nurse, and he concealed them in a cave, and he brought them their provisions monthly.

87

36 And the Lord was with Abram in the cave and he grew up, and Abram was in the cave ten years, and the king and his princes, soothsayers and sages, thought that the king had killed Abram.

Chapter 9

1 And Haran, the son of Terah, Abram's oldest brother, took a wife in those days.

2 Haran was thirty-nine years old when he took her; and the wife of Haran conceived and bare a son, and he called his name Lot.

3 And she conceived again and bare a daughter, and she called her name Milca; and she again conceived and bare a daughter, and she called her name Sarai.

4 Haran was forty-two years old when he begat Sarai, which was in the tenth year of the life of Abram; and in those days Abram and his mother and nurse went out from the cave, as the king and his subjects had forgotten the affair of Abram.

5 And when Abram came out from the cave, he went to Noah and his son Shem, and he remained with them to learn the instruction of the Lord and his ways, and no man knew where Abram was, and Abram served Noah and Shem his son for a long time.

C.1 This verse is quite exceptional, as it is proclaiming that Abraham who was in fact the 10th generation from Noah, was instructed by both Noah and Shem. That explains why Abraham became so wise.

6 And Abram was in Noah's house thirty-nine years, and Abram knew the Lord from three years old, and he went in the ways of the Lord until the day of his death, as Noah and his son Shem had taught him; and all the sons of the earth in those days greatly transgressed against the Lord, and they rebelled against him and they served other gods, and they forgot the Lord who had created them in the earth; and the inhabitants of the earth made unto themselves, at that time, every man his god; gods of wood and stone which could neither speak, hear, nor deliver, and the sons of men served them and they became their gods.

7 And the king and all his servants, and Terah with all his household were then the first of those that served gods of wood and stone.

8 And Terah had twelve gods of large size, made of wood and stone, after the twelve months of the year, and he served each one monthly, and every month Terah would bring his meat offering and drink offering to his gods; thus did Terah all the days.

9 And all that generation were wicked in the sight of the Lord, and they thus made every man his god, but they forsook the Lord who had created them.

10 And there was not a man found in those days in the whole earth, who knew the Lord (for they served each man his own God) except Noah and his household, and all those who were under his counsel knew the Lord in those days.

11 And Abram the son of Terah was waxing great in those days in the house of Noah, and no man knew it, and the Lord was with him.

12 And the Lord gave Abram an understanding heart, and he knew all the works of that generation were vain, and that all their gods were vain and were of no avail.

13 And Abram saw the sun shining upon the earth, and Abram said unto himself Surely now this sun that shines upon the earth is God, and him will I serve.

14 And Abram served the sun in that day and he prayed to him, and when evening came the sun set as usual, and Abram said within himself, Surely this cannot be God?

15 And Abram still continued to speak within himself, 'Who is he who made the heavens and the earth? who created upon earth? where is he?'

16 And night darkened over him, and he lifted up his eyes toward the west, north, south, and east, and he saw that the sun had vanished from the earth, and the day became dark.

17 And Abram saw the stars and moon before him, and he said, 'Surely this is the God who created the whole earth as well as man and behold

these his servants are gods around him': and Abram served the moon and prayed to it all that night.

18 And in the morning when it was light and the sun shone upon the earth as usual, Abram saw all the things that the Lord God had made upon earth.

19 And Abram said unto himself Surely these are not gods that made the earth and all mankind, but these are the servants of God, and Abram remained in the house of Noah and there knew the Lord and his ways' and he served the Lord all the days of his life, and all that generation forgot the Lord, and served other gods of wood and stone, and rebelled all their days.

20 And king Nimrod reigned securely, and all the earth was under his control, and all the earth was of one tongue and words of union.

C.2 At this particular time Nimrod was an emperor of the whole earth and yet this was a few hundred years after the Great Flood circa 2100 BC & well before the famous 7 Empires of mankind in Egypt, Assyria, Babylon, Medio-Persia, Greece, Rome and the final 7th Empire of the coming Anti-Christ. Notice that in this time-period there is not much evidence for very advanced ancient technology unlike before the Great Flood. Somehow after the Flood, God himself limited the quick technological advances that we have now seen in modern times in only the past 150 years. (For more on this topic see: http://www.outofthebottomlesspit.co.uk/413536147)

21 And all the princes of Nimrod and his great men took counsel together; Phut, Mitzraim, Cush and Canaan with their families, and they said to each other, Come let us build ourselves a city and in it a strong tower, and its top reaching heaven, and we will make ourselves famed, so that we may reign upon the whole world, in order that the evil of our enemies may cease from us, that we may reign mightily over them, and that we may not become scattered over the earth on account of their wars.

C.3 Notice that it was the *sons of Ham* who counselled together with Nimrod the son of Cush to build the Tower of Babel in *rebellion against God*. Canaan had already been cursed by Noah and now they all become cursed by building the tower. The Canaanities along with other sons of Ham had obviously been cursed by God and now in their rebellion they brought back the powers of the Nephilim and also brought back the Rephaim giants.

91

Nimrod was the son of Cush, the son of Ham, who somehow 'became a giant'. In other words, he had Nephilim (Satan's seed) blood in him. More about the history of Nephilim seed: https://beginningandend.com/bloodlines-of-the-nephilim-a-biblical-study/

LXX SEPTUAGINT GENESIS 9.8 'Nimrod began to be a giant upon the earth'

The sons of Canaan, who himself was a son of Ham, were also of Nephilim (Fallen angel) D.N.A and there were thus giants after the Great flood as well as before the Great flood.

C.4 The Tower of Babel was built by a race of giants, thus explaining how they managed to build it so high. (8000 feet high in 43 years)

> 22 And they all went before the king, and they told the king these words, and the king agreed with them in this affair, and he did so.
>
> 23 And all the families assembled consisting of about six hundred thousand men, and they went to seek an extensive piece of ground to build the city and the tower, and they sought in the whole earth and they found none like one valley at the east of the land of Shinar, about two days' walk, and they journeyed there and they dwelt there.

C.5 Now there are 750.000 men to help Nimrod build the Tower of Babel. If we go back a few chapters to just maybe 100 years after the Great Flood, Nimrod only had 'about 460 men' as mentioned in Jasher 7.35. this means that in Nimrod's time mankind grew from around 1000 plus people to numbering in the millions in just a few hundred years. Obviously Nimrod lived a very long time for Post-Flood times. It is stated that Nimrod lived to be around 230 years old. According to this book of Jasher it was Esau who killed Nimrod in around 2126. The Great Flood was in 1658. Nimrod was the son of Cush who was the son of Ham. Ham was born circa the exact year of the Great Flood. Cush was born around 35 years after the Flood. It is stated that Nimrod was born when Cush was old. People lived to be around 460 years old at the time of Cush. So, if Cush was old and was around 250 years old, then that would mean that Nimrod was born circa the year 1880 or in the time of Abraham's father Terah, which does make sense according to the Book of Jasher as Terah was Nimrud's top general in his army.

C.6 There should have been many more people by Nimrod's time to have joined his army in chapter 7.35 instead of just a few hundred? Is it just possible that Nimrod was actually born much closer to the Great Flood? Instead of Nimrod living only 230 years old as stated in this Book of Jasher, that in fact he lived like Eber, be around 400 years old. This would then make sense as to how his army could grow from only 460 men in chapter 7 of this book to 750,000 by the time of the Tower of Babel or chapter 9 of this book. Think of it, when Nimrod was young, there were only thousands of people on the earth. When he was old there were millions of people on the earth. So, he must have lived a very long time. Nimrod also descended from Nephilim which could perhaps have given him longevity?

> 24 And they began to make bricks and burn fires to build the city and the tower that they had imagined to complete.

GEN.11:1 And the whole earth was of one language, and of one speech.

GEN.11:2 And it came to pass, as they journeyed from the east, that they found a plain in the land of Shinar; and they dwelt there.

GEN.11:3 And they said one to another, 'Go to, let us make brick, and burn them thoroughly'. And they had brick for stone, and slime had they for mortar.

GEN.11:4 And they said, 'Go to, let us build us a city and a tower, whose top may reach unto heaven; and let us make us a name, lest we be scattered abroad upon the face of the whole earth'.

Book of Jubilees 10: 19-21

19 For they departed from the land of Ararat eastward to Shinar; for in his days they built the city and the tower, saying, 'Go to, let us ascend thereby into heaven.'

20 And they began to build, and in the fourth week they made brick with fire, and the bricks served them for stone, and the clay with which they cemented them together was asphalt which comes out of the sea, and out of the fountains of water in the land of Shinar.

21 And they built it: *forty and three years* [1645-1688 A.M.] were they building it; its breadth was 203 bricks, and the height (of a brick) was the third of one; *its height amounted to 5433 cubits* and 2 palms*1, and (the extent of one wall was) thirteen stades (and of the other thirty stades).

C.7 This date from the Book of Jubilees is not correct as the correct date according to the Bible was around 1900 A.M.

C.8 *1 The height of the tower was around *8000 feet high* according to these measurements of 5433 cubits. [A cubit being normally between 18-21 inches]

What did Nimrod and his people think to gain by building such a tall tower? There must have been some important reason for them to spend 43 years building this massive structure. Did they actually believe that they could reach up to heaven itself and throw God out and put their own Idols and gods there instead? Well that's at least that's what they boasted that they would do.

> 25 And the building of the tower was unto them a transgression and a sin, and they began to build it, and whilst they were building against the Lord God of heaven, they imagined in their hearts to war against him and to ascend into heaven.

C.9 How insane are the people who rebel against God in their hearts. How can a *puny human* or even a *Fallen angel* or *giant* or *demon* fight against God?

> 26 And all these people and all the families divided themselves in three parts; the first said We will ascend into heaven and fight against him; the second said, We will ascend to heaven and place our own gods there and serve them; and the third part said, We will ascend to heaven and smite him with bows and spears; and God knew all their works and all their evil thoughts, and he saw the city and the tower which they were building.
>
> 27 And when they were building they built themselves a great city and a very high and strong tower; and on account of its height the mortar and bricks did not reach the builders in their ascent to it, until those who went up had completed a full year, and after that, they reached to the builders and gave them the mortar and the bricks; thus was it done daily.

C.10 Here are some very important points to ponder: Before the Great Flood many amazing monuments, structures and pyramids and tunnels were built. There was a very advanced technology which was even more advanced then what mankind has today in modern times. We also know that when the original builders in Pre-Flood times, built structures like the pyramids that they used a form of anti-gravity or levitation in order to put the massive blocks or slabs of stone in place. Millions of them, each weighing at least several tons and sometimes up to hundreds of tons, one on top of the other with such great precision, that even today in modern times with all of our technology, we cannot duplicate them.

C.11 Apparently, the Great Pyramid in Egypt is quite an enigma. Strangely enough it is said that there is another pyramid just like it on the planet Mars, but which is ten times bigger. The Great Pyramid is 500 feet, but apparently the similar Pyramid on Mars is 5000 feet high. That sort of reminds us of the type of height that the Tower of Babel was, although apparently the Tower of / Babel was closer to 8000 feet high. On the planet Mars has also been found a Giza-like pyramid and a Sphinx. According to Tom Horn and Steve Quayle the Great Pyramid has many Secrets of Absolute Mathematical constants, and the Sacred Cubit built into its very structure. The pyramids are both aligned with True North & to the stars of Orion's Belt. (See the book The Cloud-Eaters by Tom Horn and Steve Quayle for a fantastic amount of info on this topic)

C.12 From this above verse it mentioned that *'completed a full year, and after that, they reached to the builders and gave them the mortar and the bricks'.* In other words, by the time of the tower of Babel, mankind no longer had the powers of levitation as afforded him in Pre-Flood times even though Nimrod himself was of Nephilim blood and he had giants working for him.

C.13 This clearly shows than mankind and the giants after the Great Flood did not equal the people and giants who had come before the Great flood. God obviously took away some of their powers and started to limit mankind more and more such as the length of his life and which powers he would be allowed to use such as 'levitation'.

C.14 It would seem that at the time of the Great Flood mankind became much more restricted and also the Fallen angels who had led mankind astray were also much more restricted including Satan himself. Certain activities and powers could no longer be demonstrated publicly in from of mankind as to quickly both deceive them and lead them astray.

C.15 Starting at the Great Flood mankind has actually become weaker and weaker and smaller in stature and living to now in modern times only around 70 years on average as God can't trust mankind to behave himself and if he had lived much longer then he would committed too many crimes.

C.16 Today is the 'harvest of crimes' and 'total wickedness', as you see the very wicked elite or the Merchants mentioned in Revelations 17-18, who run this planet and often live into their nineties and who subjugate the nations of the world. They themselves are led by the demonic powers of the Fallen angels.

---

28 And behold these ascended and others descended the whole day; and if a brick should fall from their hands and get broken, they would all weep over it, and if a man fell and died, none of them would look at him.

29 And the Lord knew their thoughts, and it came to pass when they were building they cast the arrows toward the heavens, and all the arrows fell upon them filled with blood, and when they saw them they said to each other, Surely we have slain all those that are in heaven.

30 For this was from the Lord in order to cause them to err, and in order; to destroy them from off the face of the ground.

31 And they built the tower and the city, and they did this thing daily until many days and years were elapsed.

C.17 There was a *rapid descent into great spiritual darkness* once the Nephilim and their sons the Rephaim had returned to the earth. So, shall it also be in man's last days on earth when Pandora's box of total Evil will be opened *in the reign of the coming worldwide dictator the Satanic Anti-Christ.*

C.18 Those people described as building the Tower of Babel, sounded more like *drones* of a Beehive, in other words *mindless zombies*. So, shall it also be in man's last days upon earth when eventually all order will break down and total chaos will descend and consume the whole earth in the time when mankind is forced to be branded with the 'Mark of the Beast' implants and thereby making him a *mindless zombie*. A time when a man shall not regard his neighbour or relative, but it shall be every man for himself. A spirit of *unrest* will come upon the whole earth:

II EZDRAS 15.19 'A man shall have no pity upon his neighbours but shall make an assault upon their houses with the sword and plunder their goods. Because of hunger for bread and because of Great Tribulation'.

II EZDRAS 15.15 'Alas for the world and for those who live in it! For the sword and misery draw near them, and *nation shall rise up against nation* with swords in their hands. For there shall be *unrest* among men...'

> 32 And God said to the seventy angels who stood foremost before him, to those who were near to him, saying, 'Come let us descend and confuse their tongues, that one man shall not understand the language of his neighbour, and they did so unto them.'

GEN.11:5 And the LORD came down to see the city and the tower, which the children of men builded.

GEN.11:6 And the LORD said, Behold, the people is one, and they have all one language; and this they begin to do: and now nothing will be restrained from them, which they have imagined to do.

GEN.11:7 Go to, let us go down, and there confound their language, that they may not understand one another's speech.

GEN.11:8 So the LORD scattered them abroad from thence upon the face of all the earth: and they left off to build the city.

> 33 And from that day following, they forgot each man his neighbour's tongue, and they could not understand to speak in one tongue, and when the builder took from the hands of his neighbour lime or stone which he did not order, the builder would cast it away and throw it upon his neighbour, that he would die.
>
> 34 And they did so many days, and they killed many of them in this manner.
>
> 35 And the Lord smote the three divisions that were there, and he

punished them according to their works and designs; those who said, We will ascend to heaven and serve our gods, became like apes and elephants; and those who said, We will smite the heaven with arrows, the Lord killed them, one man through the hand of his neighbour; and the third division of those who said, We will ascend to heaven and fight against him, the Lord scattered them throughout the earth.

36 And those who were left amongst them, when they knew and understood the evil which was coming upon them, they forsook the building, and they also became scattered upon the face of the whole earth.

37 And they ceased building the city and the tower; therefore, he called that place Babel, for there the Lord confounded the Language of the whole earth; behold it was at the east of the land of Shinar.

GEN.11:9 Therefore is the name of it called Babel; because the LORD did there confound the language of all the earth: and from thence did the LORD scatter them abroad upon the face of all the earth.

38 And as to the tower which the sons of men built, the earth opened its mouth and swallowed up one third part thereof, and a fire also descended from heaven and burned another third, and the other third is left to this day, and it is of that part which was aloft, and its circumference is three days' walk.

39 And many of the sons of men died in that tower, a people without number.

Chapter 10

1 And Peleg the son of Eber died in those days, in the forty-eighth year of the life of Abram son of Terah, and all the days of Peleg were two hundred and thirty-nine years.

2 And when the Lord had scattered the sons of men on account of their sin at the tower, behold they spread forth into many divisions, and all the sons of men were dispersed into the four corners of the earth.

Comment:1: *'All the sons of men were dispersed into the four corners of the earth'*. God forcibly moved the continents with the peoples that were on them; so obviously it happened sometime *after* the collapse of the Tower of Babel. It is stated in the Bible that the earth was divided in the days of Peleg. At one time apparently, all the continents of the planet were joined together. At the time after the destruction of the Tower of Babel by God Himself, the lands were separated from each other very suddenly, as they moved apart at around 50 miles/hour. This is indeed an amazing concept, as if all the continents were moving apart relative to each other immediately after the collapse of the Tower of Babel because of God's judgements, then how did the peoples of the earth survive the gargantuan movement of the earth's crust without being killed? A very good question. According to the Hydro-plate theory. The original mass of the earth was separated into 7 continents all joined together rather like the seams on a baseball. All it took, was for another major calamity some 250 years after the Great Flood, right in the centre of all the land masses and then all the continents started moving apart. Probably quite rapidly at first and eventually they slowed down drastically. This also explains many of things and animals found common to all the continents [SEE Walt Brown's Hydro-plate theory: https://youtu.be/sD9ZGt9UA-U?t=36]

3 And all the families became each according to its language, its land, or its city.

4 And the sons of men built many cities according to their families, in all the places where they went, and throughout the earth where the Lord had scattered them.

C.2 Note it says '*throughout the earth where the Lord had scattered them*'

5 And some of them built cities in places from which they were afterward extirpated, and they called these cities after their own names, or the names of their children, or after their particular occurrences.

C.3 Why does this above verse state: '*built cities in places from which they were afterward extirpated*'? If you look up maps of ancient times such as the ones I mentioned in the previous chapter 7, then you might find it confusing when you notice that one of the maps puts the location of say Magog or Gomer in a very different location than another map. The reason for this is simple. The different maps are showing different time periods.

C.4 At the time of the Tower of Babel mankind was 'blown to the 4 winds' so to speak by God himself. At first the nations were not so far away, but with time other nations 'took over their lands' which in turn forced them to move further outwards in relationship to their original location in Shinar at the Tower of Babel. http://www.marketing-und-vertrieb-international.com/images/gog-magog.jpg

---

6 And the sons of Japheth the son of Noah went and built themselves cities in the places where they were scattered, and they called all their cities after their names, and the sons of Japheth were divided upon the face of the earth into many divisions and languages.

7 And these are the sons of Japheth according to their families, Gomer, Magog, Medai, Javan, Tubal, Meshech and Tiras; these are the children of Japheth according to their generations.

8 And the children of Gomer, according to their cities, were the Francum, who dwell in the land of Franza, by the river Franza, by the river Senah.

9 And the children of Rephath are the Bartonim, who dwell in the land of Bartonia by the river Ledah, which empties its waters in the great sea Gihon, that is, oceanus.

10 And the children of Tugarma are ten families, and these are their names: Buzar, Parzunac, Balgar, Elicanum, Ragbib, Tarki, Bid, Zebuc, Ongal and Tilmaz; all these spread and rested in the north and built themselves cities.

11 And they called their cities after their own names, those are they who abide by the rivers Hithlah and Italac unto this day.

12 But the families of Angoli, Balgar and Parzunac, they dwell by the great river Dubnee; and the names of their cities are also according to their own names.

---

13 And the children of Javan are the Javanim who dwell in the land of Makdonia, and the children of Medaiare are the Orelum that dwell in the land of Curzon, and the children of Tubal are those that dwell in the land of Tuskanah by the river Pashiah.

14 And the children of Meshech are the Shibashni and the children of Tiras are Rushash, Cushni, and Ongolis; all these went and built themselves cities; those are the cities that are situate by the sea Jabus by the river Cura, which empties itself in the river Tragan.

15 And the children of Elishah are the Almanim, and they also went and built themselves cities; those are the cities situate between the mountains of Job and Shibathmo; and of them were the people of Lumbardi who dwell opposite the mountains of Job and Shibathmo, and they conquered the land of Italia and remained there unto this day.

16 And the children of Chittim are the Romim who dwell in the valley of Canopia by the river Tibreu.

17 And the children of Dudonim are those who dwell in the cities of the sea Gihon, in the land of Bordna.

18 These are the families of the children of Japheth according to their cities and languages, when they were scattered after the tower, and they called their cities after their names and occurrences; and these are the names of all their cities according to their families, which they built in those days after the tower.

19 And the children of Ham were Cush, Mitzraim, Phut and Canaan according to their generation and cities.

C.5 All the sons of the now cursed Canaan, the son of Ham became the Post-Flood Giants and were the beginning of all the Giant races in the middle East that the Israelites later were ordered by God to completely slaughter including the men, women and children. Why? Because they were totally corrupted with Nephilim DNA. (http://www.outofthebottomlesspit.co.uk/413536147)

C.6 According to the book of Jubilees, Canaan was not only cursed by Noah but also later cursed again by own his brethren for disobedience to his grandfather Noah's command after the Flood for Noah's son to be assigned certain territories and to not to inhabit the assigned territories of their brethren.

Jubilees 10. 31 *Cursed art thou, and cursed shalt thou be* beyond all the sons of Noah, by the curse by which we bound ourselves by an oath in the presence and the presence of the holy judge, and in the presence of Noah our father. But he did not harken unto them.

C.7 Much later after the death of Joshua it is stated in the Bible that the Israelites *drove out the Canaanities* from their newly acquired lands.

Book of Joshua: At that time, after the death of Joshua, the children of the Canaanites were still in the land, and the Israelites resolved to drive them out.

C.8 Following Bible history forwards all the way to the Millennium with Christ reigning in Jerusalem in Israel, we can clearly see that the descendants of Canaan were indeed cursed because they had Nephilim blood and had finally been eradicated.

ZEC.14:21 Yea, every pot in Jerusalem and in Judah shall be holiness unto the LORD of hosts: and all they that sacrifice shall come and take of them, and seethe therein: and in that day there shall be *no more the Canaanite* in the house of the LORD of hosts.

---

20 All these went and built themselves cities as they found fit places for them, and they called their cities after the names of their fathers Cush, Mitzraim, Phut and Canaan.

21 And the children of Mitzraim are the Ludim, Anamim, Lehabim, Naphtuchim, Pathrusim, Casluchim and Caphturim, seven families.

22 All these dwell by the river Sihor, that is the brook of Egypt, and they built themselves cities and called them after their own names.

23 And the children of Pathros and Casloch intermarried together, and from them went forth the Pelishtim, the Azathim, and the Gerarim, the Githim and the Ekronim, in all five families; these also built themselves cities, and they called their cities after the names of their fathers unto this day.

24 And the children of Canaan also built themselves cities, and they called their cities after their names, eleven cities and others without number.

25 And four men from the family of Ham went to the land of the plain; these are the names of the four men, Sodom, Gomorrah, Admah and Zeboyim.

C.9 It was five men from the family of Ham that built the five cities of Sodom , Gomorrah, Admah & Zeboyim, and Bela, which God later destroyed by the hands of his angels for their cruelty to strangers who visited their cities, and for their sexual depravity.

26 And these men built themselves four cities in the land of the plain, and they called the names of their cities after their own names.

27 And they and their children and all belonging to them dwelt in those cities, and they were fruitful and multiplied greatly and dwelt peaceably.

28 And Seir the son of Hur, son of Hivi, son of Canaan, went and found a valley opposite to Mount Paran, and he built a city there, and he and his seven sons and his household dwelt there, and he called the city which he built Seir, according to his name; that is the land of Seir unto this day.

29 These are the families of the children of Ham, according to their languages and cities, when they were scattered to their countries after the tower.

30 And some of the children of Shem son of Noah, father of all the children of Eber, also went and built themselves cities in the places wherein they were scattered, and they called their cities after their names.

31 And the sons of Shem were Elam, Ashur, Arpachshad, Lud and Aram, and they built themselves cities and called the names of all their cities after their names.

32 And Ashur son of Shem and his children and household went forth at that time, a very large body of them, and they went to a distant land that they found, and they met with a very extensive valley in the land that they went to, and they built themselves four cities, and they called them after their own names and occurrences.

33 And these are the names of the cities which the children of Ashur built, Ninevah, Resen, Calach and Rehobother; and the children of Ashur dwell there unto this day.

34 And the children of Aram also went and built themselves a city, and they called the name of the city Uz after their eldest brother, and they dwell therein; that is the land of Uz to this day.

C.10 The following is incidental information about the great patriarch Job & exactly what was the time-period in which he lived: The city of Uz was built relatively early on after the Great Flood or around 2400 BC. The great patriarch Job came from the city of Uz and therefore it is likely that he lived even earlier than Abraham who lived in 2000 BC.

JOB.1:1 There was a man in the land of Uz, whose name was Job; and that man was perfect and upright, and one that feared God, and eschewed evil.

35 And in the second year after the tower a man from the house of Ashur, whose name was Bela, went from the land of Ninevah to sojourn with his household wherever he could find a place; and they came until opposite the cities of the plain against Sodom, and they dwelt there.

36 And the man rose up and built there a small city, and called its name Bela, after his name; that is the land of Zoar unto this day.

37 And these are the families of the children of Shem according to their language and cities, after they were scattered upon the earth after the tower.

38 And every kingdom, city, and family of the families of the children of Noah built themselves many cities after this.

39 And they established governments in all their cities, in order to be regulated by their orders; so did all the families of the children of Noah forever.

Chapter 11

Abraham the *Idol Smasher*

> 1 And Nimrod son of Cush was still in the land of Shinar, and he reigned over it and dwelt there, and he built cities in the land of Shinar.

Comment:1: The Bible states that the earth was divided in the days of Peleg. Peleg was born close to the time of Nimrod and was born 250 years after the Great Flood. Peleg lived to be around the same age as Nimrod at 239 years according to Bible Timeframe charts but died earlier than Nimrod according to this book. This book of Jasher states that Abraham was born before the Tower of Babel in the time of Nimrod. We know that the dispersion of the peoples of the earth by God happened after the Tower of Babel in around 1950 A.C. (After creation). Apparently a little later the continents moved apart. Nimrod is said to have lived for 230 years, so Abraham would have indeed been born in the time of Nimrod. (Note: Bible charts differ slightly in the time sequence as in comparison with this Book of Jasher. The Bible puts Abraham as born after the Tower of Babel.)

C.2 In all honesty, it would have been very difficult to keep exact and accurate records of the exact times and dates to events many thousands of years ago. I think that the ancient scholars and scribes did a fantastic job of preserving the ancient books and handing them down to other generations. When you consider that a book made of paper will disintegrate in 200 years. Think how many times these ancient manuscripts such as this Book of Jasher have had to be re-written for our benefit. I think it is quite amazing that the Bible (Old testament) and the Septuagint version of the Old Testament as well as the Apocryphal books of both Jasher and Jubilees largely agree in most points. The *only thing not 100% accurate are the dates* of the events. But that is to be expected and, in my opinion, this does not alter the beauty of these ancient texts, which do indeed reveal a lot of information as to how the peoples of the earth lived many thousands of years ago.

C.3 This book of Jasher, is in my opinion, absolutely fascinating, as it has more information about Pre-Flood times than any other book except the Book of Enoch. (See my book '**Enoch Insights**') The book of Jasher also has more information about Nimrod and the Tower of Babel than any other book that I have ever read.

> 2 And these are the names of the four cities which he built, and he called their names after the occurrences that happened to them in the building of the tower.
>
> 3 And he called the first Babel, saying, Because the Lord there

> confounded the language of the whole earth; and the name of the second he called Erech, because from there God dispersed them.

C.4 Here we can clearly see that in the far past names of people and even cities were determined by the events that were happening at the time. Babel was first called Babel by king Nimrod after the Tower of Babel had been destroyed by God's angels. He built a city there instead with the same name. Babel means 'Confusion of Tongues'. The 2nd city that Nimrod built was called Erech which means 'Dispersion of the Peoples'.

> 4 And the third he called Eched, saying there was a great battle at that place; and the fourth he called Calnah, because his princes and mighty men were consumed there, and they vexed the Lord, they rebelled and transgressed against him.

C.5 The third city that Nimrod had built after the collapse of the Tower of Babel was Eched. Eched meaning – 'Place of Great Battle'. Fourthly Nimrod had the city of Calnah built. Meaning of Calnah = 'Consumed by Rebellion'.

> 5 And when Nimrod had built these cities in the land of Shinar, he placed in them the remainder of his people, his princes and his mighty men that were left in his kingdom.
>
> 6 And Nimrod dwelt in Babel, and he there renewed his reign over the rest of his subjects, and he reigned securely, and the subjects and princes of Nimrod called his name Amraphel, saying that at the tower his princes and men fell through his means.

GEN.11:9 Therefore is the name of it called Babel; because the LORD did there confound the language of all the earth: and from thence did the LORD scatter them abroad upon the face of all the earth.

C.6 This other name of Nimrod i.e. Amraphel is also mentioned in the Book of Jubilees:

JUBILEES:13.23 And in this year came Chedorlaomer, king of Elam, and Amraphel, king of Shinar, and Arioch king of Sellasar, and Tergal, king of nations, and slew the king of Gomorrah, and the king of Sodom fled, and many fell through wounds in the vale of Siddim, by the Salt Sea.

> 7 And notwithstanding this, Nimrod did not return to the Lord, and he continued in wickedness and teaching wickedness to the sons of men; and Mardon, his son, was worse than his father, and continued to add to the abominations of his father.

Jubilees 11.2 And the sons of Noah began to war on each other, to take captive and to slay one another, and to shed the blood of men upon the earth and to eat blood and to build strong cities and walls and towers and individuals began to exalt themselves above the nation and to found the beginnings of Kingdoms ...

8 And he caused the sons of men to sin, therefore it is said, From the wicked go forth wickedness.

9 At that time there was war between the families of the children of Ham, as they were dwelling in the cities which they had built.

10 And Chedorlaomer, king of Elam, went away from the families of the children of Ham, and he fought with them and he subdued them, and he went to the five cities of the plain and he fought against them and he subdued them, and they were under his control.

11 And they served him twelve years, and they gave him a yearly tax.

12 At that time died Nahor, son of Serug, in the forty-ninth year of the life of Abram son of Terah.

13 And in the fiftieth year of the life of Abram son of Terah, Abram came forth from the house of Noah, and went to his father's house.

14 And Abram knew the Lord, and he went in his ways and instructions, and the Lord his God was with him.

15 And Terah his father was in those days, still captain of the host of king Nimrod, and he still followed strange gods.

16 And Abram came to his father's house and saw twelve gods standing there in their temples, and the anger of Abram was kindled when he saw these images in his father's house.

17 And Abram said, As the Lord lives these images shall not remain in my father's house; so shall the Lord who created me do unto me if in three days' time I do not break them all.

18 And Abram went from them, and his anger burned within him.

And Abram hastened and went from the chamber to his father's outer court, and he found his father sitting in the court, and all his servants with him, and Abram came and sat before him.

19 And Abram asked his father, saying, Father, tell me where is God who created heaven and earth, and all the sons of men upon earth, and who created thee and me. And Terah answered his son Abram and said, 'Behold those who created us are all with us in the house.'

20 And Abram said to his father, My lord, shew them to me I pray thee; and Terah brought Abram into the chamber of the inner court, and Abram saw, and behold the whole room was full of gods of wood and stone, twelve great images and others less than they without number.

21 And Terah said to his son, 'Behold these are they which made all you see upon earth, and which created me and thee, and all mankind.'

22 And Terah bowed down to his gods, and he then went away from them, and Abram, his son, went away with him.

23 And when Abram had gone from them he went to his mother and sat before her, and he said to his mother, 'Behold, my father has shown me those who made heaven and earth, and all the sons of men.'

24 Now, therefore, hasten and fetch a kid from the flock, and make of it savoury meat, that I may bring it to my father's gods as an offering for them to eat; perhaps I may thereby become acceptable to them.

25 And his mother did so, and she fetched a kid, and made savoury meat thereof, and brought it to Abram, and Abram took the savoury meat from his mother and brought it before his father's gods, and he drew nigh to them that they might eat; and Terah his father, did not know of it.

26 And Abram saw on the day when he was sitting amongst them, that they had no voice, no hearing, no motion, and not one of them could stretch forth his hand to eat.

27 And Abram mocked them, and said, Surely the savoury meat that I prepared has not pleased them, or perhaps it was too little for them, and for that reason they would not eat; therefore tomorrow I will prepare fresh savoury meat, better and more plentiful than this, in order that I may see the result.

28 And it was on the next day that Abram directed his mother concerning the savoury meat, and his mother rose and fetched three fine kids from the flock, and she made of them some excellent savoury meat, such as her son was fond of, and she gave it to her son Abram; and Terah his father did not know of it.

29 And Abram took the savoury meat from his mother and brought it before his father's gods into the chamber; and he came nigh unto them that they might eat, and he placed it before them, and Abram sat before them all day, thinking perhaps they might eat.

30 And Abram viewed them, and behold they had neither voice nor hearing, nor did one of them stretch forth his hand to the meat to eat.

31 And in the evening of that day in that house Abram was clothed with the spirit of God.

32 And he called out and said, Woe unto my father and this wicked generation, whose hearts are all inclined to vanity, who serve these idols of wood and stone which can neither eat, smell, hear nor speak, who have mouths without speech, eyes without sight, ears without hearing, hands without feeling, and legs which cannot move; like them are those that made them and that trust in them.

Jubilees 11.3 'And they made for themselves molten images and worshipped each idol and they began to make graven images and unclean simulacra and malignant spirits assisted and seduced them into committing transgression and uncleanness.

33 And when Abram saw all these things his anger was kindled against his father, and he hastened and took a hatchet in his hand, and came unto the chamber of the gods, and he broke all his father's gods.

C.7 Abraham was in fact an Idol Smasher. What he started to do with his father's idols, he continued to do for the rest of his life. (See my book

34 And when he had done breaking the images, he placed the hatchet in the hand of the great god which was there before them, and he went out; and Terah his father came home, for he had heard at the door the sound of the striking of the hatchet; so Terah came into the house to know what this was about.

35 And Terah, having heard the noise of the hatchet in the room of images, ran to the room to the images, and he met Abram going out.

36 And Terah entered the room and found all the idols fallen down and broken, and the hatchet in the hand of the largest, which was not broken, and the savoury meat which Abram his son had made was still before them.

37 And when Terah saw this his anger was greatly kindled, and he hastened and went from the room to Abram.

38 And he found Abram his son still sitting in the house; and he said to him, What is this work thou hast done to my gods?

39 And Abram answered Terah his father and he said, Not so my lord, for I brought savoury meat before them, and when I came nigh to them with the meat that they might eat, they all at once stretched forth their hands to eat before the great one had put forth his hand to eat.

40 And the large one saw their works that they did before him, and his anger was violently kindled against them, and he went and took the hatchet that was in the house and came to them and broke them all, and behold the hatchet is yet in his hand as you see.

41 And Terah's anger was kindled against his son Abram, when he spoke this; and Terah said to Abram his son in his anger, 'What is this tale that thou hast told? You speak lies to me.

42 Is there in these gods spirit, soul or power to do all thou hast told me? Are they not wood and stone, and have I not myself made them,

and canst thou speak such lies, saying that the large god that was with them smote them? It is thou that didst place the hatchet in his hands, and then say he smote them all.

43 And Abram answered his father and said to him, 'And how canst thou then serve these idols in whom there is no power to do anything? Can those idols in which thou trust deliver thee? can they hear thy prayers when thou call upon them? Can they deliver thee from the hands of thy enemies, or will they fight thy battles for thee against thy enemies, that thou should serve wood and stone which can neither speak nor hear?'

44 And now surely it is not good for thee nor for the sons of men that are connected with thee, to do these things; are you so silly, so foolish or so short of understanding that you will serve wood and stone, and do after this manner?

45 And forget the Lord God who made heaven and earth, and who created you in the earth, and thereby bring a great evil upon your souls in this matter by serving stone and wood?

46 Did not our fathers in days of old sin in this matter, and the Lord God of the universe brought the waters of the flood upon them and destroyed the whole earth?

47 And how can you continue to do this and serve gods of wood and stone, who cannot hear, or speak, or deliver you from oppression, thereby bringing down the anger of the God of the universe upon you?

48 Now therefore my father refrain from this and bring not evil upon thy soul and the souls of thy household.

49 And Abram hastened and sprang from before his father, and took the hatchet from his father's largest idol, with which Abram broke it and ran away.

50 And Terah, seeing all that Abram had done, hastened to go from his house, and he went to the king and he came before Nimrod and stood before him, and he bowed down to the king; and the king said, 'What

dost thou want?'

51 And he said, I beseech thee my lord, to hear me. Now fifty years back a child was born to me, and thus has he done to my gods and thus has he spoken; and now therefore, my lord and king, send for him that he may come before thee, and judge him according to the law, that we may be delivered from his evil.

52 And the king sent three men of his servants, and they went and brought Abram before the king. And Nimrod and all his princes and servants were that day sitting before him, and Terah sat also before them.

53 And the king said to Abram, 'What is this that thou hast done to thy father and to his gods? And Abram answered the king in the words that he spoke to his father, and he said, 'The large god that was with them in the house did to them what thou hast heard.'

54 And the king said to Abram, 'Had they power to speak and eat and do as thou hast said?' And Abram answered the king, saying, 'And if there be no power in them why dost thou serve them and cause the sons of men to err through thy follies?'

55 Dost thou imagine that they can deliver thee or do anything small or great, that you should serve them? And why wilt thou not sense the God of the whole universe, who created thee and in whose power it is to kill and keep alive?

56 0 foolish, simple, and ignorant king, woe unto thee forever.

57 I thought thou wouldst teach thy servants the upright way, but thou hast not done this, but hast filled the whole earth with thy sins and the sins of thy people who have followed thy ways.

58 Dost thou not know, or hast thou not heard, that this evil which you do, our ancestors sinned therein in days of old, and the eternal God brought the waters of the flood upon them and destroyed them all, and also destroyed the whole earth on their account? And wilt thou and thy

people rise up now and do like unto this work, in order to bring down the anger of the Lord God of the universe, and to bring evil upon thee and the whole earth?

59 Now therefore put away this evil deed which you do, and serve the God of the universe, as thy soul is in his hands, and then it will be well with thee.

60 And if thy wicked heart will not hearken to my words to cause thee to forsake thy evil ways, and to serve the eternal God, then wilt thou die in shame in the latter days, thou, thy people and all who are connected with thee, hearing thy words or walking in thy evil ways.

61 And when Abram had ceased speaking before the king and princes, Abram lifted up his eyes to the heavens, and he said, 'The Lord sees all the wicked, and he will judge them.

C.8 Here we can clearly see that God Himself is speaking directly through Abraham in what is called prophecy. Sadly, today the king, like most people, don't recognise that it is God speaking to them as they have 'ears that cannot hear' and spiritual 'eyes that refuse to see'.

C.9 In spite of Nimrod's unbelief, all that Abraham prophesied before king Nimrod did indeed come to pass. See Chapter 27 of this book where Nimrod himself is killed by Esau the grandson of Abraham.

C.10 The problem with kings and leaders and the rich and powerful is that they often think that they themselves are far too high and mighty to have to listen to one of God's prophets, often with disastrous consequences for the king and his empire as shown clearly throughout history.

C.11 Enoch was the first to warn people of coming disaster and that God's Judgements would come in the form a Great Flood. He warned the nations of the world for 243 years. He also rebuked the first 200 Fallen angels to their faces on behalf of God

JUD.1:14 And Enoch also, the seventh from Adam, prophesied of these, saying, Behold, the Lord cometh with ten thousand of his saints,

JUD.1:6 And the angels which kept not their first estate, but left their own habitation, he hath reserved in everlasting chains under darkness unto the judgment of the great day.

C.12 Noah and Methuselah warned the nations for 120 years of the imminent Great Flood without anyone listening, with the exception of 8 souls who went together with Noah on the Ark

GEN.6:13 And God said unto Noah, 'The end of all flesh is come before me; for the earth is filled with violence through them; and, behold, I will destroy them with the earth'.

C.13 Moses warned Pharaoh of impending disaster for Egypt, but Pharaoh wouldn't listen. As a direct result - he lost Egypt.

EXO.6:1 Then the LORD said unto Moses, 'Now shalt thou see what I will do to Pharaoh: for with a strong hand shall he let them go, and with a strong hand shall he drive them out of his land'.

EXO.7:19 And the LORD spoke unto Moses, Say unto Aaron, Take thy rod, and stretch out thine hand upon the waters of Egypt, upon their streams, upon their rivers, and upon their ponds, and upon all their pools of water, that they may become blood; and that there may be blood throughout all the land of Egypt, both in vessels of wood, and in vessels of stone.

C.14 Daniel the prophet warned Nebuchadnezzar king of Babylon in Daniel chapter 4 that he needed to humble his pride and take care of the poor; he didn't listen and within a year was turned into a beast for 7 years.

DAN.4:25 That they shall drive thee (Nebuchadnezzar) from men, and thy dwelling shall be with the beasts of the field, and they shall make thee to eat grass as oxen, and they shall wet thee with the dew of heaven, and seven times (7 years) shall pass over thee, till thou know that the most High rules in the kingdom of men, and giveth it to whomsoever he will.

DAN.4:27 Wherefore, O king, let my counsel be acceptable unto thee, and break off thy sins by righteousness, and thine iniquities by shewing mercy to the poor; if it may be a lengthening of thy tranquillity.

C.15 Another prophecy in the Book of Daniel saved Israel from Alexander the Great the Grecian Empire's first king when he came to Israel. Israel showed him the ancient prophecies showing his conquests in the Book of Daniel chapter 8. He was so impressed that he left Israel alone and moved on in his conquests to neighbouring lands. This prophecy was given at least 200 years before the Grecian Empire even existed:

DAN.8:3 Then I lifted up mine eyes, and saw, and, behold, there stood before the river a ram which had two horns: and the two horns were high; but one was higher than the other, and the higher came up last.

DAN.8:5 And as I was considering, behold, an he goat came from the west on the face of the whole earth, and touched not the ground: and the goat had a notable horn between his eyes.

DAN.8:6 And he came to the ram that had two horns, which I had seen standing before the river, and ran unto him in the fury of his power.

DAN.8:7 And I saw him come close unto the ram, and he was moved with choler against him, and smote the ram, and brake his two horns: and there was no power in the ram to stand before him, but he cast him down to the ground, and stamped upon him: and there was none that could deliver the ram out of his hand.

DAN.8:8 Therefore the he goat waxed very great: and when he was strong, the great horn was broken; and for it came up four notable ones toward the four winds of heaven.

INTERPETATION

DAN.8:20 The ram which thou saw having two horns are the kings of Media and Persia.

DAN.8:21 And the rough goat is the king of Grecia (Alexander the Great): and the great horn that is between his eyes is the first king.

C.16 All the other major and minor prophets in the Bible warned nations to repent or perish and what was prophesied has already come to pass or will indeed yet come to pass in the future.

C.17 Jesus told the Pharisees in Matthew 23 that Israel would soon be destroyed by the Romans. They obviously didn't want to listen and soon thereafter had Jesus crucified for his warnings. However, 40 years later, the Romans came and crucified 100,000 Jews outside the walls of Jerusalem and slaughtered another million Jews and drove those not slaughtered out of Israel. Israel ceased being a nation for almost 2000 years after that.

MAT.24:1 And Jesus went out and departed from the temple: and his disciples came to him for to shew him the buildings of the temple.

MAT.24:2 And Jesus said unto them, 'See ye not all these things? verily I say unto you, 'There shall not be left here one stone upon another, that shall not be thrown down'. - *fulfilled 40 years later*

C.18 In the past 2000 years since Christ there have been many prophets also. One that everyone knows is Nostradamus

C.19 In Conclusion: Why do I mention all of the above? Because it shows the grave danger of not taking God's prophets seriously. It leads to disaster to those with deaf ears including kings and even whole nations and empires. Prophets are often not appreciated in their own time. It is only later that people recognise that they must have been a prophet because what they prophesied did come to pass.

Chapter 12

1 And when the king heard the words of Abram he ordered him to be put into prison; and Abram was ten days in prison.

2 And at the end of those days the king ordered that all the kings, princes and governors of different provinces and the sages should come before him, and they sat before him, and Abram was still in the house of confinement.

3 And the king said to the princes and sages, 'Have you heard what Abram, the son of Terah, has done to his father? 'Thus has he done to him, and I ordered him to be brought before me, and thus has he spoken; his heart did not misgive him, neither did he stir in my presence, and behold now he is confined in the prison.'

Comment:1: The Elite don't want to be reminded that there really is a God in the Heavens, as that would mean that they might owe Him some sort of obedience, especially if you are supposed to be someone high and mighty and a demi-god like Nimrod and therefore answerable to no man or God.

4 And therefore decide what judgment is due to this man who reviled the king; who spoke and did all the things that you heard.

5 And they all answered the king saying, 'The man who reviles the king should be hanged upon a tree; but having done all the things that he said, and having despised our gods, he must therefore be burned to death, for this is the law in this matter.

C.2 This story shows very clearly how twisted are those who deliberately follow the ways of darkness. Right is Wrong and Wrong is Right to the kings of the past and the leaders & Merchants of the countries of the world today who are just like Nimrod; acting as gods or demi-gods, and the Truth is whatever those in power declare. As one can see, things haven't changed much in the modern world of today. It is just the about the same, but on a much bigger scale. When a man like Abraham stands up with conviction against the status quo he is immediately imprisoned and hooted down like a lunatic, and in this story, they tried to burn him in a big fiery oven.

PSA.37:14 The wicked have drawn out the sword, and have bent their bow, to cast down the poor and needy, and to slay such as be of upright conversation.

PSA.37:15 Their sword shall enter into their own heart, and their bows shall be broken.

> 6 If it pleases the king to do this, let him order his servants to kindle a fire both night and day in thy brick furnace, and then we will cast this man into it. And the king did so, and he commanded his servants that they should prepare a fire for three days and three nights in the king's furnace, that is in Casdim; and the king ordered them to take Abram from prison and bring him out to be burned.

C.3 How many innocent people have been burned at the stake by the Catholic church during the 600-year period of the Inquisition?

We find out that in modern times that every time there was a *mini Ice-age* such as in the 14th, 17th & 18th centuries, that the bad weather was typically blamed on the local witch. If there wasn't one, then the Catholic church would find some innocents that they didn't like and blame them for the Ice-age. Many times, so-called witches that were burned were actually a group of Christians that the Catholic church had no jurisdiction over and probably other independent groups. Tens of thousands of innocent people were blamed and probably even many more people who were burned at the stake during the Mini Ice-ages of the past 700 years.

PSA.37:35 I have seen the wicked in great power and spreading himself like a green bay tree.

PSA.37:36 Yet he passed away, and, lo, he was not: yea, I sought him, but he could not be found.

> 7 And all the king's servants, princes, lords, governors, and judges, and all the inhabitants of the land, about nine hundred thousand men, stood opposite the furnace to see Abram.
>
> 8 And all the women and little ones crowded upon the roofs and towers to see what was doing with Abram, and they all stood together at a distance; and there was not a man left that did not come on that day to behold the scene.

C.4 People also started sacrificing their children to the Idol of Molech, one of the Fallen Angels.

Imagine what sick beings these Fallen angels like Lucifer and Molech are like. Requiring men & women to cast their innocent children and babies into the fire to satisfy the perverted lusts and grotesque cravings of Devils and Demons.

9 And when Abram was come, the conjurors of the king and the sages saw Abram, and they cried out to the king, saying, 'Our sovereign lord, surely this is the man whom we know to have been the child at whose birth the great star swallowed the four stars, which we declared to the king now fifty years since.'

10 And behold now his father has also transgressed thy commands, and mocked thee by bringing thee another child, which you did kill.

PSA.37:32 The wicked watch the righteous, and seeketh to slay him.

11 And when the king heard their words, he was exceedingly wroth, and he ordered Terah to be brought before him.

12 And the king said, 'Hast thou heard what the conjurors have spoken? Now tell me truly, how didst thou; and if thou shalt speak truth thou shalt be acquitted'.

13 And seeing that the king's anger was so much kindled, Terah said to the king, 'My lord and king, thou hast heard the truth, and what the sages have spoken is right. And the king said, 'How could you do this thing, to transgress my orders and to give me a child that thou didst not beget, and to take value for him?

14 And Terah answered the king, 'Because my tender feelings were excited for my son, at that time, and I took a son of my handmaid, and I brought him to the king.'

15 And the king said Who advised thee to this? Tell me, do not hide aught from me, and then thou shalt not die.

16 And Terah was greatly terrified in the king's presence, and he said to the king, It was Haran my eldest son who advised me to this; and Haran was in those days that Abram was born, two and thirty years old.

17 But Haran did not advise his father to anything, for Terah said this to the king in order to deliver his soul from the king, for he feared greatly; and the king said to Terah, 'Haran thy son who advised thee to this shall die through fire with Abram; for the sentence of death is upon him for

having rebelled against the king's desire in doing this thing.'

18 And Haran at that time felt inclined to follow the ways of Abram, but he kept it within himself.

19 And Haran said in his heart, 'Behold now the king has seized Abram on account of these things which Abram did, and it shall come to pass, that if Abram prevail over the king I will follow him, but if the king prevail I will go after the king.''

20 And when Terah had spoken this to the king concerning Haran his son, the king ordered Haran to be seized with Abram.

21 And they brought them both, Abram and Haran his brother, to cast them into the fire; and all the inhabitants of the land and the king's servants and princes and all the women and little ones were there, standing that day over them.

C.5 ABORTION: In modern times it is slightly different. Now there is a new way to get rid of children and it is called Abortion.

One billion aborted babies in the past 60 years on this planet. In reality our world is just as barbaric as in the time of Nimrod and it will soon be as barbaric as in the times before the Great Flood, when it descended into total anarchy and chaos. Why? Because so-called enlightened modern men are deliberately taking away all of the safeguards that God had put in place to teach people how-to live in love and consideration for one another. The exact stats? 41,000,000 abortions in the year 2018 alone. Actually 60,000,000 in 2018 by another official count. At the current rate that represents 410-600 Million in 10 years. 1 Billion in less than 25 years. It is also circa one out of every three pregnancies that was terminated in 2018

Source: ABORTION WAS NO.1 CAUSE OF DEATH IN 2018: //www.breitbart. com/health/2018/12/31/abortion-leading-cause-of-death-in-2018-with-41-million-killed/ >

22 And the king's servants took Abram and his brother, and they stripped them of all their clothes excepting their lower garments which were upon them.

PSA.37:12 The wicked plots against the just, and gnashes upon him with his teeth.

23 And they bound their hands and feet with linen cords, and the servants of the king lifted them up and cast them both into the furnace.

> 24 And the Lord loved Abram and he had compassion over him, and the Lord came down and delivered Abram from the fire and he was not burned.
>
> 25 But all the cords with which they bound him were burned, while Abram remained and walked about in the fire.

C.6 This account of Abraham being thrown into the fire is very similar to the story of Shadrach, Meshech and Abendigo in the Book of Daniel.

DAN.3:23 And these three men, Shadrach, Meshach, and Abednego, fell down bound into the midst of the burning fiery furnace.

> 26 And Haran died when they had cast him into the fire, and he was burned to ashes, for his heart was not perfect with the Lord; and those men who cast him into the fire, the flame of the fire spread over them, and they were burned, and twelve men of them died.
>
> 27 And Abram walked in the midst of the fire three days and three nights, and all the servants of the king saw him walking in the fire, and they came and told the king, saying, 'Behold we have seen Abram walking about in the midst of the fire, and even the lower garments which are upon him are not burned, but the cord with which he was bound is burned.'

DAN.3:25 He answered and said, Lo, I see four men loose, walking in the midst of the fire, and they have no hurt; and the form of the *fourth is like the Son of God.*

C.7 In the story of Shadrach, Meshech and Abendigo the Bible specifically mentions that it was Jesus, the Son of God protected His servants, whilst they were going through this terrible ordeal of going through the fire!

> 28 And when the king heard their words his heart fainted and he would not believe them; so he sent other faithful princes to see this matter, and they went and saw it and told it to the king; and the king rose to go and see it, and he saw Abram walking to and fro in the midst of the fire, and he saw Haran's body burned, and the king wondered greatly.

C.8 At the time of writing this: All Judeo/Christian beliefs & morals are rapidly being eroded and deliberately destroyed as we speak. There are over 180,000 Christian martyrs around the world every year right now, mostly in the Middle East, Africa and the Far East in countries such as Communist China. Today there are more Christians killed than any other religion. It has never been so bad in all of history unto this day!

119

29 And the king ordered Abram to be taken out from the fire; and his servants approached to take him out and they could not, for the fire was round about and the flame ascending toward them from the furnace.

30 And the king's servants fled from it, and the king rebuked them, saying, 'Make haste and bring Abram out of the fire that you shall not die.'

31 And the servants of the king again approached to bring Abram out, and the flames came upon them and burned their faces so that eight of them died.

DAN.3:22 Therefore because the king's commandment was urgent, and the furnace exceeding hot, the flames of the fire slew those men that took up Shadrach, Meshach, and Abednego.

32 And when the king saw that his servants could not approach the fire lest they should be burned, the king called to Abram, O servant of the God who is in heaven, go forth from amidst the fire and come hither before me; and Abram hearkened to the voice of the king, and he went forth from the fire and came and stood before the king.

33 And when Abram came out the king and all his servants saw Abram coming before the king, with his lower garments upon him, for they were not burned, but the cord with which he was bound was burned.

34 And the king said to Abram, 'How is it that thou was not burned in the fire?'

35 And Abram said to the king, 'The God of heaven and earth in whom I trust and who has all in his power, he delivered me from the fire into which thou didst cast me'.

36 And Haran the brother of Abram was burned to ashes, and they sought for his body, and they found it consumed.

37 And Haran was eighty-two years old when he died in the fire of Casdim. And the king, princes, and inhabitants of the land, seeing that Abram was delivered from the fire, they came and bowed down to Abram.

C.9 This is so sickening to see that Terah, who was Abraham's own father would lie about his son Haran, to the point of letting him get burned at the stake, in order to save his own neck. Nimrod was also in on the plot, as he was offering Terah 'a way out', if he could find a good excuse for why Abraham was *not killed* as ordered *when he was born* 50 years previously. Nimrod did not want to lose Terah, who was his top general.

C.10 The shenanigans and compromises that go on in high places, even today, where the lives of poor of the world end up being sacrificed in all of man's hellish wars, which are again sacrifices to *'the demon gods of War'*, just so that one rich nation can rob, steal and murder & plunder another one. All for what? Mammon! Another *awful demon god*.

C.11 The rich and wealthy today, are still worshipping hellish Idols and trying to get favours of these Fallen Demon gods, which still involves some sort of human sacrifices like World War I & World War II and all the other hellish and totally unnecessary and totally avoidable wars fought on this planet. The war machine: The Military Industrial Complex in the U.S.A today has the motto of 'Eternal Wars must be waged to maintain our economy and all our almighty god the Dollar'- which is yet another sibling of the demon god Mammon.

---

38 And Abram said to them, 'Do not bow down to me, but bow down to the God of the world who made you, and serve him, and go in his ways for it is he who delivered me from out of this fire, and it is he who created the souls and spirits of all men, and formed man in his mother's womb, and brought him forth into the world, and it is he who will deliver those who trust in him from all pain.'

39 And this thing seemed very wonderful in the eyes of the king and princes, that Abram was saved from the fire and that Haran was burned; and the king gave Abram many presents and he gave him his two head servants from the king's house; the name of one was Oni and the name of the other was Eliezer.

C.12 Eliezer became Abraham's top man and who would have inherited Abraham's kingdom if he had produced no heir in Isaac. It is interesting to see that it was Nimrod who gave his servant Eliezer to Abraham. This interesting detail is not mentioned in the Bible.

---

40 And all the kings, princes and servants gave Abram many gifts of silver and gold and pearl, and the king and his princes sent him away, and he went in peace.

41 And Abram went forth from the king in peace, and many of the king's servants followed him, and about three hundred men joined him.

---

42 And Abram returned on that day and went to his father's house, he and the men that followed him, and Abram served the Lord his God all the days of his life, and he walked in his ways and followed his law.

43 And from that day forward Abram inclined the hearts of the sons of men to serve the Lord.

44 And at that time Nahor and Abram took unto themselves wives, the daughters of their brother Haran; the wife of Nahor was Milca and the name of Abram's wife was Sarai. And Sarai, wife of Abram, was barren; she had no offspring in those days.

45 And at the expiration of two years from Abram's going out of the fire, that is in the fifty-second year of his life, behold king Nimrod sat in Babel upon the throne, and the king fell asleep and dreamed that he was standing with his troops and hosts in a valley opposite the king's furnace.

46 And he lifted up his eyes and saw a man in the likeness of Abram coming forth from the furnace, and that he came and stood before the king with his drawn sword, and then sprang to the king with his sword, when the king fled from the man, for he was afraid; and while he was running, the man threw an egg upon the king's head, and the egg became a great river.

47 And the king dreamed that all his troops sank in that river and died, and the king took flight with three men who were before him and he escaped.

48 And the king looked at these men and they were clothed in princely dresses as the garments of kings and had the appearance and majesty of kings.

49 And while they were running, the river again turned to an egg before the king, and there came forth from the egg a young bird which came before the king and flew at his head and plucked out the king's eye.

50 And the king was grieved at the sight, and he awoke out of his sleep and his spirit was agitated; and he felt a great terror.

C.13 It would seem in hindsight that this dream was indeed a warning that Nimrod would be killed by Abraham or his descendants.

C14 FACT: The dream did come to pass.

C.15 INTERPRETATION: The egg changing into a river is probably talking about the passage of time. As Nimrod lived to be around 220. At the time of this dream he was around 102 years old. This dream is really remarkable because it is describing that on two occasions Nimrod would be in danger from both Abraham and from his descendants.

C.16 Firstly, Abraham almost killed Nimrod in the famous 'Slaughter of the 5 kings' when Abraham went to retrieve his captured nephew Lot from 5 kings who had captured him and many other people. However, in this Book of Jasher, somehow Nimrod escaped on that occasion with a few of his men just like in the dream above.

GEN.14:14 And when Abram heard that his brother was taken captive, he armed his trained servants, born in his own house, three hundred and eighteen, and pursued them unto Dan.

GEN.14:15 And he divided himself against them, he and his servants, by night, and smote them, and pursued them unto Hobah, which is on the left hand of Damascus.

GEN.14:16 And he brought back all the goods, and also brought again his brother Lot, and his goods, and the women also, and the people.

C.17 Much later in time - Abraham's grandson Esau was the one who ended up fighting and killing both of Nimrod's two bodyguards as well as Nimrod himself.

C.18 (INTERPRETATION of dream): According to this Book of Jasher it was Esau who chopped off Nimrod's head. Maybe, that is what was the meaning of the 'bird plucking out 'Nimrod's eye' in his dream. Esau was perhaps the young bird that came from the yoke after the passage of time (118 years later) and was only around 18 years old when he killed Nimrod.

See Nimrod killed by Esau in this book in chapter 27

C.19 Esau himself was a very violent man and he also attempted many times to kill his own twin brother Jacob. Some say that Esau was a lot like Cain from before the Great Flood and was very evil and not at all like his righteous brother Jacob.

51 And in the morning the king rose from his couch in fear, and he ordered all the wise men and magicians to come before him, when the king related his dream to them.

52 And a wise servant of the king, whose name was Anuki, answered the king, saying, 'This is nothing else but the evil of Abram and his

seed which will spring up against my Lord and king in the latter days.'

53 And behold the day will come when Abram and his seed and the children of his household will war with my king, and they will smite all the king's hosts and his troops.

54 And as to what thou hast said concerning three men which thou didst see like unto thyself, and which did escape, this means that only thou wilt escape with three kings from the kings of the earth who will be with thee in battle.

55 And that which thou saw of the river which turned to an egg as at first, and the young bird plucking out thine eye, this means nothing else but the seed of Abram which will slay the king in latter days.

C.20 This vision is fulfilled later in this Book of Jasher, when it turns out to be Esau, the great-grand-son of Abraham who kills king Nimrod.

56 This is my king's dream, and this is its interpretation, and the dream is true, and the interpretation which thy servant has given thee is right.

57 Now therefore my king, surely thou know that it is now fifty-two years since thy sages saw this at the birth of Abram, and if my king will suffer Abram to live in the earth it will be to the injury of my lord and king, for all the days that Abram lives neither thou nor thy kingdom will be established, for this was known formerly at his birth; and why will not my king slay him, that his evil may be kept from thee in latter days?

58 And Nimrod hearkened to the voice of Anuki, and he sent some of his servants in secret to go and seize Abram and bring him before the king to suffer death.

59 And Eliezer, Abram's servant whom the king had given him, was at that time in the presence of the king, and he heard what Anuki had advised the king, and what the king had said to cause Abram's death.

60 And Eliezer said to Abram, 'Hasten, rise up and save thy soul, that

thou mayest not die through the hands of the king, for thus did he see in a dream concerning thee, and thus did Anuki interpret it, and thus also did Anuki advise the king concerning thee.'

61 And Abram hearkened to the voice of Eliezer, and Abram hastened and ran for safety to the house of Noah and his son Shem, and he concealed himself there and found a place of safety; and the king's servants came to Abram's house to seek him, but they could not find him, and they searched throughout the country and he was not to be found, and they went and searched in every direction and he was not to be met with.

C.21 The big question is: How could Abraham be alive at the same time as both Noah and Shem? (**See the APPENDIX**) concerning this matter.

62 And when the king's servants could not find Abram they returned to the king, but the king's anger against Abram was stilled, as they did not find him, and the king drove from his mind this matter concerning Abram.

63 And Abram was concealed in Noah's house for one month, until the king had forgotten this matter, but Abram was still afraid of the king; and Terah came to see Abram his son secretly in the house of Noah, and Terah was very great in the eyes of the king.

64 And Abram said to his father, 'Dost thou not know that the king thinketh to slay me, and to annihilate my name from the earth by the advice of his wicked counsellors?'

65 Now whom hast thou here and what hast thou in this land? Arise, let us go together to the land of Canaan, that we may be delivered from his hand, lest thou perish also through him in the latter days.

66 Dost thou not know or hast thou not heard, that it is not through love that Nimrod giveth thee all this honour, but it is only for his benefit that he bestows all this good upon thee?

67 And if he do unto thee greater good than this, surely these are only vanities of the world, for wealth and riches cannot avail in the day of wrath and anger.

125

68 Now therefore hearken to my voice and let us arise and go to the land of Canaan, out of the reach of injury from Nimrod; and serve thou the Lord who created thee in the earth and it will be well with thee; and cast away all the vain things which thou pursues.

69 And Abram ceased to speak, when Noah and his son Shem answered Terah, saying, True is the word which Abram hath said unto thee.

70 And Terah hearkened to the voice of his son Abram, and Terah did all that Abram said, for this was from the Lord, that the king should not cause Abram's death.

GEN.11:31 And Terah took Abram his son, and Lot the son of Haran his son's son, and Sarai his daughter in law, his son Abram's wife; and they went forth with them from Ur of the Chaldees, to go into the land of Canaan; and they came unto Haran, and dwelt there.

GEN.11:32 And the days of Terah were two hundred and five years: and Terah died in Haran.

Chapter 13

1 And Terah took his son Abram and his grandson Lot, the son of Haran, and Sarai his daughter-in-law, the wife of his son Abram, and all the souls of his household and went with them from Ur Casdim to go to the land of Canaan. And when they came as far as the land of Haran they remained there, for it was exceedingly good land for pasture, and of sufficient extent for those who accompanied them.

2 And the people of the land of Haran saw that Abram was good and upright with God and men, and that the Lord his God was with him, and some of the people of the land of Haran came and joined Abram, and he taught them the instruction of the Lord and his ways; and these men remained with Abram in his house and they adhered to him.

Comment:1: *'And some of the people of the land of Haran came and joined Abram, and he taught them the instruction of the Lord and his ways'* Here we can see the beginnings of the Tribe of Abraham; all being people who were taught the 'instruction of the Lord' by Abraham himself.

C.2 This is interesting how that even some of the people of the land of Canaan really liked Abraham and wanted to become part of his tribe. Abraham won quite a few people to his tribe on his first stay of 3 years in Haran but years later he returned for five years on his 2nd trip to Haran and even more people joined his tribe. Why did people of another race want to join Abraham's tribe? Well it says it so well in verse 2 *'The people of the land of Haran saw that Abram was good and upright with God and men, and that the Lord his God was with him'*

3 And Abram remained in the land three years, and at the expiration of three years the Lord appeared to Abram and said to him; I am the Lord who brought thee forth from Ur Casdim and delivered thee from the hands of all thine enemies.

C.3 The Lord starts to speak to Abraham quite frequently and here he promises Abraham that he is going to multiply Abraham's seed like the sand on the seashore or as the 'stars of heaven'

4 And now therefore if thou wilt hearken to my voice and keep my commandments, my statutes and my laws, then will I cause thy enemies to fall before thee, and I will multiply thy seed like the stars of heaven, and I will send my blessing upon all the works of thy hands, and thou shalt lack nothing.

GEN.12:1 Now the LORD had said unto Abram, 'Get thee out of thy country, and from thy kindred, and from thy father's house, unto a land that I will shew thee':

GEN.12:2 And I will make of thee a great nation, and I will bless thee, and make thy name great; and thou shalt be a blessing:

GEN.12:3 And I will bless them that bless thee and curse him that curseth thee: and in thee shall all families of the earth be blessed.

GEN.12:4 So Abram departed, as the LORD had spoken unto him; and Lot went with him: and Abram was seventy and five years old when he departed out of Haran.

> 5 Arise now, take thy wife and all belonging to thee and go to the land of Canaan and remain there, and I will there be unto thee for a God, and I will bless thee. And Abram rose and took his wife and all belonging to him, and he went to the land of Canaan as the Lord had told him; and Abram was fifty years old when he went from Haran.

GEN.12:5 And Abram took Sarai his wife, and Lot his brother's son, and all their substance that they had gathered, and the souls that they had gotten in Haran; and they went forth to go into the land of Canaan; and into the land of Canaan they came.

> 6 And Abram came to the land of Canaan and dwelt in the midst of the city, and he there pitched his tent amongst the children of Canaan, inhabitants of the land.
>
> 7 And the Lord appeared to Abram when he came to the land of Canaan, and said to him, This is the land which I gave unto thee and to thy seed after thee forever, and I will make thy seed like the stars of heaven, and I will give unto thy seed for an inheritance all the lands which thou seest.

GEN.12:7a And the LORD appeared unto Abram, and said, 'Unto thy seed will I give this land'.

> 8 And Abram built an altar in the place where God had spoken to him, and Abram there called upon the name of the Lord.

GEN.12:7b And there builded he an altar unto the LORD, who appeared unto him.

> 9 At that time, at the end of three years of Abram's dwelling in the land of Canaan, in that year Noah died, which was the fifty-eighth year of the life of Abram; and all the days that Noah lived were nine hundred and fifty years and he died.

C.4 This time description corresponds exactly with the TIMELINE of events in the Bible itself.

(See the **APPENDIX** for **KING JAMES BIBLE TIMECHART**)

> 10 And Abram dwelt in the land of Canaan, he, his wife, and all belonging to him, and all those that accompanied him, together with those that joined him from the people of the land; but Nahor, Abram's brother, and Terah his father, and Lot the son of Haran and all belonging to them dwelt in Haran.

HEB.11:8 By faith Abraham, when he was called to go out into a place which he should after receive for an inheritance, obeyed; and he went out, not knowing whither he went.

HEB.11:9 By faith he sojourned in the land of promise, as in a strange country, dwelling in tabernacles with Isaac and Jacob, the heirs with him of the same promise:

HEB.11:10 For he looked for a city which hath foundations, whose builder and maker is God.

> 11 In the fifth year of Abram's dwelling in the land of Canaan the people of Sodom and Gomorrah and all the cities of the plain revolted from the power of Chedorlaomer, king of Elam; for all the kings of the cities of the plain had served Chedorlaomer for twelve years, and given him a yearly tax, but in those days in the thirteenth year, they rebelled against him.
>
> 12 And in the tenth year of Abram's dwelling in the land of Canaan there was war between Nimrod king of Shinar and Chedorlaomer king of Elam, and Nimrod came to fight with Chedorlaomer and to subdue him.
>
> 13 For Chedorlaomer was at that time one of the princes of the hosts of Nimrod, and when all the people at the tower were dispersed and those that remained were also scattered upon the face of the earth, Chedorlaomer went to the land of Elam and reigned over it and rebelled against his lord.
>
> 14 And in those days when Nimrod saw that the cities of the plain had rebelled, he came with pride and anger to war with Chedorlaomer, and Nimrod assembled all his princes and subjects, about seven hundred

> thousand men, and went against Chedorlaomer, and Chedorlaomer went out to meet him with five thousand men, and they prepared for battle in the valley of Babel which is between Elam and Shinar.

C.5 The numbers don't make much sense. Nimrod assembled 700,000 and Chedorlaomer met him with only 5000. I don't think that sounds very likely or logical. It probably should read that Chedorlaomer had at least 50,000 or even 500,000. Chedorlaomer must have had a lot of confidence in his army to go and fight against his previous over-Lord Nimrod; and thus, must have had quite a formidable army - otherwise he wouldn't have had the confidence to rebel against his former master. Why do some of the numbers in this Book of Jasher appear to have been altered? We can only speculate or guestimate as to why. Perhaps it was a mistranslation, where some of the zeros got missed out. We have witnessed this in some places throughout this book.

> 15 And all those kings fought there, and Nimrod and his people were smitten before the people of Chedorlaomer, and there fell from Nimrud's men about six hundred thousand, and Mardon the king's son fell amongst them.
>
> 16 And Nimrod fled and returned in shame and disgrace to his land, and he was under subjection to Chedorlaomer for a long time, and Chedorlaomer returned to his land and sent princes of his host to the kings that dwelt around him, to Arioch king of Elasar, and to Tidal king of Goyim, and made a covenant with them, and they were all obedient to his commands.

C.6 Apparently as you will see later on in this book Nimrod escaped from being under the jurisdiction and subservience to Chedorlaomer when Abraham later came to rescue his nephew from these kings who warred against Sodom and Gomorrah and the other 2 kings of the plain. Chedorlaomer was killed in that battle.

GEN.14:17 And the king of Sodom went out to meet him after his return from the slaughter of *Chedorlaomer,* and of the kings that were with him, at the valley of Shaveh, which is the king's dale.

> 17 And it was in the fifteenth year of Abram's dwelling in the land of Canaan, which is the seventieth year of the life of Abram, and the Lord appeared to Abram in that year and he said to him, I am the Lord who brought thee out from Ur Casdim to give thee this land for an inheritance.

130

18 Now therefore walk before me and be perfect and keep my commands, for to thee and to thy seed I will give this land for an inheritance, from the river Mitzraim unto the great river Euphrates.

19 And thou shalt come to thy fathers in peace and in good age, and the fourth generation shall return here in this land and shall inherit it forever; and Abram built an altar, and he called upon the name of the Lord who appeared to him, and he brought up sacrifices upon the altar to the Lord.

20 At that time Abram returned and went to Haran to see his father and mother, and his father's household, and Abram and his wife and all belonging to him returned to Haran, and Abram dwelt in Haran five years.

21 And many of the people of Haran, about seventy-two men, followed Abram and Abram taught them the instruction of the Lord and his ways, and he taught them to know the Lord.

22 In those days the Lord appeared to Abram in Haran, and he said to him, Behold, I spoke unto thee these twenty years back saying,

23 Go forth from thy land, from thy birth-place and from thy father's house, to the land which I have shown thee to give it to thee and to thy children, for there in that land will I bless thee, and make thee a great nation, and make thy name great, and in thee shall the families of the earth be blessed.

24 Now therefore arise, go forth from this place, thou, thy wife, and all belonging to thee, also everyone born in thy house and all the souls thou hast made in Haran, and bring them out with thee from here, and rise to return to the land of Canaan.

25 And Abram arose and took his wife Sarai and all belonging to him and all that were born to him in his house and the souls which they had made in Haran, and they came out to go to the land of Canaan.

26 And Abram went and returned to the land of Canaan, according to the word of the Lord. And Lot the son of his brother Haran went with

him, and Abram was seventy-five years old when he went forth from Haran to return to the land of Canaan.

27 And he came to the land of Canaan according to the word of the Lord to Abram, and he pitched his tent and he dwelt in the plain of Mamre, and with him was Lot his brother's son, and all belonging to him.

28 And the Lord again appeared to Abram and said, 'To thy seed will I give this land'; and he there built an altar to the Lord who appeared to him, which is still to this day in the plains of Mamre.

C.7 MAP of ABRAHAM'S JOURNEYS: https://uk.images.search.yahoo.com/search/images?p=map+of+abrahams+journeys

Chapter 14

1 In those days there was in the land of Shinar a wise man who had understanding in all wisdom, and of a beautiful appearance, but he was poor and indigent; his name was Rikayon and he was hard set to support himself.

2 And he resolved to go to Egypt, to Oswiris the son of Anom king of Egypt, to show the king his wisdom; for perhaps he might find grace in his sight, to raise him up and give him maintenance; and Rikayon did so.

3 And when Rikayon came to Egypt he asked the inhabitants of Egypt concerning the king, and the inhabitants of Egypt told him the custom of the king of Egypt, for it was then the custom of the king of Egypt that he went from his royal palace and was seen abroad only one day in the year, and after that the king would return to his palace to remain there.

4 And on the day when the king went forth he passed judgment in the land, and everyone having a suit came before the king that day to obtain his request.

5 And when Rikayon heard of the custom in Egypt and that he could not come into the presence of the king, he grieved greatly and was very sorrowful.

6 And in the evening Rikayon went out and found a house in ruins, formerly a bake house in Egypt, and he abode there all night in bitterness of soul and pinched with hunger, and sleep was removed from his eyes.

7 And Rikayon considered within himself what he should do in the town until the king made his appearance, and how he might maintain himself there.

8 And he rose in the morning and walked about and met in his way those who sold vegetables and various sorts of seed with which they supplied the inhabitants.

9 And Rikayon wished to do the same in order to get a maintenance in the city, but he was unacquainted with the custom of the people, and he was like a blind man among them.

10 And he went and obtained vegetables to sell them for his support, and the rabble assembled about him and ridiculed him, and took his vegetables from him and left him nothing.

11 And he rose up from there in bitterness of soul and went sighing to the bake house in which he had remained all the night before, and he slept there the second night.

12 And on that night again he reasoned within himself how he could save himself from starvation, and he devised a scheme how to act.

13 And he rose up in the morning and acted ingeniously and went and hired thirty strong men of the rabble, carrying their war instruments in their hands, and he led them to the top of the Egyptian sepulchre, and he placed them there.

14 And he commanded them, saying, 'Thus saith the king, 'Strengthen yourselves and be valiant men, and let no man be buried here until two hundred pieces of silver be given, and then he may be buried; and those men did according to the order of Rikayon to the people of Egypt the whole of that year.'

15 And in eight month's time Rikayon and his men gathered great riches of silver and gold, and Rikayon took a great quantity of horses and other animals, and he hired more men, and he gave them horses and they remained with him.

16 And when the year came around at the time the king went forth into the town, all the inhabitants of Egypt assembled together to speak to him concerning the work of Rikayon and his men.

17 And the king went forth on the appointed day, and all the Egyptians came before him and cried unto him, saying,

18 May the king live forever. What is this thing thou do in the town to thy servants, not to suffer a dead body to be buried until so much silver and gold be given? Was there ever the like unto this done in the whole earth, from the days of former kings yea even from the days of Adam, unto this day, that the dead should not be buried only for a set price?

19 We know it to be the custom of kings to take a yearly tax from the living, but thou dost not only do this, but from the dead also thou exactest a tax day by day.

20 Now, O king, we can no more bear this, for the whole city is ruined on this account, and dost thou not know it?

21 And when the king heard all that they had spoken he was very wroth, and his anger burned within him at this affair, for he had known nothing of it.

22 And the king said, Who and where is he that dares to do this wicked thing in my land without my command? Surely you will tell me.

23 And they told him all the works of Rikayon and his men, and the king's anger was aroused, and he ordered Rikayon and his men to be brought before him.

24 And Rikayon took about a thousand children, sons and daughters, and clothed them in silk and embroidery, and he set them upon horses and sent them to the king by means of his men, and he also took a great quantity of silver and gold and precious stones, and a strong and beautiful horse, as a present for the king, with which he came before the king and bowed down to the earth before him; and the king, his servants and all the inhabitants of Egypt wondered at the work of Rikayon, and they saw his riches and the present that he had brought to the king.

25 And it greatly pleased the king and he wondered at it; and when Rikayon sat before him the king asked him concerning all his works, and Rikayon spoke all his words wisely before the king, his servants and all the inhabitants of Egypt.

26 And when the king heard the words of Rikayon and his wisdom, Rikayon found grace in his sight, and he met with grace and kindness from all the servants of the king and from all the inhabitants of Egypt, on account of his wisdom and excellent speeches, and from that time they loved him exceedingly.

27 And the king answered and said to Rikayon, 'Thy name shall no more be called Rikayon but Pharaoh shall be thy name, since thou didst exact a tax from the dead; and he called his name Pharaoh.'

28 And the king and his subjects loved Rikayon for his wisdom, and they consulted with all the inhabitants of Egypt to make him prefect under the king.

29 And all the inhabitants of Egypt and its wise men did so, and it was made a law in Egypt.

30 And they made Rikayon Pharaoh prefect under Oswiris king of Egypt, and Rikayon Pharaoh governed over Egypt, daily administering justice to the whole city, but Oswiris the king would judge the people of the land one day in the year, when he went out to make his appearance.

31 And Rikayon Pharaoh cunningly usurped the government of Egypt, and he exacted a tax from all the inhabitants of Egypt.

32 And all the inhabitants of Egypt greatly loved Rikayon Pharaoh, and they made a decree to call every king that should reign over them and their seed in Egypt, Pharaoh.

33 Therefore all the kings that reigned in Egypt from that time forward were called Pharaoh unto this day.

ANALYSIS OF 'RIKAYON'

THE WORD 'RIKAYON' & 'PHAROAH'

C.1 The 'Origin of the word Pharaoh means 'a great house' (ref. Wikipedia) However it is indeed possible that if such a character as Rikayon ever existed, it is likely that he, being given the title of Pharaoh, would be more remembered for his *'great wealth'* and thus the definition of the word 'Pharaoh' is given in modern times as simply *'great House'*.

C.2 The fact that Rikayon levied a *'Dead Persons Tax'* on the people of ancient times wouldn't be remembered so much, because he became very popular with both the King and the people of Egypt, in spite of his great deceit. The word 'pharaoh' eventually came to represent *'great power'* and *'great wealth'*. Eventually adopted as a title for kings. Rikayon became rich by both deceitful & corruptible means and was actually rewarded for his wickedness instead of punished.

C.3 *Word definitions*: the word 'Rika': def. *popularity-eternal ruler, charismatic, intuitive pleasant personality.* The definition goes far back in time and is mentioned in the language of many countries. The word 'Ayon': def: meaning *'To agree to conform' 'to go along with'. It also means 'to arrange according to size' 'to size up-form an opinion.* I found it very unusual obtaining these definitions of the word *'Rikayon'* and they certainly all more than apply to the character of the Rikayon mentioned in the Book of Jasher.

C.4 *Other observations.* The Egyptians 'glorified the *dead*' both as the *gods of the underworld* and with the hope of *'resurrection'*. They mummified the dead and so Rikayon's tricks to not allow the dead to be buried until the people paid him 200 pieces of silver each, was a terrible insult to the Egyptians; so much so that they would have indeed been willingly to pay the tax, as they wanted their relatives to be buried in the correct manner, in order for them to be ready for the resurrection in the after-life. So, it was indeed a *very cunning and crafty plan* that Rikayon made.

C.5 The word *'Pharaoh'* means 'a 'Great House'. I would presume to imagine that here it is referring to the great *'Pyramids of Egypt'*.

C.6 From my research, I do not believe that the Egyptians actually built the pyramids. I believe they were built by a very advanced Pre-Flood civilization such as the Atlanteans. The Egyptians merely adopted the Pyramids and used them to bury their Pharaohs, but that was not the main purpose of the pyramids which are aligned to the stars, when they were originally build before the Flood.

C.7 What was the originally purpose of the pyramids? That itself is a very good question, which I will not attempt to answer in this particular study.

C.8 The fact that Rikayon was named the first Pharaoh by the King of Egypt who was in fact called Osiris. Osiris ended up making Rikayon his prefect and 2nd under himself. Rikayon ended up taking over the whole government of Egypt through deceit and through his smooth tongue. He continued to tax the entire population of Egypt and yet it says that the people loved him!

C.9 Rikayon sounds more like a *deceptive* and very *manipulative prankster* that everyone came to admire, in the same morbid way that people today admire a very evil person who is in fact a prankster, like the Joker character in Batman. Whether the story of Rikayon is true or just perhaps a parable, it is however very true to life on earth and how the planet is indeed run by pranksters such as the *'Elite rich Merchants'*. Thus, is the way of this physical world, which constantly rewards the evil and wicked violent doers such as the Merchants who *rule the planet by deceit and violent oppression* of all with all their orchestrated wars.

Hosea 12.7 'He is a merchant. He loves to oppress'.

C.10 According to the following *link*, eventually after the death of Osiris, Rikayon became the Ruler of Egypt, and was the Pharaoh of Egypt at the time that Abram and Sarai his wife went to live in Egypt because of a famine in the land of Caanan.

C.11 We shall see in the next chapter how 'Rikayon Pharaoh', became struck with the beauty of Sarai Abram's wife which did cause some serious problems for both Abram and Rikayon.

C.12 MORE INFO about RIKAYON:- (http://musingsofawinsomeheart.blog-spot.co.uk/2011/07/first-pharoh-rikayon-abraham-astronomy.html)

C.13 RELATED: See: the History of the Rich and their oppression of the Poor throughout history: http://www.peopleofthekeys.com/news/docs/library/Rich+Man%2C+Poor+Man

Chapter 15

1 And in that year, there was a heavy famine throughout the land of Canaan, and the inhabitants of the land could not remain on account of the famine for it was very grievous.

GEN.12:10 And there was a famine in the land: and Abram went down into Egypt to sojourn there; for the famine was grievous in the land.

2 And Abram and all belonging to him rose and went down to Egypt on account of the famine, and when they were at the brook Mitzraim they remained there some time to rest from the fatigue of the road.

3 And Abram and Sarai were walking at the border of the brook Mitzraim, and Abram beheld his wife Sarai that she was very beautiful.

4 And Abram said to his wife Sarai, Since God has created thee with such a beautiful countenance, I am afraid of the Egyptians lest they should slay me and take thee away, for the fear of God is not in these places.

5 Surely then thou shalt do this, 'Say thou art my sister to all that may ask thee, in order that it may be well with me, and that we may live and not be put to death.'

GEN.12:11 And it came to pass, when he was come near to enter into Egypt, that he said unto Sarai his wife, 'Behold now, I know that thou art a fair woman to look upon':

GEN.12:12 Therefore it shall come to pass, when the Egyptians shall see thee, that they shall say, 'This is his wife: and they will kill me, but they will save thee alive'.

6 And Abram commanded the same to all those that came with him to Egypt on account of the famine; also, his nephew Lot he commanded, saying, If the Egyptians ask thee concerning Sarai say she is the sister of Abram.

7 And yet with all these orders Abram did not put confidence in them, but he took Sarai and placed her in a chest and concealed it amongst their vessels, for Abram was greatly concerned about Sarai on account of the wickedness of the Egyptians.

C.1 Poor Sarah, having to be hidden away in a box just so that the king of Egypt and other men would not desire her and take her away from her husband Abraham by force. Well the trick apparently didn't work, as the Egyptians found her anyway, and did indeed end up taking her to the pharaoh, so that she could become his wife. It seemed to be the custom of the very rich of nations back then, to just steal other men's wife's when it suited their purpose.

8 And Abram and all belonging to him rose up from the brook Mitzraim and came to Egypt; and they had scarcely entered the gates of the city when the guards stood up to them saying, Give tithe to the king from what you have, and then you may come into the town; and Abram and those that were with him did so.

9 And Abram with the people that were with him came to Egypt, and when they came they brought the chest in which Sarai was concealed and the Egyptians saw the chest.

10 And the king's servants approached Abram, saying, 'What hast thou here in this chest which we have not seen? Now open thou the chest and give tithe to the king of all that it contains'.

11 And Abram said, 'This chest I will not open, but all you demand upon it I will give.' And Pharaoh's officers answered Abram, saying, 'It is a chest of precious stones, give us the tenth thereof.'

12 Abram said, 'All that you desire I will give, but you must not open the chest.'

13 And the king's officers pressed Abram, and they reached the chest and opened it with force, and they saw, and behold a beautiful woman was in the chest.

14 And when the officers of the king beheld Sarai they were struck with admiration at her beauty, and all the princes and servants of Pharaoh assembled to see Sarai, for she was very beautiful. And the king's officers ran and told Pharaoh all that they had seen, and they praised Sarai to the king; and Pharaoh ordered her to be brought, and the woman came before the king.

GEN.12:14 And it came to pass, that, when Abram was come into Egypt, the Egyptians beheld the woman that she was very fair.

15 And Pharaoh beheld Sarai and she pleased him exceedingly, and he was struck with her beauty, and the king rejoiced greatly on her account, and made presents to those who brought him the tidings concerning her.

16 And the woman was then brought to Pharaoh's house, and Abram grieved on account of his wife, and he prayed to the Lord to deliver her from the hands of Pharaoh.

GEN.12:15 The princes also of Pharaoh saw her and commended her before Pharaoh: and the woman was taken into Pharaoh's house.

17 And Sarai also prayed at that time and said, O Lord God thou didst tell my Lord Abram to go from his land and from his father's house to the land of Canaan, and thou didst promise to do well with him if he would perform thy commands; now behold we have done that which thou didst command us, and we left our land and our families, and we went to a strange land and to a people whom we have not known before.

18 And we came to this land to avoid the famine, and this evil accident has befallen me; now therefore, O Lord God, deliver us and save us from the hand of this oppressor, and do well with me for the sake of thy mercy.

19 And the Lord hearkened to the voice of Sarai, and the Lord sent an angel to deliver Sarai from the power of Pharaoh.

20 And the king came and sat before Sarai and behold an angel of the Lord was standing over them, and he appeared to Sarai and said to her, 'Do not fear, for the Lord has heard thy prayer'.

21 And the king approached Sarai and said to her, 'What is that man to thee who brought thee hither? and she said, He is my brother.'

22 And the king said, It is incumbent upon us to make him great, to elevate him and to do unto him all the good which thou shalt command us; and at that time the king sent to Abram silver and gold and precious

stones in abundance, together with cattle, men servants and maid servants; and the king ordered Abram to be brought, and he sat in the court of the king's house, and the king greatly exalted Abram on that night.

23 And the king approached to speak to Sarai, and he reached out his hand to touch her, when the angel smote him heavily, and he was terrified, and he refrained from reaching to her.

24 And when the king came near to Sarai, the angel smote him to the ground, and acted thus to him the whole night, and the king was terrified.

25 And the angel on that night smote heavily all the servants of the king, and his whole household, on account of Sarai, and there was a great lamentation that night amongst the people of Pharaoh's house.

26 And Pharaoh, seeing the evil that befell him, said, 'Surely on account of this woman has this thing happened to me, and he removed himself at some distance from her and spoke pleasing words to her.'

27 And the king said to Sarai, 'Tell me I pray thee concerning the man with whom thou came here'; and Sarai said, 'This man is my husband, and I said to thee that he was my brother for I was afraid, lest thou should put him to death through wickedness'.

28 And the king kept away from Sarai, and the plagues of the angel of the Lord ceased from him and his household; and Pharaoh knew that he was smitten on account of Sarai, and the king was greatly astonished at this.

29 And in the morning the king called for Abram and said to him, 'What is this thou hast done to me? Why didst thou say, 'She is my sister, owing to which I took her unto me for a wife, and this heavy plague has therefore come upon me and my household.'

GEN.12:17 And the LORD plagued Pharaoh and his house with great plagues because of Sarai Abram's wife.

GEN.12:18 And Pharaoh called Abram and said, 'What is this that thou hast done unto me? why didst thou not tell me that she was thy wife'?

GEN.12:19 Why said thou, 'She is my sister? so I might have taken her to me to wife: now therefore behold thy wife, take her, and go thy way'.

---

30 'Now therefore here is thy wife, take her and go from our land lest we all die on her account.' And Pharaoh took more cattle, men servants and maid servants, and silver and gold, to give to Abram, and he returned unto him Sarai his wife.

31 And the king took a maiden whom he begat by his concubines, and he gave her to Sarai for a handmaid. (Hagar)

32 And the king said to his daughter, 'It is better for thee my daughter to be a handmaid in this man's house than to be mistress in my house, after we have beheld the evil that befell us on account of this woman.'

33 And Abram arose, and he and all belonging to him went away from Egypt; and Pharaoh ordered some of his men to accompany him and all that went with him.

GEN.12:20 And Pharaoh commanded his men concerning him: and they sent him away, and his wife, and all that he had.

GEN.13:1 And Abram went up out of Egypt, he, and his wife, and all that he had, and Lot with him, into the south.

GEN.13:2 And Abram was very rich in cattle, in silver, and in gold.

C.2 If you are wondering why God allowed a famine and for poor Sarah to go through such an ordeal then it might be good to examine the bigger picture.

C.3 God had promised great things to his servant Abraham. So, God set up the exact conditions that would make it happen. The net effect of Abraham and Sarah's short visit to Egypt was that they 'spoiled Egypt' and were sent away with much gold and silver and cattle and women servants and more men servants. All to start increasing the tribe of Abraham.

C.4 When one thinks about it in depth: Firstly, Abraham was living in Haran with his father and brother. Then God told him to move south. At Haran Abraham's name was much set by because he was a godly man and had both integrity and was also a kind and generous person. Therefore, quite a few people joined Abram's budding tribe there.

C.5 After moving to the land of Canaan in the lands to the South, even more people joined him for one reason or another; and then when the famine came and he was forced to temporarily move to Egypt, he soon returned to the land of Canaan much better off. Who could pull something like that off? Where even the Pharaoh was handing out lots of gold and goodies. Well it was God who was behind it all!

C.6 This pattern continued throughout Abraham's life, because he and Sarah were both faithful and loyal to God.

C.7 God was doing all He could to both test Abraham in all things and at the same time prepare the future for the coming of Abraham's descendants in Jacob and His 12 sons - the beginning of the Children of Israel. So, in spite of the inconvenience to poor Sarah and Abraham, actually all things worked out for good in the end!

ROM.8:28 And we know that all things work together for good to them that love God, to them who are the called according to his purpose.

---

34 And Abram returned to the land of Canaan, to the place where he had made the altar, where he at first had pitched his tent.

35 And Lot the son of Haran, Abram's brother, had a heavy stock of cattle, flocks and herds and tents, for the Lord was bountiful to them on account of Abram.

36 And when Abram was dwelling in the land the herdsmen of Lot quarrelled with the herdsmen of Abram, for their property was too great for them to remain together in the land, and the land could not bear them on account of their cattle.

37 And when Abram's herdsmen went to feed their flock they would not go into the fields of the people of the land, but the cattle of Lot's herdsmen did otherwise, for they were suffered to feed in the fields of the people of the land.

38 And the people of the land saw this occurrence daily, and they came to Abram and quarrelled with him on account of Lot's herdsmen.

39 And Abram said to Lot, 'What is this thou art doing to me, to make me despicable to the inhabitants of the land, that thou order thy herdsman to feed thy cattle in the fields of other people? Dost thou not know that I am a stranger in this land amongst the children of Canaan, and why wilt thou do this unto me?'

40 And Abram quarrelled daily with Lot on account of this, but Lot would not listen to Abram, and he continued to do the same and the

---

inhabitants of the land came and told Abram.

41 And Abram said unto Lot, 'How long wilt thou be to me for a stumbling block with the inhabitants of the land? Now I beseech thee let there be no more quarrelling between us, for we are kinsmen'.

42 'But I pray thee separate from me, go and choose a place where thou mayest dwell with thy cattle and all belonging to thee, but Keep thyself at a distance from me, thou and thy household.'

43 And be not afraid in going from me, for if anyone do an injury to thee, let me know and I will avenge thy cause from him, only remove from me.

44 And when Abram had spoken all these words to Lot, then Lot arose and lifted up his eyes toward the plain of Jordan.

45 And he saw that the whole of this place was well watered, and good for man as well as affording pasture for the cattle.

46 And Lot went from Abram to that place, and he there pitched his tent and he dwelt in Sodom, and they were separated from each other.

47 And Abram dwelt in the plain of Mamre, which is in Hebron, and he pitched his tent there, and Abram remained in that place many years.

Chapter 16

1 At that time Chedorlaomer king of Elam sent to all the neighbouring kings, to Nimrod, king of Shinar who was then under his power, and to Tidal, king of Goyim, and to Arioch, king of Elasar, with whom he made a covenant, saying, Come up to me and assist me, that we may smite all the towns of Sodom and its inhabitants, for they have rebelled against me these thirteen years.

2 And these four kings went up with all their camps, about eight hundred thousand men, and they went as they were, and smote every man they found in their road.

3 And the five kings of Sodom and Gomorrah, Shinab king of Admah, Shemeber king of Zeboyim, Bera king of Sodom, Bersha king of Gomorrah, and Bela king of Zoar, went out to meet them, and they all joined together in the valley of Siddim.

4 And these nine kings made war in the valley of Siddim; and the kings of Sodom and Gomorrah were smitten before the kings of Elam.

5 And the valley of Siddim was full of lime pits and the kings of Elam pursued the kings of Sodom, and the kings of Sodom with their camps fled and fell into the lime pits, and all that remained went to the mountain for safety, and the five kings of Elam came after them and pursued them to the gates of Sodom, and they took all that there was in Sodom.

6 And they plundered all the cities of Sodom and Gomorrah, and they also took Lot, Abram's brother's son, and his property, and they seized all the goods of the cities of Sodom, and they went away; and Unic, Abram's servant, who was in the battle, saw this, and told Abram all that the kings had done to the cities of Sodom, and that Lot was taken captive by them.

7 And Abram heard this, and he rose up with about three hundred and eighteen men that were with him, and he that night pursued these kings and smote them, and they all fell before Abram and his men, and there

> was none remaining but the four kings who fled, and they went each his own road.

Comment:1: Here we see that Abraham didn't kill the kings. The 4 kings actually fled from him including Nimrod, just as had been prophesied many years before in a vision of that star of Abraham devouring the 4 Stars of Nimrod.

> 8 And Abram recovered all the property of Sodom, and he also recovered Lot and his property, his wives and little ones and all belonging to him, so that Lot lacked nothing.
>
> 9 And when he returned from smiting these kings, he and his men passed the valley of Siddim where the kings had made war together.
>
> 10 And Bera king of Sodom, and the rest of his men that were with him, went out from the lime pits into which they had fallen, to meet Abram and his men.
>
> 11 And Adonizedek king of Jerusalem, the same was Shem, went out with his men to meet Abram and his people, with bread and wine, and they remained together in the valley of Melech.
>
> 12 And Adonizedek blessed Abram, and Abram gave him a tenth from all that he had brought from the spoil of his enemies, for Adonizedek was a priest before God.

C.2. Here it calls this High Priest Adonizedek. In the Bible it calls him Melkizedek. However, Melkizedek as mentioned in the Bible was *certainly not Shem.* Here is an exact description of Melkizedek according to the New Testament book of Hebrews:

HEB.6:20 Jesus, made a high priest for ever after the order of Melchisedec.

HEB.7:1 For this Melchisedec, king of Salem, priest of the most high God, who met Abraham returning from the slaughter of the kings and blessed him.

C.3 This is where the custom of *Tithing* began. Tithing predated the Mosaic law by some 500 years and was started by Abraham. Later Tithing was introduced into Egypt where all peoples had to tithe 20% to Pharaoh.

HEB.7:2 To whom also Abraham gave a tenth part of all; first being by interpretation King of righteousness, and after that also King of Salem, which is, King of peace;

HEB.7:3 *Without father, without mother, without descent,* having *neither beginning of days,* nor end of life; but made *like unto the Son of God;* abides a priest continually.

147

HEB.7:4 Now consider how great this man was, unto whom even the patriarch Abraham gave the tenth of the spoils.

HEB.7:15 And it is yet far more evident: for that after the similitude of Melchisedec there ariseth another priest,

HEB.7:16 Who is made, not after the law of a carnal commandment, but after the power of an endless life.

C.4 *'Adonizedek'*: meaning: 'lord of justice' The Amorite king of Jerusalem who organized a league with four other Amorite princes against Joshua. The confederate kings having laid siege to Gibeon, Joshua marched to the relief of his new allies and put the besiegers to flight. The five kings took refuge in a cave at Makkedah, whence they were taken and slain, their bodies hung on trees, and then buried in the place of their concealment. **Joshua 10: 1-27** (B.C. 1450.)

C.5 It sounds like the Melchisedec who met Abraham was in fact Jesus, the Son of God putting in one of those rare appearances, before actually being born in the flesh upon earth.

C.6 Why would this otherwise excellent Book of Jasher be altered? Some deceitful person has deliberately changed Melchisedec (The Son of God) to Adonizedec, who was an actual physical Amorite king of Jerusalem, in the time of Joshua. He lived around 500 years after Abraham's meeting with Melchisedec.

---

13 And all the kings of Sodom and Gomorrah who were there, with their servants, approached Abram and begged of him to return them their servants whom he had made captive, and to take unto himself all the property.

14 And Abram answered the kings of Sodom, saying, As the Lord liveth who created heaven and earth, and who redeemed my soul from all affliction, and who delivered me this day from my enemies, and gave them into my hand, I will not take anything belonging to you, that you may not boast tomorrow, saying, Abram became rich from our property that he saved.

15 For the Lord my God in whom I trust said unto me, 'Thou shalt lack nothing, for I will bless thee in all the works of thy hands.'

16 And now therefore behold, here is all belonging to you, take it and go; as the Lord lives I will not take from you from a living soul down to a shoe-tie or thread, excepting the expense of the food of those who went

out with me to battle, as also the portions of the men who went with me, Anar, Ashcol, and Mamre, they and their men, as well as those also who had remained to watch the baggage, they shall take their portion of the spoil.

17 And the kings of Sodom gave Abram according to all that he had said, and they pressed him to take of whatever he chose, but he would not.

18 And he sent away the kings of Sodom and the remainder of their men, and he gave them orders about Lot, and they went to their respective places.

19 And Lot, his brother's son, he also sent away with his property, and he went with them, and Lot returned to his home, to Sodom, and Abram and his people returned to their home to the plains of Mamre, which is in Hebron.

20 At that time the Lord again appeared to Abram in Hebron, and he said to him, 'Do not fear, thy reward is very great before me, for I will not leave thee, until I shall have multiplied thee, and blessed thee and made thy seed like the stars in heaven, which cannot be measured nor numbered.'

21 And I will give unto thy seed all these lands that you see with your eyes, to them will I give them for an inheritance forever, only be strong and do not fear, walk before me and be perfect.

22 And in the seventy-eighth year of the life of Abram, in that year died Reu, the son of Peleg, and all the days of Reu were two hundred and thirty-nine years, and he died.

23 And Sarai, the daughter of Haran, Abram's wife, was still barren in those days; she did not bear to Abram either son or daughter.

24 And when she saw that she bare no children she took her handmaid Hagar, whom Pharaoh had given her, and she gave her to Abram her husband for a wife.

25 For Hagar learned all the ways of Sarai as Sarai taught her, she was not in any way deficient in following her good ways.

C.7 Here Sarah is about to make a very big mistake. Instead of trusting God concerning her and Abraham having a son she took matters into her own hands and it made one big mess that she later really regretted. By offering Hagar as an additional wife to Abraham she didn't take into account that Hagar was an Egyptian. Egyptians don't have the same morals as what God had taught Abraham. Hagar was more like a slave who as soon as she was given more freedom turned around and despised her own mistress and berated her. Her son also would cause lots of trouble in the future for Abraham and Sarah's own son yet to be born Isaac who was the true promised seed by God Himself.

26 And Sarai said to Abram, 'Behold here is my handmaid Hagar, go to her that she may bring forth upon my knees, that I may also obtain children through her.'

27 And at the end of ten years of Abram's dwelling in the land of Canaan, which is the eighty-fifth year of Abram's life, Sarai gave Hagar unto him.

28 And Abram hearkened to the voice of his wife Sarai, and he took his handmaid Hagar and Abram came to her and she conceived.

C.8 Hagar conceived pretty much right away after Abraham had taken her as an additional wife, but unfortunately, she did not have the good manners to treat Sarah with respect but instead despised her thinking that Abraham would now favour her instead of Sarah. How wrong she was and obviously didn't realize how much Abraham really loved his first wife Sarah.

29 And when Hagar saw that she had conceived she rejoiced greatly, and her mistress was despised in her eyes, and she said within herself, 'This can only be that I am better before God than Sarai my mistress, for all the days that my mistress has been with my lord, she did not conceive, but me the Lord has caused in so short a time to conceive by him.'

30 And when Sarai saw that Hagar had conceived by Abram, Sarai was jealous of her handmaid, and Sarai said within herself, 'This is surely nothing else but that she must be better than I am.'

31 And Sarai said unto Abram, 'My wrong be upon thee, for at the

time when thou didst pray before the Lord for children why didst thou not pray on my account, that the Lord should give me seed from thee?'

32 And when I speak to Hagar in thy presence, she despises my words, because she has conceived, and thou wilt say nothing to her; may the Lord judge between me and thee for what thou hast done to me.

C 9 Poor Sarah is having a great battle with jealousy which is not at all surprising. She is afraid that Abraham is favouring his now second wife Hagar, but she needn't have feared as Abraham turns around the situation and tells his wife 'Look Hagar is your handmaiden to do what you want to with her'. Abraham held Sarah in much higher esteem than Hagar; as Hagar was to Abraham merely just a surrogate mother.

33 And Abram said to Sarai, 'Behold thy handmaid is in thy hand, do unto her as it may seem good in thy eyes; and Sarai afflicted her, and Hagar fled from her to the wilderness.

C.10 Well Sarah took advantage of that statement from her husband and made life rough for Hagar. So much so that she fled at least for a little while from the face of Sarah her mistress.

34 And an angel of the Lord found her in the place where she had fled, by a well, and he said to her, 'Do not fear, for I will multiply thy seed, for thou shalt bear a son and thou shalt call his name Ishmael; now then return to Sarai thy mistress, and submit thyself under her hands.'

35 And Hagar called the place of that well Beer-lahai-roi, it is between Kadesh and the wilderness of Bered.

36 And Hagar at that time returned to her master's house, and at the end of days Hagar bare a son to Abram, and Abram called his name Ishmael; and Abram was eighty-six years old when he begat him.

C. 11 Hagar ended up staying with Abraham and Sarah and her baby boy Ismael was born when Abraham was 86 years old. Abraham was 100 when his son Isaac was born, so that Ismael was already 14 by the time Isaac was born. As we will yet read this is going to cause some rivalry.

Chapter 17

1 And in those days, in the ninety-first year of the life of Abram, the children of Chittim made war with the children of Tubal, for when the Lord had scattered the sons of men upon the face of the earth, the children of Chittim went and embodied themselves in the plain of Canopia, and they built themselves cities there and dwelt by the river Tibreu.

2 And the children of Tubal dwelt in Tuscanah, and their boundaries reached the river Tibreu, and the children of Tubal built a city in Tuscanan, and they called the name Sabinah, after the name of Sabinah son of Tubal their father, and they dwelt there unto this day.

3 And it was at that time the children of Chittim made war with the children of Tubal, and the children of Tubal were smitten before the children of Chittim, and the children of Chittim caused three hundred and seventy men to fall from the children of Tubal.

4 And at that time the children of Tubal swore to the children of Chittim, saying, 'You shall not intermarry amongst us, and no man shall give his daughter to any of the sons of Chittim'.

5 For all the daughters of Tubal were in those days fair, for no women were then found in the whole earth so fair as the daughters of Tubal.

6 And all who delighted in the beauty of women went to the daughters of Tubal and took wives from them, and the sons of men, kings and princes, who greatly delighted in the beauty of women, took wives in those days from the daughters of Tubal.

7 And at the end of three years after the children of Tubal had sworn to the children of Chittim not to give them their daughters for wives, about twenty men of the children of Chittim went to take some of the daughters of Tubal, but they found none.

8 For the children of Tubal kept their oaths not to intermarry with them, and they would not break their oaths.

9 And in the days of harvest the children of Tubal went into their fields to get in their harvest, when the young men of Chittim assembled and went to the city of Sabinah, and each man took a young woman from the daughters of Tubal, and they came to their cities.

10 And the children of Tubal heard of it and they went to make war with them, and they could not prevail over them, for the mountain was exceedingly high from them, and when they saw they could not prevail over them they returned to their land.

11 And at the revolution of the year the children of Tubal went and hired about ten thousand men from those cities that were near them, and they went to war with the children of Chittim.

12 And the children of Tubal went to war with the children of Chittim, to destroy their land and to distress them, and in this engagement the children of Tubal prevailed over the children of Chittim, and the children of Chittim, seeing that they were greatly distressed, lifted up the children which they had had by the daughters of Tubal, upon the wall which had been built, to be before the eyes of the children of Tubal.

13 And the children of Chittim said to them, 'Have you come to make war with your own sons and daughters, and have we not been considered your flesh and bones from that time till now'?

14 And when the children of Tubal heard this they ceased to make war with the children of Chittim, and they went away.

15 And they returned to their cities, and the children of Chittim at that time assembled and built two cities by the sea, and they called one Purtu and the other Ariza.

16 And Abram the son of Terah was then ninety-nine years old.

C.1 Now we find Abraham is 99 that God makes the 'Covenant of Circumcision' with him as well all of his tribe, and for all future generations of the children of Israel. It was supposed to be an indication that the 'Children of Israel' were to be dedicated to serving God and not to false gods and idols.

> 17 At that time the Lord appeared to him and he said to him, I will make my covenant between me and thee, and I will greatly multiply thy seed, and this is the covenant which I make between me and thee, that every male child be circumcised, thou and thy seed after thee.
>
> 18 At eight days old shall it be circumcised, and this covenant shall be in your flesh for an everlasting covenant.

C.2 here it was also established that baby boys were to be circumcised on the 8th day. I suspect that God stated that it should be done *exactly on the 8th day* for some health reasons.

GEN.17:10 This is my covenant, which ye shall keep, between me and you and thy seed after thee; Every man child among you shall be circumcised.

GEN.17:11 And ye shall circumcise the flesh of your foreskin; and it shall be a token of the covenant betwixt me and you.

GEN.17:12 And he that is eight days old shall be circumcised among you, every man child in your generations, he that is born in the house, or bought with money of any stranger, which is not of thy seed.

GEN.17:13 He that is born in thy house, and he that is bought with thy money, must needs be circumcised: and my covenant shall be in your flesh for an everlasting covenant.

> 19 And now therefore thy name shall no more be called Abram but Abraham, and thy wife shall no more be called Sarai but Sarah.
>
> 20 For I will bless you both, and I will multiply your seed after you that you shall become a great nation, and kings shall come forth from you.

GEN.17:15 And God said unto Abraham, 'As for Sarai thy wife, thou shalt not call her name Sarai, but Sarah shall her name be'.

GEN.17:16 And I will bless her and give thee a son also of her: yea, I will bless her, and she shall be a mother of nations; kings of people shall be of her.

GEN.17:17 Then Abraham fell upon his face, and laughed, and said in his heart, 'Shall a child be born unto him that is an hundred years old? and shall Sarah, that is ninety years old, bear'?

C.3 What a test for Abraham and Sarah with God promising them that many people would come from their seed. Well, it turns out that it was only one year later when Abraham was 100 years old that Isaac the 'promised seed' would indeed be born when Abraham and Sarah were relatively old.

Chapter 18

SODOM AND GOMORRAH

Comment:1: This chapter describes the terrible depravity and perversions of the cities of the plain: Sodom and Gomorrah. It also shows their final destruction by God Himself in chapter 19 by the hand of two of his angels because of the peoples' repeated wickedness.

1 And Abraham rose and did all that God had ordered him, and he took the men of his household and those bought with his money, and he circumcised them as the Lord had commanded him.

2 And there was not one left whom he did not circumcise, and Abraham and his son Ishmael were circumcised in the flesh of their foreskin; thirteen years old was Ishmael when he was circumcised in the flesh of his foreskin.

3 And in the third day Abraham went out of his tent and sat at the door to enjoy the heat of the sun, during the pain of his flesh.

4 And the Lord appeared to him in the plain of Mamre, and sent three of his ministering angels to visit him, and he was sitting at the door of the tent, and he lifted his eyes and saw, and lo three men were coming from a distance, and he rose up and ran to meet them, and he bowed down to them and brought them into his house.

5 And he said to them, 'If now I have found favour in your sight, turn in and eat a morsel of bread; and he pressed them, and they turned in and he gave them water and they washed their feet, and he placed them under a tree at the door of the tent.'

6 And Abraham ran and took a calf, tender and good, and he hastened to kill it, and gave it to his servant Eliezer to dress.

7 And Abraham came to Sarah into the tent, and he said to her, 'Make ready quickly three measures of fine meal, knead it and make cakes to cover the pot containing the meat', and she did so.

8 And Abraham hastened and brought before them butter and milk, beef and mutton, and gave it before them to eat before the flesh of the calf was sufficiently done, and they did eat.

9 And when they had done eating one of them said to him, I will return to thee according to the time of life, and Sarah thy wife shall have a son.

10 And the men afterward departed and went their ways, to the places to which they were sent.

11 In those days all the people of Sodom and Gomorrah, and of the whole five cities, were exceedingly wicked and sinful against the Lord and they provoked the Lord with their abominations, and they strengthened in aging abominably and scornfully before the Lord, and their wickedness and crimes were in those days great before the Lord.

C.2 *'they strengthened in aging abominably'* What could that mean? Perhaps this simply means that they committed more and more abominations as they got older. They abused more and more people and more frequently and intensely as you will see in the rest of this chapter and the next. (including their own wives and daughters by allowing other men to be with them upon occasion) This was very much shown to be the case, when two angels came to deliver Lot from Sodom before they destroyed, it for all of its sexual perversions and cruelties to strangers.

12 And they had in their land a very extensive valley, about half a day's walk, and in it there were fountains of water and a great deal of herbage surrounding the water.

13 And all the people of Sodom and Gomorrah went there four times in the year, with their wives and children and all belonging to them, and they rejoiced there with timbrels and dances.

14 And in the time of rejoicing they would all rise and lay hold of their neighbour's wives, and some, the virgin daughters of their neighbours, and they enjoyed them, and each man saw his wife and daughter in the hands of his neighbour and did not say a word.

ROM.1:24 Wherefore God also gave them up to uncleanness through the lusts of their own hearts, to dishonour their own bodies between themselves:

C.3 The tragedy today in modern times is that the idea of rules and regulations seems archaic to many. Those who are so liberal in their views, are becoming increasing amoral, meaning 'anything goes', as 'there is no God' and 'no absolutes'. They will bring about exactly what is described in this last verse. By that time, it will be time for the Wrath of God.

> 15 And they did so from morning to night, and they afterward returned home each man to his house and each woman to her tent; so, they always did four times in the year.

C.4 Why does it say that the men returned to their houses and the women to their tents? It would appear that the women were treated like an inferior species, (just because they are weaker physically?) and that the men ruled by violence and force. The women were treated like inferiors for the convenience of the men and were some of the time kept in inferior quarters such as a tent whilst the men of Sodom and Gomorrah lived in fine houses. The women were but slaves to the men and nothing more. After all it says about Sodom what Paul described so well in the New Testament in the Book of Romans:

ROM.1:21 Because that, when they knew God, they glorified him not as God, neither were thankful; but became vain in their imaginations, and their foolish heart was darkened.

ROM.1:26 For this cause God gave them up unto vile affections: for even their women did change the natural use into that which is against nature:

C.5 God originally stated in Genesis 3 that *a woman's desire would be towards her husband* and not that she was to get raped by other men frequently.

GEN.3:16 Unto the woman he said, I will greatly multiply thy sorrow and thy conception; in sorrow thou shalt bring forth children; and *thy desire shall be to thy husband*, and he shall rule over thee.

C.6 The husband is supposed to protect and care for his wife even as does Christ the church of true believers. The husband is not supposed to indiscriminately throw his wife to other men who want and desire her.

EPH.5:25 Husbands, *love your wives*, even as Christ also loved the church, and gave himself for it;

C.7 Obviously the men of Sodom did not honour their wives; and in fact, they became more and more depraved and *'lusted after strange flesh'*

JUD.1:7 Even as Sodom and Gomorrah, and the cities about them in like manner, giving themselves over to fornication, and going after strange flesh, are set forth for an example, suffering the vengeance of eternal fire.

2PE.2:12 But these, as natural brute beasts, made to be taken and destroyed, and shall utterly perish in their own corruption.

ROM.1:27 And likewise also the men, *leaving the natural use of the woman, burned in their lust one toward another*; men with men working that which is unseemly, and receiving in themselves that recompense of their error which was meet.

C.8 What happened to Sodom and Gomorrah *had* happened before! When? Before the Great Flood. See my book '**Enoch Insights**' for how conditions were upon the earth for the women who the Fallen angels made love with and fathered giants with. The giants also became demons when they died. The women that the Fallen angels made love with became Sirens and fore-mothers of the Mermaid race, but that's another story.

C.9 The point here is that first of all - the Fallen angels had seemingly normal sex with the women...but their union was not blessed by God and their sons became giants and demi-gods who in turn changed into monsters who devoured mankind. The Fallen angels in turn eventually became more and more depraved and left the use of the women and started to become totally perverse and mated with both men and animals. How does this above scenario all start? Three words: *Rebellion against God!*

The men of Sodom kept rebelling against God's Holy Spirit who would have tried to tell them to be kind to those who visited their city, but they would not listen. The last straw according to this book of Jasher was when they started to burn innocent and kind people to death for helping a stranger.

MAT.25:42 For I was hungry, and ye gave me no meat: I was thirsty, and ye gave me no drink:

MAT.25:43 I was a stranger, and ye took me not in: naked, and ye clothed me not: sick, and in prison, and ye visited me not.

C.10 As they showed more and more cruelty to others for no reason whatsoever, they lost God's blessing and the Devils angels literally just took over and made the men just as perverse as they had been before the Great Flood. This shows how dangerous it is to have no rules and to ignore God and His Holy Spirit, who is always trying to talk with each one of us and show us what is right and wrong. Call it your conscience if you will; I would call it 'Guardian angels' and 'spirit helpers'. God has warned us that there is a limit to resisting His Holy Spirit and that there are dire consequences for so doing!

C.11 The following verses show clearly how that we are tested in this life to see how we will treat others and in particular strangers. 'whatsoever a man soweth that shall he also reap' In the story of Sodom and Gomorrah they were very guilty of the following which became worse and worse until there was no remedy.

PRO.29:1 He, that being often reproved hardeneth his neck, shall suddenly be destroyed, and that without remedy.

HEB.13:2 Be not forgetful to entertain strangers: for thereby some have entertained angels unawares.

16 Also when a stranger came into their cities and brought goods which he had purchased with a view to dispose of there, the people of these cities would assemble, men, women and children, young and old, and go to the man and take his goods by force, giving a little to each man until there was an end to all the goods of the owner which he had brought into the land.

17 And if the owner of the goods quarrelled with them, saying, What is this work which you have done to me, then they would approach to him one by one, and each would show him the little which he took and taunt him, saying, I only took that little which thou didst give me; and when he heard this from them all, he would arise and go from them in sorrow and bitterness of soul, when they would all arise and go after him, and drive him out of the city with great noise and tumult.

18 And there was a man from the country of Elam who was leisurely going on the road, seated upon his ass, which carried a fine mantle of divers colours, and the mantle was bound with a cord upon the ass.

19 And the man was on his journey passing through the street of Sodom when the sun set in the evening, and he remained there in order to abide during the night, but no one would let him into his house; and at that time there was in Sodom a wicked and mischievous man, one skilful to do evil, and his name was Hedad.

20 And he lifted up his eyes and saw the traveller in the street of the city, and he came to him and said, 'Whence comest thou and whither dost thou go'?

21 And the man said to him, I am traveling from Hebron to Elam where I belong, and as I passed the sun set and no one would suffer me to enter his house, though I had bread and water and also straw and provender for my ass and am short of nothing.

22 And Hedad answered and said to him, 'All that thou shalt want shall be supplied by me, but in the street thou shalt not abide all night'.

23 And Hedad brought him to his house, and he took off the mantle

from the ass with the cord, and brought them to his house, and he gave the ass straw and provender whilst the traveller ate and drank in He dad's house, and he abode there that night.

24 And in the morning the traveller rose up early to continue his journey, when Hedad said to him, Wait, comfort thy heart with a morsel of bread and then go, and the man did so; and he remained with him, and they both ate and drank together during the day, when the man rose up to go.

25 And Hedad said to him, 'Behold now the day is declining, thou hadst better remain all night that thy heart may be comforted'; and he pressed him so that he tarried there all night, and on the second day he rose up early to go away, when Hedad pressed him, saying, 'Comfort thy heart with a morsel of bread and then go', and he remained and ate with him also the second day, and then the man rose up to continue his journey.

C.12 This guy Hedad was a real deceiver and certainly not one to be trusted. It is surprising that this visitor blindly went to the city of Sodom. Why didn't he know of the reputation of Sodom before considering going there?

26 And Hedad said to him, 'Behold now the day is declining, remain with me to comfort thy heart and in the morning rise up early and go thy way'.

27 And the man would not remain, but rose and saddled his ass, and whilst he was saddling his ass the wife of Hedad said to her husband, Behold this man has remained with us for two days eating and drinking and he has given us nothing, and now shall he go away from us without giving anything? and Hedad said to her, Be silent.

28 And the man saddled his ass to go, and he asked Hedad to give him the cord and mantle to tie it upon the ass.

29 And Hedad said to him, What sayest thou? And he said to him, 'That thou my lord shalt give me the cord and the mantle made with divers colours which thou didst conceal with thee in thy house to take care of it'.

30 And Hedad answered the man, saying, 'This is the interpretation

of thy dream, the cord which thou didst see, means that thy life will be lengthened out like a cord, and having seen the mantle coloured with all sorts of colours, means that thou shalt have a vineyard in which thou wilt plant trees of all fruits'.

31 And the traveller answered, saying, 'Not so my lord, for I was awake when I gave thee the cord and also a mantle woven with different colours, which thou didst take off the ass to put them by for me'; and Hedad answered and said, 'Surely I have told thee the interpretation of thy dream and it is a good dream, and this is the interpretation thereof'.

32 Now the sons of men give me four pieces of silver, which is my charge for interpreting dreams, and of thee only I require three pieces of silver.

33 And the man was provoked at the words of Hedad, and he cried bitterly, and he brought Hedad to Serak judge of Sodom.

34 And the man laid his cause before Serak the judge, when Hedad replied, saying, 'It is not so, but thus the matter stands'; and the judge said to the traveller, 'This man Hedad telleth thee truth, for he is famed in the cities for the accurate interpretation of dreams'.

35 And the man cried at the word of the judge, and he said, 'Not so my Lord, for it was in the day that I gave him the cord and mantle which was upon the ass, in order to put them by in his house'; and they both disputed before the judge, the one saying, 'Thus the matter was, and the other declaring otherwise'.

36 And Hedad said to the man, 'Give me four pieces of silver that I charge for my interpretations of dreams; I will not make any allowance; and give me the expense of the four meals that thou didst eat in my house'.

37 And the man said to Hedad, 'Truly I will pay thee for what I ate in thy house, only give me the cord and mantle which thou didst conceal in thy house'.

38 And Hedad replied before the judge and said to the man, 'Did I not

tell thee the interpretation of thy dream? The cord means that thy days shall be prolonged like a cord, and the mantle, that thou wilt have a vineyard in which thou wilt plant all kinds of fruit trees'.

39 'This is the proper interpretation of thy dream, now give me the four pieces of silver that I require as a compensation, for I will make thee no allowance'.

40 And the man cried at the words of Hedad and they both quarrelled before the judge, and the judge gave orders to his servants, who drove them rashly from the house.

41 And they went away quarrelling from the judge, when the people of Sodom heard them, and they gathered about them and they exclaimed against the stranger, and they drove him rashly from the city.

42 And the man continued his journey upon his ass with bitterness of soul, lamenting and weeping.

43 And whilst he was going along, he wept at what had happened to him in the corrupt city of Sodom.

Chapter 19

FIRE FROM HEAVEN RAINS UPON SODOM & GOMORRAH

1 And the cities of Sodom had four judges to four cities, and these were their names, Serak in the city of Sodom, Sharkad in Gomorrah, Zabnac in Admah, and Menon in Zeboyim.

2 And Eliezer Abraham's servant applied to them different names, and he converted Serak to Shakra, Sharkad to Shakrura, Zebnac to Kezobim, and Menon to Matzlodin.

3 And by desire of their four judges the people of Sodom and Gomorrah had beds erected in the streets of the cities, and if a man came to these places they laid hold of him and brought him to one of their beds, and by force made him to lie in them.

4 And as he lay down, three men would stand at his head and three at his feet, and measure him by the length of the bed, and if the man was less than the bed these six men would stretch him at each end, and when he cried out to them they would not answer him.

5 And if he was longer than the bed they would draw together the two sides of the bed at each end, until the man had reached the gates of death.

Comment:1: Such extreme cruelty and for no logical reason. These people of Sodom were clearly not the children of God, but were of the 'Seed of Satan', and behaved just like the Devil himself. Cain was the first Seed of Satan and was the first murderer, and also went on to kill, rape and pillage others as a way of living.

6 And if he continued to cry out to them, they would answer him, saying, 'Thus shall it be done to a man that cometh into our land'.

7 And when men heard all these things that the people of the cities of Sodom did, they refrained from coming there.

8 And when a poor man came to their land they would give him silver and gold, and cause a proclamation in the whole city not to give him a morsel of bread to eat, and if the stranger should remain there some days, and die from hunger, not having been able to obtain a morsel of bread, then at his death all the people of the city would come and take their silver and gold which they had given to him.

C.2 A very dangerous place to visit where you would be stripped and robed blind, starved to death, and probably abused or even gang-raped if you were a woman and sodomized if you were a man.

9 And those that could recognize the silver or gold which they had given him took it back, and at his death they also stripped him of his garments, and they would fight about them, and he that prevailed over his neighbour took them.

10 They would after that carry him and bury him under some of the shrubs in the deserts; so, they did all the days to anyone that came to them and died in their land.

11 And in the course of time Sarah sent Eliezer to Sodom, to see Lot and inquire after his welfare.

12 And Eliezer went to Sodom, and he met a man of Sodom fighting with a stranger, and the man of Sodom stripped the poor man of all his clothes and went away.

13 And this poor man cried to Eliezer and supplicated his favour on account of what the man of Sodom had done to him.

14 And he said to him, 'Why dost thou act thus to the poor man who came to thy land'?

15 And the man of Sodom answered Eliezer, saying, 'Is this man thy brother, or have the people of Sodom made thee a judge this day, that thou speakest about this man'?

16 And Eliezer strove with the man of Sodom on account of the poor man, and when Eliezer approached to recover the poor man's clothes

from the man of Sodom, he hastened and with a stone smote Eliezer in the forehead.

17 And the blood flowed copiously from Eliezer's forehead, and when the man saw the blood he caught hold of Eliezer, saying, Give me my hire for having rid thee of this bad blood that was in thy forehead, for such is the custom and the law in our land.

C.3 What utter madness that the man smote Eliezer and asked him to pay for the wound that he had just inflicted? Today we would say that such a person should be arrested and that he be taken to the loony bin.

18 And Eliezer said to him, 'Thou hast wounded me and requirest me to pay thee thy hire'; and Eliezer would not hearken to the words of the man of Sodom.

19 And the man laid hold of Eliezer and brought him to Shakra the judge of Sodom for judgment.

20 And the man spoke to the judge, saying, I beseech thee my lord, thus has this man done, for I smote him with a stone that the blood flowed from his forehead, and he is unwilling to give me my hire.

21 And the judge said to Eliezer, 'This man speaks truth to thee, give him his hire, for this is the custom in our land'; and Eliezer heard the words of the judge, and he lifted up a stone and smote the judge, and the stone struck on his forehead, and the blood flowed copiously from the forehead of the judge, and Eliezer said, 'If this then is the custom in your land give thou unto this man what I should have given him, for this has been thy decision, thou didst decree it'.

C.4 What utter insanity! Even the so-called judge of the city of Sodom was a total nut-job. These people were totally depraved and without any sense of right and wrong.

22 And Eliezer left the man of Sodom with the judge, and he went away.

23 And when the kings of Elam had made war with the kings of Sodom, the kings of Elam captured all the property of Sodom, and they took Lot captive, with his property, and when it was told to Abraham he

> went and made war with the kings of Elam, and he recovered from their hands all the property of Lot as well as the property of Sodom.

C.5 Good to see Abraham rescue Lot from the army of the 5 kings who had fought against Sodom and Gomorrah.

> 24 At that time the wife of Lot bare him a daughter, and he called her name Paltith, saying, Because God had delivered him and his whole household from the kings of Elam; and Paltith daughter of Lot grew up, and one of the men of Sodom took her for a wife.
>
> 25 And a poor man came into the city to seek a maintenance, and he remained in the city some days, and all the people of Sodom caused a proclamation of their custom not to give this man a morsel of bread to eat, until he dropped dead upon the earth, and they did so.
>
> 26 And Paltith the daughter of Lot saw this man lying in the streets starved with hunger, and no one would give him anything to keep him alive, and he was just upon the point of death.
>
> 27 And her soul was filled with pity on account of the man, and she fed him secretly with bread for many days, and the soul of this man was revived.

C.6 Now here was a gem in the dung heaps! What a sweetheart, the daughter of Lot was. Such a sad, and tragic story!

> 28 For when she went forth to fetch water, she would put the bread in the water pitcher, and when she came to the place where the poor man was, she took the bread from the pitcher and gave it him to eat; so, she did many days.
>
> 29 And all the people of Sodom and Gomorrah wondered how this man could bear starvation for so many days.
>
> 30 And they said to each other, This can only be that he eats and drinks, for no man can bear starvation for so many days or live as this man has, without even his countenance changing; and three men concealed themselves in a place where the poor man was stationed, to know who it was that brought him bread to eat.

31 And Paltith daughter of Lot went forth that day to fetch water, and she put bread into her pitcher of water, and she went to draw water by the poor man's place, and she took out the bread from the pitcher and gave it to the poor man and he ate it.

32 And the three men saw what Paltith did to the poor man, and they said to her, 'It is thou then who hast supported him, and therefore has he not starved, nor changed in appearance nor died like the rest'.

33 And the three men went out of the place in which they were concealed, and they seized Paltith and the bread which was in the poor man's hand.

34 And they took Paltith and brought her before their judges, and they said to them, Thus did she do, and it is she who supplied the poor man with bread, therefore did he not die all this time; now therefore declare to us the punishment due to this woman for having transgressed our law.

35 And the people of Sodom and Gomorrah assembled and kindled a fire in the street of the city, and they took the woman and cast her into the fire, and she was burned to ashes.

C.7 Imagine seeing a kind person helping someone who falls on the city street today in modern times. Everyone almost without exception, would applaud such a kind person for their kind deed. What in heaven's name was wrong with those who were the inhabitants of Sodom, Gomorrah and the cities of the plain? These people were all descendants of Ham. His sons were cursed because of Noah's curse on Ham and his son Canaan.

C.8 This race was originally cursed because Ham committed an act of sodomy against his own father when he was drunk and naked. Noah then cursed Ham and his sons. It was 5 of the descendants of Ham who founded the 5 cities of the plain -Sodom, Gomorrah, Zeboim, Admah and Bela.

C.9 Because of the rebellion of some of the sons of Ham a negative spiritual portal was opened after the Great Flood, which allowed evil entities back into our physical world. These evil entities or demons would seek people to possess and would look for those who tended to like being evil and would possess them.

C.10 Because of the depravity of certain races, it brought back the Nephilim and their sons the giants. Thus, the Canaanites were races of Giants. The entities from hell were bent on doing everything in opposition to God and His rules of love, kindness, consideration and humility. The ways of Satan are pride, arrogancy, cruelty, violence, forced control of others, heartless, perversion, depravity, and above all deception & doubt sowing.

C.11 It is hard to believe that a people could be so cruel. Obviously, the men of Sodom kept the women as slaves. They had them abused by other men in orgies 4 times a year. They were cruel and barbaric to those who happened to visit their cities and had crazy ideas of both judgment and suitable punishments for things that weren't even crimes! What utter madness and in fact total insanity ruled in Sodom and Gomorrah, not to mention their sexual loudness and total depravity and debauchery. No one was safe in Sodom as shown what happened when the angels of Judgment came to judge the cities of the plain.

C.12 FEMINISM There is probably a deeper reason why races of the past treated women as inferiors. If we go back before the times of the Great Flood, we find that *feminism* was very dominant. What did that mean? We know that many Fallen angels came to the earth especially during the 500 years before the Great Flood. The first Fallen angels had seduced the women in the time of Jared. Later on, in time, or around 1000 years later closer to the actual Great Flood, it became the other way around, where the women started seducing the Fallen angels and had sex with them. When the beautiful women saw that they were able to have sex with angels rather than men, then in some cases they *abandoned the normal men in favour of having sex with Fallen angels*, who after the Great Flood became known as devils and demons.

C13 This essentially was the beginning of Witchcraft, and the same rituals of sex are still performed to this day, although it appears that God has severely restricted Satan and the Fallen angels in this department, as Witchcraft and sexual orgies in sacrifice to Fallen Angels (Devils) is not yet as rampant as it was before the Great Flood. Or am I wrong in assuming that?

C.14 Before the Great Flood the women could actually see the entities or Fallen angels that they were having sex with. After the Great Flood, it was much more difficult, as they couldn't actually see them anymore as God had restricted the Fallen angels from having easy contact with humans. However, the witches learned to use seances and spells and sex debauchery with certain selected men who were into dark arts and this in turn calls those entities from the hidden realm or the negative spirit world or even Hell itself to join in the orgy.

C.15 MACHOISM My argument as to why after the Great Flood many races *subjugated the women* into 2nd class citizens is because they *didn't want the women dominating them again* as in what happened to some of the men before the Great Flood. The men after the Great Flood didn't want the women abandoning them again as before the Great Flood. In fact, many cultures adopted severe laws against witches who performed such sexual acts and they were to be burned to at the stake according to the Laws of Moses.

36 And in the city of Admah there was a woman to whom they did the like.

37 For a traveller came into the city of Admah to abide there all night, with the intention of going home in the morning, and he sat opposite the door of the house of the young woman's father, to remain there, as the sun had set when he had reached that place; and the young woman saw him sitting by the door of the house.

38 And he asked her for a drink of water and she said to him, Who art thou? and he said to her, I was this day going on the road, and reached here when the sun set, so I will abide here all night, and in the morning I will arise early and continue my journey.

39 And the young woman went into the house and fetched the man bread and water to eat and drink.

C.16 Here we can see what a charitable person would do in order to help those around them. However, the inhabitants of Sodom and the other cities of the plain were anything but charitable, even though as God Himself said in effect that they had everything and nothing lacking and yet they chose to be evil and cruel and violent and deceitful to any strangers who happened to travel through their land and would rob them of all they had. No wonder God totally destroyed them as they were more like children from hell.

40 And this affair became known to the people of Admah, and they assembled and brought the young woman before the judges, that they should judge her for this act.

41 And the judge said, 'The judgment of death must pass upon this woman because she transgressed our law, and this therefore is the decision concerning her'.

42 And the people of those cities assembled and brought out the young woman, and anointed her with honey from head to foot, as the judge had decreed, and they placed her before a swarm of bees which were then in their hives, and the bees flew upon her and stung her that her whole body was swelled.

43 And the young woman cried out on account of the bees, but no one

took notice of her or pitied her, and her cries ascended to heaven.

44 And the Lord was provoked at this and at all the works of the cities of Sodom, for they had abundance of food, and had tranquillity amongst them, and still would not sustain the poor and the needy, and in those days their evil doings and sins became great before the Lord.

45 And the Lord sent for two of the angels that had come to Abraham's house, to destroy Sodom and its cities.

46 And the angels rose up from the door of Abraham's tent, after they had eaten and drunk, and they reached Sodom in the evening, and Lot was then sitting in the gate of Sodom, and when he saw them he rose to meet them, and he bowed down to the ground.

47 And he pressed them greatly and brought them into his house, and he gave them victuals which they ate, and they abode all night in his house.

C.17 The men of the city surrounded Lot's house and demanded that he bring the angels out to them so that they could gang sodomize the angels. Instead the angels blinded all the men and dragged Lot and his family out of Sodom and then raining fire and brimstone on the disgusting depraved city. That was the end of the cities of the plain.

GEN.19:4 But before they lay down, the men of the city, even the men of Sodom, compassed the house round, both old and young, all the people from every quarter:

GEN.19:5 And they called unto Lot, and said unto him, 'Where are the men (the 2 angels) which came in to thee this night? bring them out unto us, that we may know them'. (sodomize them).

GEN.19:6 And Lot went out at the door unto them, and shut the door after him,

GEN.19:7 And said, I pray you, brethren, do not so wickedly.

GEN.19:8 Behold now, I have two daughters which have not known man; let me, I pray you, bring them out unto you, and do ye to them as is good in your eyes: only unto these men do nothing; for therefore came they under the shadow of my roof.

GEN.19:9 And they said, Stand back. And they said again, 'This one fellow came in to sojourn, and he will needs be a judge: now will we deal worse with thee, than with them. And they pressed sore upon the man, even Lot, and came near to break the door'.

GEN.19:10 But the men put forth their hand, and pulled Lot into the house to them, and shut to the door.

GEN.19:11 And they smote the men that were at the door of the house with blindness, both small and great: so that they wearied themselves to find the door.

2 Ezdras 2.8 Woe to you, Assyria, who conceal the unrighteous within you! 'O wicked nation remember what I did to Sodom and Gomorrah'.

> 49 And the angels laid hold upon the hand of Lot and upon the hand of his wife, and upon the hands of his children, and all belonging to him, and they brought him forth and set him without the cities.
>
> 50 And they said to Lot, 'Escape for thy life'; and he fled and all belonging to him.
>
> 51 Then the Lord rained upon Sodom and upon Gomorrah and upon all these cities brimstone and fire from the Lord out of heaven.

C.18 Here we see another excellent description of the destruction of the cities of the plain:

Book of Jubilees 16.5-6 The Lord executed His judgements on Sodom and Gomorrah and Zeboim and all the regions of the Jordan and He burned them with *fire and brimstone* and destroyed them until this day, and lo I have declared unto thee all their works, that they are wicked and sinners exceedingly, and that they defile themselves commit fornication in their flesh and work uncleanness on the earth. 6. And in like manner, God will execute His judgement on the places where they have done according to the uncleanness of the Sodomites, like unto the judgment of Sodom.

> 52 And he overthrew these cities, all the plain and all the inhabitants of the cities, and that which grew upon the ground; and Ado the wife of Lot looked back to see the destruction of the cities, for her compassion was moved on account of her daughters who remained in Sodom, for they did not go with her.

C.19 For more info see the following *link* for 100 Bible verses concerning Sodom and Gomorrah: https://www.openbible.info/topics/sodom

> 53 And when she looked back, she became a pillar of salt, and it is yet in that place unto this day.
>
> 54 And the oxen which stood in that place daily licked up the salt to

the extremities of their feet, and in the morning, it would spring forth afresh, and they again licked it up unto this day.

55 And Lot and two of his daughters that remained with him fled and escaped to the cave of Adullam, and they remained there for some time.

56 And Abraham rose up early in the morning to see what had been done to the cities of Sodom; and he looked and beheld the smoke of the cities going up like the smoke of a furnace.

57 And Lot and his two daughters remained in the cave, and they made their father drink wine, and they lay with him, for they said there was no man upon earth that could raise up seed from them, for they thought that the whole earth was destroyed.

58 And they both lay with their father, and they conceived and bare sons, and the first born called the name of her son Moab, saying, 'From my father did I conceive him; he is the father of the Moabites unto this day'.

C.20 Here is a very strange situation which would certainly not be officially tolerated in our modern society and which would have caused Lot to be put in jail. Well at least that's how it used to be 50 years ago. Today, there is a lot of depravity. I was working one time to help a certain charity here where I live, and the woman in charge told me that here in Scotland ¼ young women and girls and even children are sexually abused by someone in their own families! I was absolutely shocked. She also told me that 1/5 boys under 18 are also abused by their own families. What are the stats in other countries? So, as one can see our society in modern times is going the way of Sodom and Gomorrah - slowly but surely.

59 And the younger also called her son Benami; he is the father of the children of Ammon unto this day.

60 And after this Lot and his two daughters went away from there, and he dwelt on the other side of the Jordan with his two daughters and their sons, and the sons of Lot grew up, and they went and took themselves wives from the land of Canaan, and they begat children and they were fruitful and multiplied.

Chapter 20

1 And at that time Abraham journeyed from the plain of Mamre, and he went to the land of the Philistines, and he dwelt in Gerar; it was in the twenty-fifth year of Abraham's being in the land of Canaan, and the hundredth year of the life of Abraham, that he came to Gerar in the land of the Philistines.

GEN.20:1 And Abraham journeyed from thence toward the south country, and dwelled between Kadesh and Shur, and sojourned in Gerar.

2 And when they entered the land, he said to Sarah his wife, say thou art my sister, to any one that shall ask thee, in order that we may escape the evil of the inhabitants of the land.

3 And as Abraham was dwelling in the land of the Philistines, the servants of Abimelech, king of the Philistines, saw that Sarah was exceedingly beautiful, and they asked Abraham concerning her, and he said, 'She is my sister'.

Comment:1: This is one of the rare occasions where Abraham was leaning to his own understanding and not really trusting the Lord. Doing things his own way didn't give the desired result and he was found out anyway.

PRO.3:5 Trust in the LORD with all thine heart; and lean not unto thine own understanding.

PRO.3:6 In all thy ways acknowledge him, and he shall direct thy paths.

4 And the servants of Abimelech went to Abimelech, saying, A man from the land of Canaan is come to dwell in the land, and he has a sister that is exceeding fair.

GEN.20:2 And Abraham said of Sarah his wife, 'She is my sister': and Abimelech king of Gerar sent and took Sarah.

5 And Abimelech heard the words of his servants who praised Sarah to him, and Abimelech sent his officers, and they brought Sarah to the king.

6 And Sarah came to the house of Abimelech, and the king saw that Sarah was beautiful, and she pleased him exceedingly.

7 And he approached her and said to her, 'What is that man to thee with whom thou didst come to our land?' and Sarah answered and said 'He is my brother, and we came from the land of Canaan to dwell wherever we could find a place'.

8 And Abimelech said to Sarah, 'Behold my land is before thee, place thy brother in any part of this land that pleases thee, and it will be our duty to exalt and elevate him above all the people of the land since he is thy brother'.

9 And Abimelech sent for Abraham, and Abraham came to Abimelech.

10 And Abimelech said to Abraham, Behold I have given orders that thou shalt be honoured as thou desirest on account of thy sister Sarah.

11 And Abraham went forth from the king, and the king's present followed him.

12 As at evening time, before men lie down to rest, the king was sitting upon his throne, and a deep sleep fell upon him, and he lay upon the throne and slept till morning.

13 And he dreamed that an angel of the Lord came to him with a drawn sword in his hand, and the angel stood over Abimelech, and wished to slay him with the sword, and the king was terrified in his dream, and said to the angel, In what have I sinned against thee that thou comest to slay me with thy sword?

GEN.20:3 But God came to Abimelech in a dream by night, and said to him, Behold, thou art but a dead man, for the woman which thou hast taken; for she is a man's wife.

GEN.20:5 Said he not unto me, 'She is my sister? and she, even she herself said, He is my brother: in the integrity of my heart and innocence of my hands have I done this'.

GEN.20:6 And God said unto him in a dream, Yea, I know that thou didst this in the integrity of thy heart; for I also withheld thee from sinning against me: therefore, suffered I thee not to touch her.

GEN.20:7 Now therefore restore the man his wife; for he is a prophet, and he shall pray for thee, and thou shalt live: and if thou restore her not, know thou that thou shalt surely die, thou, and all that are thine.

> 14 And the angel answered and said to Abimelech, Behold thou diest on account of the woman which thou didst yesternight bring to thy house, for she is a married woman, the wife of Abraham who came to thy house; now therefore return that man his wife, for she is his wife; and shouldst thou not return her, know that thou wilt surely die, thou and all belonging to thee.

GEN.20:4 But Abimelech had not come near her: and he said, LORD, wilt thou slay also a righteous nation?

> 15 And on that night there was a great outcry in the land of the Philistines, and the inhabitants of the land saw the figure of a man standing with a drawn sword in his hand, and he smote the inhabitants of the land with the sword, yea he continued to smite them.

GEN.20:7 Now therefore restore the man his wife; for he is a prophet, and he shall pray for thee, and thou shalt live: and if thou restore her not, know thou that thou shalt surely die, thou, and all that are thine.

GEN.20:8 Therefore Abimelech rose early in the morning, and called all his servants, and told all these things in their ears: and the men were sore afraid.

> 16 And the angel of the Lord smote the whole land of the Philistines on that night, and there was a great confusion on that night and on the following morning.
>
> 17 And every womb was closed, and all their issues, and the hand of the Lord was upon them on account of Sarah, wife of Abraham, whom Abimelech had taken.
>
> 18 And in the morning, Abimelech rose with terror and confusion and with a great dread, and he sent and had his servants called in, and he related his dream to them, and the people were greatly afraid.
>
> 19 And one man standing amongst the servants of the king answered the king, saying, O sovereign king, restore this woman to her husband, for he is her husband, for the like happened to the king of Egypt when this man came to Egypt.

20 And he said concerning his wife, 'She is my sister, for such is his manner of doing when he cometh to dwell in the land in which he is a stranger'.

21 And Pharaoh sent and took this woman for a wife and the Lord brought upon him grievous plagues until he returned the woman to her husband.

22 Now therefore, O sovereign king, know what happened yesternight to the whole land, for there was a very great consternation and great pain and lamentation, and we know that it was on account of the woman which thou didst take.

23 Now, therefore, restore this woman to her husband, lest it should befall us as it did to Pharaoh king of Egypt and his subjects, and that we may not die; and Abimelech hastened and called and had Sarah called for, and she came before him, and he had Abraham called for, and he came before him.

24 And Abimelech said to them, 'What is this work you have been doing in saying you are brother and sister, and I took this woman for a wife?'

25 And Abraham said, Because I thought I should suffer death on account of my wife; and Abimelech took flocks and herds, and men servants and maid servants, and a thousand pieces of silver, and he gave them to Abraham, and he returned Sarah to him.

C.2 Because Abraham was afraid that he would be killed and his wife taken away from him by the rich or wealthy such as the king, it shows that back then the people living in the land were dangerous and unpredictable. Abraham need not have feared as the angels of God were always with him and Sarah.

GEN.20:9 Then Abimelech called Abraham, and said unto him, What hast thou done unto us? and what have I offended thee, that thou hast brought on me and on my kingdom a great sin? thou hast done deeds unto me that ought not to be done.

GEN.20:10 And Abimelech said unto Abraham, 'What saw thou, that thou hast done this thing'?

GEN.20:11 And Abraham said, Because I thought, Surely the fear of God is not in this place; and they will slay me for my wife's sake.

GEN.20:12 And yet indeed she is my sister; she is the daughter of my father, but not the daughter of my mother; and she became my wife.

---

26 And Abimelech said to Abraham, Behold the whole land is before thee, dwell in it wherever thou shalt choose.

27 And Abraham and Sarah, his wife, went forth from the king's presence with honour and respect, and they dwelt in the land, even in Gerar.

28 And all the inhabitants of the land of the Philistines and the king's servants were still in pain, through the plague which the angel had inflicted upon them the whole night on account of Sarah.

29 And Abimelech sent for Abraham, saying, 'Pray now for thy servants to the Lord thy God, that he may put away this mortality from amongst us'.

30 And Abraham prayed on account of Abimelech and his subjects, and the Lord heard the prayer of Abraham, and he healed Abimelech and all his subjects.

C.3 It is true that the Lord did end up destroying Egypt by his Judgements 400 years after Abraham in the time of Moses.

C.4 God also destroyed the Philistines in the time of Samson, around 250 years after Moses time in around 1170 BCE because of their customs and because of their wickedness, just like Sodom and Gomorrah.

C.5 God also destroyed most of the lands through which the children of Israel passed through on their way to the Promised Land at some time or other as God had instructed Israel to wipe out the Canaanites.

C.6 The Canaanites who lived anywhere from the land of the Phoenicians in the north and the Philistines in the West down to Egypt in the south were eventually totally destroyed by the sons of Jacob and their descendants.

C.7 Israel who acted like the 'Sword of the Lord' in the very Hand of God in the time of Gideon and the Midianites. It would appear that God would tolerate the nations surrounding Israel to live as long as they did not harm Israel. Those that tried to destroy Israel were themselves often destroyed. Of course, throughout time Israel went astray as happened more often than not under certain king's influence, then God would allow their enemies to capture Israel for a season until his people cried out to God for deliverance & fully repented and then He would rescue them time and time again.

Chapter 21

1 And it was at that time at the end of a year and four months of Abraham's dwelling in the land of the Philistines in Gerar, that God visited Sarah, and the Lord remembered her, and she conceived and bare a son to Abraham.

Comment:1: Such a miracle to be able to have a baby at 90 years old. Putting things into the proper perspective. Abraham fathered Israel at the age of 100 when he thought that he was already old, and yet he lived to the ripe old age of 175. Sarah on the other hand only lived to be 127. In modern terms it would be as if the average person today lives to be 80 then having a child in one's late 40's would be considered too old to have a child in the case of most women.

ROM.4:18 Abraham…Who against hope believed in hope, that he might become the father of many nations, according to that which was spoken, 'So shall thy seed be'.

ROM.4:19 And being not weak in faith, he considered not his own body now dead, when he was about a hundred years old, neither yet the deadness of Sarah's womb:

ROM.4:20 He staggered not at the promise of God through unbelief; but was strong in faith, giving glory to God;

ROM.4:21 And being fully persuaded that, what he had promised, he was able also to perform.

ROM.4:22 And therefore it was imputed to him for righteousness.

2 And Abraham called the name of the son which was born to him, which Sarah bare to him, Isaac.

3 And Abraham circumcised his son Isaac at eight days old, as God had commanded Abraham to do unto his seed after him; and Abraham was one hundred, and Sarah ninety years old, when Isaac was born to them.

4 And the child grew up and he was weaned, and Abraham made a great feast upon the day that Isaac was weaned.

5 And Shem and Eber and all the great people of the land, and Abimelech king of the Philistines, and his servants, and Phicol, the captain of his host, came to eat and drink and rejoice at the feast which Abraham made upon the day of his son Isaac's being weaned.

C.2 This book along with the Bible mentions that Shem and Eber were actually still alive in the time of Abraham, although the Biblical Time charts also do show that they were indeed alive at the same time.

6 Also Terah, the father of Abraham, and Nahor his brother, came from Haran, they and all belonging to them, for they greatly rejoiced on hearing that a son had been born to Sarah.

7 And they came to Abraham, and they ate and drank at the feast which Abraham made upon the day of Isaac's being weaned.

8 And Terah and Nahor rejoiced with Abraham, and they remained with him many days in the land of the Philistines.

9 At that time Serug the son of Reu died, in the first year of the birth of Isaac son of Abraham.

10 And all the days of Serug were two hundred and thirty-nine years, and he died.

C.3 These are the generations from Noah to Abraham according to the King James Bible: Noah-Shem-Arphaxad-Salah-Eber-Peleg-Reu-Serug-Nahor- Terah – Abraham. Shem lived longer than his son Arphaxad and his grandson Salah and also Peleg, Reu, Serug, Nahor, Terah and Abraham. Eber lived longer than all of those mentioned in the lineage from Noah to Abraham. How was such a thing even possible? God had stated at the Judgement of the Great Flood that a man's life would be 120 years. Man's life started to be reduced drastically from the Flood onwards. Noah lived to be 950 years old. Shem his son 600 years old. Arphaxad, Salah and Eber around 438 years, Peleg & Reu 239, Serug 230, Nahor 148, Terah 205, Abraham 175, Isaac 180, Jacob 147, Joseph 110. Most of Joseph's 11 brothers died around 120 years old. It took 550 years for the lifespan of mankind to be reduced from 950 years old down to only 120 years old. It then took another 800 years to further reduce the age of man from 120 down to 70 as in the case of King David. The average age since of mankind has been around 70-80 years old.

11 And Ishmael the son of Abraham was grown up in those days; he was fourteen years old when Sarah bare Isaac to Abraham.

12 And God was with Ishmael the son of Abraham, and he grew up, and he learned to use the bow and became an archer.

13 And when Isaac was five years old, he was sitting with Ishmael at the door of the tent.

14 And Ishmael came to Isaac and seated himself opposite to him, and he took the bow and drew it and put the arrow in it and intended to slay Isaac.

15 And Sarah saw the act which Ishmael desired to do to her son Isaac, and it grieved her exceedingly on account of her son, and she sent for Abraham, and said to him, 'Cast out this bondwoman and her son, for her son shall not be heir with my son, for thus did he seek to do unto him this day'.

GEN.21:10 Wherefore she said unto Abraham, 'Cast out this bondwoman and her son: for the son of this bondwoman shall not be heir with my son, even with Isaac'.

16 And Abraham hearkened to the voice of Sarah, and he rose up early in the morning, and he took twelve loaves and a bottle of water which he gave to Hagar, and sent her away with her son, and Hagar went with her son to the wilderness, and they dwelt in the wilderness of Paran with the inhabitants of the wilderness, and Ishmael was an archer, and he dwelt in the wilderness a long time.

GEN.21:11 And the thing was very grievous in Abraham's sight because of his son.

GEN.21:12 And God said unto Abraham, 'Let it not be grievous in thy sight because of the lad, and because of thy bondwoman; in all that Sarah hath said unto thee, hearken unto her voice; for in Isaac shall thy seed be called.'

GEN.21:13 And also of the son of the bondwoman will I make a nation, because he is thy seed.

C.4 It would seem to us in modern times, that initially, this episode sounds very cruel, at least on first hearing this particular part of the story. To send a woman out alone with her young son into the wilderness with nowhere to go and no place to take shelter and with next to no provisions? However, Abraham is sending Hagar away against his better judgement because of his wife's desire to get rid of Hagar, and because God's angel told him too. Abraham knew that if he sent Hagar away that God had promised to take care of her and her son. In fact, God promised to make 12 nations arise from her son Ishmael – the 12 Arab nations. So, stepping out by faith into what to most would seem total 'abandonment of all reason', actually gets the 'desired results' that God is looking for. If Hagar and Ismael had not been 'kicked out' of the nest, perhaps Ishmael would never have fathered the 12 Arab nations?

HAB.2:4 Behold the just shall live by his faith

ROM.1:17 For therein is the righteousness of God revealed from faith to faith: as it is written, 'The just shall live by faith'.

---

17 And he and his mother afterward went to the land of Egypt, and they dwelt there, and Hagar took a wife for her son from Egypt, and her name was Meribah.

18 And the wife of Ishmael conceived and bare four sons and two daughters, and Ishmael and his mother and his wife and children afterward went and returned to the wilderness.

19 And they made themselves tents in the wilderness, in which they dwelt, and they continued to travel and then to rest monthly and yearly.

20 And God gave Ishmael flocks and herds and tents on account of Abraham his father, and the man increased in cattle.

21 And Ishmael dwelt in deserts and in tents, traveling and resting for a long time, and he did not see the face of his father.

22 And in some time after, Abraham said to Sarah his wife, I will go and see my son Ishmael, for I have a desire to see him, for I have not seen him for a long time.

23 And Abraham rode upon one of his camels to the wilderness to seek his son Ishmael, for he heard that he was dwelling in a tent in the wilderness with all belonging to him.

24 And Abraham went to the wilderness, and he reached the tent of Ishmael about noon, and he asked after Ishmael, and he found the wife of Ishmael sitting in the tent with her children, and Ishmael her husband and his mother were not with them.

25 And Abraham asked the wife of Ishmael, saying, 'Where has Ishmael gone? and she said, He has gone to the field to hunt, and Abraham was still mounted upon the camel, for he would not get off to the ground as he had sworn to his wife Sarah that he would not get off from the camel'.

26 And Abraham said to Ishmael's wife, 'My daughter, give me a little water that I may drink, for I am fatigued from the journey'.

27 And Ishmael's wife answered and said to Abraham, 'We have neither water nor bread, and she continued sitting in the tent and did not notice Abraham, neither did she ask him who he was'.

28 But she was beating her children in the tent, and she was cursing them, and she also cursed her husband Ishmael and reproached him, and Abraham heard the words of Ishmael's wife to her children, and he was very angry and displeased.

29 And Abraham called to the woman to come out to him from the tent, and the woman came and stood opposite to Abraham, for Abraham was still mounted upon the camel.

30 And Abraham said to Ishmael's wife, 'When thy husband Ishmael returneth home say these words to him,

31 A very old man from the land of the Philistines came hither to seek thee, and thus was his appearance and figure'; I did not ask him who he was, and seeing thou wast not here he spoke unto me and said, 'When Ishmael thy husband returneth tell him thus did this man say, 'When thou comest home put away this nail of the tent which thou hast placed here, and place another nail in its stead'.

32 And Abraham finished his instructions to the woman, and he turned and went off on the camel homeward.

33 And after that Ishmael came from the chase, he and his mother, and returned to the tent, and his wife spoke these words to him,

34 A very old man from the land of the Philistines came to seek thee, and thus was his appearance and figure; I did not ask him who he was, and seeing thou wast not at home he said to me, When thy husband cometh home tell him, thus saith the old man, Put away the nail of the tent which thou hast placed here and place another nail in its stead.

35 And Ishmael heard the words of his wife, and he knew that it was his father, and that his wife did not honour him.

36 And Ishmael understood his father's words that he had spoken to his wife, and Ishmael hearkened to the voice of his father, and Ishmael cast off that woman and she went away.

37 And Ishmael afterward went to the land of Canaan, and he took another wife and he brought her to his tent to the place where he then dwelt.

38 And at the end of three years Abraham said, I will go again and see Ishmael my son, for I have not seen him for a long time.

39 And he rode upon his camel and went to the wilderness, and he reached the tent of Ishmael about noon.

40 And he asked after Ishmael, and his wife came out of the tent and she said, He is not here my lord, for he has gone to hunt in the fields, and to feed the camels, and the woman said to Abraham, Turn in my lord into the tent, and eat a morsel of bread, for thy soul must be wearied on account of the journey.

41 And Abraham said to her, I will not stop for I am in haste to continue my journey, but give me a little water to drink, for I have thirst; and the woman hastened and ran into the tent and she brought out water and bread to Abraham, which she placed before him and she urged him to eat, and he ate and drank and his heart was comforted and he blessed his son Ishmael.

42 And he finished his meal and he blessed the Lord, and he said to Ishmael's wife, When Ishmael cometh home say these words to him,

43 A very old man from the land of the Philistines came hither and asked after thee, and thou wast not here; and I brought him out bread and water and he ate and drank, and his heart was comforted.

44 And he spoke these words to me: When Ishmael thy husband cometh

home, say unto him, 'The nail of the tent which thou hast is very good, do not put it away from the tent'.

45 And Abraham finished commanding the woman, and he rode off to his home to the land of the Philistines; and when Ishmael came to his tent his wife went forth to meet him with joy and a cheerful heart.

46 And she said to him, 'An old man came here from the land of the Philistines and thus was his appearance, and he asked after thee and thou wast not here, so I brought out bread and water, and he ate and drank and his heart was comforted.'

47 And he spoke these words to me, 'When Ishmael thy husband cometh home say to him, 'The nail of the tent which thou hast is very good, do not put it away from the tent.'

48 And Ishmael knew that it was his father, and that his wife had honoured him, and the Lord blessed Ishmael.

Chapter 22

1 And Ishmael then rose up and took his wife and his children and his cattle and all belonging to him, and he journeyed from there and he went to his father in the land of the Philistines.

2 And Abraham related to Ishmael his son the transaction with the first wife that Ishmael took, according to what she did.

3 And Ishmael and his children dwelt with Abraham many days in that land, and Abraham dwelt in the land of the Philistines a long time.

4 And the days increased and reached twenty six years, and after that Abraham with his servants and all belonging to him went from the land of the Philistines and removed to a great distance, and they came near to Hebron, and they remained there, and the servants of Abraham dug wells of water, and Abraham and all belonging to him dwelt by the water, and the servants of Abimelech king of the Philistines heard the report that Abraham's servants had dug wells of water in the borders of the land.

5 And they came and quarrelled with the servants of Abraham, and they robbed them of the great well which they had dug.

6 And Abimelech king of the Philistines heard of this affair, and he with Phicol the captain of his host and twenty of his men came to Abraham, and Abimelech spoke to Abraham concerning his servants, and Abraham rebuked Abimelech concerning the well of which his servants had robbed him.

7 And Abimelech said to Abraham, As the Lord lives who created the whole earth, I did not hear of the act which my servants did unto thy servants until this day.

8 And Abraham took seven ewe lambs and gave them to Abimelech, saying, 'Take these, I pray thee, from my hands that it may be a testimony for me that I dug this well'.

9 And Abimelech took the seven ewe lambs which Abraham had given to him, for he had also given him cattle and herds in abundance, and Abimelech swore to Abraham concerning the well, therefore he called that well Beersheba, for there they both swore concerning it.

10 And they both made a covenant in Beersheba, and Abimelech rose up with Phicol the captain of his host and all his men, and they returned to the land of the Philistines, and Abraham and all belonging to him dwelt in Beersheba and he was in that land a long time.

11 And Abraham planted a large grove in Beersheba, and he made to it four gates facing the four sides of the earth, and he planted a vineyard in it, so that if a traveller came to Abraham he entered any gate which was in his road and remained there and ate and drank and satisfied himself and then departed.

12 For the house of Abraham was always open to the sons of men that passed and repassed, who came daily to eat and drink in the house of Abraham.

13 And any man who had hunger and came to Abraham's house, Abraham would give him bread that he might eat and drink and be satisfied, and any one that came naked to his house he would clothe with garments as he might choose, and give him silver and gold and make known to him the Lord who had created him in the earth; this did Abraham all his life.

Comment:1: Abraham was a kind and generous man & he set a sample of being compassionate. For this reason, his name was much set by all who met him.

HEB.11:8 By faith Abraham, when he was called to go out into a place which he should after receive for an inheritance, obeyed; and he went out, not knowing whither he went.

HEB.11:9 By faith he sojourned in the land of promise, as in a strange country, dwelling in tabernacles with Isaac and Jacob, the heirs with him of the same promise:

HEB.11:10 For he looked for a city which hath foundations, whose builder and maker is God.

14 And Abraham and his children and all belonging to him dwelt in Beersheba, and he pitched his tent as far as Hebron.

15 And Abraham's brother Nahor and his father and all belonging to them dwelt in Haran, for they did not come with Abraham to the land of Canaan.

16 And children were born to Nahor which Milca the daughter of Haran, and sister to Sarah, Abraham's wife, bare to him.

17 And these are the names of those that were born to him, Uz, Buz, Kemuel, Kesed, Chazo, Pildash, Tidlaf, and Bethuel, being eight sons, these are the children of Milca which she bare to Nahor, Abraham's brother.

C.2 TIMEFRAME: In the Bible it talks about a man called Job whom it says came from the land of Uz. The name Uz is mentioned 3 times in the Bible & was first mentioned in the Bible as the grandson of Shem, which means he lived around the same time as Salah. Since back in those times cities were often built and the given the name of someone's son, it could mean that the city if Uz was built just after the Great Flood or *within a hundred years of the Great Flood*. It also means that Job could have predated Abraham. Most Bible scholars state there is no real evidence to prove when Job actually lived, but I disagree due to the mention of the word Uz. Uz was built just after the Great Flood and Job came from that city. It is therefore very likely that he was around about 2000 BCE or even earlier and not 400-1000 BCE as quoted by some as in the following source: (https://www.quora.com/When-did-Job-of-the-Bible-live)

JOB.1:1 There was a man in the *land of Uz*, whose name was Job; and that man was perfect and upright, and one that feared God, and eschewed evil.

C.3 The Book of Jubilees mentions a man called Job as also coming from the city of Uz. The timeframe from that book, if it was indeed the same man mentioned in the Bible was as follows. There was an advisor to one of the Pharaohs in the time before the *days of Moses* who advised the Pharaoh to afflict the 'Children of Israel'

18 And Nahor had a concubine and her name was Reumah, and she also bare to Nahor, Zebach, Gachash, Tachash and Maacha, being four sons.

19 And the children that were born to Nahor were twelve sons besides his daughters, and they also had children born to them in Haran.

20 And the children of Uz the first born of Nahor were Abi, Cheref, Gadin, Melus, and Deborah their sister.

21 And the sons of Buz were Berachel, Naamath, Sheva, and Madonu.

22 And the sons of Kemuel were Aram and Rechob.

23 And the sons of Kesed were Anamlech, Meshai, Benon and Yifi; and the sons of Chazo were Pildash, Mechi and Opher.

24 And the sons of Pildash were Arud, Chamum, Mered and Moloch.

25 And the sons of Tidlaf were Mushan, Cushan and Mutzi.

26 And the children of Bethuel were Sechar, Laban and their sister Rebecca.

27 These are the families of the children of Nahor, that were born to them in Haran; and Aram the son of Kemuel and Rechob his brother went away from Haran, and they found a valley in the land by the river Euphrates.

28 And they built a city there, and they called the name of the city after the name of Pethor the son of Aram, that is Aram Naharayim unto this day.

29 And the children of Kesed also went to dwell where they could find a place, and they went and they found a valley opposite to the land of Shinar, and they dwelt there.

30 And they there built themselves a city, and they called the name at the city Kesed after the name of their father, that is the land Kasdim unto this day, and the Kasdim dwelt in that land and they were fruitful and multiplied exceedingly.

31 And Terah, father of Nahor and Abraham, went and took another wife in his old age, and her name was Pelilah, and she conceived and bare him a son and he called his name Zoba.

32 And Terah lived twenty-five years after he begat Zoba.

33 And Terah died in that year, that is in the thirty-fifth year of the birth of Isaac son of Abraham.

34 And the days of Terah were two hundred and five years, and he was buried in Haran.

35 And Zoba the son of Terah lived thirty years and he begat Aram, Achlis and Merik.

36 And Aram son of Zoba son of Terah, had three wives and he begat twelve sons and three daughters; and the Lord gave to Aram the son of Zoba, riches and possessions, and abundance of cattle, and flocks and herds, and the man increased greatly.

37 And Aram the son of Zoba and his brother and all his household journeyed from Haran, and they went to dwell where they should find a place, for their property was too great to remain in Haran; for they could not stop in Haran together with their brethren the children of Nahor.

38 And Aram the son of Zoba went with his brethren, and they found a valley at a distance toward the eastern country and they dwelt there.

39 And they also built a city there, and they called the name thereof Aram, after the name of their eldest brother; that is Aram Zoba to this day.

40 And Isaac the son of Abraham was growing up in those days, and Abraham his father taught him the way of the Lord to know the Lord, and the Lord was with him.

41 And when Isaac was thirty-seven years old, Ishmael his brother was going about with him in the tent.

42 And Ishmael boasted of himself to Isaac, saying, I was thirteen years old when the Lord spoke to my father to circumcise us, and I did according to the word of the Lord which he spoke to my father, and I

gave my soul unto the Lord, and I did not transgress his word which he commanded my father.

43 And Isaac answered Ishmael, saying, 'Why dost thou boast to me about this, about a little bit of thy flesh which thou didst take from thy body, concerning which the Lord commanded thee?'

44 As the Lord lives, the God of my father Abraham, if the Lord should say unto my father, 'Take now thy son Isaac and bring him up an offering before me, I would not refrain but I would joyfully accede to it.'

45 And the Lord heard the word that Isaac spoke to Ishmael, and it seemed good in the sight of the Lord, and he thought to try Abraham in this matter.

46 And the day arrived when the sons of God came and placed themselves before the Lord, and Satan also came with the sons of God before the Lord.

JOB.1:6 Now there was a day when the sons of God came to present themselves before the LORD, and Satan came also among them.

47 And the Lord said unto Satan, 'Whence comest thou? and Satan answered the Lord and said, 'From going to and fro in the earth, and from walking up and down in it'.

JOB.1:7 And the LORD said unto Satan, Whence comest thou? Then Satan answered the LORD, and said, 'From going to and fro in the earth, and from walking up and down in it'.

48 And the Lord said to Satan, 'What is thy word to me concerning all the children of the earth?' and Satan answered the Lord and said, 'I have seen all the children of the earth who serve thee and remember thee when they require anything from thee'.

49 And when thou givest them the thing which they require from thee, they sit at their ease, and forsake thee and they remember thee no more.

50 Hast thou seen Abraham the son of Terah, who at first had no children, and he served thee and erected altars to thee wherever he came,

and he brought up offerings upon them, and he proclaimed thy name continually to all the children of the earth.

51 And now that his son Isaac is born to him, he has forsaken thee, he has made a great feast for all the inhabitants of the land, and the Lord he has forgotten.

52 For amidst all that he has done he brought thee no offering; neither burnt offering nor peace offering, neither ox, lamb nor goat of all that he killed on the day that his son was weaned.

53 Even from the time of his son's birth till now, being thirty-seven years, he built no altar before thee, nor brought any offering to thee, for he saw that thou didst give what he requested before thee, and he therefore forsook thee.

54 And the Lord said to Satan, Hast thou thus considered my servant Abraham? for there is none like him upon earth, a perfect and an upright man before me, one that feareth God and avoideth evil; as I live, were I to say unto him, Bring up Isaac thy son before me, he would not withhold him from me, much more if I told him to bring up a burnt offering before me from his flock or herds.

JOB.1:8 And the LORD said unto Satan, Hast thou considered my servant Job, that there is none like him in the earth, a perfect and an upright man, one that feareth God, and escheweth evil?

55 And Satan answered the Lord and said, 'Speak then now unto Abraham as thou hast said, and thou wilt see whether he will not this day transgress and cast aside thy words.'

JOB.1:9 Then Satan answered the LORD, and said, Doth Job fear God for nought?

JOB.1:10 Hast not thou made an hedge about him, and about his house, and about all that he hath on every side? thou hast blessed the work of his hands, and his substance is increased in the land.

JOB.1:11 But put forth thine hand now, and touch all that he hath, and he will curse thee to thy face.

Chapter 23

1 At that time the word of the Lord came to Abraham, and he said unto him, Abraham, and he said, Here I am.

2 And he said to him, 'Take now thy son, thine only son whom thou love, even Isaac, and go to the land of Moriah, and offer him there for a burnt offering upon one of the mountains which shall be shown to thee, for there wilt thou see a cloud and the glory of the Lord.'

GEN.22:2 And he said, 'Take now thy son, thine only son Isaac, whom thou lovest, and get thee into the land of Moriah; and offer him there for a burnt offering upon one of the mountains which I will tell thee of'.

3 And Abraham said within himself, 'How shall I separate my son Isaac from Sarah his mother, in order to bring him up for a burnt offering before the Lord?'

4 And Abraham came into the tent, and he sat before Sarah his wife, and he spoke these words to her,

5 My son Isaac is grown up and he has not for some time studied the service of his God, now tomorrow I will go and bring him to Shem, and Eber his son, and there he will learn the ways of the Lord, for they will teach him to know the Lord as well as to know that when he prays continually before the Lord, he will answer him, therefore there he will know the way of serving the Lord his God.

MAN'S AGE DEGRADATION FROM 950 YEARS OLD DOWN TO 70 - IN JUST 1000 YEARS.

Comment:1: According to this book of Jasher & the Masoretic text used in the K.J.V of the Bible, Shem and Eber were still alive when Abraham's son Isaac was in his thirties. It must have been a very strange time back then when generation after generation were dying younger and younger and Abraham actually died before Shem even though he came nine generations after Shem. Shem having lived to be a ripe old 600 years old and Abraham died a young sprout at only 175 years old. Abraham also predicted that the time would come when any man who reached 75 would be considered old! Sounds like our modern times! On my biblical chart, which I have here on my wall in front of me, even Arphaxad and Salah were still alive at this time. Arphaxad lived to be 438 and was the son of Shem. Salah the son of

Arphaxad lived to be 433. Eber the son of Salah lived to be 464 years old. Peleg the son of Eber only lived to be 239 years. Peleg's son Reu live to be 239 years. Reu's son Serug live to be 230 years. Serug's son Nahor lived to be 148 years. Nahor's son Terah (Father of Abraham) lived to be 206 years. Abraham 175. Isaac 180. His son Jacob 146 years. The sons of Jacob around 120 years with Joseph only 110 years old. Around 500 years later Moses lived to be120 years old. 1000 years after Abraham, King David stated that a man's years shall be 70 years and strangely he himself lived to be exactly 70 years old. From Noah being 950 years old (2000 B.C.E) when he died, down to King David being only 70 years old at his death, took just 1000 years. (1000 B.C.E) for this serious degradation of the age of man.

PSA.90:10 The days of our years are threescore years and ten; and if by reason of strength they be fourscore years yet is their strength labour and sorrow; for it is soon cut off, and we fly away.

---

6 And Sarah said, 'Thou hast spoken well, go my lord and do unto him as thou hast said, but remove him not at a great distance from me, neither let him remain there too long, for my soul is bound within his soul'.

7 And Abraham said unto Sarah, 'My daughter, let us pray to the Lord our God that he may do good with us.'

8 And Sarah took her son Isaac and he abode all that night with her, and she kissed and embraced him, and gave him instructions till morning.

9 And she said to him, O my son, how can my soul separate itself from thee? And she still kissed him and embraced him, and she gave Abraham instructions concerning him.

10 And Sarah said to Abraham, O my lord, I pray thee take heed of thy son, and place thine eyes over him, for I have no other son nor daughter but him.

11 O forsake him not. If he be hungry give him bread, and if he be thirsty give him water to drink; do not let him go on foot, neither let him sit in the sun.

12 Neither let him go by himself in the road, neither force him from whatever he may desire, but do unto him as he may say to thee.

13 And Sarah wept bitterly the whole night on account of Isaac, and she gave him instructions till morning.

14 And in the morning, Sarah selected a very fine and beautiful garment from those garments which she had in the house, that Abimelech had given to her.

15 And she dressed Isaac her son therewith, and she put a turban upon his head, and she enclosed a precious stone in the top of the turban, and she gave them provision for the road, and they went forth, and Isaac went with his father Abraham, and some of their servants accompanied them to see them off the road.

16 And Sarah went out with them, and she accompanied them upon the road to see them off, and they said to her, Return to the tent.

17 And when Sarah heard the words of her son Isaac she wept bitterly, and Abraham her husband wept with her, and their son wept with them a great weeping; also, those who went with them wept greatly.

18 And Sarah caught hold of her son Isaac, and she held him in her arms, and she embraced him and continued to weep with him, and Sarah said, 'Who knoweth if after this day I shall ever see thee again?'

19 And they still wept together, Abraham, Sarah and Isaac, and all those that accompanied them on the road wept with them, and Sarah afterward turned away from her son, weeping bitterly, and all her men servants and maid servants returned with her to the tent.

20 And Abraham went with Isaac his son to bring him up as an offering before the Lord, as He had commanded him.

GEN.22:3 And Abraham rose up early in the morning, and saddled his ass, and took two of his young men with him, and Isaac his son, and clave the wood for the burnt offering, and rose up, and went unto the place of which God had told him.

21 And Abraham took two of his young men with him, Ishmael the son of Hagar and Eliezer his servant, and they went together with them, and whilst they were walking in the road the young men spoke these words to themselves,

22 And Ishmael said to Eliezer, 'Now my father Abraham is going with Isaac to bring him up for a burnt offering to the Lord, as He commanded him.'

23 Now when he returns, he will give unto me all that he possesses, to inherit after him, for I am his first born.

24 And Eliezer answered Ishmael and said, Surely Abraham did cast thee away with thy mother, and swear that thou should not inherit any thing of all he possesses, and to whom will he give all that he has, with all his treasures, but unto me his servant, who has been faithful in his house, who has served him night and day, and has done all that he desired me? To me will he bequeath at his death all that he possesses.

25 And whilst Abraham was proceeding with his son Isaac along the road, Satan came and appeared to Abraham in the figure of a very aged man, humble and of contrite spirit, and he approached Abraham and said to him, Art thou silly or brutish, that thou goest to do this thing this day to thine only son?

26 For God gave thee a son in thy latter days, in thy old age, and wilt thou go and slaughter him this day because he committed no violence, and wilt thou cause the soul of thine only son to perish from the earth?

27 Dost thou not know and understand that this thing cannot be from the Lord? for the Lord cannot do unto man such evil upon earth to say to him, 'Go slaughter thy child'.

C.2 This is quite an amazing comment. Ever since Satan fell along with his Fallen angels, one of the things that they insist on from their most dedicated disciples is 'human sacrifice'. Apparently, some people *make a pact with Satan to become rich and famous* in this world and the price is either to give their very soul to Satan or to make some sort of human sacrifice. This has been a common practice for millennia to sacrifice innocent people unto Satan and his fallen angels such as Moloch, Baal, Beelzebub [New movie about exactly this concerning becoming a famous Rock Star:] I suppose this is the greatest insult against God: to *persuade foolish and devilish men to kill the innocent and God's highest creation*: Mankind.

C.3 See how Satan has tricked the world into believing that it is ok to murder your own unborn children in the womb. What absolute fools and blind! Then there are the incessant wars on this planet which in the last century alone slaughtered over 100 million people. For what? Was it all part of a massive 'human sacrifice', in order for men to gain more *evil knowledge*? More people died in the 20th century than in any other century in the whole of history since the Great Flood. On the other side of the coin *knowledge increased exponentially*. Why? There is a lot of evidence that the followers of Satan are rewarded with 'advanced science and knowledge for doing satanic practices such as human sacrifices. This explains how that the Nazis in Germany had much more advanced technology than other countries because they were satanic in nature. (**Nazi Technology:** https://www.ancient-code.com/ declassified-cia-documents-suggest-the-nazis-successfully-built-ufos-2/)

---

28 And Abraham heard this and knew that it was the word of Satan who endeavoured to draw him aside from the way of the Lord, but Abraham would not hearken to the voice of Satan, and Abraham rebuked him so that he went away.

29 And Satan returned and came to Isaac; and he appeared unto Isaac in the figure of a young man comely and well favoured.

C.4 These above examples concerning Satan, show that he can change form at will and appear in any form that he wishes to be in.

---

30 And he approached Isaac and said unto him, Dost thou not know and understand that thy old silly father bringeth thee to the slaughter this day for naught?

31 Now therefore, my son, do not listen nor attend to him, for he is a silly old man, and let not thy precious soul and beautiful figure be lost from the earth.

C.5 Especially when one is trying to obey God, Satan will come along and try to accuse you & also try to persuade both you yourself and everyone around you that you are but a fool for following God; and it would be better to just 'do your own thing' which in fact is often 'Satan's thing' = disobedience and rebellion against God and his Holy Spirit. Sadly, many people don't get to do what God would like them to do, simply because they are too in tune with Satan's lies and condemnation. One has to be like Abraham, who simply turned around and rebuked the Devil to his face and then the Devil left!

2CO.10:4 For the weapons of our warfare are not carnal, but mighty through God to the pulling down of strong holds.

It is essential for God's people to tank up on the Word of God and to memorise God's Words. It is a weapon against Satan. As someone once wisely stated. 'What you memorise will motivate you when the chips are down'. So, when Satan shows up in your life then rebuke him in the Name of Jesus and he will flee.

HEB.4:12 For the word of God is quick, and powerful, and sharper than any two-edged sword, piercing even to the dividing asunder of soul and spirit, and of the joints and marrow, and is a discerner of the thoughts and intents of the heart.

ISA.59:19 When the enemy shall come in like a flood, the Spirit of the LORD shall lift up a standard against him.

1TI.4:15 Meditate upon these things; give thyself wholly to them; that thy profiting may appear to all.

[See APPENDIX for HOW TO FIGHT SATAN]

---

32 And Isaac heard this, and said unto Abraham, Hast thou heard, my father, that which this man has spoken? even thus has he spoken.

33 And Abraham answered his son Isaac and said to him, 'Take heed of him and do not listen to his words, nor attend to him, for he is Satan, endeavouring to draw us aside this day from the commands of God.'

34 And Abraham still rebuked Satan, and Satan went from them, and seeing he could not prevail over them he hid himself from them, and he went and passed before them in the road; and he transformed himself to a large brook of water in the road, and Abraham and Isaac and his two young men reached that place, and they saw a brook large and powerful as the mighty waters.

C.6 In this example Satan not only changes his appearance into the form of an old or young person, but now transforms himself into a deep stream of water. Sounds really far out and very unusual!

---

35 And they entered the brook and passed through it, and the waters at first reached their legs.

36 And they went deeper in the brook and the waters reached up to their necks, and they were all terrified-on account of the water; and whilst they were going over the brook Abraham recognized that place, and he knew that there was no water there before.

37 And Abraham said to his son Isaac, I know this place in which there was no brook nor water, now therefore it is this Satan who does all this

---

197

to us, to draw us aside this day from the commands of God.

38 And Abraham rebuked him and said unto him, The Lord rebuke thee, O Satan, begone from us for we go by the commands of God.

C.7 Abraham clearly takes a stand of faith and rebukes Satan to his face, and because he takes the time to actually confront Satan directly, therefore the devil becomes afraid and hides himself away somewhere else.

1PE.5:8 Be sober, be vigilant; because your adversary the devil, as a roaring lion, walketh about, seeking whom he may devour:

1PE.5:9 Whom resist steadfast in the faith, knowing that the same afflictions are accomplished in your brethren that are in the world.

39 And Satan was terrified at the voice of Abraham, and he went away from them, and the place again became dry land as it was at first.

C.8 This shows that it pays to rebuke Satan upon occasion, as he could indeed be hindering any one of us in a number of ways that we are not even aware of.

EPH.4:27 Neither give place to the devil.

40 And Abraham went with Isaac toward the place that God had told him.

41 And on the third day Abraham lifted up his eyes and saw the place at a distance which God had told him of.

42 And a pillar of fire appeared to him that reached from the earth to heaven, and a cloud of glory upon the mountain, and the glory of the Lord was seen in the cloud.

43 And Abraham said to Isaac, 'My son, dost thou see in that mountain, which we perceive at a distance, that which I see upon it?'

44 And Isaac answered and said unto his father, I see and lo a pillar of fire and a cloud, and the glory of the Lord is seen upon the cloud.

45 And Abraham knew that his son Isaac was accepted before the Lord for a burnt offering.

46 And Abraham said unto Eliezer and unto Ishmael his son, 'Do you also see that which we see upon the mountain which is at a distance?'

47 And they answered and said, 'We see nothing more than like the other mountains of the earth.' And Abraham knew that they were not accepted before the Lord to go with them, and Abraham said to them, 'Abide ye here with the ass whilst I and Isaac my son will go to yonder mount and worship there before the Lord and then return to you'.

48 And Eliezer and Ishmael remained in that place, as Abraham had commanded.

49 And Abraham took wood for a burnt offering and placed it upon his son Isaac, and he took the fire and the knife, and they both went to that place.

50 And when they were going along Isaac said to his father, Behold, I see here the fire and wood, and where then is the lamb that is to be the burnt offering before the Lord?

51 And Abraham answered his son Isaac, saying, The Lord has made choice of thee my son, to be a perfect burnt offering instead of the lamb.

52 And Isaac said unto his father, I will do all that the Lord spoke to thee with joy and cheerfulness of heart.

53 And Abraham again said unto Isaac his son, 'Is there in thy heart any thought or counsel concerning this, which is not proper? tell me my son, I pray thee, O my son conceal it not from me.'

54 And Isaac answered his father Abraham and said unto him, O my father, as the Lord liveth and as thy soul liveth, there is nothing in my heart to cause me to deviate either to the right or to the left from the word that he has spoken to thee.

55 Neither limb nor muscle has moved or stirred at this, nor is there in my heart any thought or evil counsel concerning this.

56 But I am of joyful and cheerful heart in this matter, and I say, 'Blessed is the Lord who has this day chosen me to be a burnt offering before Him.'

57 And Abraham greatly rejoiced at the words of Isaac, and they went on and came together to that place that the Lord had spoken of.

58 And Abraham approached to build the altar in that place, and Abraham was weeping, and Isaac took stones and mortar until they had finished building the altar.

59 And Abraham took the wood and placed it in order upon the altar which he had built.

60 And he took his son Isaac and bound him in order to place him upon the wood which was upon the altar, to slay him for a burnt offering before the Lord.

61 And Isaac said to his father, 'Bind me securely and then place me upon the altar lest I should turn and move and break loose from the force of the knife upon my flesh and thereof profane the burnt offering; and Abraham did so.

62 And Isaac still said to his father, O my father, when thou shalt have slain me and burnt me for an offering, take with thee that which shall remain of my ashes to bring to Sarah my mother, and say to her, This is the sweet smelling savor of Isaac; but do not tell her this if she should sit near a well or upon any high place, lest she should cast her soul after me and die.

63 And Abraham heard the words of Isaac, and he lifted up his voice and wept when Isaac spake these words; and Abraham's tears gushed down upon Isaac his son, and Isaac wept bitterly, and he said to his father, Hasten thou, O my father, and do with me the will of the Lord our God as He has commanded thee.

64 And the hearts of Abraham and Isaac rejoiced at this thing which the Lord had commanded them; but the eye wept bitterly whilst the heart rejoiced.

C.9 We see here how that both Abraham and Isaac are totally yielded to God's will even though they really don't understand what God has asked them to do and why? We know in hindsight that the Bible says that it was all a test to see if Abraham would obey anything that God told him to do! Today in modern times, if one of us thought that God had spoken to one of us and asked of us the same thing that He asked of Abraham concerning his son, we would immediately rightly state 'That must be Satan talking to me'. We know today that killing your own son cannot be justified under any modern circumstances. So, what was different in the times of Abraham?

C.10 In Abraham's time Idol worshipping was rampant. It was indeed a very common practice for the wicked to sacrifice their sons and daughters to the fiery Image of Molech.

C.11 With God's asking Abraham to sacrifice his only son, and then telling Abraham not to kill him, God Himself was making several very important points to all of mankind both in Abraham's time and for all future generations:1) It is not God's will for people to sacrifice their children to either God Himself, no matter how dedicated to God Himself you are, or even sacrificing to the lesser gods and demons as the Canaanites were doing in Abraham's time. 2) Abraham taking his only son of his wife Sarah and being willing to sacrifice him on the altar of sacrifice as a burnt offering, was a forerunner of God Himself sacrificing His only begotten Son Jesus on the altar of the cross of Calvary, for the Redemption of all mankind for eternity. The difference was that Abraham didn't have to kill his son, but God had to sacrifice His only Begotten Son for all of us, so that we could have eternal life together with Him. Such Love God has for us all.

ROM.5:8 But God commended his love toward us, in that, while we were yet sinners, Christ died for us.

JOH.3:16 For God so loved the world, that he gave his only begotten Son, that whosoever believeth in him should not perish, but have everlasting life.

JOH.3:17 For God sent not his Son into the world to condemn the world; but that the world through him might be saved.

---

65 And Abraham bound his son Isaac, and placed him on the altar upon the wood, and Isaac stretched forth his neck upon the altar before his father, and Abraham stretched forth his hand to take the knife to slay his son as a burnt offering before the Lord.

66 At that time the angels of mercy came before the Lord and spake to him concerning Isaac, saying,

67 0 Lord, thou art a merciful and compassionate King over all that thou hast created in heaven and in earth, and thou support them all;

---

give therefore ransom and redemption instead of thy servant Isaac, and pity and have compassion upon Abraham and Isaac his son, who are this day performing thy commands.

68 Hast thou seen, O Lord, how Isaac the son of Abraham thy servant is bound down to the slaughter like an animal? now therefore let thy pity be roused for them, O Lord.

C.12 This is beautiful how that many 'angels of mercy' became very concerned about what was happening down on the earth with Abraham being a just man about to sacrifice his only son Isaac.

God Himself of course knew that it was all a test, and for a much greater testimony than anyone understood back then, including God's angels.

C.13 This very much reminds me of a similar situation in the Book of Enoch which I covered in my book 'Enoch Insights' Here is a quote: *'It is very interesting to see here, how that God was apparently waiting, until His top officers or arch-angels had realized how evil the earth had become and came to report to Him about it. God doesn't usually do things suddenly and rashly, without involving the counsel of others. In the above verse, it is almost as if God has been thinking and pondering His options concerning the horrors of violence going on down below on the earth, when His angels mentioned the very grave nature and condition of the fallen earth to God, it triggers a pre-planned response from God Himself. It is almost as if He was saying, "Ah, I have been waiting for you archangels to be concerned enough about the situation on earth, to challenge me to do something about it!" And of course, He did immediately react strongly!'*

69 At that time the Lord appeared unto Abraham, and called to him, from heaven, and said unto him, 'Lay not thine hand upon the lad, neither do thou anything unto him, for now I know that thou fear God in performing this act, and in not withholding thy son, thine only son, from me'.

GEN.22:10 And Abraham stretched forth his hand and took the knife to slay his son.

GEN.22:11 And the angel of the LORD called unto him out of heaven, and said, Abraham, Abraham: and he said, 'Here am I'.

GEN.22:12 And he said, 'Lay not thine hand upon the lad, neither do thou anything unto him: for now, I know that thou fear God, seeing thou hast not withheld thy son, thine only son from me.'

70 And Abraham lifted up his eyes and saw, and behold, a ram was caught in a thicket by his horns; that was the ram which the Lord God had created in the earth in the day that he made earth and heaven.

> 71 For the Lord had prepared this ram from that day, to be a burnt offering instead of Isaac.
>
> 72 And this ram was advancing to Abraham when Satan caught hold of him and entangled his horns in the thicket, that he might not advance to Abraham, in order that Abraham might slay his son.

C.14 Here it clearly shows the spiritual fight going on in actual physical form.

1PE.5:8 Be sober, be vigilant; because your adversary the devil, as a roaring lion, walketh about, seeking whom he may devour:

1PE.5:9 Whom resist steadfast in the faith, knowing that the same afflictions are accomplished in your brethren that are in the world.

> 73 And Abraham, seeing the ram advancing to him and Satan withholding him, fetched him and brought him before the altar, and he loosened his son Isaac from his binding, and he put the ram in his stead, and Abraham killed the ram upon the altar, and brought it up as an offering in the place of his son Isaac.
>
> 74 And Abraham sprinkled some of the blood of the ram upon the altar, and he exclaimed and said, 'This is in the place of my son, and may this be considered this day as the blood of my son before the Lord.'

C.15 Notice how that Abraham was given a ram instead of his having to sacrifice his son. This is also symbolic of how God would 2000 years later offer His Only Begotten Son Jesus as a Blood Sacrifice to take away all the sins of mankind. Abraham didn't have to sacrifice his physical son as *God had paid for the sacrifice* by offering a ram instead. (Symbolic of the Lamb of God)

JOH.1:29 The next day John seeth Jesus coming unto him, and saith, Behold the Lamb of God, which *taketh away the sin of the world*

ISA.53:7 He was oppressed, and he was afflicted, yet he opened not his mouth: he is brought as a *lamb to the slaughter*, and as a sheep before her shearers is dumb, so he opened not his mouth.

> 75 And all that Abraham did on this occasion by the altar, he would exclaim and say, This is in the room of my son, and may it this day be considered before the Lord in the place of my son; and Abraham finished the whole of the service by the altar, and the service was accepted before the Lord, and was accounted as if it had been Isaac; and the Lord blessed Abraham and his seed on that day.

76 And Satan went to Sarah, and he appeared to her in the figure of an old man very humble and meek, and Abraham was yet engaged in the burnt offering before the Lord.

77 And he said unto her, Dost thou not know all the work that Abraham has made with thine only son this day? for he took Isaac and built an altar, and killed him, and brought him up as a sacrifice upon the altar, and Isaac cried and wept before his father, but he looked not at him, neither did he have compassion over him.

C.16 What a nasty vicious little pest Satan really is. He is a lying deceitful scumbag, and we have to get rid of him each and every day, as *he is exactly as shown in this chapter of Jasher*, a real pest if you let him be, by not rebuking him in the Name of Jesus and sending him away from you. Satan generally doesn't have to pester you directly himself, unless you are doing the right thing and moreover you are working for God and doing something to help God's work.

JAM.4:7 Submit yourselves therefore to God. *Resist the devil*, and he will flee from you.

1JN.3:8. For this purpose the Son of God was manifested, that he might *destroy the works of the devil.*

78 And Satan repeated these words, and he went away from her, and Sarah heard all the words of Satan, and she imagined him to be an old man from amongst the sons of men who had been with her son and had come and told her these things.

79 And Sarah lifted up her voice and wept and cried out bitterly on account of her son; and she threw herself upon the ground and she cast dust upon her head, and she said, O my son, Isaac my son, O that I had this day died instead of thee. And she continued to weep and said, 'It grieves me for thee, O my son, my son Isaac, O that I had died this day in thy stead.'

C.17 Sadly according to this book of Jasher, Sarah was very weak at this particular time, and did not resist the Devil but started to believe his lies which in this case was her downfall and resultant death. She was too on the defensive. A tragic story. Is it just possible that after these *direct confrontations of Satan* with both Abraham and Sarah that God started to limit Satan's powers more than before, so that he was not actually allowed to appear unto mankind in the physical plain, as he had done in the above story? Was Satan perhaps from that time on limited to the negative spirit world, where he was now only allowed to talk to the minds of those on earth and tempt them, but not anymore allowed to disguise himself and trick people such as he had both Eve and now Sara with his lies in person.

2CO.10:3 For though we walk in the flesh, we do not war after the flesh:

2CO.10:4 (For the weapons of our warfare are not carnal, but mighty through God to the pulling down of strong holds;)

2CO.10:5 Casting down imaginations, and every high thing that exalts itself against the knowledge of God, and bringing into captivity every thought to the obedience of Christ;

---

80 And she still continued to weep, and said, It grieves me for thee after that I have reared thee and have brought thee up; now my joy is turned into mourning over thee, I that had a longing for thee, and cried and prayed to God till I bare thee at ninety years old; and now hast thou served this day for the knife and the fire, to be made an offering.

81 But I console myself with thee, my son, in its being the word of the Lord, for thou didst perform the command of thy God; for who can transgress the word of our God, in whose hands is the soul of every living creature?

82 Thou art just, O Lord our God, for all thy works are good and righteous; for I also am rejoiced with thy word which thou didst command, and whilst mine eye weeps bitterly my heart rejoices.

83 And Sarah laid her head upon the bosom of one of her handmaids, and she became as still as a stone.

84 She afterward rose up and went about making inquiries till she came to Hebron, and she inquired of all those whom she met walking in the road, and no one could tell her what had happened to her son.

85 And she came with her maid servants and men servants to Kireath-arba, which is Hebron, and she asked concerning her Son, and she remained there while she sent some of her servants to seek where Abraham had gone with Isaac; they went to seek him in the house of Shem and Eber, and they could not find him, and they sought throughout the land and he was not there.

> 86 And behold, Satan came to Sarah in the shape of an old man, and he came and stood before her, and he said unto her, I spoke falsely unto thee, for Abraham did not kill his son and he is not dead; and when she heard the word her joy was so exceedingly violent on account of her son, that her soul went out through joy; she died and was gathered to her people.

C.18 This part of the story is indeed a little unusual. People don't normally *die from joy* although they can die from grief and sorrow. Sarah was very old being 127 years old. She was probably very fragile physically at this time and probably would have died one way or the other as it was clearly her time to die. Better to die from fits of laughter and happiness than from grief and sorrow. I looked this up and apparently people have been known to die from laughter when they have a medical condition such as heart failure or a stroke. **SOURCE**: < https://www.unbelievable-facts.com/2017/11/people-who-died-laughing.html>

> 87 And when Abraham had finished his service, he returned with his son Isaac to his young men, and they rose up and went together to Beer-sheba, and they came home.
>
> 88 And Abraham sought for Sarah, and could not find her, and he made inquiries concerning her, and they said unto him, 'She went as far as Hebron to seek you both where you had gone, for thus was she informed.'
>
> 89 And Abraham and Isaac went to her to Hebron, and when they found that she was dead they lifted up their voices and wept bitterly over her; and Isaac fell upon his mother's face and wept over her, and he said, O my mother, my mother, how hast thou left me, and where hast thou gone? O how, how hast thou left me!
>
> 90 And Abraham and Isaac wept greatly, and all their servants wept with them on account of Sarah, and they mourned over her a great and heavy mourning.

GEN.23:1 And Sarah was a hundred and seven and twenty years old: these were the years of the life of Sarah.

GEN.23:2 And Sarah died in Kirjatharba; the same is Hebron in the land of Canaan: and Abraham came to mourn for Sarah, and to weep for her.

Chapter 24

1 And the life of Sarah was one hundred and twenty-seven years, and Sarah died; and Abraham rose up from before his dead to seek a burial place to bury his wife Sarah; and he went and spoke to the children of Heth, the inhabitants of the land, saying,

Comments:1: Analysis Of Sarah: When we consider the time period in which Abraham himself lived to be 175 and Isaac his son 180 and even his grandson Jacob 146, why did Sarah only live to be 127-years-old at a time when she should have lived much longer?

C.2 In order to live, psychologists today tell us that one has to have the *'will to live'*. Sarah obviously lost the will to live, because her soul was 'all wrapped up in Isaac'. This is indeed a very strange concept to us in modern times. No mother clings to her 38-year-old son! It would appear according to this story of Jasher, that Abraham was a man indeed very dedicated to God. Willing to do even God's slightest commands.

C.3 What about Sarah, was she actually the same? After God had already promised Abraham that through his seed many nations would be born, it turned out Sarah herself was barren. She certainly had her share of hard trials, such as having to tell Abraham her husband to marry another woman-Hagar in other to perhaps have children by her, and thus fulfil God's promise, at least that was the original plan of Sarah.

C.4 God however had another plan. When three angels came to Abraham & Sarah to announce that in one year, his wife Sarah would stop being barren and conceive and have a baby, it states that Sarah didn't believe this and *laughed*. Is it just possible, that Abraham had actually spoiled Sarah, as she was very beautiful, and he was very rich, and they had many servants? It says in verse 13 of this very chapter: *'And Abraham buried Sarah with pomp as observed at the interment of kings, and she was buried in very fine and beautiful garments.'*

C.5 Sarah obviously didn't have enough to do to occupy her time, or at least let's say, she didn't have an active ministry of her own. Everyone has to have something important to do, and to occupy their time. Everyone needs to feel important and useful.

It states that **Sarah's heart was all caught up in Isaac**, which just does not sound right. She should have put her heart into God and His Word and His promises and not been all emotional about her son. She should have trusted God concerning her son Isaac. She should have trusted Abraham that he was following God and doing what God had told her to do. It is possible that they didn't have much 'written Word of God to hold onto in those days'?

C.6 This book of Jasher tends to indicate, that in actuality Sarah 'lost the will to live' at some point, because she believed the lie that Satan told her, that her husband had murdered her son Isaac, when it was not true at all. That of course caused her great sorrow, but it wasn't enough to kill her, so Satan came back and told her that he had lied to Sarah, and that in fact Isaac was still very much alive. Then apparently Sarah got *so ecstatically happy,* that she *supposedly died from laughter!* A very strange end to the story concerning Sarah. [It is true that people have been known to die from *laughing too much* because of internal problems that they already had] What a way to go! **SOURCE**: < https://www.unbelievable-facts.com/2017/11/people-who-died-laughing.html>

C.7 In conclusion, I think that it is very likely that God deliberately took Sarah back home to heaven early at only 127 years old, so that *Abraham could remarry and yet have many sons*; and thus *fulfilling God's promises* to *Abraham that he would indeed be the father of many nations.*

> 2 I am a stranger and a sojourner with you in your land; give me a possession of a burial place in your land, that I may bury my dead from before me.
>
> 3 And the children of Heth said unto Abraham, behold the land is before thee, in the choice of our sepulchres bury thy dead, for no man shall withhold thee from burying thy dead.
>
> 4 And Abraham said unto them, If you are agreeable to this go and entreat for me to Ephron, the son of Zochar, requesting that he may give me the cave of Machpelah, which is in the end of his field, and I will purchase it of him for whatever he desire for it.

C.8 SECRETS OF THE CAVE OF MACHPELAH: according to ancient Jewish text Abraham bought himself a trans-dimensional doorway, vortex, stargate: https://godssecret.wordpress.com/category/hebron-machpelah/

> 5 And Ephron dwelt among the children of Heth, and they went and called for him, and he came before Abraham, and Ephron said unto Abraham, 'Behold all thou requirest thy servant will do; and Abraham said, No, but I will buy the cave and the field which thou hast for value, In order that it may be for a possession of a burial place for ever.'
>
> 6 And Ephron answered and said, 'Behold the field and the cave are before thee, give whatever thou desirest'; and Abraham said, 'Only at full value will I buy it from thy hand, and from the hands of those that go in at the gate of thy city, and from the hand of thy seed for ever.'

7 And Ephron and all his brethren heard this, and Abraham weighed to Ephron four hundred shekels of silver in the hands of Ephron and in the hands of all his brethren; and Abraham wrote this transaction, and he wrote it and testified it with four witnesses.

8 And these are the names of the witnesses, Amigal son of Abishna the Hittite, Adichorom son of Ashunach the Hivite, Abdon son of Achiram the Gomerite, Bakdil the son of Abudish the Zidonite.

9 And Abraham took the book of the purchase, and placed it in his treasures, and these are the words that Abraham wrote in the book, namely:

10 That the cave and the field Abraham bought from Ephron the Hittite, and from his seed, and from those that go out of his city, and from their seed for ever, are to be a purchase to Abraham and to his seed and to those that go forth from his loins, for a possession of a burial place for ever; and he put a signet to it and testified it with witnesses.

11 And the field and the cave that was in it and all that place were made sure unto Abraham and unto his seed after him, from the children of Heth; behold it is before Mamre in Hebron, which is in the land of Canaan.

12 And after this Abraham buried his wife Sarah there, and that place and all its boundary became to Abraham and unto his seed for a possession of a burial place.

13 And Abraham buried Sarah with pomp as observed at the interment of kings, and she was buried in very fine and beautiful garments.

14 And at her bier was Shem, his sons Eber and Abimelech, together with Anar, Ashcol and Mamre, and all the grandees of the land followed her bier.

15 And the days of Sarah were one hundred and twenty-seven years and she died, and Abraham made a great and heavy mourning, and he performed the rites of mourning for seven days.

16 And all the inhabitants of the land comforted Abraham and Isaac his son on account of Sarah.

17 And when the days of their mourning passed by Abraham sent away his son Isaac, and he went to the house of Shem and Eber, to learn the ways of the Lord and his instructions, and Abraham remained there three years.

18 At that time Abraham rose up with all his servants, and they went and returned homeward to Beersheba, and Abraham and all his servants remained in Beersheba.

19 And at the revolution of the year Abimelech king of the Philistines died in that year; he was one hundred and ninety-three years old at his death; and Abraham went with his people to the land of the Philistines, and they comforted the whole household and all his servants, and he then turned and went home.

20 And it was after the death of Abimelech that the people of Gerar took Benmalich his son, and he was only twelve years old, and they made him king in the place of his father.

21 And they called his name Abimelech after the name of his father, for thus was it their custom to do in Gerar, and Abimelech reigned instead of Abimelech his father, and he sat upon his throne.

22 And Lot the son of Haran also died in those days, in the thirty-ninth year of the life of Isaac, and all the days that Lot lived were one hundred and forty years and he died.

23 And these are the children of Lot, that were born to him by his daughters, the name of the first born was Moab, and the name of the second was Benami.

24 And the two sons of Lot went and took themselves wives from the land of Canaan, and they bare children to them, and the children of Moab were Ed, Mayon, Tarsus, and Kanvil, four sons, these are fathers to the children of Moab unto this day.

25 And all the families of the children of Lot went to dwell wherever they should light upon, for they were fruitful and increased abundantly.

26 And they went and built themselves cities in the land where they dwelt, and they called the names of the cities which they built after their own names.

27 And Nahor the son of Terah, brother to Abraham, died in those days in the fortieth year of the life of Isaac, and all the days of Nahor were one hundred and seventy-two years and he died and was buried in Haran.

28 And when Abraham heard that his brother was dead, he grieved sadly, and he mourned over his brother many days.

29 And Abraham called for Eliezer his head servant, to give him orders concerning his house, and he came and stood before him.

30 And Abraham said to him, Behold I am old, I do not know the day of my death; for I am advanced in days; now therefore rise up, go forth and do not take a wife for my son from this place and from this land, from the daughters of the Canaanites amongst whom we dwell.

31 But go to my land and to my birthplace, and take from thence a wife for my son, and the Lord God of Heaven and earth who took me from my father's house and brought me to this place, and said unto me, To thy seed will I give this land for an inheritance for ever, he will send his angel before thee and prosper thy way, that thou mayest obtain a wife for my son from my family and from my father's house.

32 And the servant answered his master Abraham and said, Behold I go to thy birthplace and to thy father's house, and take a wife for thy son from there; but if the woman be not willing to follow me to this land, shall I take thy son back to the land of thy birthplace?

33 And Abraham said unto him, 'Take heed that thou bring not my son hither again, for the Lord before whom I have walked, he will send his angel before thee and prosper thy way.'

34 And Eliezer did as Abraham ordered him, and Eliezer swore unto Abraham his master upon this matter; and Eliezer rose up and took ten camels of the camels of his master, and ten men from his master's servants with him, and they rose up and went to Haran, the city of Abraham and Nahor, in order to fetch a wife for Isaac the son of Abraham; and whilst they were gone Abraham sent to the house of Shem and Eber, and they brought from thence his son Isaac.

35 And Isaac came home to his father's house to Beersheba, whilst Eliezer and his men came to Haran; and they stopped in the city by the watering place, and he made his camels to kneel down by the water and they remained there.

36 And Eliezer, Abraham's servant, prayed and said, O God of Abraham my master; send me I pray thee good speed this day and show kindness unto my master, that thou shalt appoint this day a wife for my master's son from his family.

37 And the Lord hearkened to the voice of Eliezer, for the sake of his servant Abraham, and he happened to meet with the daughter of Bethuel, the son of Milcah, the wife of Nahor, brother to Abraham, and Eliezer came to her house.

38 And Eliezer related to them all his concerns, and that he was Abraham's servant, and they greatly rejoiced at him.

39 And they all blessed the Lord who brought this thing about, and they gave him Rebecca, the daughter of Bethuel, for a wife for Isaac.

40 And the young woman was of very comely appearance, she was a virgin, and Rebecca was ten years old in those days.

41 And Bethuel and Laban and his children made a feast on that night, and Eliezer and his men came and ate and drank and rejoiced there on that night.

42 And Eliezer rose up in the morning, he and the men that were with him, and he called to the whole household of Bethuel, saying, Send

me away that I may go to my master; and they rose up and sent away Rebecca and her nurse Deborah, the daughter of Uz, and they gave her silver and gold, men servants and maid servants, and they blessed her.

43 And they sent Eliezer away with his men; and the servants took Rebecca, and he went and returned to his master to the land of Canaan.

44 And Isaac took Rebecca and she became his wife, and he brought her into the tent.

45 And Isaac was forty years old when he took Rebecca, the daughter of his uncle Bethuel, for a wife.

Chapter 25

1 And it was at that time that Abraham again took a wife in his old age, and her name was Keturah, from the land of Canaan.

2 And she bare unto him Zimran, Jokshan, Medan, Midian, Ishbak and Shuach, being six sons. And the children of Zimran were Abihen, Molich and Narim.

3 And the sons of Jokshan were Sheba and Dedan, and the sons of Medan were Amida, Joab, Gochi, Elisha and Nothach; and the sons of Midian were Ephah, Epher, Chanoch, Abida and Eldaah.

4 And the sons of Ishbak were Makiro, Beyodua and Tator.

5 And the sons of Shuach were Bildad, Mamdad, Munan and Meban; all these are the families of the children of Keturah the Canaanitish woman which she bare unto Abraham the Hebrew.

GEN.25:5 And Abraham gave all that he had unto Isaac.

GEN.25:6 But unto the sons of the concubines, which Abraham had, Abraham gave gifts, and sent them away from Isaac his son, while he yet lived, eastward, unto the east country.

GEN.25:7 And these are the days of the years of Abraham's life which he lived, an hundred threescore and fifteen years.

Comment:1: This chapter proves that God's promises to Abraham that he would become the father of many nations is being amazingly fulfilled in detail. Sheba and Dedan is what we call Saudi Arabia today. Abraham became both the father of the Jews and the Arabs.

C.2 Notice how that Abraham's 3rd wife was a Canaanite. He obviously witnessed to her and brought her into God's camp. Remember how God had told Abraham that the Canaanites would one day be purged from the land, which was fulfilled in the time of Israel coming out of Egypt into the Promised land with both Moses and Joshua some 500 years later.

C.3 The fact that Abraham married a *Canaanite woman* shows that God can have compassion on any race or creed and bring them unto Himself in spirit. God is not a harsh cruel religionist as many have portrayed Him to be. He is the spirit of Love. Obviously, not all of the Canaanites were totally evil and monstrous people, but some were but in particular those with Nephilim blood in their veins.

C.4 In a way God telling Abraham that his descendants would wipe out the Canaanites was symbolic of how God Himself would have to wipe out the terrible corruption that is in our world today in modern times.

C.5 Do we think that the Canaanites were worse with their Idolatry than modern man is today? I don't think so! Today it is even worse because millions, if not billions of people have been blindly led astray by Satan and his minions.

C.6 Every day this planet is getting more satanic and confusing. Human sacrifices still happen today with child-trafficking, slave traffic, paedophilia and satanic human sacrifices, just as with the Canaanites. Most of the evil is hidden away, but God sees it all and will soon arise to wipe out the wicked rulers of this planet:

REV.11:18 And the nations were angry, and thy wrath is come, and the time of the dead, that they should be judged, and that thou shouldest give reward unto thy servants the prophets, and to the saints, and them that fear thy name, small and great; and shouldest destroy them which destroy the earth.

---

6 And Abraham sent all these away, and he gave them gifts, and they went away from his son Isaac to dwell wherever they should find a place.

7 And all these went to the mountain at the east, and they built themselves six cities in which they dwelt unto this day.

8 But the children of Sheba and Dedan, children of Jokshan, with their children, did not dwell with their brethren in their cities, and they journeyed and encamped in the countries and wildernesses unto this day.

9 And the children of Midian, son of Abraham, went to the east of the land of Cush, and they there found a large valley in the eastern country, and they remained there and built a city, and they dwelt therein, that is the land of Midian unto this day.

10 And Midian dwelt in the city which he built, he and his five sons and all belonging to him.

11 And these are the names of the sons of Midian according to their names in their cities, Ephah, Epher, Chanoch, Abida and Eldaah.

12 And the sons of Ephah were Methach, Meshar, Avi and Tzanua, and the sons of Epher were Ephron, Zur, Alirun and Medin, and the sons of Chanoch were Reuel, Rekem, Azi, Alyoshub and Alad.

13 And the sons of Abida were Chur, Melud, Kerury, Molchi; and the sons of Eldaah were Miker, and Reba, and Malchiyah and Gabol; these are the names of the Midianites according to their families; and afterward the families of Midian spread throughout the land of Midian.

14 And these are the generations of Ishmael the son Abraham, whom Hagar, Sarah's handmaid, bare unto Abraham.

15 And Ishmael took a wife from the land of Egypt, and her name was Ribah, the same is Meribah.

16 And Ribah bare unto Ishmael Nebayoth, Kedar, Adbeel, Mibsam and their sister Bosmath.

17 And Ishmael cast away his wife Ribah, and she went from him and returned to Egypt to the house of her father, and she dwelt there, for she had been very bad in the sight of Ishmael, and in the sight of his father Abraham.

18 And Ishmael afterward took a wife from the land of Canaan, and her name was Malchuth, and she bare unto him Nishma, Dumah, Masa, Chadad, Tema, Yetur, Naphish and Kedma.

19 These are the sons of Ishmael, and these are their names, being twelve princes according to their nations; and the families of Ishmael afterward spread forth, and Ishmael took his children and all the property that he had gained, together with the souls of his household and all belonging to him, and they went to dwell where they should find a place.

20 And they went and dwelt near the wilderness of Paran, and their dwelling was from Havilah unto Shur, that is before Egypt as thou comest toward Assyria.

21 And Ishmael and his sons dwelt in the land, and they had children born to them, and they were fruitful and increased abundantly.

22 And these are the names of the sons of Nebayoth the first born of Ishmael; Mend, Send, Mayon; and the sons of Kedar were Alyon, Kezem, Chamad and Eli.

23 And the sons of Adbeel were Chamad and Jabin; and the sons of Mibsam were Obadiah, Ebedmelech and Yeush; these are the families of the children of Ribah the wife of Ishmael.

24 And the sons of Mishma the son of Ishmael were Shamua, Zecaryon and Obed; and the sons of Dumah were Kezed, Eli, Machmad and Amed.

25 And the sons of Masa were Melon, Mula and Ebidadon; and the sons of Chadad were Azur, Minzar and Ebedmelech; and the sons of Tema were Seir, Sadon and Yakol.

26 And the sons of Yetur were Merith, Yaish, Alyo, and Pachoth; and the sons of Naphish were Ebed-Tamed, Abiyasaph and Mir; and the sons of Kedma were Calip, Tachti, and Omir; these were the children of Malchuth the wife of Ishmael according to their families.

27 All these are the families of Ishmael according to their generations, and they dwelt in those lands wherein they had built themselves cities unto this day.

28 And Rebecca the daughter of Bethuel, the wife of Abraham's son Isaac, was barren in those days, she had no offspring; and Isaac dwelt with his father in the land of Canaan; and the Lord was with Isaac; and Arpachshad the son of Shem the son of Noah died in those days, in the forty-eighth year of the life of Isaac, and all the days that Arpachshad lived were four hundred and thirty-eight years, and he died.

Chapter 26

1 And in the fifty-ninth year of the life of Isaac the son of Abraham, Rebecca his wife was still barren in those days.

2 And Rebecca said unto Isaac, Truly I have heard, my lord, that thy mother Sarah was barren in her days until my Lord Abraham, thy father, prayed for her and she conceived by him.

3 Now therefore stand up, pray thou also to God and he will hear thy prayer and remember us through his mercies.

4 And Isaac answered his wife Rebecca, saying, Abraham has already prayed for me to God to multiply his seed, now therefore this barrenness must proceed to us from thee.

5 And Rebecca said unto him, But arise now thou also and pray, that the Lord may hear thy prayer and grant me children, and Isaac hearkened to the words of his wife, and Isaac and his wife rose up and went to the land of Moriah to pray there and to seek the Lord, and when they had reached that place Isaac stood up and prayed to the Lord on account of his wife because she was barren.

Comment:1: Notice how that Sarah and her daughter in law Rebecka as well as Rebecka's daughter in law Rachel or three generations of women one after the other were all barren until God Himself intervened because of desperate prayers on behalf of the Patriarchs. My wife was just mentioning how that back then the men liked their women being beautiful and having children, but the question to be asked is: Did they really make sure that their wives learned to be spiritual and also totally dedicated to God? In the times before the Great Flood it stated that the men preferred the beautiful women who didn't have children and kept their figures. How did they avoid having children?

C.2 I was just pondering what it must have felt like being Sarah? Back in those times, a rich and powerful man would often steal a beautiful woman away from husband.

Here she is one of the most beautiful women around and desired probably by all men who saw her including Pharaoh of Egypt and the King of the Philistines. Couldn't Sarah have been tempted to feel that because she being as beautiful as she was and constantly desired, maybe it would be safer for her to take herbs that would stop her from getting pregnant in case any man other than her husband forced himself upon her. Perhaps she didn't tell her husband Abraham.

C.3 How about Abraham hiding his beautiful wife in a box whilst moving down to Egypt. That must have made Sarah feel very insecure Do you think she even agreed to being put in a box for Abraham's convenience. What happened to his great faith? He didn't even have the faith that God would protect his wife! Since Abraham had shown such great faith in many other areas, why couldn't he have trusted God about his wife, instead of on two occasions lying about his wife, and stating that she was his sister.

Well the answer to that question is simple: We are all human and we all make dumb mistakes. Even Abraham who is 'lifted up' as being the 'great patriarch' and origin of Israel. Even he had to learn from his mistakes and lack of faith in God upon occasions.

ROM.3:23 For all have sinned, and come short of the glory of God;

SELF-RIGHTEOUS RELIGIONS versus 'SAVED ONLY BY GRACE'

Religious people often really miss the point that God's people were not perfect but sinful just like them. The Religious people (those who follow the 'letter of the law' but have not the spirit of God's love in them) try to make the patriarchs look so perfect and wise that they themselves could never attain to such sainthood, and therefore that gives them an excuse to not even try to obey the Lord's Word and to follow God closely. In this manner they often excuse their flocks as well.

Those in the Bible were anything but perfect, but they all turned to God for forgiveness and mercy and that's what makes the difference. Notice how 'religious' people are often the most inflexible, intolerant, judgemental, unmerciful, and often act as if they themselves are so 'righteous' that they don't need God's forgiveness.

IT WAS THE 'RELIGIOUS' WHO HAD SO MANY INNOCENT PEOPLE 'BURNED AT THE STAKE IN THE MIDDLE AGES due to their superstitions and fears. Jesus told the Pharisees to their faces that they were hypocrites just like so many 'religious' people today.

Stephen the very first Christian martyr put it so well as to what he thought of so-called goody-goody religionists:

ACT.7:51 Ye stiff-necked and uncircumcised in heart and ears, ye do always resist the Holy Ghost: as your fathers did, so do ye.

ACT.7:52 Which of the prophets have not your fathers persecuted? and they have slain them which shewed before of the coming of the Just One; of whom ye have been now the betrayers and murderers:

ACT.7:53 Who have received the law by the disposition of angels (Fallen Angels =Devils) and have not kept it.

Not much has changed as there are still so many goody-goody religious people who go around feeling superior about themselves that they go to church or to a synagogue or Mosque, but are they really obeying and doing what God has told all of us His children to do?

MAT.22:37 Jesus said unto him, 'Thou shalt love the Lord thy God with all thy heart, and with all thy soul, and with all thy mind'.

MAT.22:38 This is the first and great commandment.

MAT.22:39 And the second is like unto it, 'Thou shalt love thy neighbour as thyself.'

MAT.22:40 On these two commandments hang all the law and the prophets.

C.4 As to those of us who follow God, we are to judge no man. Let God be the judge:

MAT.7:1 Judge not, that ye be not judged.

MAT.7:2 For with what judgment ye judge, ye shall be judged: and with what measure ye mete, it

C.5 ABRAHAM LEARNT TO TRUST GOD IN ALL THINGS

Abraham had to learn to totally trust God in seemingly impossible and daunting situations. I can't help but feel that the men of the past were far too macho and didn't confide in the women as they should have done. The women needed to be reassured that their lives were also very important and that they were not just there for the convenience of the men, as is still the case in Arab & Muslim countries. God made the woman to be the equal of man in many ways and to be his helpmeet. The man was not supposed to push the woman around and the woman was not supposed to be a big nag either. Man and wife should get on together in perfect harmony with each one doing their different, but equally important ministries.

C.6 In the story of Lamech a descendant of Cain, it states that he had two wives. One of which took a concoction of herbs to both stop her from getting pregnant and to help her stay beautiful. It states that they took special herbs that rendered them barren. Is this also possibly why the three women mentioned above were also barren? Was it because of vain beauty?

JASHER 2 2F0-21 And some of the sons of men caused their wives to drink a draught that would render them barren, in order that they might retain their figures and whereby their beautiful appearance might not fade. And when the sons of men caused some of their wives to drink, Zillah drank with them.

C.7 Isn't that exactly how many people see things today. Better not to have children and let the women stay beautiful. Perhaps the Patriarchs beautiful wives were tempted to take a drink which made them barren.? In the case of Sarah, who was indeed very beautiful she seems to have lacked spiritual depth and died because of it at the early age of only 127, whilst her husband outlived her and lived to be 175.

C.8 In Isaac's case, it was Rebecka's request that her husband get desperate in prayer for her to be able to have children. It was considered a curse for women not to be able to have children in those days. In the case of Rachel who also died very young, why was she also initially barren? Well we know that Rachel hid the idols of her father in her saddle bag which was certainly not a good idea.

C.9 We have to remember that up until Abraham, all his ancestors for at least three to four generations before him were all Idol worshippers. Laban the father of Rachel was certainly an ungodly man who cheated Jacob many times and who would have killed him if God had not intervened.

C.10 Abraham was the first man to be called a Hebrew, because he was the very first of his race to have lived in Hebron. Abraham being a righteous man didn't mean that all of his life was perfect, or his brethren and descendants were perfectly righteous. They didn't yet have the Saviour and the Messiah to save mankind from their sins. We are all imperfect without the Saviour. It was in the New Testament that it stated:

GAL.3:29 And if ye be Christ's, then are ye Abraham's seed, and heirs according to the promise.

C.11 Why is it that the descendants of Abraham as in both the Jews and Arabs have treated women as second-class citizens. Why is it today that in both cases of Jews and Arabs it is only the men that go to prayer? This is certainly not what the Messiah taught us! In the New testament the *women* were often *spiritual leaders*.

GAL.3:28 There is neither Jew nor Greek, there is neither bond nor free, there is *neither male nor* female: for ye are all one in Christ Jesus.

C.12 MACHO MEN: I suspect that the real reason can be traced to the far past when a man had to be a warrior who could keep his family safe from marauders. So, a man had to be both tough and strong and well able to protect his wife. The only problem with that is that it is giving too much emphasis to the strength and prowess of a physical man and not enough credit given to God and his angels and spirit helpers who are always in the background trying to help each of his children to make the right choices.

C.13 MEN BECAME FAR TOO PHYSICAL AND UN-PRAYERFUL. Thus, probably out of seeming necessity, as there were constant dangers around them, the women got pushed into the background as mothers and carers of children. They weren't included in meetings when different heads of families got together. Very strange, as it turns out *women are often more in tune spiritually* than men in many areas.

C.14 The Lord tells us to put our confidence only in Him in times of great turmoil and danger and not to take matters into our own physical hands, which would probably lead to disaster and often does.

PSA.91:1 He that dwelleth in the secret place of the most High shall abide under the shadow of the Almighty.

PSA.91:2 I will say of the LORD, He is my refuge and my fortress: my God; in him will I trust.

PSA.91:3 Surely, he shall deliver thee from the snare of the fowler, and from the noisome pestilence.

C.15 PERSONAL RELATIONSHIP WITH GOD

God wants every person on earth to connect directly to Himself through the reading of His Word without the interference of other human beings who tend to just get in the way. God desires a link with each of our hearts in a very personal way. Bye - bye religions – They are simply not needed and tend to be just another *claptrap; a control mechanism* that Satan uses against the peoples of the earth.

JOHN.4:23 But the hour cometh, and now is, when the true worshippers shall worship the Father in spirit and in truth: for the Father seeketh such to worship him.

JOHN.4:24 God is a Spirit: and they that worship him must worship him in spirit and in truth.

---

6 And Isaac said, O Lord God of heaven and earth, whose goodness and mercies fill the earth, thou who didst take my father from his father's house and from his birthplace, and didst bring him unto this land, and didst say unto him, To thy seed will I give the land, and thou didst promise him and didst declare unto him, I will multiply thy seed as the stars of heaven and as the sand of the sea, now may thy words be verified which thou didst speak unto my father.

7 For thou art the Lord our God, our eyes are toward thee to give us seed of men, as thou didst promise us, for thou art the Lord our God and our eyes are directed toward thee only.

8 And the Lord heard the prayer of Isaac the son of Abraham, and the Lord was entreated of him and Rebecca his wife conceived.

9 And in about seven months after the children struggled together within her, and it pained her greatly that she was wearied on account of them, and she said to all the women who were then in the land, Did such a thing happen to you as it has to me? and they said unto her, No.

10 And she said unto them, Why am I alone in this amongst all the women that were upon earth? and she went to the land of Moriah to

---

seek the Lord on account of this; and she went to Shem and Eber his son to make inquiries of them in this matter, and that they should seek the Lord in this thing respecting her.

11 And she also asked Abraham to seek and inquire of the Lord about all that had befallen her.

12 And they all inquired of the Lord concerning this matter, and they brought her word from the Lord and told her, Two children are in thy womb, and two nations shall rise from them; and one nation shall be stronger than the other, and the greater shall serve the younger.

13 And when her days to be delivered were completed, she knelt down, and behold there were twins in her womb, as the Lord had spoken to her.

14 And the first came out red all over like a hairy garment, and all the people of the land called his name Esau, saying, 'That this one was made complete from the womb.'

15 And after that came his brother, and his hand took hold of Esau's heel, therefore they called his name Jacob.

16 And Isaac, the son of Abraham, was sixty years old when he begat them.

17 And the boys grew up to their fifteenth year, and they came amongst the society of men. Esau was a designing and deceitful man, and an expert hunter in the field, and Jacob was a man perfect and wise, dwelling in tents, feeding flocks and learning the instructions of the Lord and the commands of his father and mother.

18 And Isaac and the children of his household dwelt with his father Abraham in the land of Canaan, as God had commanded them.

19 And Ishmael the son of Abraham went with his children and all belonging to them, and they returned there to the land of Havilah, and they dwelt there.

20 And all the children of Abraham's concubines went to dwell in the land of the east, for Abraham had sent them away from his son, and had given them presents, and they went away.

C.16 Interesting how some of God's great men had many women such was the case with Abraham. Maybe, that is where the Muslims, who are descendants of Abraham, got the idea that they should have 4 wives. Well, if they can all get along with each other fine. In modern times, however, most men can hardly take care of one woman never mind 2 or more. As we can see in the case of Sarah and Hagar, jealousy is the big problem in having more than one wife. Although Jacob managed alright with his 4 wives, and I suspect that it was from Jacob that the Muslim tradition of being able to have 4 wives came. Of course, Solomon held the record in the Bible for the most wives and it is listed as around 1000 wives. I felt sorry for his wives as they would not be seen or loved very often, but around once every 3-4 years. Ha! Most women are not going to like that, as they need a lot more attention! Rightly so!

21 And Abraham gave all that he had to his son Isaac, and he also gave him all his treasures.

22 And he commanded him saying, Dost thou not know and understand the Lord is God in heaven and in earth, and there is no other beside him?

23 And it was he who took me from my father's house, and from my birth place, and gave me all the delights upon earth; who delivered me from the counsel of the wicked, for in him did I trust.

24 And he brought me to this place, and he delivered me from Ur Casdim; and he said unto me, To thy seed will I give all these lands, and they shall inherit them when they keep my commandments, my statutes and my judgments that I have commanded thee, and which I shall command them.

25 Now therefore my son, hearken to my voice, and keep the commandments of the Lord thy God, which I commanded thee, do not turn from the right way either to the right or to the left, in order that it may be well with thee and thy children after thee forever.

26 And remember the wonderful works of the Lord, and his kindness that he has shown toward us, in having delivered us from the hands of

our enemies, and the Lord our God caused them to fall into our hands; and now therefore keep all that I have commanded thee, and turn not away from the commandments of thy God, and serve none beside him, in order that it may be well with thee and thy seed after thee.

27 And teach thou thy children and thy seed the instructions of the Lord and his commandments and teach them the upright way in which they should go, in order that it may be well with them forever.

1TI.4:15 Meditate upon these things; give thyself wholly to them; that thy profiting may appear to all.

28 And Isaac answered his father and said unto him, That which my Lord has commanded that will I do, and I will not depart from the commands of the Lord my God, I will keep all that he commanded me; and Abraham blessed his son Isaac, and also his children; and Abraham taught Jacob the instruction of the Lord and his ways.

29 And it was at that time that Abraham died, in the fifteenth year of the life of Jacob and Esau, the sons of Isaac, and all the days of Abraham were one hundred and seventy-five years, and he died and was gathered to his people in good old age, old and satisfied with days, and Isaac and Ishmael his sons buried him.

30 And when the inhabitants of Canaan heard that Abraham was dead, they all came with their kings and princes and all their men to bury Abraham.

31 And all the inhabitants of the land of Haran, and all the families of the house of Abraham, and all the princes and grandees, and the sons of Abraham by the concubines, all came when they heard of Abraham's death, and they requited Abraham's kindness, and comforted Isaac his son, and they buried Abraham in the cave which he bought from Ephron the Hittite and his children, for the possession of a burial place.

32 And all the inhabitants of Canaan, and all those who had known Abraham, wept for Abraham a whole year, and men and women mourned over him.

33 And all the little children, and all the inhabitants of the land wept on account of Abraham, for Abraham had been good to them all, and because he had been upright with God and men.

34 And there arose not a man who feared God like unto Abraham, for he had feared his God from his youth, and had served the Lord, and had gone in all his ways during his life, from his childhood to the day of his death.

C.17 Here are some wonderful verses about Abraham in the New testament.

HEB.11:8 By faith Abraham, when he was called to go out into a place which he should after receive for an inheritance, obeyed; and he went out, not knowing whither he went.

HEB.11:9 By faith he sojourned in the land of promise, as in a strange country, dwelling in tabernacles with Isaac and Jacob, the heirs with him of the same promise:

HEB.11:10 For he looked for a city which hath foundations, whose builder and maker is God.

35 And the Lord was with him and delivered him from the counsel of Nimrod and his people, and when he made war with the four kings of Elam he conquered them.

36 And he brought all the children of the earth to the service of God, and he taught them the ways of the Lord, and caused them to know the Lord.

37 And he formed a grove and he planted a vineyard therein, and he had always prepared in his tent meat and drink to those that passed through the land, that they might satisfy themselves in his house.

C.18 Abraham was a kind and generous man, who always took care of those who came to him and were in need. So much so that His name was much set by. When he died, he was honoured by many kings and even peoples of Canaan.

38 And the Lord God delivered the whole earth on account of Abraham.

39 And it was after the death of Abraham that God blessed his son Isaac and his children, and the Lord was with Isaac as he had been with his father Abraham, for Isaac kept all the commandments of the Lord as Abraham his father had commanded him; he did not turn to the right or to the left from the right path which his father had commanded him.

Chapter 27

Comment:1: The following story concerning Esau and Nimrod is not mentioned in the Bible as is the case with many of the stories in this very interesting Book of Jasher. However just because many of these stories in this Book of Jasher are not mentioned in the Bible, doesn't really mean that they are not real or even important.

It is very important not to be narrow-mined and the fact that *you* are reading this book, shows that you certainly are *not* narrow-mined. As I have always stated: 'Know the Bible really well first, and then study the very interesting Apocryphal books, which are most definitely inspired, but perhaps have a few details that are different. Even John the who wrote the Book of Revelation states at the end of the Gospel of John, that it is *impossible to write and contain all the stories of God to just one book!*

JOH.21:25 And there are also many other things which Jesus did, the which, if they should be written every one, I suppose that even the world itself could *not contain the books that should be written.* Amen.

ECC.12:12 And further, by these, my son, be admonished: of *making many books there is no end*; and much study is a weariness of the flesh.

ECC.12:13 Let us hear the conclusion of the whole matter: *'Fear God and keep his commandments: for this is the whole duty of man.*

ESAU SLAYS NIMROD

1 And Esau at that time, after the death of Abraham, frequently went in the field to hunt.

2 And Nimrod king of Babel, the same was Amraphel, also frequently went with his mighty men to hunt in the field, and to walk about with his men in the cool of the day.

3 And Nimrod was observing Esau all the days, for a jealousy was formed in the heart of Nimrod against Esau all the days.

4 And on a certain day Esau went in the field to hunt, and he found Nimrod walking in the wilderness with his two men.

5 And all his mighty men and his people were with him in the wilderness, but they removed at a distance from him, and they went from

him in different directions to hunt, and Esau concealed himself from Nimrod, and he lurked for him in the wilderness.

6 And Nimrod and his men that were with him did not know him, and Nimrod and his men frequently walked about in the field at the cool of the day, and to know where his men were hunting in the field.

7 And Nimrod and two of his men that were with him came to the place where they were, when Esau started suddenly from his lurking place, and drew his sword, and hastened and ran to Nimrod and cut off his head.

8 And Esau fought a desperate fight with the two men that were with Nimrod, and when they called out to him, Esau turned to them and smote them to death with his sword.

9 And all the mighty men of Nimrod, who had left him to go to the wilderness, heard the cry at a distance, and they knew the voices of those two men, and they ran to know the cause of it, when they found their king and the two men that were with him lying dead in the wilderness.

10 And when Esau saw the mighty men of Nimrod coming at a distance, he fled, and thereby escaped; and Esau took the valuable garments of Nimrod, which Nimrod's father had bequeathed to Nimrod, and with which Nimrod prevailed over the whole land, and he ran and concealed them in his house.

11 And Esau took those garments and ran into the city on account of Nimrod's men, and he came unto his father's house wearied and exhausted from fight, and he was ready to die through grief when he approached his brother Jacob and sat before him.

12 And he said unto his brother Jacob, Behold I shall die this day, and wherefore then do I want the birthright? And Jacob acted wisely with Esau in this matter, and Esau sold his birthright to Jacob, for it was so brought about by the Lord.

GEN.25:29 And Jacob sod pottage: and Esau came from the field, and he was faint:

GEN.25:30 And Esau said to Jacob, 'Feed me, I pray thee, with that same red pottage; for I am faint': therefore, was his name called Edom.

GEN.25:31 And Jacob said, Sell me this day thy birthright.

GEN.25:32 And Esau said, Behold, I am at the point to die: and what profit shall this birthright do to me?

---

13 And Esau's portion in the cave of the field of Machpelah, which Abraham had bought from the children of Heth for the possession of a burial ground, Esau also sold to Jacob, and Jacob bought all this from his brother Esau for value given.

14 And Jacob wrote the whole of this in a book, and he testified the same with witnesses, and he sealed it, and the book remained in the hands of Jacob.

15 And when Nimrod the son of Cush died, his men lifted him up and brought him in consternation, and buried him in his city, and all the days that Nimrod lived were two hundred and fifteen years and he died.

C.2 Here it states that Nimrod was two hundred and fifteen years old and he died. It states in the Bible that Nimrod was the son of Cush. Nimrod was the grandson of Ham. In this book of Jasher it states that Nimrod was a child of Cush in his old age. Ham was born at the time as the Great Flood around 4500 years ago. His great grandson was Nimrod who was alive in the time of Abraham and supposedly killed by Abraham's grandson Esau. Was that actually possible in time sequence? According to the current biblical time chart (See Appendix in this book) Nimrod would have been born around 1950 A.C or around 50 years before Abraham. Nimrod could have been killed by Esau as he outlived Abraham but not Isaac. Abraham was 175 when he died. Nimrod lived 40 years longer than Abraham It is possible according to current Biblical Time Charts, that he could have been killed by Esau even when initially that would seem impossible, but because people lived for such a very long time in those first days after the Great Flood and also the fact that Nimrod was born to Cush when he was old is the reason why it was indeed possible.

C.3 If indeed Esau killed Nimrod, then he was still quite young at the time, because right after killing Nimrod, was the time when Jacob deceived Esau and cheated him out of his 'birthright' for a mess a pottage.

---

16 And the days that Nimrod reigned upon the people of the land were one hundred and eighty-five years; and Nimrod died by the sword of Esau in shame and contempt, and the seed of Abraham caused his

---

death as he had seen in his dream.

C.4 The original 'vision' seen by the wise men of Nimrod on the night of the birth of Abraham was fulfilled. Nimrod came close to being killed by Abraham himself in the 'Slaughter of the kings' at the time of the 5 kings raid on Sodom and Gomorrah. Nimrod somehow escaped death the first time. However, he was later killed by Abraham's grandson Esau, just as the original vision had prophesied that Nimrod would be killed by one of the descendants of Abraham.

17 And at the death of Nimrod his kingdom became divided into many divisions, and all those parts that Nimrod reigned over were restored to the respective kings of the land, who recovered them after the death of Nimrod, and all the people of the house of Nimrod were for a long time enslaved to all the other kings of the land.

C.5 Nimrod died around 2120 After Creation according to Biblical time Charts or about 1900 B.C.

Chapter 28

1 And in those days, after the death of Abraham, in that year the Lord brought a heavy famine in the land, and whilst the famine was raging in the land of Canaan, Isaac rose up to go down to Egypt on account of the famine, as his father Abraham had done.

2 And the Lord appeared that night to Isaac and he said to him, 'Do not go down to Egypt but rise and go to Gerar, to Abimelech king of the Philistines, and remain there till the famine shall cease.'

GEN.26:1 And there was a famine in the land, beside the first famine that was in the days of Abraham. And Isaac went unto Abimelech king of the Philistines unto Gerar.

GEN.26:2 And the LORD appeared unto him, and said, 'Go not down into Egypt; dwell in the land which I shall tell thee of.'

GEN.26:3 Sojourn in this land, and I will be with thee, and will bless thee; for unto thee, and unto thy seed, I will give all these countries, and I will perform the oath which I swore unto Abraham thy father;

GEN.26:4 And I will make thy seed to multiply as the stars of heaven, and will give unto thy seed all these countries; and in thy seed shall all the nations of the earth be blessed;

GEN.26:5 Because that Abraham obeyed my voice, and kept my charge, my commandments, my statutes, and my laws.

GEN.26:6 And Isaac dwelt in Gerar:

3 And Isaac rose up and went to Gerar, as the Lord commanded him, and he remained there a full year.

4 And when Isaac came to Gerar, the people of the land saw that Rebecca his wife was of a beautiful appearance, and the people of Gerar asked Isaac concerning his wife, and he said, She is my sister, for he was afraid to say she was his wife lest the people of the land should slay him on account of her.

GEN.26:7 And the men of the place asked him of his wife; and he said, She is my sister: for he feared to say, She is my wife; lest, said he, the men of the place should kill me for Rebekah; because she was fair to look upon

5 And the princes of Abimelech went and praised the woman to the king, but he answered them not, neither did he attend to their words.

6 But he heard them say that Isaac declared her to be his sister, so the king reserved this within himself.

7 And when Isaac had remained three months in the land, Abimelech looked out at the window, and he saw, and behold Isaac was sporting with Rebecca his wife, for Isaac dwelt in the outer house belonging to the king, so that the house of Isaac was opposite the house of the king.

GEN.26:8 And it came to pass, when he had been there a long time, that Abimelech king of the Philistines looked out at a window, and saw, and, behold, Isaac was sporting with Rebekah his wife.

8 And the king said unto Isaac, 'What is this thou hast done to us in saying of thy wife, 'She is my sister'? how easily might one of the great men of the people have lain with her, and thou wouldst then have brought guilt upon us.'

GEN.26:9 And Abimelech called Isaac, and said, Behold, of a surety she is thy wife; and how said thou, 'She is my sister?' And Isaac said unto him, Because I said, Lest I die for her.

GEN.26:10 And Abimelech said, 'What is this thou hast done unto us? One of the people might lightly have lien with thy wife, and thou shouldest have brought guiltiness upon us'.

9 And Isaac said unto Abimelech, Because I was afraid lest I die on account of my wife, therefore I said, 'She is my sister'.

10 At that time Abimelech gave orders to all his princes and great men, and they took Isaac and Rebecca his wife and brought them before the king.

11 And the king commanded that they should dress them in princely garments, and make them ride through the streets of the city, and proclaim before them throughout the land, saying, This is the man and this is his wife; whoever toucheth this man or his wife shall surely die. And Isaac returned with his wife to the king's house, and the Lord was with Isaac and he continued to wax great and lacked nothing.

GEN.26:11 And Abimelech charged all his people, saying, He that touches this man or his wife shall surely be put to death.

Comment:1: It never ceases to amaze me how God so lovingly and faithfully protected His Patriarchs and their beautiful wives from being harmed. Both in the cases of Abraham and Isaac God fully protected them and would not let any man harm them in any way, even though back then it was commonplace for a powerful ruler to steal another man's beautiful wife away from him. God Himself fought for both Abraham and Isaac, as they were the beginning of the nation of Israel.

---

12 And the Lord caused Isaac to find favour in the sight of Abimelech, and in the sight of all his subjects, and Abimelech acted well with Isaac, for Abimelech remembered the oath and the covenant that existed between his father and Abraham.

13 And Abimelech said unto Isaac, Behold the whole earth is before thee; dwell wherever it may seem good in thy sight until thou shalt return to thy land; and Abimelech gave Isaac fields and vineyards and the best part of the land of Gerar, to sow and reap and eat the fruits of the ground until the days of the famine should have passed by.

14 And Isaac sowed in that land and received a hundred-fold in the same year, and the Lord blessed him.

15 And the man waxed great, and he had possession of flocks and possession of herds and great store of servants.

16 And when the days of the famine had passed away the Lord appeared to Isaac and said unto him, Rise up, go forth from this place and return to thy land, to the land of Canaan; and Isaac rose up and returned to Hebron which is in the land of Canaan, he and all belonging to him as the Lord commanded him.

17 And after this Shelach the son at Arpachshad died in that year, which is the eighteenth year of the lives of Jacob and Esau; and all the days that Shelach lived were four hundred and thirty-three years and he died.

C.2 This is exactly what is also written in the King James Bible as well, except it calls Shelach – Salah.

18 At that time Isaac sent his younger son Jacob to the house of Shem and Eber, and he learned the instructions of the Lord, and Jacob remained in the house of Shem and Eber for thirty-two years, and Esau his brother did not go, for he was not willing to go, and he remained in his father's house in the land of Canaan.

19 And Esau was continually hunting in the fields to bring home what he could get, so did Esau all the days.

20 And Esau was a designing and deceitful man, one who hunted after the hearts of men and inveigled them, and Esau was a valiant man in the field, and in the course of time went as usual to hunt; and he came as far as the field of Seir, the same is Edom.

21 And he remained in the land of Seir hunting in the field a year and four months.

22 And Esau there saw in the land of Seir the daughter of a man of Canaan, and her name was Jehudith, the daughter of Beeri, son of Epher, from the families of Heth the son of Canaan.

23 And Esau took her for a wife, and he came unto her; forty years old was Esau when he took her, and he brought her to Hebron, the land of his father's dwelling place, and he dwelt there.

24 And it came to pass in those days, in the hundred and tenth year of the life of Isaac, that is in the fiftieth year of the life of Jacob, in that year died Shem the son of Noah; Shem was six hundred years old at his death.

25 And when Shem died Jacob returned to his father to Hebron which is in the land of Canaan.

26 And in the fifty-sixth year of the life of Jacob, people came from Haran, and Rebecca was told concerning her brother Laban the son of Bethuel.

27 For the wife of Laban was barren in those days, and bare no children, and also all his handmaids bare none to him.

28 And the Lord afterward remembered Adinah the wife of Laban, and she conceived and bare twin daughters, and Laban called the names of his daughters, the name of the elder Leah, and the name of the younger Rachel.

29 And those people came and told these things to Rebecca, and Rebecca rejoiced greatly that the Lord had visited her brother and that he had gotten children.

Chapter 29

> 1 And Isaac the son of Abraham became old and advanced in days, and his eyes became heavy through age; they were dim and could not see.

Comment:1: In many of these stories in the Book of Jasher which parallel the Bible sometimes putting in extra details not contained in the Bible but also leaving out other important details. For this reason, I have put in the Bible verses where this Book of Jasher has left out those details.

GEN.27:1 And it came to pass, that when Isaac was old, and his eyes were dim, so that he could not see, he called Esau his eldest son, and said unto him, My son: and he said unto him, Behold, here am I.

GEN.27:2 And he said, 'Behold now, I am old, I know not the day of my death':

> 2 At that time Isaac called unto Esau his son, saying, Get I pray thee thy weapons, thy quiver and thy bow, rise up and go forth into the field and get me some venison, and make me savoury meat and bring it to me, that I may eat in order that I may bless thee before my death, as I have now become old and grey-headed.
>
> 3 And Esau did so; and he took his weapon and went forth into the field to hunt for venison, as usual, to bring to his father as he had ordered him, so that he might bless him.
>
> 4 And Rebecca heard all the words that Isaac had spoken unto Esau, and she hastened and called her son Jacob, saying, Thus did thy father speak unto thy brother Esau, and thus did I hear, now therefore hasten thou and make that which I shall tell thee.

GEN.27:11 And Jacob said to Rebekah his mother, 'Behold, Esau my brother is a hairy man, and I am a smooth man':

GEN.27:12 My father peradventure will feel me, and I shall seem to him as a deceiver; and I shall bring a curse upon me, and not a blessing.

> 5 Rise up and go, I pray thee, to the flock and fetch me two fine kids of the goats, and I will get the savoury meat for thy father, and thou shalt bring the savoury meat that he may eat before thy brother shall have come from the chase, in order that thy father may bless thee.

GEN.27:15 And Rebekah took goodly raiment of her eldest son Esau, which were with her in the house, and put them upon Jacob her younger son:

GEN.27:16 And she put the skins of the kids of the goats upon his hands, and upon the smooth of his neck:

> 6 And Jacob hastened and did as his mother had commanded him, and he made the savoury meat and brought it before his father before Esau had come from his chase.
>
> 7 And Isaac said unto Jacob, Who art thou, my son? And he said, I am thy first-born Esau, I have done as thou didst order me, now therefore rise up I pray thee, and eat of my hunt, in order that thy soul may bless me as thou didst speak unto me.
>
> 8 And Isaac rose up and he ate and he drank, and his heart was comforted, and he blessed Jacob and Jacob went away from his father; and as soon as Isaac had blessed Jacob and he had gone away from him, behold Esau came from his hunt from the field, and he also made savoury meat and brought it to his father to eat thereof and to bless him.

GEN.27:20 And Isaac said unto his son, 'How is it that thou hast found it so quickly, my son?' And he said, 'Because the LORD thy God brought it to me'.

GEN.27:21 And Isaac said unto Jacob, 'Come near, I pray thee, that I may feel thee, my son, whether thou be my very son Esau or not'.

GEN.27:22 And Jacob went near unto Isaac his father; and he felt him, and said, 'The voice is Jacob's voice, but the hands are the hands of Esau'.

GEN.27:23 And he discerned him not, because his hands were hairy, as his brother Esau's hands: so, he blessed him

> 9 And Isaac said unto Esau, 'And who was he that has taken venison and brought it me before thou camest and whom I did bless? And Esau knew that his brother Jacob had done this, and the anger of Esau was kindled against his brother Jacob that he had acted thus toward him.'

GEN.27:30 And it came to pass, as soon as Isaac had made an end of blessing Jacob, and Jacob was yet scarce gone out from the presence of Isaac his father, that Esau his brother came in from his hunting.

GEN.27:31 And he also had made savoury meat, and brought it unto his father, and said unto his father, 'Let my father arise, and eat of his son's venison, that thy soul may bless me'.

GEN.27:32 And Isaac his father said unto him, Who art thou? And he said, I am thy son, thy firstborn Esau.

GEN.27:33 And Isaac trembled very exceedingly, and said, 'Who? where is he that hath taken venison, and brought it me, and I have eaten of all before thou came, and have blessed him? yea, and he shall be blessed.'

10 And Esau said, Is he not rightly called Jacob? for he has supplanted me twice, he took away my birthright and now he has taken away my blessing; and Esau wept greatly; and when Isaac heard the voice of his son Esau weeping, Isaac said unto Esau, What can I do, my son, thy brother came with subtlety and took away thy blessing; and Esau hated his brother Jacob on account of the blessing that his father had given him, and his anger was greatly roused against him.

GEN.27:39 And Isaac his father answered and said unto him, Behold, thy dwelling shall be the fatness of the earth, and of the dew of heaven from above;

GEN.27:40 And by thy sword shalt thou live, and shalt serve thy brother; and it shall come to pass when thou shalt have the dominion, that thou shalt break his yoke from off thy neck.

GEN.27:41 And Esau hated Jacob because of the blessing wherewith his father blessed him: and Esau said in his heart, 'The days of mourning for my father are at hand; then will I slay my brother Jacob'.

11 And Jacob was very much afraid of his brother Esau, and he rose up and fled to the house of Eber the son of Shem, and he concealed himself there on account of his brother, and Jacob was sixty-three years old when he went forth from the land of Canaan from Hebron, and Jacob was concealed in Eber's house fourteen years on account of his brother Esau, and he there continued to learn the ways of the Lord and his commandments.

12 And when Esau saw that Jacob had fled and escaped from him, and that Jacob had cunningly obtained the blessing, then Esau grieved exceedingly, and he was also vexed at his father and mother; and he also rose up and took his wife and went away from his father and mother to the land of Seir, and he dwelt there; and Esau saw there a woman from amongst the daughters of Heth whose name was

Bosmath, the daughter of Elon the Hittite, and he took her for a wife in addition to his first wife, and Esau called her name Adah, saying the blessing had in that time passed from him.

13 And Esau dwelt in the land of Seir six months without seeing his father and mother, and afterward Esau took his wives and rose up and returned to the land of Canaan, and Esau placed his two wives in his father's house in Hebron.

14 And the wives of Esau vexed and provoked Isaac and Rebecca with their works, for they walked not in the ways of the Lord but served their father's gods of wood and stone as their father had taught them, and they were more wicked than their father.

15 And they went according to the evil desires of their hearts, and they sacrificed and burnt incense to the Baalim, and Isaac and Rebecca became weary of them.

16 And Rebecca said, I am weary of my life because of the daughters of Heth; if Jacob take a wife of the daughters of Heth, such as these which are of the daughters of the land, what good then is life unto me?

17 And in those days Adah the wife of Esau conceived and bare him a son, and Esau called the name of the son that was born unto him Eliphaz, and Esau was sixty-five years old when she bare him.

18 And Ishmael the son of Abraham died in those days, in the sixty-forth year of the life of Jacob, and all the days that Ishmael lived were one hundred and thirty-seven years and he died.

C.2 Ismael lived to be 137. That sounds about right, as Jacob himself lived to be 147.

19 And when Isaac heard that Ishmael was dead, he mourned for him, and Isaac lamented over him many days.

20 And at the end of fourteen years of Jacob's residing in the house of Eber, Jacob desired to see his father and mother, and Jacob came to the house of his father and mother to Hebron, and Esau had in those days

240

forgotten what Jacob had done to him in having taken the blessing from him in those days.

21 And when Esau saw Jacob coming to his father and mother, he remembered what Jacob had done to him, and he was greatly incensed against him and he sought to slay him.

22 And Isaac the son of Abraham was old and advanced in days, and Esau said, 'Now my father's time is drawing nigh that he must die, and when he shall die, I will slay my brother Jacob.'

23 And this was told to Rebecca, and she hastened and sent and called for Jacob her son, and she said unto him, Arise, go and flee to Haran to my brother Laban, and remain there for some time, until thy brother's anger be turned from thee and then shalt thou come back.

24 And Isaac called unto Jacob and said unto him, Take not a wife from the daughters of Canaan, for thus did our father Abraham command us according to the word of the Lord which he had commanded him, saying, Unto thy seed will I give this land; if thy children keep my covenant that I have made with thee, then will I also perform to thy children that which I have spoken unto thee and I will not forsake them.

25 Now therefore my son hearken to my voice, to all that I shall command thee, and refrain from taking a wife from amongst the daughters of Canaan; arise, go to Haran to the house of Bethuel thy mother's father, and take unto thee a wife from there from the daughters of Laban thy mother's brother.

26 Therefore take heed lest thou shouldst forget the Lord thy God and all his ways in the land to which thou goest, and shouldst get connected with the people of the land and pursue vanity and forsake the Lord thy God.

27 But when thou comest to the land serve there the Lord, do not turn to the right or to the left from the way which I commanded thee and which thou didst learn.

28 And may the Almighty God grant thee favour in the sight of the people of the earth, that thou mayest take there a wife according to thy choice; one who is good and upright in the ways of the Lord.

29 And may God give unto thee and thy seed the blessing of thy father Abraham, and make thee fruitful and multiply thee, and mayest thou become a multitude of people in the land whither thou goest, and may God cause thee to return to this land, the land of thy father's dwelling, with children and with great riches, with joy and with pleasure.

30 And Isaac finished commanding Jacob and blessing him, and he gave him many gifts, together with silver and gold, and he sent him away; and Jacob hearkened to his father and mother; he kissed them and arose and went to Padan-aram; and Jacob was seventy-seven years old when he went out from the land of Canaan from Beersheba.

31 And when Jacob went away to go to Haran Esau called unto his son Eliphaz, and secretly spoke unto him, saying, Now hasten, take thy sword in thy hand and pursue Jacob and pass before him in the road, and lurk for him, and slay him with thy sword in one of the mountains, and take all belonging to him and come back.

C.3 Here is yet another story concerning Jacob and Esau not told in the Bible: that Esau sent his son Eliphaz to kill Esau's brother Jacob. Although, fortunately for Jacob, he did not succeed in killing him

32 And Eliphaz the son of Esau was an active man and expert with the bow as his father had taught him, and he was a noted hunter in the field and a valiant man.

33 And Eliphaz did as his father had commanded him, and Eliphaz was at that time thirteen years old, and Eliphaz rose up and went and took ten of his mother's brothers with him and pursued Jacob.

34 And he closely followed Jacob, and he lurked for him in the border of the land of Canaan opposite to the city of Shechem.

35 And Jacob saw Eliphaz and his men pursuing him, and Jacob stood still in the place in which he was going, in order to know what this was, for he did not know the thing; and Eliphaz drew his sword and he went

on advancing, he and his men, toward Jacob; and Jacob said unto them, What is to do with you that you have come hither, and what meaneth it that you pursue with your swords.

36 And Eliphaz came near to Jacob and he answered and said unto him, Thus did my father command me, and now therefore I will not deviate from the orders which my father gave me; and when Jacob saw that Esau had spoken to Eliphaz to employ force, Jacob then approached and supplicated Eliphaz and his men, saying to him,

37 Behold all that I have and which my father and mother gave unto me, that take unto thee and go from me, and do not slay me, and may this thing be accounted unto thee a righteousness.

38 And the Lord caused Jacob to find favour in the sight of Eliphaz the son of Esau, and his men, and they hearkened to the voice of Jacob, and they did not put him to death, and Eliphaz and his men took all belonging to Jacob together with the silver and gold that he had brought with him from Beersheba; they left him nothing.

39 And Eliphaz and his men went away from him and they returned to Esau to Beersheba, and they told him all that had occurred to them with Jacob, and they gave him all that they had taken from Jacob.

40 And Esau was indignant at Eliphaz his son, and at his men that were with him, because they had not put Jacob to death.

41 And they answered and said unto Esau, Because Jacob supplicated us in this matter not to slay him, our pity was excited toward him, and we took all belonging to him and brought it unto thee; and Esau took all the silver and gold which Eliphaz had taken from Jacob and he put them by in his house.

42 At that time when Esau saw that Isaac had blessed Jacob, and had commanded him, saying, 'Thou shalt not take a wife from amongst the daughters of Canaan, and that the daughters of Canaan were bad in the sight of Isaac and Rebecca,'

43 Then he went to the house of Ishmael his uncle, and in addition to his older wives he took Machlath the daughter of Ishmael, the sister of Nebayoth, for a wife.

Chapter 30

1 And Jacob went forth continuing his road to Haran, and he came as far as mount Moriah, and he tarried there all night near the city of Luz; and the Lord appeared there unto Jacob on that night, and he said unto him, I am the Lord God of Abraham and the God of Isaac thy father; the land upon which thou liest I will give unto thee and thy seed.

2 And behold I am with thee and will keep thee wherever thou goest, and I will multiply thy seed as the stars of Heaven, and I will cause all thine enemies to fall before thee; and when they shall make war with thee they shall not prevail over thee, and I will bring thee again unto this land with joy, with children, and with great riches.

3 And Jacob awoke from his sleep and he rejoiced greatly at the vision which he had seen; and he called the name of that place Bethel.

Comment:1: On this occasion many important details are left out in this book of Jasher concerning Jacob's dream and vision. Here is the full description from the Bible:

GEN.28:11 And he lighted upon a certain place, and tarried there all night, because the sun was set; and he took of the stones of that place, and put them for his pillows, and lay down in that place to sleep.

GEN.28:12 And he dreamed, and behold a ladder set up on the earth, and the top of it reached to heaven: and behold the angels of God ascending and descending on it.

GEN.28:13 And, behold, the LORD stood above it, and said, I am the LORD God of Abraham thy father, and the God of Isaac: the land whereon thou liest, to thee will I give it, and to thy seed;

GEN.28:14 And thy seed shall be as the dust of the earth, and thou shalt spread abroad to the west, and to the east, and to the north, and to the south: and in thee and in thy seed shall all the families of the earth be blessed.

GEN.28:15 And, behold, I am with thee, and will keep thee in all places whither thou go, and will bring thee again into this land; for I will not leave thee, until I have done that which I have spoken to thee of.

GEN.28:16 And Jacob awaked out of his sleep, and he said, Surely the LORD is in this place; and I knew it not.

GEN.28:17 And he was afraid, and said, 'How dreadful is this place! this is none other but the house of God, and this is the gate of heaven'.

GEN.28:18 And Jacob rose up early in the morning and took the stone that he had put for his pillows, and set it up for a pillar, and poured oil upon the top of it.

GEN.28:19 And he called the name of that place Bethel: but the name of that city was called Luz at the first.

GEN.28:20 And Jacob vowed a vow, saying, If God will be with me, and will keep me in this way that I go, and will give me bread to eat, and raiment to put on,

GEN.28:21 So that I come again to my father's house in peace; then shall the LORD be my God:

GEN.28:22 And this stone, which I have set for a pillar, shall be God's house: and of all that thou shalt give me I will surely give the tenth unto thee.

---

4 And Jacob rose up from that place quite rejoiced, and when he walked his feet felt light to him for joy, and he went from there to the land of the children of the East, and he returned to Haran and he set by the shepherd's well.

5 And he there found some men; going from Haran to feed their flocks, and Jacob made inquiries of them, and they said, 'We are from Haran.'

6 And he said unto them, 'Do you know Laban, the son of Nahor?' and they said, 'We know him, and behold his daughter Rachel is coming along to feed her father's flock'.

7 Whilst he was yet speaking with them, Rachel the daughter of Laban came to feed her father's sheep, for she was a shepherdess.

8 And when Jacob saw Rachel, the daughter of Laban, his mother's brother, he ran and kissed her, and lifted up his voice and wept.

9 And Jacob told Rachel that he was the son of Rebecca, her father's sister, and Rachel ran and told her father, and Jacob continued to cry because he had nothing with him to bring to the house of Laban.

10 And when Laban heard that his sister's son Jacob had come, he ran and kissed him and embraced him and brought him into the house and gave him bread, and he ate.

11 And Jacob related to Laban what his brother Esau had done to him, and what his son Eliphaz had done to him in the road.

12 And Jacob resided in Laban's house for one month, and Jacob ate and drank in the house of Laban, and afterward Laban said unto Jacob, 'Tell me what shall be thy wages, for how canst thou serve me for nought?'

13 And Laban had no sons but only daughters, and his other wives and handmaids were still barren in those days; and these are the names of Laban's daughters which his wife Adinah had borne unto him; the name of the elder was Leah and the name of the younger was Rachel; and Leah was tender-eyed, but Rachel was beautiful and well favoured, and Jacob loved her.

14 And Jacob said unto Laban, I will serve thee seven years for Rachel thy younger daughter; and Laban consented to this and Jacob served Laban seven years for his daughter Rachel.

15 And in the second year of Jacob's dwelling in Haran, that is in the seventy ninth year of the life of Jacob, in that year died Eber the son of Shem, he was four hundred and sixty-four years old at his death.

C.2 Here it is stating that Eber was alive at the same time as Jacob and that he died aged 464 years old when Jacob was 79. Jacob was the 8th generation from Eber who was the grandson of Arphaxad who the son of Shem was who was the son of Noah. According to the Bible chart on my wall Eber died when Jacob was 79. So, this above verse agrees with the Bible.

16 And when Jacob heard that Eber was dead, he grieved exceedingly, and he lamented and mourned over him many days.

17 And in the third year of Jacob's dwelling in Haran, Bosmath, the daughter of Ishmael, the wife of Esau, bare unto him a son, and Esau called his name Reuel.

18 And in the fourth year of Jacob's residence in the house of Laban, the Lord visited Laban and remembered him on account of Jacob, and sons were born unto him, and his first born was Beor, his second was Alib, and the third was Chorash.

19 And the Lord gave Laban riches and honor, sons and daughters, and the man increased greatly on account of Jacob.

20 And Jacob in those days served Laban in all manner of work, in the house and in the field, and the blessing of the Lord was in all that belonged to Laban in the house and in the field.

21 And in the fifth year died Jehudith, the daughter of Beeri, the wife of Esau, in the land of Canaan, and she had no sons but daughters only.

22 And these are the names of her daughters which she bare to Esau, the name of the elder was Marzith, and the name of the younger was Puith.

23 And when Jehudith died, Esau rose up and went to Seir to hunt in the field, as usual, and Esau dwelt in the land of Seir for a long time.

24 And in the sixth year Esau took for a wife, in addition to his other wives, Ahlibamah, the daughter of Zebeon the Hivite, and Esau brought her to the land of Canaan.

25 And Ahlibamah conceived and bare unto Esau three sons, Yeush, Yaalan, and Korah.

26 And in those days, in the land of Canaan, there was a quarrel between the herdsmen of Esau and the herdsmen of the inhabitants of the land of Canaan, for Esau's cattle and goods were too abundant for him to remain in the land of Canaan, in his father's house, and the land of Canaan could not bear him on account of his cattle.

27 And when Esau saw that his quarrelling increased with the inhabitants of the land of Canaan, he rose up and took his wives and his sons and his daughters, and all belonging to him, and the cattle which he possessed, and all his property that he had acquired in the land of Canaan, and he went away from the inhabitants of the land to the land of Seir, and Esau and all belonging to him dwelt in the land of Seir.

28 But from time to time Esau would go and see his father and mother in the land of Canaan, and Esau intermarried with the Horites, and he gave his daughters to the sons of Seir, the Horite.

29 And he gave his elder daughter Marzith to Anah, the son of Zebeon, his wife's brother, and Puith he gave to Azar, the son of Bilhan the Horite; and Esau dwelt in the mountain, he and his children, and they were fruitful and multiplied.

Chapter 31

1 And in the seventh year, Jacob's service which he served Laban was completed, and Jacob said unto Laban, Give me my wife, for the days of my service are fulfilled; and Laban did so, and Laban and Jacob assembled all the people of that place and they made a feast.

2 And in the evening, Laban came to the house, and afterward Jacob came there with the people of the feast, and Laban extinguished all the lights that were there in the house.

Comment:1: What trick is Laban up to this time? Jacob thought that he himself was a trickster in cheating his brother Esau out of his birthright and inheritance, but his uncle Laban was an even bigger deceiver. The word Jacob means deceiver, and thus eventually when Jacob had learned some very important lessons through working under a rogue such as his cheating uncle, he was finally ready for God to change his name to Israel meaning 'He fought with God' when he had to wrestle with one of God's angels. That is when he was changed to a 'Prince of Israel' instead of 'Jacob the deceiver'.

3 And Jacob said unto Laban, 'Wherefore dost thou do this thing unto us?' And Laban answered, 'Such is our custom to act in this land'.

4 And afterward Laban took his daughter Leah, and he brought her to Jacob, and he came to her and Jacob did not know that she was Leah.

5 And Laban gave his daughter Leah his maid Zilpah for a handmaid.

6 And all the people at the feast knew what Laban had done to Jacob, but they did not tell the thing to Jacob.

7 And all the neighbours came that night to Jacob's house, and they ate and drank and rejoiced, and played before Leah upon timbrels, and with dances, and they responded before Jacob, Heleah, Heleah.

8 And Jacob heard their words but did not understand their meaning, but he thought such might be their custom in this land.

9 And the neighbours spoke these words before Jacob during the night, and all the lights that were in the house Laban had that night extinguished.

10 And in the morning, when daylight appeared, Jacob turned to his wife and he saw, and behold it was Leah that had been lying in his bosom, and Jacob said, Behold now I know what the neighbours said last night, Heleah, they said, and I knew it not.

11 And Jacob called unto Laban, and said unto him, 'What is this that thou didst unto me? Surely, I served thee for Rachel, and why didst thou deceive me and didst give me Leah?'

12 And Laban answered Jacob, saying, Not so is it done in our place to give the younger before the elder now therefore if thou desirest to take her sister likewise, take her unto thee for the service which thou wilt serve me for another seven years.

C.2 Imagine a father in law who slipped the wrong girl into the marriage bed at the last minute. What a rogue! Poor girl being treated like that. I suppose it was easier for Lamech to play that trick on Jacob as Leah was the twin sister of Rachel. Perhaps they looked alike but not identical. In the dim light which Laban had created at the marriage Feast it was difficult for Jacob to see who was who?

13 And Jacob did so, and he also took Rachel for a wife, and he served Laban seven years more, and Jacob also came to Rachel, and he loved Rachel more than Leah, and Laban gave her his maid Bilhah for a handmaid.

C.3 Notice how God Himself obviously set things up, so that Jacob would actually end up with four wives so that he would have 12 sons, who became the 12 Tribes of Israel. It is very unusual how that these 12 sons got on well with each other considering they were from 4 different mothers. They had their share of troubles with each other and in particular the episode with Joseph because of jealousy of him and the fact that he was obviously a spoiled brat, but in general they got on very well with each other, which I'm sure was only a miracle of God.

14 And when the Lord saw that Leah was hated, the Lord opened her womb, and she conceived and bare Jacob four sons in those days.

15 And these are their names, Reuben Simeon, Levi, and Judah, and she afterward left bearing.

16 And at that time Rachel was barren, and she had no offspring, and

251

Rachel envied her sister Leah, and when Rachel saw that she bare no children to Jacob, she took her handmaid Bilhah, and she bare Jacob two sons, Dan and Naphtali.

17 And when Leah saw that she had left bearing, she also took her handmaid Zilpah, and she gave her to Jacob for a wife, and Jacob also came to Zilpah, and she also bare Jacob two sons, Gad and Asher.

18 And Leah again conceived and bare Jacob in those days two sons and one daughter, and these are their names, Issachar, Zebulon, and their sister Dinah.

19 And Rachel was still barren in those days, and Rachel prayed unto the Lord at that time, and she said, O Lord God remember me and visit me, I beseech thee, for now my husband will cast me off, for I have borne him no children.

20 Now O Lord God hear my supplication before thee, and see my affliction, and give me children like one of the handmaids, that I may no more bear my reproach.

21 And God heard her and opened her womb, and Rachel conceived and bare a son, and she said, The Lord has taken away my reproach, and she called his name Joseph, saying, May the Lord add to me another son; and Jacob was ninety-one years old when she bare him.

22 At that time Jacob's mother, Rebecca, sent her nurse Deborah the daughter of Uz, and two of Isaac's servants unto Jacob.

23 And they came to Jacob to Haran and they said unto him, Rebecca has sent us to thee that thou shalt return to thy father's house to the land of Canaan; and Jacob hearkened unto them in this which his mother had spoken.

24 At that time, the other seven years which Jacob served Laban for Rachel were completed, and it was at the end of fourteen years that he had dwelt in Haran that Jacob said unto Laban, give me my wives and send me away, that I may go to my land, for behold my mother did send

unto me from the land at Canaan that I should return to my father's house.

25 And Laban said unto him, 'Not so I pray thee; if I have found favour in thy sight do not leave me; appoint me thy wages and I will give them and remain with me.'

26 And Jacob said unto him, This is what thou shalt give me for wages, that I shall this day pass through all thy flock and take away from them every lamb that is speckled and spotted and such as are brown amongst the sheep, and amongst the goats, and if thou wilt do this thing for me I will return and feed thy flock and keep them as at first.

27 And Laban did so, and Laban removed from his flock all that Jacob had said and gave them to him.

28 And Jacob placed all that he had removed from Laban's flock in the hands of his sons, and Jacob was feeding the remainder of Laban's flock.

29 And when the servants of Isaac which he had sent unto Jacob saw that Jacob would not then return with them to the land of Canaan to his father, they then went away from him, and they returned home to the land of Canaan.

30 And Deborah remained with Jacob in Haran, and she did not return with the servants of Isaac to the land of Canaan, and Deborah resided with Jacob's wives and children in Haran.

31 And Jacob served Laban six years longer, and when the sheep brought forth, Jacob removed from them such as were speckled and spotted, as he had determined with Laban, and Jacob did so at Laban's for six years, and the man increased abundantly and he had cattle and maid servants and men servants, camels, and asses.

32 And Jacob had two hundred drove of cattle, and his cattle were of large size and of beautiful appearance and were very productive, and all the families of the sons of men desired to get some of the cattle of Jacob, for they were exceedingly prosperous.

33 And many of the sons of men came to procure some of Jacob's flock, and Jacob gave them a sheep for a man servant or a maid servant or for an ass or a camel, or whatever Jacob desired from them they gave him.

34 And Jacob obtained riches and honor and possessions by means of these transactions with the sons of men, and the children of Laban envied him of this honor.

35 And in the course of time he heard the words of Laban's sons, saying, Jacob has taken away all that was our father's, and of that which was our father has he acquired all this glory.

36 And Jacob beheld the countenance of Laban and of his children, and behold it was not toward him in those days as it had been before.

37 And the Lord appeared to Jacob at the expiration of the six years, and said unto him, Arise, go forth out of this land, and return to the land of thy birthplace and I will be with thee.

38 And Jacob rose up at that time and he mounted his children and wives and all belonging to him upon camels, and he went forth to go to the land of Canaan to his father Isaac.

39 And Laban did not know that Jacob had gone from him, for Laban had been that day sheep-shearing.

40 And Rachel stole her father's images, and she took them, and she concealed them upon the camel upon which she sat, and she went on.

C.4 Rachel steals her father's images. This was a big mistake, that perhaps brought a curse upon Rachel as she died at a very young age in the childbirth of her second son Benjamin. In the next verse we see how bad these images actually were made from the scalp of a dead man! Sounds ghastly:

41 And this is the manner of the images; in taking a man who is the first born and slaying him and taking the hair off his head, and taking salt and salting the head and anointing it in oil, then taking a small tablet of copper or a tablet of gold and writing the name upon it, and placing the tablet under his tongue, and taking the head with the tablet under the tongue and putting it in the house, and lighting up lights before it and bowing down to it.

C.5 Here, we can clearly see how some people can 'divine' things through idols. The idols attract evil spirits, which can sometimes talk and reveal secrets. However as is written 'The borrower becomes servant of the lender' and there always strings attached in getting favours from demons which possess idols.

42 And at the time when they bow down to it, it speaks to them in all matters that they ask of it, through the power of the name which is written in it.

43 And some make them in the figures of men, of gold and silver, and go to them in times known to them, and the figures receive the influence of the stars, and tell them future things, and in this manner were the images which Rachel stole from her father.

44 And Rachel stole these images which were her father's, in order that Laban might not know through them where Jacob had gone.

C.6 Rachel's motive was not to worship the same idols as her father, but to stop him from using the idols to discern where she and Jacob had gone,

45 And Laban came home and he asked concerning Jacob and his household, and he was not to be found, and Laban sought his images to know where Jacob had gone, and could not find them, and he went to some other images, and he inquired of them and they told him that Jacob had fled from him to his father's, to the land of Canaan.

46 And Laban then rose up and he took his brothers and all his servants, and he went forth and pursued Jacob, and he overtook him in mount Gilead.

47 And Laban said unto Jacob, 'What is this thou hast done to me to flee and deceive me, and lead my daughters and their children as captives taken by the sword?'

48 And thou didst not suffer me to kiss them and send them away with joy, and thou didst steal my gods and didst go away.

49 And Jacob answered Laban, saying, Because I was afraid lest thou wouldst take thy daughters by force from me; and now with whomsoever thou find thy gods he shall die.

50 And Laban searched for the images and he examined in all Jacob's tents and furniture but could not find them.

51 And Laban said unto Jacob, 'We will make a covenant together and it shall be a testimony between me and thee; if thou shalt afflict my daughters, or shalt take other wives besides my daughters, even God shall be a witness between me and thee in this matter.'

52 And they took stones and made a heap, and Laban said, 'This heap is a witness between me and thee, therefore he called the name thereof Gilead.'

53 And Jacob and Laban offered sacrifice upon the mount, and they ate there by the heap, and they tarried in the mount all night, and Laban rose up early in the morning, and he wept with his daughters and he kissed them, and he returned unto his place.

54 And he hastened and sent off his son Beor, who was seventeen years old, with Abichorof the son of Uz, the son of Nahor, and with them were ten men.

55 And they hastened and went and passed on the road before Jacob, and they came by another road to the land of Seir.

56 And they came unto Esau and said unto him, 'Thus saith thy brother and relative, thy mother's brother Laban, the son of Bethuel, saying,

57 Hast thou heard what Jacob thy brother has done unto me, who first came to me naked and bare, and I went to meet him, and brought him to my house with honor, and I made him great, and I gave him my two daughters for wives and also two of my maids.'

58 And God blessed him on my account, and he increased abundantly, and had sons, daughters and maid servants.

59 He has also an immense stock of flocks and herds, camels and asses, also silver and gold in abundance; and when he saw that his

wealth increased, he left me whilst I went to shear my sheep, and he rose up and fled in secrecy.

60 And he lifted his wives and children upon camels, and he led away all his cattle and property which he acquired in my land, and he lifted up his countenance to go to his father Isaac, to the land of Canaan.

61 And he did not suffer me to kiss my daughters and their children, and he led my daughters as captives taken by the sword, and he also stole my gods and he fled.

62 And now I have left him in the mountain of the brook of Jabuk, him and all belonging to him; he lacketh nothing.

63 If it be thy wish to go to him, go then and there wilt thou find him, and thou canst do unto him as thy soul desireth; and Laban's messengers came and told Esau all these things.

64 And Esau heard all the words of Laban's messengers, and his anger was greatly kindled against Jacob, and he remembered his hatred, and his anger burned within him.

65 And Esau hastened and took his children and servants and the souls of his household, being sixty men, and he went and assembled all the children of Seir the Horite and their people, being three hundred and forty men, and took all this number of four hundred men with drawn swords, and he went unto Jacob to smite him.

66 And Esau divided this number into several parts, and he took the sixty men of his children and servants and the souls of his household as one head and gave them in care of Eliphaz his eldest son.

67 And the remaining heads he gave to the care of the six sons of Seir the Horite, and he placed every man over his generations and children.

68 And the whole of this camp went as it was, and Esau went amongst them toward Jacob, and he conducted them with speed.

69 And Laban's messengers departed from Esau and went to the land

of Canaan, and they came to the house of Rebecca the mother of Jacob and Esau.

70 And they told her saying, 'Behold thy son Esau has gone against his brother Jacob with four hundred men, for he heard that he was coming, and he is gone to make war with him, and to smite him and to take all that he has.'

71 And Rebecca hastened and sent seventy-two men from the servants of Isaac to meet Jacob on the road; for she said, Peradventure, Esau may make war in the road when he meets him.

72 And these messengers went on the road to meet Jacob, and they met him in the road of the brook on the opposite side of the brook Jabuk, and Jacob said when he saw them, This camp is destined to me from God, and Jacob called the name of that place Machnayim.

73 And Jacob knew all his father's people, and he kissed them and embraced them and came with them, and Jacob asked them concerning his father and mother, and they said, 'They were well.'

74 And these messengers said unto Jacob, Rebecca thy mother has sent us to thee, saying, I have heard, my son, that thy brother Esau has gone forth against thee on the road with men from the children of Seir the Horite.

75 And therefore, my son, hearken to my voice and see with thy counsel what thou wilt do, and when he cometh up to thee, supplicate him, and do not speak rashly to him, and give him a present from what thou possesses, and from what God has favoured thee with.

76 And when he asketh thee concerning thy affairs, conceal nothing from him, perhaps he may turn from his anger against thee and thou wilt thereby save thy soul, thou and all belonging to thee, for it is thy duty to honor him, for he is thy elder brother.

77 And when Jacob heard the words of his mother which the messengers had spoken to him, Jacob lifted up his voice and wept bitterly, and did as his mother then commanded him.

Chapter 32

1 And at that time Jacob sent messengers to his brother Esau toward the land of Seir, and he spoke to him words of supplication.

2 And he commanded them, saying, 'Thus shall ye say to my lord, to Esau, 'Thus saith thy servant Jacob, 'Let not my lord imagine that my father's blessing with which he did bless me has proved beneficial to me.'

3 For I have been these twenty years with Laban, and he deceived me and changed my wages ten times, as it has all been already told unto my lord.

4 And I served him in his house very laboriously, and God afterward saw my affliction, my labour and the work of my hands, and he caused me to find grace and favour in his sight.

5 And I afterward through God's great mercy and kindness acquired oxen and asses and cattle, and men servants and maid servants.

6 And now I am coming to my land and my home to my father and mother, who are in the land of Canaan; and I have sent to let my lord know all this in order to find favour in the sight of my lord, so that he may not imagine that I have of myself obtained wealth, or that the blessing with which my father blessed me has benefited me.

7 And those messengers went to Esau and found him on the borders of the land of Edom going toward Jacob, and four hundred men of the children of Seir the Horite were standing with drawn swords.

8 And the messengers of Jacob told Esau all the words that Jacob had spoken to them concerning Esau.

9 And Esau answered them with pride and contempt, and said unto them, Surely I have heard and truly it has been told unto me what Jacob has done to Laban, who exalted him in his house and gave him his daughters for wives, and he begat sons and daughters, and abundantly increased in wealth and riches in Laban's house through his means.

> 10 And when he saw that his wealth was abundant and his riches great, he fled with all belonging to him, from Laban's house, and he led Laban's daughters away from the face of their father, as captives taken by the sword without telling him of it.

Comment:1: Laban was a nasty piece of work and was an opportunist. He knew that God had blessed him for Jacob's sake and yet he sought to slay Jacob through the hand of his brother Esau by giving a false report to Esau. Even though God had increased Laban many times over in the 20 years that Jacob had faithfully worked for him, yet he was full of jealously and hatred towards Jacob, instead of thankfulness to the God of heaven.

ISA.26:10 Let favour be shewed to the wicked, yet will he not learn righteousness: in the land of uprightness will he deal unjustly and will not behold the majesty of the LORD.

> 11 And not only to Laban has Jacob done thus but also unto me has he done so and has twice supplanted me, and shall I be silent?
>
> 12 Now therefore I have this day come with my camps to meet him, and I will do unto him according to the desire of my heart.
>
> 13 And the messengers returned and came to Jacob and said unto him, 'We came to thy brother, to Esau, and we told him all thy words, and thus has he answered us, and behold he cometh to meet thee with four hundred men.'

GEN.33:1 And Jacob lifted up his eyes, and looked, and, behold, Esau came, and with him four hundred men

> 14 Now then know and see what thou shalt do and pray before God to deliver thee from him.
>
> 15 And when he heard the words of his brother which he had spoken to the messengers of Jacob, Jacob was greatly afraid, and he was distressed.
>
> 16 And Jacob prayed to the Lord his God, and he said, O Lord God of my fathers, Abraham and Isaac, thou didst say unto me when I went away from my father's house, saying,
>
> 17 I am the Lord God of thy father Abraham and the God of Isaac, unto thee do I give this land and thy seed after thee, and I will make thy

seed as the stars of heaven, and thou shalt spread forth to the four sides of heaven, and in thee and in thy seed shall all the families of the earth be blessed.

18 And thou didst establish thy words, and didst give unto me riches and children and cattle, as the utmost wishes of my heart didst thou give unto thy servant; thou didst give unto me all that I asked from thee, so that I lacked nothing.

19 And thou didst afterward say unto me, 'Return to thy parents and to thy birthplace and I will still do well with thee'.

20 And now that I have come, and thou didst deliver me from Laban, I shall fall in the hands of Esau who will slay me, yea, together with the mothers of my children.

21 Now therefore, O Lord God, deliver me, I pray thee, also from the hands of my brother Esau, for I am greatly afraid of him.

22 And if there is no righteousness in me, do it for the sake of Abraham and my father Isaac.

23 For I know that through kindness and mercy have I acquired this wealth; now therefore I beseech thee to deliver me this day with thy kindness and to answer me.

24 And Jacob ceased praying to the Lord, and he divided the people that were with him with the flocks and cattle into two camps, and he gave the half to the care of Damesek, the son of Eliezer, Abraham's servant, for a camp, with his children, and the other half he gave to the care of his brother Elianus the son of Eliezer, to be for a camp with his children.

25 And he commanded them, saying, 'Keep yourselves at a distance with your camps, and do not come too near each other, and if Esau come to one camp and slay it, the other camp at a distance from it will escape him.'

26 And Jacob tarried there that night, and during the whole night he gave his servants instructions concerning the forces and his children.

27 And the Lord heard the prayer of Jacob on that day, and the Lord then delivered Jacob from the hands of his brother Esau.

C.2 So wonderful to see how God again protected the Patriarch Jacob from his twin brother Esau's intention to kill him, in revenge for Jacob having tricked Esau out of his birthright some twenty years previously.

28 And the Lord sent three angels of the angels of heaven, and they went before Esau and came to him.

29 And these angels appeared unto Esau and his people as two thousand men, riding upon horses furnished with all sorts of war instruments, and they appeared in the sight of Esau and all his men to be divided into four camps, with four chiefs to them.

30 And one camp went on and they found Esau coming with four hundred men toward his brother Jacob, and this camp ran toward Esau and his people and terrified them, and Esau fell off the horse in alarm, and all his men separated from him in that place, for they were greatly afraid.

31 And the whole of the camp shouted after them when they fled from Esau, and all the warlike men answered, saying,

32 Surely, we are the servants of Jacob, who is the servant of God, and who then can stand against us? And Esau said unto them, O then, my lord and brother Jacob is your lord, whom I have not seen for these twenty years, and now that I have this day come to see him, do you treat me in this manner?

33 And the angels answered him saying, As the Lord liveth, were not Jacob of whom thou speaketh thy brother, we had not let one remaining from thee and thy people, but only on account of Jacob we will do nothing to them.

34 And this camp passed from Esau and his men and it went away, and Esau and his men had gone from them about a league when the second camp came toward him with all sorts of weapons, and they also did unto Esau and his men as the first camp had done to them.

35 And when they had left it to go on, behold the third camp came toward him and they were all terrified, and Esau fell off the horse, and the whole camp cried out, and said, Surely we are the servants of Jacob, who is the servant of God, and who can stand against us?

36 And Esau again answered them saying, O then, Jacob my lord and your lord is my brother, and for twenty years I have not seen his countenance and hearing this day that he was coming, I went this day to meet him, and do you treat me in this manner?

37 And they answered him, and said unto him, As the Lord liveth, were not Jacob thy brother as thou didst say, we had not left a remnant from thee and thy men, but on account of Jacob of whom thou speakest being thy brother, we will not meddle with thee or thy men.

38 And the third camp also passed from them, and he still continued his road with his men toward Jacob, when the fourth camp came toward him, and they also did unto him and his men as the others had done.

39 And when Esau beheld the evil which the four angels had done to him and to his men, he became greatly afraid of his brother Jacob, and he went to meet him in peace.

40 And Esau concealed his hatred against Jacob, because he was afraid of his life on account of his brother Jacob, and because he imagined that the four camps that he had lighted upon were Jacob's servants.

41 And Jacob tarried that night with his servants in their camps, and he resolved with his servants to give unto Esau a present from all that he had with him, and from all his property; and Jacob rose up in the morning, he and his men, and they chose from amongst the cattle a present for Esau.

42 And this is the amount of the present which Jacob chose from his flock to give unto his brother Esau: and he selected two hundred and forty head from the flocks, and he selected from the camels and asses thirty each, and of the herds he chose fifty kine.

43 And he put them all in ten droves, and he placed each sort by itself, and he delivered them into the hands of ten of his servants, each drove by itself.

44 And he commanded them, and said unto them, Keep yourselves at a distance from each other, and put a space between the droves, and when Esau and those who are with him shall meet you and ask you, saying, Whose are you, and whither do you go, and to whom belongeth all this before you, you shall say unto them, We are the servants of Jacob, and we come to meet Esau in peace, and behold Jacob cometh behind us.

45 And that which is before us is a present sent from Jacob to his brother Esau.

46 And if they shall say unto you, Why doth he delay behind you, from coming to meet his brother and to see his face, then you shall say unto them, Surely he cometh joyfully behind us to meet his brother, for he said, I will appease him with the present that goeth to him, and after this I will see his face, peradventure he will accept of me.

47 So the whole present passed on in the hands of his servants, and went before him on that day, and he lodged that night with his camps by the border of the brook of Jabuk, and he rose up in the midst of the night, and he took his wives and his maid servants, and all belonging to him, and he that night passed them over the ford Jabuk.

48 And when he passed all belonging to him over the brook, Jacob was left by himself, and a man met him, and he wrestled with him that night until the breaking of the day, and the hollow of Jacob's thigh was out of joint through wrestling with him.

49 And at the break of day the man left Jacob there, and he blessed him and went away, and Jacob passed the brook at the break of day, and he halted upon his thigh.

50 And the sun rose upon him when he had passed the brook, and he came up to the place of his cattle and children.

51 And they went on till midday, and whilst they were going the present was passing on before them.

52 And Jacob lifted up his eyes and looked, and behold Esau was at a distance, coming along with many men, about four hundred, and Jacob was greatly afraid of his brother.

GEN.33:1 And Jacob lifted up his eyes, and looked, and, behold, Esau came, and with him four hundred men

53 And Jacob hastened and divided his children unto his wives and his handmaids, and his daughter Dinah he put in a chest, and delivered her into the hands of his servants.

C.3 Poor Dinah, Jacob's only daughter! Oh No! Not the chest thing again, that Abraham also used to hide his beautiful wife Sarah when travelling over the Egyptian border. What is it with these Patriarchs that they would hide their beautiful women in chests?

54 And he passed before his children and wives to meet his brother, and he bowed down to the ground, yea he bowed down seven times until he approached his brother, and God caused Jacob to find grace and favour in the sight of Esau and his men, for God had heard the prayer of Jacob.

55 And the fear of Jacob and his terror fell upon his brother Esau, for Esau was greatly afraid of Jacob for what the angels of God had done to Esau, and Esau's anger against Jacob was turned into kindness.

C.4 This story really is very touching, as it shows that even in the midst of very great adversity, God can turn things around by the help of His agents the angels and influence people and in this particular case Esau, to behave in the opposite way from what he originally intended. God's Spirit was able to turn hatred into love. Wow! What an amazing example of a miraculous answer to both the prayers of Jacob and all of his godly relatives, who were also praying desperately for him, his wives and children when they were yet young and very vulnerable. His sons had not yet grown into might warriors as they were destined yet to become.

56 And when Esau saw Jacob running toward him, he also ran toward him and he embraced him, and he fell upon his neck, and they kissed, and they wept.

GEN.33:3 And he passed over before them, and bowed himself to the ground seven times, until he came near to his brother.

GEN.33:4 And Esau ran to meet him, and embraced him, and fell on his neck, and kissed him: and they wept.

> 57 And God put fear and kindness toward Jacob in the hearts of the men that came with Esau, and they also kissed Jacob and embraced him.
>
> 58 And also Eliphaz, the son of Esau, with his four brothers, sons of Esau, wept with Jacob, and they kissed him and embraced him, for the fear of Jacob had fallen upon them all.

PRO.14:26 In the fear of the LORD is strong confidence: and his children shall have a place of refuge.

PRO.14:27 The fear of the LORD is a fountain of life, to depart from the snares of death.

> 59 And Esau lifted up his eyes and saw the women with their offspring, the children of Jacob, walking behind Jacob and bowing along the road to Esau.
>
> 60 And Esau said unto Jacob, 'Who are these with thee, my brother? are they thy children or thy servants? and Jacob answered Esau and said, 'They are my children which God hath graciously given to thy servant.'

GEN.33:5 And he lifted up his eyes, and saw the women and the children; and said, 'Who are those with thee?' And he said, 'The children which God hath graciously given thy servant.'

> 61 And whilst Jacob was speaking to Esau and his men, Esau beheld the whole camp, and he said unto Jacob, Whence didst thou get the whole of the camp that I met yesternight? and Jacob said, To find favour in the sight of my lord, it is that which God graciously gave to thy servant.
>
> 62 And the present came before Esau, and Jacob pressed Esau, saying, Take I pray thee the present that I have brought to my lord, and Esau said, 'Wherefore is this my purpose? keep that which thou hast unto thyself.'

63 And Jacob said, 'It is incumbent upon me to give all this, since I have seen thy face, that thou still live in peace.'

64 And Esau refused to take the present, and Jacob said unto him, I beseech thee my lord, if now I have found favour in thy sight, then receive my present at my hand, for I have therefore seen thy face, as though I had seen a god-like face, because thou wast pleased with me.

65 And Esau took the present, and Jacob also gave unto Esau silver and gold and bdellium, for he pressed him so much that he took them.

66 And Esau divided the cattle that were in the camp, and he gave the half to the men who had come with him, for they had come on hire, and the other half he delivered unto the hands of his children.

67 And the silver and gold and bdellium he gave in the hands of Eliphaz his eldest son, and Esau said unto Jacob, Let us remain with thee, and we will go slowly along with thee until thou come to my place with me, that we may dwell there together.

68 And Jacob answered his brother and said, I would do as my lord speak unto me, but my lord know that the children are tender, and the flocks and herds with their young who are with me, go but slowly, for if they went swiftly they would all die, for thou know their burdens and their fatigue.

69 Therefore let my lord pass on before his servant, and I will go on slowly for the sake of the children and the flock, until I come to my lord's place to Seir.

70 And Esau said unto Jacob, I will place with thee some of the people that are with me to take care of thee in the road, and to bear thy fatigue and burden, and he said, What need it my lord, if I may find grace in thy sight?

71 Behold I will come unto thee to Seir to dwell there together as thou hast spoken, go thou then with thy people for I will follow thee.

72 And Jacob said this to Esau in order to remove Esau and his men from him, so that Jacob might afterward go to his father's house to the land of Canaan.

73 And Esau hearkened to the voice of Jacob, and Esau returned with the four hundred men that were with him on their road to Seir, and Jacob and all belonging to him went that day as far as the extremity of the land of Canaan in its borders, and he remained there some time.

GEN.33:13 And he said unto him, 'My lord knows that the children are tender, and the flocks and herds with young are with me: and if men should overdrive them one day, all the flock will die.'

GEN.33:14 Let my lord, I pray thee, pass over before his servant: and I will lead on softly, according as the cattle that goes before me and the children be able to endure, until I come unto my lord unto Seir.

GEN.33:15 And Esau said, 'Let me now leave with thee some of the folk that are with me. And he said, 'What needs it? Let me find grace in the sight of my lord'.

GEN.33:16 So Esau returned that day on his way unto Seir.

Chapter 33

SHECHEM

THE ROOT CAUSE FOR THE DESTRUCTION OF THE CAANANITIES

Comment:1: This front cover picture of this book is dedicated to the following on-going story, which starts in this 33rd chapter and ends in the 40th chapter. It occupies a whole 8 chapters of the book of Jasher. This destruction of the Canaanites is also continued 500 years later under Moses and the Children of Israel. (See this Book of JASHER chapter 85-91 for the completion of the total destruction of the Canaanites from the land.)

[**JASHER 89.51** So Joshua and all the children of Israel smote the whole land of Canaan as the Lord had commanded them, and smote all their kings, being thirty and one kings, and the children of Israel took their whole country.]

C.2 God had promised to Abraham that he would drive out the Canaanites from the lands which were supposed to belong to the descendants of Shem according to the original agreement of Noah with his three sons, Shem, Ham and Japheth right after the Great flood.

1 And in some time after Jacob went away from the borders of the land, and he came to the land of Shalem, that is the city of Shechem, which is in the land of Canaan, and he rested in front of the city.

2 And he bought a parcel of the field which was there, from the children of Hamor the people of the land, for five shekels.

3 And Jacob there built himself a house, and he pitched his tent there, and he made booths for his cattle, therefore he called the name of that place Succoth.

4 And Jacob remained in Succoth a year and six months.

5 At that time some of the women of the inhabitants of the land went to the city of Shechem to dance and rejoice with the daughters of the people of the city, and when they went forth then Rachel and Leah the wives of Jacob with their families also went to behold the rejoicing of the daughters of the city.

6 And Dinah the daughter of Jacob also went along with them and saw the daughters of the city, and they remained there before these

daughters whilst all the people of the city were standing by them to behold their rejoicings, and all the great people of the city were there.

7 And Shechem the son of Hamor, the prince of the land was also standing there to see them.

8 And Shechem beheld Dinah the daughter of Jacob sitting with her mother before the daughters of the city, and the damsel pleased him greatly, and he there asked his friends and his people, saying, Whose daughter is that sitting amongst the women, whom I do not know in this city?

9 And they said unto him, Surely this is the daughter of Jacob the son of Isaac the Hebrew, who has dwelt in this city for some time, and when it was reported that the daughters of the land were going forth to rejoice she went with her mother and maid servants to sit amongst them as thou seest.

10 And Shechem beheld Dinah the daughter of Jacob, and when he looked at her his soul became fixed upon Dinah.

11 And he sent and had her taken by force, and Dinah came to the house of Shechem and he seized her forcibly and lay with her and humbled her, and he loved her exceedingly and placed her in his house.

C.3 Shechem himself being a prince of this city sets a very bad example to everyone by forcing himself on the daughter of Jacob. A very serious mistake which is going to both cost him his life and the lives of all who lived in that city. God's plan for the totally destruction of the Canaanites is beginning to happen as God had promised to his servant Abraham.

12 And they came and told the thing unto Jacob, and when Jacob heard that Shechem had defiled his daughter Dinah, Jacob sent twelve of his servants to fetch Dinah from the house of Shechem, and they went and came to the house of Shechem to take away Dinah from there.

13 And when they came Shechem went out to them with his men and drove them from his house, and he would not suffer them to come before Dinah, but Shechem was sitting with Dinah kissing and embracing her before their eyes.

C.4 What a totally arrogant reprobate sicko this prince Shechem was with no respect for Dinah, her father or her brethren. Shechem sounds just like the typical rich man's kid. A big spoilt brat that has never been made to learn anything. Especially no self-discipline, manners, courtesy or kindness. It is very easy to see why God would end up totally destroying Shechem and his city. In kissing and embracing Dinah before Jacob's men, it was as if he was deliberately challenging and goading on Jacob and his family.

---

14 And the servants of Jacob came back and told him, saying, 'When we came, he and his men drove us away, and thus did Shechem do unto Dinah before our eyes'.

15 And Jacob knew moreover that Shechem had defiled his daughter, but he said nothing, and his sons were feeding his cattle in the field, and Jacob remained silent till their return.

16 And before his sons came home Jacob sent two maidens from his servants' daughters to take care of Dinah in the house of Shechem, and to remain with her, and Shechem sent three of his friends to his father Hamor the son of Chiddekem, the son of Pered, saying, Get me this damsel for a wife.

C.5 This man Shechem was a nasty piece of work and here he doesn't even have the manners to speak to his father about his matter but sends his servants and pretty much commands his father to 'Get me this damsel for a wife'. The Canaanites really treated women with great disrespect back in those times.

C.6 Here is a key verse from the book of Jubilees:

JUBILESS 30.1-2 And in the first year of the sixth week [2143 A.M.] he went up to Salem, to the east of Shechem, in peace, in the fourth month. 2 And there they carried off Dinah, the daughter of Jacob, into the house of Shechem, the son of Hamor, the Hivite, the prince of the land, and he lay with her and defiled her, and she was a little girl, a child of twelve years.

C.7 This happens to be an extremely important details from the Book of Jubilees. Why? Because it specifically tells us the age of Dinah. She wasn't even a young woman but merely a child. In fact, the verse goes as far as to state that she was a little girl. No wonder both Jacob and his sons were so angry and so mad that they wiped out a whole town of people who had done nothing to protect the innocent child from a paedophile, plain and simple!

---

17 And Hamor the son of Chiddekem the Hivite came to the house of Shechem his son, and he sat before him, and Hamor said unto his son,

---

271

Shechem, Is there then no woman amongst the daughters of thy people that thou wilt take an Hebrew woman who is not of thy people?

18 And Shechem said to him, 'Her only must thou get for me, for she is delightful in my sight'; and Hamor did according to the word of his son, for he was greatly beloved by him.

19 And Hamor went forth to Jacob to commune with him concerning this matter, and when he had gone from the house of his son Shechem, before he came to Jacob to speak unto him, behold the sons of Jacob had come from the field, as soon as they heard the thing that Shechem the son of Hamor had done.

C.8 It is very hard to understand why Hamor, the father of Shechem would have the nerve to go and talk with Jacob, the father of Jacob's abused young daughter Dinah; and ask for her to be the bride of his son, when she was very underage and also the fact that his son had already raped her and abused her in public in front of Jacob's servants, when they had come to his house to take Dinah back to her father, but had been driven away by Shechem's men. Who did these arrogant people from Shechem think that they were? They obviously had no code of ethics or of decency.

20 And the men were very much grieved concerning their sister, and they all came home fired with anger, before the time of gathering in their cattle.

C.9 Not good! You don't want to get these sons of Jacob all riled up in fierce anger!

21 And they came and sat before their father and they spoke unto him kindled with wrath, saying, Surely death is due to this man and to his household, because the Lord God of the whole earth commanded Noah and his children that man shall never rob, nor commit adultery; now behold Shechem has both ravaged and committed fornication with our sister, and not one of all the people of the city spoke a word to him.

C.10 The Laws given to Noah had stated that a man should not rob, nor commit adultery, or for that matter should not rape a woman.

22 Surely, thou knowest and understandest that the judgment of death is due to Shechem, and to his father, and to the whole city on account of the thing which he has done.

23 And whilst they were speaking before their father in this matter, behold Hamor the father of Shechem came to speak to Jacob the words of his son concerning Dinah, and he sat before Jacob and before his sons.

24 And Hamor spoke unto them, saying, The soul of my son Shechem longeth for your daughter; I pray you give her unto him for a wife and intermarry with us; give us your daughters and we will give you our daughters, and you shall dwell with us in our land and we will be as one people in the land.

25 For our land is very extensive, so dwell ye and trade therein and get possessions in it, and do therein as you desire, and no one shall prevent you by saying a word to you.

26 And Hamor ceased speaking unto Jacob and his sons, and behold Shechem his son had come after him, and he sat before them.

27 And Shechem spoke before Jacob and his sons, saying, May I find favour in your sight that you will give me your daughter, and whatever you say unto me that will I do for her.

28 Ask me for abundance of dowry and gift, and I will give it, and whatever you shall say unto me that will I do, and whoever he be that will rebel against your orders, he shall die; only give me the damsel for a wife.

29 And Simeon and Levi answered Hamor and Shechem his son deceitfully, saying, 'All you have spoken unto us we will do for you'.

30 And behold our sister is in your house but keep away from her until we send to our father Isaac concerning this matter, for we can do nothing without his consent.

31 For he knoweth the ways of our father Abraham, and whatever he sayeth unto us we will tell you, we will conceal nothing from you.

32 And Simeon and Levi spoke this unto Shechem and his father in order to find a pretext, and to seek counsel what was to be done to Shechem and to his city in this matter.

C.11 Here the sons of Jacob are acting with cunning. They know that there is no way that they are going to let their little sister be the wife of this spoiled prince who has zero manners as he has already proven. First, they use the delay in order to arrive at a plan.

33 And when Shechem and his father heard the words of Simeon and Levi, it seemed good in their sight, and Shechem and his father came forth to go home.

34 And when they had gone, the sons of Jacob said unto their father, saying, Behold, we know that death is due to these wicked ones and to their city, because they transgressed that which God had commanded unto Noah and his children and his seed after them.

35 And also because Shechem did this thing to our sister Dinah in defiling her, for such vileness shall never be done amongst us.

36 Now therefore know and see what you will do and seek counsel and pretext what is to be done to them, in order to kill all the inhabitants of this city.

37 And Simeon said to them, 'Here is a proper advice for you: tell them to circumcise every male amongst them as we are circumcised, and if they do not wish to do this, we shall take our daughter from them and go away'.

C.12 Now Simeon comes up with an excellent plan to totally weaken their enemies. It is painful to get circumcised and especially after several days. It so weakens a man that there is no possibility of him being able to fight effectively as he would be severely distracted by pain. In effect they now have a method to torture their victims first before killing them outright.

38 And if they consent to do this and will do it, then when they are sunk down with pain, we will attack them with our swords, as upon one who is quiet and peaceable, and we will slay every male person amongst them.

39 And Simeon's advice pleased them, and Simeon and Levi resolved to do unto them as it was proposed.

40 And on the next morning Shechem and Hamor his father came

again unto Jacob and his sons, to speak concerning Dinah, and to hear what answer the sons of Jacob would give to their words.'

41 And the sons of Jacob spoke deceitfully to them, saying, 'We told our father Isaac all your words, and your words pleased him'.

42 But he spoke unto us, saying, 'Thus did Abraham his father command him from God the Lord of the whole earth, that any man who is not of his descendants that should wish to take one of his daughters, shall cause every male belonging to him to be circumcised, as we are circumcised, and then we may give him our daughter for a wife.

43 Now we have made known to you all our ways that our father spoke unto us, for we cannot do this of which you spoke unto us, to give our daughter to an uncircumcised man, for it is a disgrace to us.

44 But herein will we consent to you, to give you our daughter, and we will also take unto ourselves your daughters, and will dwell amongst you and be one people as you have spoken, if you will hearken to us, and consent to be like us, to circumcise every male belonging to you, as we are circumcised.

45 And if you will not hearken unto us, to have every male circumcised as we are circumcised, as we have commanded, then we will come to you, and take our daughter from you and go away'.

46 And Shechem and his father Hamor heard the words of the sons of Jacob, and the thing pleased them exceedingly, and Shechem and his father Hamor hastened to do the wishes of the sons of Jacob, for Shechem was very fond of Dinah, and his soul was riveted to her.

C.13 How could Shechem and his father be so easily deceived. How could they believe that it was in their favour to get circumcised? Shechem was so full of lust for poor little Dinah that he and his father had totally lost their senses. They should have perceived that they were quickly falling into a very well-planned trap. One from which they would not survive.

47 And Shechem and his father Hamor hastened to the gate of the city, and they assembled all the men of their city and spoke unto them the words of the sons of Jacob, saying,

275

48 We came to these men, the sons of Jacob, and we spoke unto them concerning their daughter, and these men will consent to do according to our wishes, and behold our land is of great extent for them, and they will dwell in it, and trade in it, and we shall be one people; we will take their daughters, and our daughters we will give unto them for wives.

49 But only on this condition will these men consent to do this thing, that every male amongst us be circumcised as they are circumcised, as their God commanded them, and when we shall have done according to their instructions to be circumcised, then will they dwell amongst us, together with their cattle and possessions, and we shall be as one people with them.

50 And when all the men of the city heard the words of Shechem and his father Hamor, then all the men of their city were agreeable to this proposal, and they obeyed to be circumcised, for Shechem and his father Hamor were greatly esteemed by them, being the princes of the land.

C.14 This is very unusual that all the men of the city would agree to be circumcised just to help the prince in his nasty predicament. It sounds like the people were very much under the thumb of royalty!

51 And on the next day, Shechem and Hamor his father rose up early in the morning, and they assembled all the men of their city into the middle of the city, and they called for the sons of Jacob, who circumcised every male belonging to them on that day and the next.

52 And they circumcised Shechem and Hamor his father, and the five brothers of Shechem, and then everyone rose up and went home, for this thing was from the Lord against the city of Shechem, and from the Lord was Simeon's counsel in this matter, in order that the Lord might deliver the city of Shechem into the hands of Jacob's two sons.

Chapter 34

> 1 And the number of all the males that were circumcised, were six hundred and forty-five men, and two hundred and forty-six children.

Comment:1: This so-called city actually had a very small population of 645 men. Only forty-six children and probably around 700 women. This is what we call today in modern times a village. Certainly not a 'large town'. Here is the description of Shechem in verse 40: 'How could two men lay waste such a large town as Shechem? To us today there is a very big difference between a village of 1000 people and a town of 100,000 people. Obviously at the time of Shechem the populations on the earth (which was only around 500 years after the Great Flood of Noah) had not grown to many millions yet.

> 2 But Chiddekem, son of Pered, the father of Hamor, and his six brothers, would not listen unto Shechem and his father Hamor, and they would not be circumcised, for the proposal of the sons of Jacob was loathsome in their sight, and their anger was greatly roused at this, that the people of the city had not hearkened to them.

C.2 Finally someone in this city of Shechem with their head still screwed on saying to Shechem and his father, 'What? Are you out of your minds? We are certainly not going to allow ourselves to be circumcised as it is not the custom of our peoples'.

> 3 And in the evening of the second day, they found eight small children who had not been circumcised, for their mothers had concealed them from Shechem and his father Hamor, and from the men of the city.
>
> 4 And Shechem and his father Hamor sent to have them brought before them to be circumcised, when Chiddekem and his six brothers sprang at them with their swords and sought to slay them.
>
> 5 And they sought to slay also Shechem and his father Hamor and they sought to slay Dinah with them on account of this matter.
>
> 6 And they said unto them, What is this thing that you have done? are there no women amongst the daughters of your brethren the Canaanites, that you wish to take unto yourselves daughters of the Hebrews, whom ye knew not before, and will do this act which your fathers never commanded you?

C.3 Chiddekem was 'smelling a rat' in the situation, and knew that they were now in danger, so he goes on the attack and threatens to kill both Shechem and his father if they compromise with the Hebrews over their daughter.

> 7 Do you imagine that you will succeed through this act which you have done? and what will you answer in this affair to your brethren the Canaanites, who will come tomorrow and ask you concerning this thing?

C.4 Chiddekem tells them 'You just wait until our brethren the Canaanites come to see us one of these days. They will be very angry with us about what you have done, as it is not a Canaanite custom to get circumcised - and they will *kill all of us!*

> 8 And if your act shall not appear just and good in their sight, what will you do for your lives, and me for our lives, in your not having hearkened to our voices?
>
> 9 And if the inhabitants of the land and all your brethren the children of Ham, shall hear of your act, saying,
>
> 10 On account of a Hebrew woman did Shechem and Hamor his father, and all the inhabitants of their city, do that with which they had been unacquainted and which their ancestors never commanded them, where then will you fly or where conceal your shame, all your days before your brethren, the inhabitants of the land of Canaan?
>
> 11 Now therefore we cannot bear up against this thing which you have done, neither can we be burdened with this yoke upon us, which our ancestors did not command us.
>
> 12 Behold tomorrow we will go and assemble all our brethren, the Canaanitish brethren who dwell in the land, and we will all come and smite you and all those who trust in you, that there shall not be a remnant left from you or them.
>
> 13 And when Hamor and his son Shechem and all the people of the city heard the words of Chiddekem and his brothers, they were terribly afraid of their lives at their words, and they repented of what they had done.

> 14 And Shechem and his father Hamor answered their father Chidde-kem and his brethren, and they said unto them, All the words which you spoke unto us are true.

C.5 Now see what murderous slimy snakes Shechem and his father really are:

> 15 Now do not say, nor imagine in your hearts that on account of the love of the Hebrews we did this thing that our ancestors did not command us.
>
> 16 But because we saw that it was not their intention and desire to accede to our wishes concerning their daughter as to our taking her, except on this condition, so we hearkened to their voices and did this act which you saw, in order to obtain our desire from them.
>
> 17 And when we shall have obtained our request from them, we will then return to them and do unto them that which you say unto us.
>
> 18 We beseech you then to wait and tarry until our flesh shall be healed and we again become strong, and we will then go together against them, and do unto them that which is in your hearts and in ours.
>
> 19 And Dinah the daughter of Jacob heard all these words which Chiddekem and his brothers had spoken, and what Hamor and his son Shechem and the people of their city had answered them.

C.6 These people were not so smart. It sounds as if they were too agitated and didn't concern themselves with who might have happened to be tuning in to their conversation. In this case Dinah and her maidens. These people were so over-confident in themselves that they don't take note that Dinah herself might get a message through to her own father about the intents of the men of Shechem to steal away Dinah and to kill both Jacob and his sons.

C.7 When we read about the perverse behaviour of those who lived in the city of Shechem then it does not surprise me that God wanted to destroy all of the Canaanites. They were both cruel, arrogant and had no sense of right and wrong just like the 'seed of Satan' which is what they really were, being the descendants of not just Canaan, who was himself rebellious and evil, but also the influence of the Nephilim after the Great Flood who mated with the women again, and had giants among the Canaanites such as Goliath of Gath amongst the Philistines. That happened in King David's time around 800 years after Jacob's time. So even in King David's time there were still a few giants around. (See more about Giants in the **APPENDIX**)

20 And she hastened and sent one of her maidens, that her father had sent to take care of her in the house of Shechem, to Jacob her father and to her brethren, saying:

21 Thus did Chiddekem and his brothers advise concerning you, and thus did Hamor and Shechem and the people of the city answer them.

22 And when Jacob heard these words he was filled with wrath, and he was indignant at them, and his anger was kindled against them.

23 And Simeon and Levi swore and said, As the Lord liveth, the God of the whole earth, by this time tomorrow, there shall not be a remnant left in the whole city.

24 And twenty young men had concealed themselves who were not circumcised, and these young men fought against Simeon and Levi, and Simeon and Levi killed eighteen of them, and two fled from them and escaped to some lime pits that were in the city, and Simeon and Levi sought for them, but could not find them.

25 And Simeon and Levi continued to go about in the city, and they killed all the people of the city at the edge of the sword, and they left none remaining.

26 And there was a great consternation in the midst of the city, and the cry of the people of the city ascended to heaven, and all the women and children cried aloud.

27 And Simeon and Levi slew all the city; they left not a male remaining in the whole city.

28 And they slew Hamor and Shechem his son at the edge of the sword, and they brought away Dinah from the house of Shechem and they went from there.

C.8 Shechem the prince himself, certainly got was he deserved. That is the problem in our modern society. There is no longer any real sense of 'right and wrong'. There is no sense of 'pending judgement' for committing crimes. I myself once did a Christian ministry in prisons for quite some years. I came to the conclusion as did the head of one of the prisons, that society had mostly the wrong people in the prison - petty criminals. The real monsters of the criminal world were rarely caught, as they are protected by High Society. Because of the Elites' unique position on this planet, they are able to use and abuse people at will most of the time & mostly through the power of money without retribution - at least by man. They get away with horrendous crimes for which the man on the street would be put away in prison for years or even executed. Such is the state of Justice in our modern Western Society. One set of rules for the poor and an entirely different set of rules for the rich and powerful Elite who basically do whatever they want. The Elite of our planet are very blind and don't seem to care about what they will have to give an account for when they die:

ISA.5:14 Therefore Hell hath enlarged herself and opened her mouth without measure: and their glory, and their multitude, and their pomp, and he that rejoiceth, shall descend into it.

PSA.9:17 The wicked shall be turned into Hell, and all the nations that forget God.

GAL.6:7 Be not deceived; God is not mocked: for whatsoever a man soweth, that shall he also reap.

GAL.6:8 For he that soweth to his flesh shall of the flesh reap corruption; but he that soweth to the Spirit shall of the Spirit reap life everlasting.

29 And the sons of Jacob went and returned, and came upon the slain, and spoiled all their property which was in the city and the field.

30 And whilst they were taking the spoil, three hundred men stood up and threw dust at them and struck them with stones, when Simeon turned to them and he slew them all with the edge of the sword, and Simeon turned before Levi, and came into the city.

31 And they took away their sheep and their oxen and their cattle, and also the remainder of the women and little ones, and they led all these away, and they opened a gate and went out and came unto their father Jacob with vigour.

32 And when Jacob saw all that they had done to the city, and saw the spoil that they took from them, Jacob was very angry at them, and Jacob said unto them, What is this that you have done to me? behold I obtained rest amongst the Canaanitish inhabitants of the land, and none of them meddled with me.

C.9 Here it would seem that Jacob didn't quite get the point, as he had mostly been a pacifist living in the land of the Canaanites. God Himself however, had promised to Jacob's own grandfather Abraham, that as the land of the Canaanites had been usurped from Shem's descendants that Abraham's descendants would take back the lands that had been stolen from his ancestors. Of course, Jacob probably felt very small and inadequate, & that his 'as of yet' small tribe of 218 souls couldn't tackle the large number of the Canaanite kings and their populous peoples, so he personally tried to be a pacifist in the land of Canaan. God Himself however, had other plans, and allowed Jacob's sons to stir up trouble. Eventually Jacob's small tribe grew into millions within the next 400 years and his descendants did indeed totally annihilate the Canaanites and their many kings under Moses and especially under Joshua some 500 years after Jacob's time.

33 And now you have done to make me obnoxious to the inhabitants of the land, amongst the Canaanites and the Perizzites, and I am but of a small number, and they will all assemble against me and slay me when they hear of your work with their brethren, and I and my household will be destroyed.

34 And Simeon and Levi and all their brothers with them answered their father Jacob and said unto him, Behold we live in the land, and shall Shechem do this to our sister? why art thou silent at all that Shechem has done? and shall he deal with our sister as with a harlot in the streets?

35 And the number of women whom Simeon and Levi took captives from the city of Shechem, whom they did not slay, was eighty-five who had not known man.

36 And amongst them was a young damsel of beautiful appearance and well favoured, whose name was Bunah, and Simeon took her for a wife, and the number of the males which they took captives and did not slay, was forty-seven men, and the rest they slew.

37 And all the young men and women that Simeon and Levi had taken captives from the city of Shechem, were servants to the sons of Jacob and to their children after them, until the day of the sons of Jacob going forth from the land of Egypt.

38 And when Simeon and Levi had gone forth from the city, the two young men that were left, who had concealed themselves in the city,

and did not die amongst the people of the city, rose up, and these young men went into the city and walked about in it, and found the city desolate without man, and only women weeping, and these young men cried out and said, Behold, this is the evil which the sons of Jacob the Hebrew did to this city in their having this day destroyed one of the Canaanitish cities, and were not afraid of their lives of all the land of Canaan.

39 And these men left the city and went to the city of Tapnach, and they came there and told the inhabitants of Tapnach all that had befallen them, and all that the sons of Jacob had done to the city of Shechem.

40 And the information reached Jashub king of Tapnach, and he sent men to the city of Shechem to see those young men, for the king did not believe them in this account, saying, 'How could two men lay waste such a large town as Shechem'?

41 And the messengers of Jashub came back and told him, saying, We came unto the city, and it is destroyed, there is not a man there; only weeping women; neither is any flock or cattle there, for all that was in the city the sons of Jacob took away.

42 And Jashub wondered at this, saying, 'How could two men do this thing, to destroy so large a city, and not one man able to stand against them'?

C.10 It was as if God Himself fought His enemies through the sons of Jacob, as they all had supernatural strength and powers which were manifest upon different occasions. It all started with Abraham their great-grandfather, who with only 300 men totally slaughtered a coalition of 5 kings and their armies including the ruling King Chedorlaomer at that time, who ruled over Nimrod for a season.

C.11 Jacob's sons were all so strong it was as if he had 12 Samsons for sons. They even used a 'shrieking loud voice', as in the case of Simeon, which he used as a weapon. How about that: using sound weapons in ancient times.

C.12 Imagine having 12 Samsons for your sons! No wonder their enemies were afraid of them, as just two of them were able to totally destroy a whole city and slaughter all of the male inhabitants. That was in around 1800 BCE.

C.13 Then we had Samson in around 1200 BCE who totally single-handed destroyed the kingdom of the Philistines. He literally tore apart their multi-story temple-palace with 5000 Philistine Lords and the upper-echelon of Philistia by pushing apart the two main pillars of the temple against which he was chained to.

283

C.14 Then we have the famous King David in 1000 BCE who really built the empire of Israel and expanded its borders. He also fought and defeated and subdued many kings. He also was a very prayerful king and always involved God in every battle that he was involved in.

C.15 We have king Hezekiah in around 900 BCE who was surrounded by the armies of Sennacherib when he was in reigning in Jerusalem. There are so many stories in the Bible about God fighting for Israel. God defeated His enemies in a supernatural way as long as Israel put Him first or acknowledged him.

C.16 We also have the amazing stories from the Apocryphal book of Maccabees in the times of the Grecian empire. Five brothers decided to fight back against Antiochus Epiphanes who was the Seleucid king which was one of the 4 sections of Grecian empire in around 150 BCE. Antiochus Epiphanes totally decimated Jerusalem and Israel and profaned the temple by putting a pig on the altar. It was then that God raised up the 5 Maccabee brothers. When the Maccabees brothers fought, they always included God in the picture and prayed for miracles against all odds in the numbers of their enemies and they won tremendous victories over their enemies who always outnumbered them. http://www.outofthebottomlesspit.co.uk/420555449

> 43 For the like has not been from the days of Nimrod, and not even from the remotest time, has the like taken place; and Jashub, king of Tapnach, said to his people, Be courageous and we will go and fight against these Hebrews, and do unto them as they did unto the city, and we will avenge the cause of the people of the city.

C.17 Here we see the enemies of Jacob's sons figuring out what they are supposed to do. How can they defeat a family and their small tribe, when only two of them could destroy a whole city single-handedly?

> 44 And Jashub, king of Tapnach, consulted with his counsellors about this matter, and his advisers said unto him, 'Alone thou wilt not prevail over the Hebrews, for they must be powerful to do this work to the whole city'.
>
> 45 If two of them laid waste the whole city, and no one stood against them, surely if thou wilt go against them, they will all rise against us and destroy us likewise.
>
> 46 But if thou wilt send to all the kings that surround us, and let them come together, then we will go with them and fight against the sons of Jacob; then wilt thou prevail against them.

47 And Jashub heard the words of his counsellors, and their words pleased him and his people, and he did so; and Jashub king of Tapnach sent to all the kings of the Amorites that surrounded Shechem and Tapnach, saying,

48 Go up with me and assist me, and we will smite Jacob the Hebrew and all his sons, and destroy them from the earth, for thus did he do to the city of Shechem, and do you not know of it?

49 And all the kings of the Amorites heard the evil that the sons of Jacob had done to the city of Shechem, and they were greatly astonished at them.

50 And the seven kings of the Amorites assembled with all their armies, about ten thousand men with drawn swords, and they came to fight against the sons of Jacob; and Jacob heard that the kings of the Amorites had assembled to fight against his sons, and Jacob was greatly afraid, and it distressed him.

C.18 10,000 men with drawn swords coming against Jacob and his sons. No wonder that Jacob was afraid. Jacob himself was a very good fighter, but he didn't deliberately want to stir up a hornet's next of contention leading to a great battle and terrible war.

51 And Jacob exclaimed against Simeon and Levi, saying, What is this act that you did? why have you injured me, to bring against me all the children of Canaan to destroy me and my household? for I was at rest, even I and my household, and you have done this thing to me, and provoked the inhabitants of the land against me by your proceedings.

C.19 Most of the time both Abraham and his son Isaac after him and his grandson Jacob after him, tried to avoid unnecessary conflicts, if at all possible. They only attacked their enemies when they were forced into a tight corner. This time Simeon and Levi had literally stirred up a hornet's nest by slaughtering the inhabitants of the city of Shechem. However, on this particular occasion, it would seem to be God's plan to stir up trouble as God Himself wanted to get rid of the Canaanites from the land as He had originally promised unto Abraham.

C.20 Of course, God knew that He would supernaturally take care of the situation no matter how long the odds against Jacob and his sons were. The whole point was to prove that a 'God-empowered' people could totally defeat Satan's hoards no matter what the odds!

C.21 In order to get God's power and miracles God's people had to be obedient to God's commands. God likes to 'prove' his people. When they obeyed God then He protected them and supplied abundantly for them. When they strayed away and became disobedient as happened under many of the kings of Israel, eventually their enemies got the upper had over them time and time again.

C.22 Israel was under the thumb of the Philistines for a long time around 1200 BCE, until Samson came along. The 10 Northern tribes of Israel went into captivity under the Assyrian empire in around 720 BCE. Jerusalem was taken in around 600 BCE by Nebuchadnezzar king of the Babylonian empire. Israel was still in captivity under the next empire of Medio-Persia. They finally got to go back to Israel under Nehemiah and Ezra the prophet in around 450 BCE. It wasn't more than 200 years later the Grecian empire under Antiochus Epiphanes invaded and took over Israel yet again. Sadly, Israel was finally totally destroyed by the Romans in 70 AD. Millions were butchered by the Romans and millions were kicked out of their homelands in what is known in Israel as the Diaspora. It was as if in all the time from Abraham unto Christ and the apostles (2000 years of history) there were those in Israel who were obedient to God, but the vast majority of the time most of the people of Israel, kings and leaders were disobedient. So, on the one hand God was always trying to bless Israel, but also His Wrath was also hanging over them like a 'Diocletian sword' when they had seriously departed from His ways, although God patiently often waited for centuries for a good king or prophet and leader to lead the people back to God's ways. God only judged Israel after many warnings and their blatant defiance of God is eventually what always caused their own demise. Unfortunately, this world today is very much likewise in the camp of the 'disobedient to God'. Therefore, it is inevitable that great destruction will soon come to planet earth one way or the other unless the whole world repents of all the evils. (**FOR MORE ON THIS TOPIC SEE: APPENDIX XVI**)

---

52 And Judah answered his father, saying, 'Was it for naught my brothers Simeon and Levi killed all the inhabitants of Shechem'? Surely it was because Shechem had humbled our sister and transgressed the command of our God to Noah and his children, for Shechem took our sister away by force, and committed adultery with her.

53 And Shechem did all this evil and not one of the inhabitants of his city interfered with him, to say, Why wilt thou do this? surely for this my brothers went and smote the city, and the Lord delivered it into their hands, because its inhabitants had transgressed the commands of our God. Is it then for naught that they have done all this?

54 And now why art thou afraid or distressed, and why art thou displeased at my brothers, and why is thine anger kindled against them?

---

55 Surely our God who delivered into their hand the city of Shechem and its people, he will also deliver into our hands all the Canaanitish kings who are coming against us, and we will do unto them as my brothers did unto Shechem.

56 Now be tranquil about them and cast away thy fears, but trust in the Lord our God, and pray unto him to assist us and deliver us and deliver our enemies into our hands.

57 And Judah called to one of his father's servants, 'Go now and see where those kings, who are coming against us, are situated with their armies'.

58 And the servant went and looked far off, and went up opposite Mount Sihon, and saw all the camps of the kings standing in the fields, and he returned to Judah and said, Behold the kings are situated in the field with all their camps, a people exceedingly numerous, like unto the sand upon the sea shore.

59 And Judah said unto Simeon and Levi, and unto all his brothers, 'Strengthen yourselves and be sons of valour, for the Lord our God is with us, do not fear them'.

60 Stand forth each man, girt with his weapons of war, his bow and his sword, and we will go and fight against these uncircumcised men; the Lord is our God, He will save us.

61 And they rose up, and each girt on his weapons of war, great and small, eleven sons of Jacob, and all the servants of Jacob with them.

62 And all the servants of Isaac who were with Isaac in Hebron, all came to them equipped in all sorts of war instruments, and the sons of Jacob and their servants, being one hundred and twelve men, went towards these kings, and Jacob also went with them.

63 And the sons of Jacob sent unto their father Isaac the son of Abraham to Hebron, the same is Kireath-arba, saying,

64 Pray we beseech thee for us unto the Lord our God, to protect us from the hands of the Canaanites who are coming against us, and to deliver them into our hands.

65 And Isaac the son of Abraham prayed unto the Lord for his sons, and he said, O Lord God, thou didst promise my father, saying, I will multiply thy seed as the stars of heaven, and thou didst also promise me, and establish thou thy word, now that the kings of Canaan are coming together, to make war with my children because they committed no violence.

66 Now therefore, O Lord God, God of the whole earth, pervert, I pray thee, the counsel of these kings that they may not fight against my sons.

67 And impress the hearts of these kings and their people with the terror of my sons and bring down their pride, and that they may turn away from my sons.

68 And with thy strong hand and outstretched arm deliver my sons and their servants from them, for power and might are in thy hands to do all this.

69 And the sons of Jacob and their servants went toward these kings, and they trusted in the Lord their God, and whilst they were going, Jacob their father also prayed unto the Lord and said, O Lord God, powerful and exalted God, who has reigned from days of old, from thence till now and forever;

70 Thou art He who stirreth up wars and causeth them to cease, in thy hand are power and might to exalt and to bring down; O may my prayer be acceptable before thee that thou mayest turn to me with thy mercies, to impress the hearts of these kings and their people with the terror of my sons, and terrify them and their camps, and with thy great kindness deliver all those that trust in thee, for it is thou who canst bring people under us and reduce nations under our power.

Chapter 35

1 And all the kings of the Amorites came and took their stand in the field to consult with their counsellors what was to be done with the sons of Jacob, for they were still afraid of them, saying, Behold, two of them slew the whole of the city of Shechem.

2 And the Lord heard the prayers of Isaac and Jacob, and he filled the hearts of all these kings' advisers with great fear and terror that they unanimously exclaimed,

3 Are you silly this day, or is there no understanding in you, that you will fight with the Hebrews, and why will you take a delight in your own destruction this day?

4 Behold two of them came to the city of Shechem without fear or terror, and they killed all the inhabitants of the city, that no man stood up against them, and how will you be able to fight with them all?

5 Surely, you know that their God is exceedingly fond of them, and has done mighty things for them, such as have not been done from days of old, and amongst all the gods of nations, there is none can do like unto his mighty deeds.

6 Surely, he delivered their father Abraham, the Hebrew, from the hand of Nimrod, and from the hand of all his people who had many times sought to slay him.

7 He delivered him also from the fire in which king Nimrod had cast him, and his God delivered him from it.

8 And who else can do the like? surely it was Abraham who slew the five kings of Elam, when they had touched his brother's son who in those days dwelt in Sodom.

9 And took his servant that was faithful in his house and a few of his men, and they pursued the kings of Elam in one night and killed them

and restored to his brother's son all his property which they had taken from him.

10 And surely you know the God of these Hebrews is much delighted with them, and they are also delighted with him, for they know that he delivered them from all their enemies.

11 And behold through his love toward his God, Abraham took his only and precious son and intended to bring him up as a burnt offering to his God, and had it not been for God who prevented him from doing this, he would then have done it through his love to his God.

12 And God saw all his works, and swore unto him, and promised him that he would deliver his sons and all his seed from every trouble that would befall them, because he had done this thing, and through his love to his God stifled his compassion for his child.

13 And have you not heard what their God did to Pharaoh king of Egypt, and to Abimelech king of Gerar, through taking Abraham's wife, who said of her, She is my sister, lest they might slay him on account of her, and think of taking her for a wife? and God did unto them and their people all that you heard of.

14 And behold, we ourselves saw with our eyes that Esau, the brother of Jacob, came to him with four hundred men, with the intention of slaying him, for he called to mind that he had taken away from him his father's blessing.

15 And he went to meet him when he came from Syria, to smite the mother with the children, and who delivered him from his hands but his God in whom he trusted? he delivered him from the hand of his brother and also from the hands of his enemies, and surely he again will protect them.

16 Who does not know that it was their God who inspired them with strength to do to the town of Shechem the evil which you heard of?

17 Could it then be with their own strength that two men could destroy

such a large city as Shechem had it not been for their God in whom they trusted? he said and did unto them all this to slay the inhabitants of the city in their city.

18 And can you then prevail over them who have come forth together from your city to fight with the whole of them, even if a thousand times as many more should come to your assistance?

19 Surely you know and understand that you do not come to fight with them, but you come to war with their God who made choice of them, and you have therefore all come this day to be destroyed.

20 Now therefore refrain from this evil which you are endeavouring to bring upon yourselves, and it will be better for you not to go to battle with them, although they are but few in numbers, because their God is with them.

21 And when the kings of the Amorites heard all the words of their advisers, their hearts were filled with terror, and they were afraid of the sons of Jacob and would not fight against them.

22 And they inclined their ears to the words of their advisers, and they listened to all their words, and the words of the counsellors greatly pleased the kings, and they did so.

23 And the kings turned and refrained from the sons of Jacob, for they durst not approach them to make war with them, for they were greatly afraid of them, and their hearts melted within them from their fear of them.

24 For this proceeded from the Lord to them, for he heard the prayers of his servants Isaac and Jacob, for they trusted in him; and all these kings returned with their camps on that day, each to his own city, and they did not at that time fight with the sons of Jacob.

C.1 What a demonstration of the power of prayer to do miracles. Isaac and Jacob both prayed very desperately as did their families and relatives for God to bring a mighty deliverance and He did.

2KI.19:35 And it came to pass that night, that the angel of the LORD went out, and smote in the camp of the Assyrians an hundred fourscore and five thousand: and when they arose early in the morning, behold, they were all dead corpses

C.2 This Bible verse is showing that the angel of the Lord slaughtered 185.000 men of the Assyrian army. What this clearly shows is that if you have God on your side you don't even need to fight physically. God will fight for you against your enemies - even if He has to send one of his angels to slaughter them.

---

25 And the sons of Jacob kept their station that day till evening opposite mount Sihon and seeing that these kings did not come to fight against them, the sons of Jacob returned home.

Chapter 36

1 At that time the Lord appeared unto Jacob saying, Arise, go to Bethel and remain there, and make there an altar to the Lord who appeared unto thee, who delivered thee and thy sons from affliction.

2 And Jacob rose up with his sons and all belonging to him, and they went and came to Bethel according to the word of the Lord.

3 And Jacob was ninety-nine years old when he went up to Bethel, and Jacob and his sons and all the people that were with him, remained in Bethel in Luz, and he there built an altar to the Lord who appeared unto him, and Jacob and his sons remained in Bethel six months.

4 At that time died Deborah the daughter of Uz, the nurse of Rebecca, who had been with Jacob; and Jacob buried her beneath Bethel under an oak that was there.

5 And Rebecca the daughter of Bethuel, the mother of Jacob, also died at that time in Hebron, the same is Kireath-arba, and she was buried in the cave of Machpelah which Abraham had bought from the children of Heth.

6 And the life of Rebecca was one hundred and thirty-three years, and she died and when Jacob heard that his mother Rebecca was dead he wept bitterly for his mother, and made a great mourning for her, and for Deborah her nurse beneath the oak, and he called the name of that place Allon-bachuth.

7 And Laban the Syrian died in those days, for God smote him because he transgressed the covenant that existed between him and Jacob.

8 And Jacob was a hundred years old when the Lord appeared unto him, and blessed him and called his name Israel, and Rachel the wife of Jacob conceived in those days.

9 And at that time Jacob and all belonging to him journeyed from Bethel to go to his father's house, to Hebron.

10 And whilst they were going on the road, and there was yet but a little way to come to Ephrath, Rachel bare a son and she had hard labour and she died.

11 And Jacob buried her in the way to Ephrath, which is Bethlehem, and he set a pillar upon her grave, which is there unto this day; and the days of Rachel were forty-five years and she died.

12 And Jacob called the name of his son that was born to him, which Rachel bare unto him, Benjamin, for he was born to him in the land on the right hand.

13 And it was after the death of Rachel, that Jacob pitched his tent in the tent of her handmaid Bilhah.

14 And Reuben was jealous for his mother Leah on account of this, and he was filled with anger, and he rose up in his anger and went and entered the tent of Bilhah and he thence removed his father's bed.

15 At that time the portion of birthright, together with the kingly and priestly offices, was removed from the sons of Reuben, for he had profaned his father's bed, and the birthright was given unto Joseph, the kingly office to Judah, and the priesthood unto Levi, because Reuben had defiled his father's bed.

16 And these are the generations of Jacob who were born to him in Padan-aram, and the sons of Jacob were twelve.

17 The sons of Leah were Reuben the first born, and Simeon, Levi, Judah, Issachar, Zebulun, and their sister Dinah; and the sons of Rachel were Joseph and Benjamin.

18 The sons of Zilpah, Leah's handmaid, were Gad and Asher, and the sons of Bilhah, Rachel's handmaid, were Dan and Naphtali; these are the sons of Jacob which were born to him in Padan-aram.

19 And Jacob and his sons and all belonging to him journeyed and came to Mamre, which is Kireath-arba, that is in Hebron, where Abra-

ham and Isaac sojourned, and Jacob with his sons and all belonging to him, dwelt with his father in Hebron.

20 And his brother Esau and his sons, and all belonging to him went to the land of Seir and dwelt there, and had possessions in the land of Seir, and the children of Esau were fruitful and multiplied exceedingly in the land of Seir.

21 And these are the generations of Esau that were born to him in the land of Canaan, and the sons of Esau were five.

22 And Adah bare to Esau his first born Eliphaz, and she also bare to him Reuel, and Ahlibamah bare to him Jeush, Yaalam and Korah.

23 These are the children of Esau who were born to him in the land of Canaan; and the sons of Eliphaz the son of Esau were Teman, Omar, Zepho, Gatam, Kenaz and Amalex, and the sons of Reuel were Nachath, Zerach, Shamah and Mizzah.

24 And the sons of Jeush were Timnah, Alvah, Jetheth; and the sons of Yaalam were Alah, Phinor and Kenaz.

25 And the sons of Korah were Teman, Mibzar, Magdiel and Eram; these are the families of the sons of Esau according to their dukedoms in the land of Seir.

26 And these are the names of the sons of Seir the Horite, inhabitants of the land of Seir, Lotan, Shobal, Zibeon, Anah, Dishan, Ezer and Dishon, being seven sons.

27 And the children of Lotan were Hori, Heman and their sister Timna, that is Timna who came to Jacob and his sons, and they would not give ear to her, and she went and became a concubine to Eliphaz the son of Esau, and she bare to him Amalek.

28 And the sons of Shobal were Alvan, Manahath, Ebal, Shepho, and Onam, and the sons of Zibeon were Ajah, and Anah, this was that Anah who found the Yemim in the wilderness when he fed the asses of Zibeon his father.

29 And whilst he was feeding his father's asses, he led them to the wilderness at different times to feed them.

30 And there was a day that he brought them to one of the deserts on the sea shore, opposite the wilderness of the people, and whilst he was feeding them, behold a very heavy storm came from the other side of the sea and rested upon the asses that were feeding there, and they all stood still.

31 And afterward about one hundred and twenty great and terrible animals came out from the wilderness at the other side of the sea, and they all came to the place where the asses were, and they placed themselves there.

32 And those animals, from their middle downward, were in the shape of the children of men, and from their middle upward, some had the likeness of bears, and some the likeness of the keephas, with tails behind them from between their shoulders reaching down to the earth, like the tails of the ducheephath, and these animals came and mounted and rode upon these asses, and led them away, and they went away unto this day.

Comment:1: Here we see the *chimeras*, but different from what we have heard before in mythology as the *top half* of these creatures are as *animals* and the *bottom part* as the *legs of humans*. This then enables them to ride on the backs of the asses and to lead them away. A very strange description, but not completely impossible, as many odd things happened after the Great Flood, including the same Fallen angels and demonic powers interfering with the DNA of both mankind and animals.

C.2 ORIGIN of the DEMONS: The demons originally came into being as the de-embodied spirits of the Pre-Flood giants, who were in turn, the sons of the 'union between Fallen angels and the women on the earth', according to the book of Enoch. See my book 'Enoch Insights'. This process of harvesting DNA is today in modern times known as *'Alien Abductions'* and *'cattle-mutilations'*. Some non-human entities are in the 'spare body parts' business. Some say they are aliens, but I believe they are simply *demons* masquerading as *aliens* for the purpose of ensnaring & beguiling modern scientific men.

33 And one of these animals approached Anah and smote him with his tail, and then fled from that place.

C.3 These are indeed very strange verses. Where did these chimeras come from? What was the purpose in creating a type of chimera with animal heads and human legs like the Faun from the book 'The Lion the Witch and the Wardrobe' - by C.S. Lewis? Many would think 'I always thought that Fauns and other types of chimeras were creatures from mythology and were really imaginary creatures. Well, as you can see from the story above, apparently, they are in fact real.

34 And when he saw this work, he was exceedingly afraid of his life, and he fled and escaped to the city.

35 And he related to his sons and brothers all that had happened to him, and many men went to seek the asses but could not find them, and Anah and his brothers went no more to that place from that day following, for they were greatly afraid of their lives.

C.4 Why do you suppose that the men were so greatly afraid of these chimeras, to the point that the men would not go near that place where the chimeras had been seen? Is it not likely that the men had heard somewhere that chimeras were evil creatures and had something to do with the Fallen angels from before the Great Flood? These men could not explain to themselves how these creatures had come into being again and therefore they were terrified just at the thought of chimeras having returned to their lands. I suppose in modern terms it would be like if one of us saw a U.F.O at close range. We would probably try to get as far away from it as possible because in our mind 'it shouldn't exist, and it certainly shouldn't be there right in front of me!' Humans generally have a very hard time accepting the 'unknown' or paranormal. (To know more about Chimeras - see my book 'Enoch Insights')

36 And the children of Anah the son of Seir, were Dishon and his sister Ahlibamah, and the children of Dishon were Hemdan, Eshban, Ithran and Cheran, and the children of Ezer were Bilhan, Zaavan and Akan, and the children of Dishon were Uz and Aran.

37 These are the families of the children of Seir the Horite, according to their dukedoms in the land of Seir.

38 And Esau and his children dwelt in the land of Seir the Horite, the inhabitant of the land, and they had possessions in it and were fruitful and multiplied exceedingly, and Jacob and his children and all belonging to them, dwelt with their father Isaac in the land of Canaan, as the Lord had commanded Abraham their father.

Chapter 37

WARS OF JACOB & HIS SONS AGAINST THE CAANANITES

Comment:1: In chapters 37-40 we will see the wars of the Canaanites against Jacob and his sons. It was all started because two of Jacob's sons Simeon and Levi had single-handedly obliterated the town of Shechem and put around 700 men to the sword. Why did they do this horrible deed one might say? It was justifiable revenge for the rape of their sister Dinah who was only 12 years old. One evil act by the prince of Shechem ended up in the virtual annihilation of many of the Canaanites. Remember that God had prophesied through Abraham that he would obliterate the Canaanities because they were descendants of Canaan who had originally usurped the lands of Shem. God said that He would drive out the Canaanites from the lands of Shem. The rest of the Canaanities were killed in the time of Moses and Joshua some 500 years later when the Children of Israel came out of Egypt.

1 And in the one hundred and fifth year of the life of Jacob, that is the ninth year of Jacob's dwelling with his children in the land of Canaan, he came from Padan-aram.

2 And in those days Jacob journeyed with his children from Hebron, and they went and returned to the city of Shechem, they and all belonging to them, and they dwelt there, for the children of Jacob obtained good and fat pasture land for their cattle in the city of Shechem, the city of Shechem having then been rebuilt, and there were in it about three hundred men and women.

3 And Jacob and his children and all belonging to him dwelt in the part of the field which Jacob had bought from Hamor the father of Shechem, when he came from Padan-aram before Simeon and Levi had smitten the city.

4 And all those kings of the Canaanites and Amorites that surrounded the city of Shechem, heard that the sons of Jacob had again come to Shechem and dwelt there.

5 And they said, Shall the sons of Jacob the Hebrew again come to the

city and dwell therein, after that they have smitten its inhabitants and driven them out? shall they now return and also drive out those who are dwelling in the city or slay them?

6 And all the kings of Canaan again assembled, and they came together to make war with Jacob and his sons.

7 And Jashub king of Tapnach sent also to all his neighbouring kings, to Elan king of Gaash, and to Ihuri king of Shiloh, and to Parathon king of Chazar, and to Susi king of Sarton, and to Laban king of Beth-choran, and to Shabir king of Othnay-mah, saying,

8 Come up to me and assist me and let us smite Jacob the Hebrew and his sons, and all belonging to him, for they are again come to Shechem to possess it and to slay its inhabitants as before.

9 And all these kings assembled together and came with all their camps, a people exceedingly plentiful like the sand upon the seashore, and they were all opposite to Tapnach.

10 And Jashub king of Tapnach went forth to them with all his army, and he encamped with them opposite to Tapnach without the city, and all these kings they divided into seven divisions, being seven camps against the sons of Jacob.

11 And they sent a declaration to Jacob and his son, saying, Come you all forth to us that we may have an interview together in the plain, and revenge the cause of the men of Shechem whom you slew in their city, and you will now again return to the city of Shechem and dwell therein, and slay its inhabitants as before.

12 And the sons of Jacob heard this and their anger was kindled exceedingly at the words of the kings of Canaan, and ten of the sons of Jacob hastened and rose up, and each of them girt on his weapons of war; and there were one hundred and two of their servants with them equipped in battle array.

13 And all these men, the sons of Jacob with their servants, went toward these kings, and Jacob their father was with them, and they all stood upon the heap of Shechem.

14 And Jacob prayed to the Lord for his sons, and he spread forth his hands to the Lord, and he said, O God, thou art an Almighty God, thou art our father, thou didst form us and we are the works of thine hands; I pray thee deliver my sons through thy mercy from the hand of their enemies, who are this day coming to fight with them and save them from their hand, for in thy hand is power and might, to save the few from the many.

15 And give unto my sons, thy servants, strength of heart and might to fight with their enemies, to subdue them, and make their enemies fall before them, and let not my sons and their servants die through the hands of the children of Canaan.

16 But if it seemeth good in thine eyes to take away the lives of my sons and their servants, take them in thy great mercy through the hands of thy ministers, that they may not perish this day by the hands of the kings of the Amorites.

17 And when Jacob ceased praying to the Lord the earth shook from its place, and the sun darkened, and all these kings were terrified, and a great consternation seized them.

C.2 God the Almighty Warrior was directly fighting for His people. This sounds like something out of the Book of Joel:

JOEL.2:31 The sun shall be turned into darkness, and the moon into blood, before the great and terrible day of the LORD come.

18 And the Lord hearkened to the prayer of Jacob, and the Lord impressed the hearts of all the kings and their hosts with the terror and awe of the sons of Jacob.

C.3 God struck the hearts of Jacob's enemies with fear and terror so that they had no longer the fight in them to attack Jacob and his sons. God was answering the prayers of Isaac and Rebecca and those of Jacob and his sons.

> 19 For the Lord caused them to hear the voice of chariots, and the voice of mighty horses from the sons of Jacob, and the voice of a great army accompanying them.

C.4 This same tactic was used many times by God himself in the Old Testament:

2KI.6:17 And Elisha prayed, and said, LORD, I pray thee, open his eyes, that he may see. And the LORD opened the eyes of the young man; and he saw: and, behold, the mountain was full of horses and chariots of fire round about Elisha.

2KI.6:18 And when they came down to him, Elisha prayed unto the LORD, and said, 'Smite this people, I pray thee, with blindness'. And he smote them with blindness according to the word of Elisha.

> 20 And these kings were seized with great terror at the sons of Jacob, and whilst they were standing in their quarters, behold the sons of Jacob advanced upon them, with one hundred and twelve men, with a great and tremendous shouting.
>
> 21 And when the kings saw the sons of Jacob advancing toward them, they were still more panic struck, and they were inclined to retreat from before the sons of Jacob as at first, and not to fight with them.
>
> 22 But they did not retreat, saying, 'It would be a disgrace to us thus twice to retreat from before the Hebrews'.
>
> 23 And the sons of Jacob came near and advanced against all these kings and their armies, and they saw, and behold it was a very mighty people, numerous as the sand of the sea.
>
> 24 And the sons of Jacob called unto the Lord and said, 'Help us O Lord, help us and answer us, for we trust in thee, and let us not die by the hands of these uncircumcised men, who this day have come against us.'
>
> 25 And the sons of Jacob girt on their weapons of war, and they took in their hands each man his shield and his javelin, and they approached to battle.
>
> 26 And Judah, the son of Jacob, ran first before his brethren, and ten of his servants with him, and he went toward these kings.

27 And Jashub, king of Tapnach, also came forth first with his army before Judah, and Judah saw Jashub and his army coming toward him, and Judah's wrath was kindled, and his anger burned within him, and he approached to battle in which Judah ventured his life.

28 And Jashub and all his army were advancing toward Judah, and he was riding upon a very strong and powerful horse, and Jashub was a very valiant man, and covered with iron and brass from head to foot.

29 And whilst he was upon the horse, he shot arrows with both hands from before and behind, as was his manner in all his battles, and he never missed the place to which he aimed his arrows.

30 And when Jashub came to fight with Judah, and was darting many arrows against Judah, the Lord bound the hand of Jashub, and all the arrows that he shot rebounded upon his own men.

31 And notwithstanding this, Jashub kept advancing toward Judah, to challenge him with the arrows, but the distance between them was about thirty cubits, and when Judah saw Jashub darting forth his arrows against him, he ran to him with his wrath-excited might.

32 And Judah took up a large stone from the ground, and its weight was sixty shekels, and Judah ran toward Jashub, and with the stone struck him on his shield, that Jashub was stunned with the blow, and fell off from his horse to the ground.

C.5 Why were there big rocks just strewn randomly over the ground? Did that used to be a more common occurrence back then. Rocks left around for centuries even in modern times are ones which have often been spewed forth from volcanoes at some time or the other. They are often left where they landed because of their great weight and size. Perhaps there had been some great destruction in the not too distance past like the Great Flood. Judah must have been exceedingly strong to have lifted up one of these massive rocks.

C.6 Actually 60 shekels in modern terms is a very small weight. It would be like throwing the 'weight of 60 coins' at Judah's enemy's shield? The 'shekel' in olden times must have been a different measurement. One would expect the weight mentioned above to be in 'talents' One talent being around 60 kg.

REV.16:21 And there fell upon men a great hail out of heaven, every stone about the weight of a talent: and men blasphemed God because of the plague of the hail; for the plague thereof was exceeding great.

302

33 And the shield burst asunder out of the hand of Jashub, and through the force of the blow sprang to the distance of about fifteen cubits, and the shield fell before the second camp.

C.7 The force at which the massive rock hit the shield of Jashub shattered the big shield and thrown it 25 feet away. It must have been hit with a massive force to do that!

34 And the kings that came with Jashub saw at a distance the strength of Judah, the son of Jacob, and what he had done to Jashub, and they were terribly afraid of Judah.

35 And they assembled near Jashub's camp, seeing his confusion, and Judah drew his sword and smote forty-two men of the camp of Jashub, and the whole of Jashub's camp fled before Judah, and no man stood against him, and they left Jashub and fled from him, and Jashub was still prostrate upon the ground.

36 And Jashub seeing that all the men of his camp had fled from him, hastened and rose up with terror against Judah, and stood upon his legs opposite Judah.

37 And Jashub had a single combat with Judah, placing shield toward shield, and Jashub's men all fled, for they were greatly afraid of Judah.

38 And Jashub took his spear in his hand to strike Judah upon his head, but Judah had quickly placed his shield to his head against Jashub's spear, so that the shield of Judah received the blow from Jashub's spear, and the shield was split in too.

39 And when Judah saw that his shield was split, he hastily drew his sword and smote Jashub at his ankles and cut off his feet that Jashub fell upon the ground, and the spear fell from his hand.

40 And Judah hastily picked up Jashub's spear, with which he severed his head and cast it next to his feet.

41 And when the sons of Jacob saw what Judah had done to Jashub, they all ran into the ranks of the other kings, and the sons of Jacob fought with the army of Jashub, and the armies of all the kings that were there.

42 And the sons of Jacob caused fifteen thousand of their men to fall, and they smote them as if smiting at gourds, and the rest fled for their lives.

43 And Judah was still standing by the body of Jashub, and stripped Jashub of his coat of mail.

44 And Judah also took off the iron and brass that was about Jashub and behold nine men of the captains of Jashub came along to fight against Judah.

45 And Judah hastened and took up a stone from the ground, and with it smote one of them upon the head, and his skull was fractured, and the body also fell from the horse to the ground.

46 And the eight captains that remained, seeing the strength of Judah, were greatly afraid and they fled, and Judah with his ten men pursued them, and they overtook them and slew them.

47 And the sons of Jacob were still smiting the armies of the kings, and they slew many of them, but those kings daringly kept their stand with their captains, and did not retreat from their places, and they exclaimed against those of their armies that fled from before the sons of Jacob, but none would listen to them, for they were afraid of their lives lest they should die.

48 And all the sons of Jacob, after having smitten the armies of the kings, returned and came before Judah, and Judah was still slaying the eight captains of Jashub, and stripping off their garments.

49 And Levi saw Elon, king of Gaash, advancing toward him, with his fourteen captains to smite him, but Levi did not know it for certain.

50 And Elon with his captains approached nearer, and Levi looked back and saw that battle was given him in the rear, and Levi ran with twelve of his servants, and they went and slew Elon and his captains with the edge of the sword.

Chapter 38

1 And Ihuri king of Shiloh came up to assist Elon, and he approached Jacob, when Jacob drew his bow that was in his hand and with an arrow struck Ihuri which caused his death.

2 And when Ihuri king of Shiloh was dead, the four remaining kings fled from their station with the rest of the captains, and they endeavoured to retreat, saying, We have no more strength with the Hebrews after their having killed the three kings and their captains who were more powerful than we are.

1 And Ihuri king of Shiloh came up to assist Elon, and he approached Jacob, when Jacob drew his bow that was in his hand and with an arrow struck Ihuri which caused his death.

2 And when Ihuri king of Shiloh was dead, the four remaining kings fled from their station with the rest of the captains, and they endeavoured to retreat, saying, We have no more strength with the Hebrews after their having killed the three kings and their captains who were more powerful than we are.

3 And when the sons of Jacob saw that the remaining kings had removed from their station, they pursued them, and Jacob also came from the heap of Shechem from the place where he was standing, and they went after the kings and they approached them with their servants.

4 And the kings and the captains with the rest of their armies, seeing that the sons of Jacob approached them, were afraid of their lives and fled till they reached the city of Chazar.

5 And the sons of Jacob pursued them to the gate of the city of Chazar, and they smote a great smiting amongst the kings and their armies, about four thousand men, and whilst they were smiting the army of the kings, Jacob was occupied with his bow confining himself to smiting the kings, and he slew them all.

6 And he slew Parathon king of Chazar at the gate of the city of Chazar, and he afterward smote Susi king of Sarton, and Laban king of Bethchorin, and Shabir king of Machnaymah, and he slew them all with arrows, an arrow to each of them, and they died.

7 And the sons of Jacob seeing that all the kings were dead and that they were broken up and retreating, continued to carry on the battle with the armies of the kings opposite the gate of Chazar, and they still smote about four hundred of their men.

8 And three men of the servants of Jacob fell in that battle, and when Judah saw that three of his servants had died, it grieved him greatly, and his anger burned within him against the Amorites.

9 And all the men that remained of the armies of the kings were greatly afraid of their lives, and they ran and broke the gate of the walls of the city of Chazar, and they all entered the city for safety.

10 And they concealed themselves in the midst of the city of Chazar, for the city of Chazar was very large and extensive, and when all these armies had entered the city, the sons of Jacob ran after them to the city.

11 And four mighty men, experienced in battle, went forth from the city and stood against the entrance of the city, with drawn swords and spears in their hands, and they placed themselves opposite the sons of Jacob, and would not suffer them to enter the city.

12 And Naphtali ran and came between them and with his sword smote two of them and cut off their heads at one stroke.

13 And he turned to the other two, and behold they had fled, and he pursued them, overtook them, smote them and slew them.

14 And the sons of Jacob came to the city and saw, and behold there was another wall to the city, and they sought for the gate of the wall and could not find it, and Judah sprang upon the top of the wall, and Simeon and Levi followed him, and they all three descended from the wall into the city.

15 And Simeon and Levi slew all the men who ran for safety into the city, and also the inhabitants of the city with their wives and little ones, they slew with the edge of the sword, and the cries of the city ascended up to heaven.

16 And Dan and Naphtali sprang upon the wall to see what caused the noise of lamentation, for the sons of Jacob felt anxious about their brothers, and they heard the inhabitants of the city speaking with weeping and supplications, saying, Take all that we possess in the city and go away, only do not put us to death.

17 And when Judah, Simeon, and Levi had ceased smiting the inhabitants of the city, they ascended the wall and called to Dan and Naphtali, who were upon the wall, and to the rest of their brothers, and Simeon and Levi informed them of the entrance into the city, and all the sons of Jacob came to fetch the spoil.

18 And the sons of Jacob took the spoil of the city of Chazar, the flocks and herds, and the property, and they took all that could be captured, and went away that day from the city.

19 And on the next day the sons of Jacob went to Sarton, for they heard that the men of Sarton who had remained in the city were assembling to fight with them for having slain their king, and Sarton was a very high and fortified city, and it had a deep rampart surrounding the city.

20 And the pillar of the rampart was about fifty cubits and its breadth forty cubits, and there was no place for a man to enter the city on account of the rampart, and the sons of Jacob saw the rampart of the city, and they sought an entrance in it but could not find it.

21 For the entrance to the city was at the rear, and every man that wished to come into the city came by that road and went around the whole city, and he afterwards entered the city.

22 And the sons of Jacob seeing they could not find the way into the city, their anger was kindled greatly, and the inhabitants of the city seeing that the sons of Jacob were coming to them were greatly afraid of them, for they had heard of their strength and what they had done to Chazar.

23 And the inhabitants of the city of Sarton could not go out toward the sons of Jacob after having assembled in the city to fight against them, lest they might thereby get into the city, but when they saw that they were coming toward them, they were greatly afraid of them, for they had heard of their strength and what they had done to Chazar.

24 So the inhabitants of Sarton speedily took away the bridge of the road of the city, from its place, before the sons of Jacob came, and they brought it into the city.

25 And the sons of Jacob came and sought the way into the city and could not find it and the inhabitants of the city went up to the top of the wall, and saw, and behold the sons of Jacob were seeking an entrance into the city.

26 And the inhabitants of the city reproached the sons of Jacob from the top of the wall, and they cursed them, and the sons of Jacob heard the reproaches, and they were greatly incensed, and their anger burned within them.

27 And the sons of Jacob were provoked at them, and they all rose and sprang over the rampart with the force of their strength, and through their might passed the forty cubits' breadth of the rampart.

28 And when they had passed the rampart they stood under the wall of the city, and they found all the gates of the city enclosed with iron doors.

29 And the sons of Jacob came near to break open the doors of the gates of the city, and the inhabitants did not let them, for from the top of the wall they were casting stones and arrows upon them.

30 And the number of the people that were upon the wall was about four hundred men, and when the sons of Jacob saw that the men of the city would not let them open the gates of the city, they sprang and ascended the top of the wall, and Judah went up first to the east part of the city.

31 And Gad and Asher went up after him to the west corner of the city, and Simeon and Levi to the north, and Dan and Reuben to the south.

32 And the men who were on the top of the wall, the inhabitants of the city, seeing that the sons of Jacob were coming up to them, they all fled from the wall, descended into the city, and concealed themselves in the midst of the city.

33 And Issachar and Naphtali that remained under the wall approached and broke the gates of the city, and kindled a fire at the gates of the city, that the iron melted, and all the sons of Jacob came into the city, they and all their men, and they fought with the inhabitants of the city of Sarton, and smote them with the edge of the sword, and no man stood up before them.

34 And about two hundred men fled from the city, and they all went and hid themselves in a certain tower in the city, and Judah pursued them to the tower, and he broke down the tower, which fell upon the men, and they all died.

35 And the sons of Jacob went up the road of the roof of that tower, and they saw, and behold there was another strong and high tower at a distance in the city, and the top of it reached to heaven, and the sons of Jacob hastened and descended, and went with all their men to that tower, and found it filled with about three hundred men, women and little ones.

36 And the sons of Jacob smote a great smiting amongst those men in the tower and they ran away and fled from them.

37 And Simeon and Levi pursued them, when twelve mighty and valiant men came out to them from the place where they had concealed themselves.

38 And those twelve men maintained a strong battle against Simeon and Levi, and Simeon and Levi could not prevail over them, and those valiant men broke the shields of Simeon and Levi, and one of them struck at Levi's head with his sword, when Levi hastily placed his hand

to his head, for he was afraid of the sword, and the sword struck Levi's hand, and it wanted but little to the hand of Levi being cut off.

39 And Levi seized the sword of the valiant man in his hand, and took it forcibly from the man, and with it he struck at the head of the powerful man, and he severed his head.

40 And eleven men approached to fight with Levi, for they saw that one of them was killed, and the sons of Jacob fought, but the sons of Jacob could not prevail over them, for those men were very powerful.

41 And the sons of Jacob seeing that they could not prevail over them, Simeon gave a loud and tremendous shriek, and the eleven powerful men were stunned at the voice of Simeon's shrieking.

42 And Judah at a distance knew the voice of Simeon's shouting, and Naphtali and Judah ran with their shields to Simeon and Levi, and found them fighting with those powerful men, unable to prevail over them as their shields were broken.

43 And Naphtali saw that the shields of Simeon and Levi were broken, and he took two shields from his servants and brought them to Simeon and Levi.

44 And Simeon, Levi and Judah on that day fought all three against the eleven mighty men until the time of sunset, but they could not prevail over them.

45 And this was told unto Jacob, and he was sorely grieved, and he prayed unto the Lord, and he and Naphtali his son went against these mighty men.

46 And Jacob approached and drew his bow, and came nigh unto the mighty men, and slew three of their men with the bow, and the remaining eight turned back, and behold, the war waged against them in the front and rear, and they were greatly afraid of their lives, and could not stand before the sons of Jacob, and they fled from before them.

47 And in their flight, they met Dan and Asher coming toward them, and they suddenly fell upon them, and fought with them, and slew two of them, and Judah and his brothers pursued them, and smote the remainder of them, and slew them.

48 And all the sons of Jacob returned and walked about the city, searching if they could find any men, and they found about twenty young men in a cave in the city, and Gad and Asher smote them all, and Dan and Naphtali lighted upon the rest of the men who had fled and escaped from the second tower, and they smote them all.

49 And the sons of Jacob smote all the inhabitants of the city of Sarton, but the women and little ones they left in the city and did not slay them.

50 And all the inhabitants of the city of Sarton were powerful men, one of them would pursue a thousand, and two of them would not flee from ten thousand of the rest of men.

51 And the sons of Jacob slew all the inhabitants of the city of Sarton with the edge of the sword, that no man stood up against them, and they left the women in the city.

52 And the sons of Jacob took all the spoil of the city, and captured what they desired, and they took flocks and herds and property from the city, and the sons of Jacob did unto Sarton and its inhabitants as they had done to Chazar and its inhabitants, and they turned and went away.

Chapter 39

1 And when the sons of Jacob went from the city of Sarton, they had gone about two hundred cubits when they met the inhabitants of Tapnach coming toward them, for they went out to fight with them, because they had smitten the king of Tapnach and all his men.

2 So all that remained in the city of Tapnach came out to fight with the sons of Jacob, and they thought to retake from them the booty and the spoil which they had captured from Chazar and Sarton.

3 And the rest of the men of Tapnach fought with the sons of Jacob in that place, and the sons of Jacob smote them, and they fled before them, and they pursued them to the city of Arbelan, and they all fell before the sons of Jacob.

4 And the sons of Jacob returned and came to Tapnach, to take away the spoil of Tapnach, and when they came to Tapnach they heard that the people of Arbelan had gone out to meet them to save the spoil of their brethren, and the sons of Jacob left ten of their men in Tapnach to plunder the city, and they went out toward the people of Arbelan.

5 And the men of Arbelan went out with their wives to fight with the sons of Jacob, for their wives were experienced in battle, and they went out, about four hundred men and women.

6 And all the sons of Jacob shouted with a loud voice, and they all ran toward the inhabitants of Arbelan, and with a great and tremendous voice.

7 And the inhabitants of Arbelan heard the noise of the shouting of the sons of Jacob, and their roaring like the noise of lions and like the roaring of the sea and its waves.

8 And fear and terror possessed their hearts on account of the sons of Jacob, and they were terribly afraid of them, and they retreated and fled before them into the city, and the sons of Jacob pursued them to the gate of the city, and they came upon them in the city.

9 And the sons of Jacob fought with them in the city, and all their women were engaged in slinging against the sons of Jacob, and the combat was very severe amongst them the whole of that day till evening.

10 And the sons of Jacob could not prevail over them, and the sons of Jacob had almost perished in that battle, and the sons of Jacob cried unto the Lord and greatly gained strength toward evening, and the sons of Jacob smote all the inhabitants of Arbelan by the edge of the sword, men, women and little ones.

11 And also the remainder of the people who had fled from Sarton, the sons of Jacob smote them in Arbelan, and the sons of Jacob did unto Arbelan and Tapnach as they had done to Chazar and Sarton, and when the women saw that all the men were dead, they went upon the roofs of the city and smote the sons of Jacob by showering down stones like rain.

12 And the sons of Jacob hastened and came into the city and seized all the women and smote them with the edge of the sword, and the sons of Jacob captured all the spoil and booty, flocks and herds and cattle.

13 And the sons of Jacob did unto Machnaymah as they had done to Tapnach, to Chazar and to Shiloh, and they turned from there and went away.

14 And on the fifth day the sons of Jacob heard that the people of Gaash had gathered against them to battle, because they had slain their king and their captains, for there had been fourteen captains in the city of Gaash, and the sons of Jacob had slain them all in the first battle.

15 And the sons of Jacob that day girt on their weapons of war, and they marched to battle against the inhabitants of Gaash, and in Gaash there was a strong and mighty people of the people of the Amorites, and Gaash was the strongest and best fortified city of all the cities of the Amorites, and it had three walls.

16 And the sons of Jacob came to Gaash and they found the gates of the city locked, and about five hundred men standing at the top of the

outer-most wall, and a people numerous as the sand upon the sea shore were in ambush for the sons of Jacob from without the city at the rear thereof.

17 And the sons of Jacob approached to open the gates of the city, and whilst they were drawing nigh, behold those who were in ambush at the rear of the city came forth from their places and surrounded the sons of Jacob.

18 And the sons of Jacob were enclosed between the people of Gaash, and the battle was both to their front and rear, and all the men that were upon the wall, were casting from the wall upon them, arrows and stones.

19 And Judah, seeing that the men of Gaash were getting too heavy for them, gave a most piercing and tremendous shriek and all the men of Gaash were terrified at the voice of Judah's cry, and men fell from the wall at his powerful shriek, and all those that were from without and within the city were greatly afraid of their lives.

20 And the sons of Jacob still came nigh to break the doors of the city, when the men of Gaash threw stones and arrows upon them from the top of the wall and made them flee from the gate.

21 And the sons of Jacob returned against the men of Gaash who were with them from without the city, and they smote them terribly, as striking against gourds, and they could not stand against the sons of Jacob, for fright and terror had seized them at the shriek of Judah.

22 And the sons of Jacob slew all those men who were without the city, and the sons of Jacob still drew nigh to effect an entrance into the city, and to fight under the city walls, but they could not for all the inhabitants of Gaash who remained in the city had surrounded the walls of Gaash in every direction, so that the sons of Jacob were unable to approach the city to fight with them.

23 And the sons of Jacob came nigh to one corner to fight under the wall, the inhabitants of Gaash threw arrows and stones upon them like showers of rain, and they fled from under the wall.

24 And the people of Gaash who were upon the wall, seeing that the sons of Jacob could not prevail over them from under the wall, reproached the sons of Jacob in these words, saying,

25 What is the matter with you in the battle that you cannot prevail? can you then do unto the mighty city of Gaash and its inhabitants as you did to the cities of the Amorites that were not so powerful? Surely to those weak ones amongst us you did those things, and slew them in the entrance of the city, for they had no strength when they were terrified at the sound of your shouting.

26 And will you now then be able to fight in this place? Surely here you will all die, and we will avenge the cause of those cities that you have laid waste.

27 And the inhabitants of Gaash greatly reproached the sons of Jacob and reviled them with their gods and continued to cast arrows and stones upon them from the wall.

28 And Judah and his brothers heard the words of the inhabitants of Gaash and their anger was greatly roused, and Judah was jealous of his God in this matter, and he called out and said, O Lord, help, send help to us and our brothers.

29 And he ran at a distance with all his might, with his drawn sword in his hand, and he sprang from the earth and by dint of his strength, mounted the wall, and his sword fell from his hand.

30 And Judah shouted upon the wall, and all the men that were upon the wall were terrified, and some of them fell from the wall into the city and died, and those who were yet upon the wall, when they saw Judah's strength, they were greatly afraid and fled for their lives into the city for safety.

31 And some were emboldened to fight with Judah upon the wall, and they came nigh to slay him when they saw there was no sword in Judah's hand, and they thought of casting him from the wall to his brothers, and twenty men of the city came up to assist them, and they

surrounded Judah and they all shouted over him, and approached him with drawn swords, and they terrified Judah, and Judah cried out to his brothers from the wall.

32 And Jacob and his sons drew the bow from under the wall, and smote three of the men that were upon the top of the wall, and Judah continued to cry and he exclaimed, O Lord help us, O Lord deliver us, and he cried out with a loud voice upon the wall, and the cry was heard at a great distance.

33 And after this cry he again repeated to shout, and all the men who surrounded Judah on the top of the wall were terrified, and they each threw his sword from his hand at the sound of Judah's shouting and his tremor and fled.

34 And Judah took the swords which had fallen from their hands, and Judah fought with them and slew twenty of their men upon the wall.

35 And about eighty men and women still ascended the wall from the city, and they all surrounded Judah, and the Lord impressed the fear of Judah in their hearts, that they were unable to approach him.

36 And Jacob and all who were with him drew the bow from under the wall, and they slew ten men upon the wall, and they fell below the wall, before Jacob and his sons.

37 And the people upon the wall seeing that twenty of their men had fallen, they still ran toward Judah with drawn swords, but they could not approach him for they were greatly terrified at Judah's strength.

38 And one of their mighty men whose name was Arud approached to strike Judah upon the head with his sword, when Judah hastily put his shield to his head, and the sword hit the shield, and it was split in two.

39 And this mighty man after he had struck Judah ran for his life, at the fear of Judah, and his feet slipped upon the wall and he fell amongst the sons of Jacob who were below the wall, and the sons of Jacob smote him and slew him.

40 And Judah's head pained him from the blow of the powerful man, and Judah had nearly died from it.

41 And Judah cried out upon the wall owing to the pain produced by the blow, when Dan heard him, and his anger burned within him, and he also rose up and went at a distance and ran and sprang from the earth and mounted the wall with his wrath-excited strength.

42 And when Dan came upon the wall near unto Judah all the men upon the wall fled, who had stood against Judah, and they went up to the second wall, and they threw arrows and stones upon Dan and Judah from the second wall, and endeavoured to drive them from the wall.

43 And the arrows and stones struck Dan and Judah, and they had nearly been killed upon the wall, and wherever Dan and Judah fled from the wall, they were attacked with arrows and stones from the second wall.

44 And Jacob and his sons were still at the entrance of the city below the first wall, and they were not able to draw their bow against the inhabitants of the city, as they could not be seen by them, being upon the second wall.

45 And Dan and Judah when they could no longer bear the stones and arrows that fell upon them from the second wall, they both sprang upon the second wall near the people of the city, and when the people of the city who were upon the second wall saw that Dan and Judah had come to them upon the second wall, they all cried out and descended below between the walls.

46 And Jacob and his sons heard the noise of the shouting from the people of the city, and they were still at the entrance of the city, and they were anxious about Dan and Judah who were not seen by them, they are being upon the second wall.

47 And Naphtali went up with his wrath-excited might and sprang upon the first wall to see what caused the noise of shouting which they had heard in the city, and Issachar and Zebulun drew nigh to break the

doors of the city, and they opened the gates of the city and came into the city.

48 And Naphtali leaped from the first wall to the second, and came to assist his brothers, and the inhabitants of Gaash who were upon the wall, seeing that Naphtali was the third who had come up to assist his brothers, they all fled and descended into the city, and Jacob and all his sons and all their young men came into the city to them.

49 And Judah and Dan and Naphtali descended from the wall into the city and pursued the inhabitants of the city, and Simeon and Levi were from without the city and knew not that the gate was opened, and they went up from there to the wall and came down to their brothers into the city.

50 And the inhabitants of the city had all descended into the city, and the sons of Jacob came to them in different directions, and the battle waged against them from the front and the rear, and the sons of Jacob smote them terribly, and slew about twenty thousand of them men and women, not one of them could stand up against the sons of Jacob.

51 And the blood flowed plentifully in the city, and it was like a brook of water, and the blood flowed like a brook to the outer part of the city and reached the desert of Bethchorin.

52 And the people of Bethchorin saw at a distance the blood flowing from the city of Gaash, and about seventy men from amongst them ran to see the blood, and they came to the place where the blood was.

53 And they followed the track of the blood and came to the wall of the city of Gaash, and they saw the blood issue from the city, and they heard the voice of crying from the inhabitants of Gaash, for it ascended unto heaven, and the blood was continuing to flow abundantly like a brook of water.

54 And all the sons of Jacob were still smiting the inhabitants of Gaash, and were engaged in slaying them till evening, about twenty thousand men and women, and the people of Chorin said, Surely this is the work

of the Hebrews, for they are still carrying on war in all the cities of the Amorites.

55 And those people hastened and ran to Bethchorin, and each took his weapons of war, and they cried out to all the inhabitants of Bethchorin, who also girt on their weapons of war to go and fight with the sons of Jacob.

56 And when the sons of Jacob had done smiting the inhabitants of Gaash, they walked about the city to strip all the slain and coming in the innermost part of the city and farther on they met three very powerful men, and there was no sword in their hand.

57 And the sons of Jacob came up to the place where they were, and the powerful men ran away, and one of them had taken Zebulun, who he saw was a young lad and of short stature, and with his might dashed him to the ground.

58 And Jacob ran to him with his sword and Jacob smote him below his loins with the sword, and cut him in two, and the body fell upon Zebulun.

59 And the second one approached and seized Jacob to tell him to the ground, and Jacob turned to him and shouted to him, whilst Simeon and Levi ran and smote him on the hips with the sword and felled him to the ground.

60 And the powerful man rose up from the ground with wrath-excited might, and Judah came to him before he had gained his footing, and struck him upon the head with the sword, and his head was split, and he died.

61 And the third powerful man, seeing that his companions were killed, ran from before the sons of Jacob, and the sons of Jacob pursued him in the city; and whilst the powerful man was fleeing he found one of the swords of the inhabitants of the city, and he picked it up and turned to the sons of Jacob and fought them with that sword.

62 And the powerful man ran to Judah to strike him upon the head with the sword, and there was no shield in the hand of Judah; and whilst he was aiming to strike him, Naphtali hastily took his shield and put it to Judah's head, and the sword of the powerful man hit the shield of Naphtali and Judah escaped the sword.

63 And Simeon and Levi ran upon the powerful man with their swords and struck at him forcibly with their swords, and the two swords entered the body of the powerful man and divided it in two, lengthwise.

64 And the sons of Jacob smote the three mighty men at that time, together with all the inhabitants of Gaash, and the day was about to decline.

65 And the sons of Jacob walked about Gaash and took all the spoil of the city, even the little ones and women they did not suffer to live, and the sons of Jacob did unto Gaash as they had done to Sarton and Shiloh.

Chapter 40

1 And the sons of Jacob led away all the spoil of Gaash and went out of the city by night.

2 They were going out marching toward the castle of Bethchorin, and the inhabitants of Bethchorin were going to the castle to meet them, and on that night the sons of Jacob fought with the inhabitants of Bethchorin, in the castle of Bethchorin.

3 And all the inhabitants of Bethchorin were mighty men, one of them would not flee from before a thousand men, and they fought on that night upon the castle, and their shots were heard on that night from afar, and the earth quaked at their shouting.

4 And all the sons of Jacob were afraid of those men, as they were not accustomed to fight in the dark, and they were greatly confounded, and the sons of Jacob cried unto the Lord, saying, Give help to us O Lord, deliver us that we may not die by the hands of these uncircumcised men.

5 And the Lord hearkened to the voice of the sons of Jacob, and the Lord caused great terror and confusion to seize the people of Bethchorin, and they fought amongst themselves the one with the other in the darkness of night and smote each other in great numbers.

Comment:1: This happened many times in the Bible, where upon the prayers of His people, God confounded their enemies, and they started fighting among themselves in the confusion created by the Lord Himself. The following verse story is what happened when Gideon and only 300 men totally confounded their enemies who were innumerable in number, by creating a very loud noise at nigh time:

JDG.7:22 And the three hundred blew the trumpets, and the LORD set every man's sword against his fellow, even throughout all the host: and the host fled to Bethshittah in Zererath, and to the border of Abelmeholah, unto Tabbath.

6 And the sons of Jacob, knowing that the Lord had brought a spirit of perverseness amongst those men, and that they fought each man with his neighbour, went forth from among the bands of the people of Bethchorin and went as far as the descent of the castle of Bethchorin,

and farther, and they tarried there securely with their young men on that night.

7 And the people of Bethchorin fought the whole night, one man with his brother, and the other with his neighbor, and they cried out in every direction upon the castle, and their cry was heard at a distance, and the whole earth shook at their voice, for they were powerful above all the people of the earth.

8 And all the inhabitants of the cities of the Canaanites, the Hittites, the Amorites, the Hivites and all the kings of Canaan, and also those who were on the other side of the Jordan, heard the noise of the shouting on that night.

9 And they said, surely these are the battles of the Hebrews who are fighting against the seven cities, who came nigh unto them; and who can stand against those Hebrews?

10 And all the inhabitants of the cities of the Canaanites, and all those who were on the other side of the Jordan, were greatly afraid of the sons of Jacob, for they said, Behold the same will be done to us as was done to those cities, for who can stand against their mighty strength?

11 And the cries of the Chorinites were very great on that night and continued to increase; and they smote each other till morning, and numbers of them were killed.

12 And the morning appeared, and all the sons of Jacob rose up at daybreak and went up to the castle, and they smote those who remained of the Chorinites in a terrible manner, and they were all killed in the castle.

13 And the sixth day appeared, and all the inhabitants of Canaan saw at a distance all the people of Bethchorin lying dead in the castle of Bethchorin and strewed about as the carcasses of lambs and goats.

14 And the sons of Jacob led all the spoil which they had captured from Gaash and went to Bethchorin, and they found the city full of people

like the sand of the sea, and they fought with them, and the sons of Jacob smote them there till evening time.

15 And the sons of Jacob did unto Bethchorin as they had done to Gaash and Tapnach, and as they had done to Chazar, to Sarton and to Shiloh.

16 And the sons of Jacob took with them the spoil of Bethchorin and all the spoil of the cities, and on that day, they went home to Shechem.

17 And the sons of Jacob came home to the city of Shechem, and they remained without the city, and they then rested there from the war, and tarried there all night.

18 And all their servants together with all the spoil that they had taken from the cities, they left without the city, and they did not enter the city, for they said, Peradventure there may be yet more fighting against us, and they may come to besiege us in Shechem.

19 And Jacob and his sons and their servants remained on that night and the next day in the portion of the field which Jacob had purchased from Hamor for five shekels, and all that they had captured was with them.

20 And all the booty which the sons of Jacob had captured, was in the portion of the field, immense as the sand upon the seashore.

21 And the inhabitants of the land observed them from afar, and all the inhabitants of the land were afraid of the sons of Jacob who had done this thing, for no king from the days of old had ever done the like.

22 And the seven kings of the Canaanites resolved to make peace with the sons of Jacob, for they were greatly afraid of their lives, on account of the sons of Jacob.

23 And on that day, being the seventh day, Japhia king of Hebron sent secretly to the king of Ai, and to the king of Gibeon, and to the king of Shalem, and to the king of Adulam, and to the king of Lachish, and to the king of Chazar, and to all the Canaanitish kings who were under their subjection, saying,

24 Go up with me, and come to me that we may go to the sons of Jacob, and I will make peace with them, and form a treaty with them, lest all your lands be destroyed by the swords of the sons of Jacob, as they did to Shechem and the cities around it, as you have heard and seen.

25 And when you come to me, do not come with many men, but let every king bring his three head captains, and every captain bring three of his officers.

26 And come all of you to Hebron, and we will go together to the sons of Jacob and supplicate them that they shall form a treaty of peace with us.

27 And all those kings did as the king of Hebron had sent to them, for they were all under his counsel and command, and all the kings of Canaan assembled to go to the sons of Jacob, to make peace with them; and the sons of Jacob returned and went to the portion of the field that was in Shechem, for they did not put confidence in the kings of the land.

28 And the sons of Jacob returned and remained in the portion of the field ten days, and no one came to make war with them.

29 And when the sons of Jacob saw that there was no appearance of war, they all assembled and went to the city of Shechem, and the sons of Jacob remained in Shechem.

30 And at the expiration of forty days, all the kings of the Amorites assembled from all their places and came to Hebron, to Japhia, king of Hebron.

31 And the number of kings that came to Hebron, to make peace with the sons of Jacob, was twenty-one kings, and the number of captains that came with them was sixty-nine, and their men were one hundred and eighty-nine, and all these kings and their men rested by Mount Hebron.

32 And the king of Hebron went out with his three captains and nine men, and these kings resolved to go to the sons of Jacob to make peace.

33 And they said unto the king of Hebron, go thou before us with thy men, and speak for us unto the sons of Jacob, and we will come after thee and confirm thy words, and the king of Hebron did so.

34 And the sons of Jacob heard that all the kings of Canaan had gathered together and rested in Hebron, and the sons of Jacob sent four of their servants as spies, saying, Go and spy these kings, and search and examine their men whether they are few or many, and if they are but few in number, number them all and come back.

35 And the servants of Jacob went secretly to these kings, and did as the sons of Jacob had commanded them, and on that day they came back to the sons of Jacob, and said unto them, We came unto those kings, and they are but few in number, and we numbered them all, and behold, they were two hundred and eighty-eight, kings and men.

36 And the sons of Jacob said, They are but few in number, therefore we will not all go out to them; and in the morning the sons of Jacob rose up and chose sixty two of their men, and ten of the sons of Jacob went with them; and they girt on their weapons of war, for they said, They are coming to make war with us, for they knew not that they were coming to make peace with them.

37 And the sons of Jacob went with their servants to the gate of Shechem, toward those kings, and their father Jacob was with them.

38 And when they had come forth, behold, the king of Hebron and his three captains and nine men with him were coming along the road against the sons of Jacob, and the sons of Jacob lifted up their eyes, and saw at a distance Japhia, king of Hebron, with his captains, coming toward them, and the sons of Jacob took their stand at the place of the gate of Shechem, and did not proceed.

39 And the king of Hebron continued to advance, he and his captains, until he came nigh to the sons of Jacob, and he and his captains bowed down to them to the ground, and the king of Hebron sat with his captains before Jacob and his sons.

40 And the sons of Jacob said unto him, What has befallen thee, O king of Hebron? why hast thou come to us this day? what dost thou require from us? and the king of Hebron said unto Jacob, I beseech thee my lord, all the kings of the Canaanites have this day come to make peace with you.

41 And the sons of Jacob heard the words of the king of Hebron, and they would not consent to his proposals, for the sons of Jacob had no faith in him, for they imagined that the king of Hebron had spoken deceitfully to them.

42 And the king of Hebron knew from the words of the sons of Jacob, that they did not believe his words, and the king of Hebron approached nearer to Jacob, and said unto him, I beseech thee, my lord, to be assured that all these kings have come to you on peaceable terms, for they have not come with all their men, neither did they bring their weapons of war with them, for they have come to seek peace from my lord and his sons.

43 And the sons of Jacob answered the king of Hebron, saying, Send thou to all these kings, and if thou speakest truth unto us, let them each come singly before us, and if they come unto us unarmed, we shall then know that they seek peace from us.

44 And Japhia, king of Hebron, sent one of his men to the kings, and they all came before the sons of Jacob, and bowed down to them to the ground, and these kings sat before Jacob and his sons, and they spoke unto them, saying,

45 We have heard all that you did unto the kings of the Amorites with your sword and exceedingly mighty arm, so that no man could stand up before you, and we were afraid of you for the sake of our lives, lest it should befall us as it did to them.

46 So we have come unto you to form a treaty of peace between us, and now therefore contract with us a covenant of peace and truth, that you will not meddle with us, inasmuch as we have not meddled with you.

> 47 And the sons of Jacob knew that they had really come to seek peace from them, and the sons of Jacob listened to them, and formed a covenant with them.

C.2 This apparently was not to be a good idea, i.e. to make a covenant with these kings of the Canaanites

> 48 And the sons of Jacob swore unto them that they would not meddle with them, and all the kings of the Canaanites swore also to them, and the sons of Jacob made them tributary from that day forward.
>
> 49 And after this all the captains of these kings came with their men before Jacob, with presents in their hands for Jacob and his sons, and they bowed down to him to the ground.
>
> 50 And these kings then urged the sons of Jacob and begged of them to return all the spoil they had captured from the seven cities of the Amorites, and the sons of Jacob did so, and they returned all that they had captured, the women, the little ones, the cattle and all the spoil which they had taken, and they sent them off, and they went away each to his city.
>
> 51 And all these kings again bowed down to the sons of Jacob, and they sent or brought them many gifts in those days, and the sons of Jacob sent off these kings and their men, and they went peaceably away from them to their cities, and the sons of Jacob also returned to their home, to Shechem.
>
> 52 And there was peace from that day forward between the sons of Jacob and the kings of the Canaanites, until the children of Israel came to inherit the land of Canaan.

SUMMARY: WHY THE SLAUGHTER OF THE CANAANITES BY GOD'S PEOPLE?

C.3) It stated in this next chapter that Joseph was 17 years old when his brethren sold him into slavery. In this book of Jasher in chapter 43 verse 4, we hear Reuben stating about his brother Joseph 'The child is not there'. I am making this point because if Reuben considered his younger brother Joseph as a child, then how much more did the sons of Jacob consider their poor sister Dinah to be but a young child, who was only 12, when she was raped by Shechem. I think that they the sons of Jacob had every reason to be very angry and to have ended up destroying the city of Shechem.

C.4) Of course, Abraham had already prophesied that Israel would end up destroying the Canaanites. This was indeed by the hand of God Himself. The slaughter of the Canaanites just got started with the town of Shechem. When the kings of the Canaanites eventually came to fight with the sons of Jacob, many of their towns were destroyed and their inhabitants slaughtered.

C.5) Eventually the Canaanites realized that they couldn't defeat the sons of Jacob, as they were so strong and supernaturally empowered by God himself, so that they ended up making a peace pact with the sons of Jacob that lasted until Israel had become a nation and emerged from the captivity of Egypt.

C.6) After coming out of Egypt as the emerging nation of Israel, then, Israel started slaughtering the Canaanites again in the times of both Moses and Joshua, until they were made an end of.

C.7) Well that was the plan, but was it fully fulfilled?

C.8) Remember that the original reason why God had prophesied through Abraham that the Canaanites were to be driven out of the land was because the father of the Canaanites, Canaan, was told by his grandfather Noah not to take over the lands of Canaan as they were to belong to the Shemites. Also, the Canaanites brought forth Giants in the land because of them having Nephilim D.N.A.

PLEASE SEE 'JASHER INSIGHTS' BOOK II FOR THE CONCLUSION OF THIS BOOK AT AMAZON

SALVATION

JOH.3:36 He that believeth on the Son hath everlasting life: and he that believeth not the Son shall not see life; but the wrath of God abides on him.

Finally, I challenge you, that if you have not already prayed to receive Jesus into your heart, so that you can have eternal life, & be guaranteed a an eternal place in Heaven, then please do so immediately, to keep you safe from what is soon coming upon the earth!

Jesus stated in Revelations 3.20 "Behold, I stand at the door and knock, if any man hear my voice, and open the door, I will come into him and live with him and him with me".

"He who believes on the Son of God has eternal life." John 3.36. That means right now!

Once saved, you are eternally saved, and here is a very simple prayer to help you to get saved: -

"*Dear Jesus,*

Please come into my heart, forgive me all of my sins, give me eternal life, and fill me with your Holy Spirit. Please help me to love others and to read the Word of God in Jesus name, Amen.

Once you've prayed that little prayer sincerely, then you are guaranteed a wonderful future in Heaven for eternity with your creator and loved ones. "For God is Love" (1 John 4.16)

As I mentioned earlier in this book, your Salvation does not depend on you going to church, and your good works. Titus 3.5 states "Not by works of righteousness which we have done, but according to His mercy he saved us".

Your salvation only depends on receiving Christ as your saviour, not on church or religion!

(Steve: If I could get saved having been an atheist and an evolutionist whilst at university, then anyone can get saved! Just challenge God to prove He exists & ask Him into your heart! He will show up in your life & teach you the truth!) (John 14.6)

"He that comes unto Me I will in no wise cast out"- Jesus

Jesus explained that unless you become as a child you won't even understand the Kingdom of Heaven. (John 3.3)

MORE ON SALVATION: http://www.outofthebottomlesspit.co.uk/418605189

APPENDICES

I BACKGROUND INFORMATION ABOUT THE BOOK OF JASHER

'The **Book of Jasher'** is mentioned twice in the Bible. For this reason, a number of Bible teachers and others consider it to be as reliable and/or inspired as the Old Testament. Is this true?

Comment:1: I believe that there was an 'original' Book of Jasher which was probably an excellent book; but the copy that we have today has unfortunately been *altered to some extent*, although I would say that most of it is still inspired. The first mention of the Book of Jasher is in the Old Testament book of **Joshua 10.13**

JOS.10:13 And the sun stood still, and the moon stayed, until the people had avenged themselves upon their enemies. Is not this *written in the book of Jasher*? So, the sun stood still in the midst of heaven, and hasted not to go down about a whole day.

The second mention is in **2 Samuel 1:18**.

2SA.1:18 (Also he bade them teach the children of Judah the use of the bow: behold, it is *written in the book of Jasher*.)

C.2 Obviously from reading these scriptures from the Old Testament, it is clear that at one time there used to be a **Book of Jasher** that was reliable, otherwise it would not have been mentioned in both the time of Joshua and in the time of King David. As I mentioned in the Introduction of my 2nd Book **'Enoch Insights'** we *must not automatically throw out the Apocryphal Books* just because they are not perfect. Maybe they were excellent books at one time, but some powerful persons have altered the texts at some time or other.

In Conclusion, I would say that most of the Apocryphal books are largely accurate in content with a few mostly 'time discrepancies.

Unlike the Old Testament books, we have *no access to any manuscript of Jasher dating before 100 AD.*

Why that date? *Because the book we have is written in modern, square Hebrew characters without the vowel points.* The earliest manuscripts from this time are also missing the vowel points. *This points directly to Rabbi Akiba and his group's efforts to promote rabbinical leadership over Scripture.* His group, referred to as the Council of Jamnia, wanted to produce a foundation copy of the Scriptures as the original had been burned by the Romans when Jerusalem and the Temple were destroyed in 70AD. They made a number of *changes in the Scriptures* (which have come down to us as the *Masoretic Text*).'

C.3 It sounds to me, like this guy Rabbi Akiba in 100 A.D was very bitter because of the destruction of Israel in 70 A.D, in the which 100,000 Jews were crucified around Jerusalem alone, and millions driven out of the country in the famous 'Diaspora'. That was a direct fulfilment of a prophecy given by Jesus Himself 40 years earlier.

C.4 Jesus warned Israel that because they had rejected Him, as their Messiah, and that they had killed all the prophets that God had sent unto them, that *Israel would be destroyed.*

MAT.23:37 O Jerusalem, Jerusalem, thou that kills the prophets, and stones them which are sent unto thee, how often would I have gathered thy children together, even as a hen gathers her chickens under her wings, and ye would not!

MAT.23:38 Behold, your house is left unto you desolate.

C.5 The Romans came in their full might and fury in 70 AD, in the figure of general Titus, to destroy Israel completely. Normally, throughout history, when an emperor has done something like that, it is simply because that particular nation is being very difficult, rebellious & totally impossible to deal with, and this particular case, being stubbornly unwilling to submit to the Roman Rule. The same thing happened to Jerusalem in the time of Nebuchadnezzar and the Babylonian Empire, some 600 years earlier. It was much worse under the Romans though, as Israel ceased to be a nation for almost 2000 years until 1948.

C.6 What did Israel expect? They murdered their own Saviour Jesus Christ! It looks to me as if *God Himself allowed Israel to be severely judged*, and its people *cast out* for their *blatant rebellion against God Himself and His Son Jesus*. It was necessary for trials and tribulations to happen to the Messiah in order for Him to fulfil His mission on earth., but woe was unto them by whom the tribulations came. *Israel was itself annihilated* for almost 2000 years.

C.7 Apparently because Israel did get destroyed, this Rabbi Akiba obviously blamed Jesus and Christianity for the destruction of Israel and decided to try and eradicate all mention of Jesus in the Old Testament, by altering the Old Hebrew version of the Septuagint. He did this because Christians were using the Septuagint versions of the Old testament, to actually prove that Jesus was in fact mentioned in the Old Testament as the Messiah and prophesied about hundreds and even thousands of years before His actual birth on earth. Here are a couple of examples: **Isaiah 53** (whole chapter) and **Psalm 22:16.**

ISA.53:5 But he was *wounded* for our *transgressions*, he was *bruised* for our *iniquities*: the *chastisement* of *our peace* was *upon him*; and with *his stripes we are healed.*

C.8 I can't think of anyone, other than Jesus Christ himself, who could have fulfilled this Old testament verse in Isaiah written over 700 years before the birth of Christ!

PSA.22:16 For dogs have compassed me: the assembly of the wicked have enclosed me: they *pierced my hands and my feet.*

C.9 The discovery of the Dead Sea Scrolls really exposed this fake Masoretic text by clearly showing that the Septuagint version of the Old Testament is by far the most accurate, and that the Masoretic text had altered many scriptures.

SOURCE: https://theorthodoxlife.wordpress.com/2012/03/12/masoretic-text-vs-original-hebrew/

The Masoretic text has a different wording in Deuteronomy 32:43 and Psalm 40:6. In addition chapters 5 and 11 of Genesis have a much-shortened chronology. Therefore, given these and the other variations, it is a simple matter to determine if the text of a Scripture version is following that of the ancient (Septuagint LXX), used by the Apostles and Church fathers, or is following the Masoretic text which came about 400 years later. If the Bible text does not have the full chronology in Genesis 5 & 11, or the full rendering of Deuteronomy 32:43 or the correct wording for Psalm 40:6 (39:6), then it is *not following the ancient text*, but is from the *changed Masoretic text.*

C.10 The Bible is 100% accurate when it comes to the 'New Testament', but concerning the KJV of the Old Testament, which is translated from the Masoretic Text, and therefore some important things were altered, as those who devised the Masoretic text wanted to expunge all references to Jesus as mentioned in the Old Testament, as their position was anti-Christ. The only solution today in 2018 is for people to read the *Septuagint* versions of the *Old Testament* which was compiled much earlier than the infamous Masoretic text. The Septuagint was put together in around 300 BCE and the Masoretic text around 100 A.D http://www.ecclesia.org/truth/comparisons.html

C.11 Here is a website which offers the Septuagint Text alongside the King James version which I personally have found very useful: http://ecmarsh.com/lxx-kjv/

C.12 Is the real date today 5993? [See this story on my website which is taken from the APPENDIX of my other book **JUBILEES INSIGHTS**: http://www.outofthebottomlesspit.co.uk/413438217}

C.13 Is it true that it is 5993 years after Creation at this moment in this year of 2018 or is more likely around 650 years older at around 6643 years old? Find out with the following excellent thought-provoking video: https://youtu.be/VI1yRTC6kGE?t=4

▌▌ MORE BACKGROUND INFO INTO THE BOOK OF JASHER

The first mention of the Book of Jasher is in the Old Testament book of **Joshua 10.13.**

JOSH.10:13 And the sun stood still, and the moon stayed, until the people had avenged themselves upon their enemies. *Is not this written in the book of Jasher?* So, the sun stood still in the midst of heaven, and hasted not to go down about a whole day.

The second mention is in **2 Samuel 1:18**.

2SA.1:18 (Also he bade them teach the children of Judah the use of the bow: behold, it is *written in the book of Jasher*.)

Some writers minimize or make light of these two verses mentioned above, but with a deeper examination, one finds out *that these two verses* are the *perfect verses* to describe the Book of Jasher and I will now explain why:

'USE OF THE BOW'
In this Book of Jasher in Chapter 56 verses7-9 it states:

JASHER 56.7 And on the next day Jacob again called for his sons, and they all assembled and came to him and sat before him, and Jacob on that day blessed his sons before his death, each man did he bless according to his blessing; behold it is written in the book of the law of the Lord appertaining to Israel.

JASHER 56.8 And Jacob said unto Judah, I know my son that thou art a mighty man for thy brethren; reign over them, and thy sons shall reign over their sons forever.

JASHER 56.9 Only teach thy sons the bow and all the weapons of war, in order that they may fight the battles of their brother who will rule over his enemies.

C.1 The first important thing to notice is that Jacob the old Patriarch of Israel was on his deathbed and was giving his last 'Blessing' to his family.

Second: He chose Judah to be the *leader* over all of his brethren even though he wasn't the eldest. Judah from that time on (circa 1900 BC) became the leading tribe of Israel and eventually the Royal tribe from which proceeded the Kings of Judah & Israel.

Third: Let's examine the major events happening in 2SA.1:18 (Also he bade them teach the children of Judah the use of the bow: behold, it is *written in the book of Jasher)*. This verse unlike the other verses in this chapter is in (brackets), as though the Old Testament writers are pausing for a moment, to *interject the importance of the Book of Jasher* although the content of the verse does not *seem to have anything to do with the other verses around it:*

2SA.1:17 And David lamented with this lamentation over Saul and over Jonathan his son:

2SA.1:18 (Also he bade them teach the children of Judah the use of the bow: behold, it is written in the book of Jasher.)

2SA.1:19 The beauty of Israel is slain upon thy high places: how are the mighty fallen!

C.2 King David later went on to capture Jerusalem and made it his own capital city.

2SA.5:7 Nevertheless David took the strong hold of Zion: the same is the city of David

1CH.11:4,7 And David and all Israel went to Jerusalem; And David dwelt in the castle; therefore, they called it the city of David.

C.3 What is the link between 'Use of the Bow' & Leadership?

REV.6:2 And I saw and behold a white horse: and he that sat on him had a bow; and a crown was given unto him: and he went forth conquering, and to conquer.

C.4 Fourth: Let's look at:

JOSH.10:13 'And the sun stood still, and the moon stayed, until the people had avenged themselves upon their enemies. Is not this *written in the book of Jasher*? So, the sun stood still in the midst of heaven, and hasted not to go down about a whole day'.

C.5 Both of the verses mentioning the Book of Jasher are in effect pointing to the importance of *Warrior Kings* starting with Jacob, then Judah not to mention Joshua. Then the capital *Jerusalem* conquered by 'Warrior King' David

IN CONCLUSION: WHY WERE THESE PARTICULAR TWO BIBLE VERSES THAT MENTION THE BOOK OF JASHER SO IMPORTANT?

C.6 Both verses occurred at *very critical times* in Ancient Israel's History. At actual turning points that would decide the very future of the nation of Israel.

In **Joshua 10.13** a decisive battle was occurring, and Joshua asked God to do a miracle and cause the Sun to stand still over Gibeon. He did this so that he would have enough time to defeat his enemies before the sun would have set.

2SA.1:18 In the story about David, it was when King Saul and his sons were killed in battle & just before David was made King.

C.7 The implication from the two verses mentioning the Book of Jasher in the Bible is for all to read the Book of Jasher as it talks about the beginning and fulfilment of Israel in History all the way to the founding of the city of Jerusalem in King David's time. Jerusalem is also to be the capital of the King of Kings in the future. So, in effect those two verses with the relevant verses in the Book of Jasher paint the picture of God's promises to Abraham fulfilled in Jacob, Judah, Jerusalem as Israel's capital city, & eventually the Coming of Jesus (King of Kings) & New Jerusalem. As Jesus said about Himself, I am the Alpha and the Omega.

C.8 The two verses mentioning the Book of Jasher are doing exactly that: pointing to the beginning and fulfilment of Israel as God's people and nation.

C.9 Those reading those verses in the Bible about the Book of Joshua and taking the time to research the Book of Jasher would end up reading Chapter

56 verses7-9 to get the point that Jacob on his deathbed was fulfilling the promises made to his grand-father Abraham and Isaac by choosing Judah to be the Warrior King and leader of his brethren but much more importantly that *Judah* was to be the most important *Leadership* tribe of the Kings of Israel

III NUMEROLOGY

THE IMPORTANCE OF THE LETTER J AS IN FOUND IN BOTH LEADERSHIP & WARRIOR KINGS.

C.1 The first leader mentioned in the Bible with a name beginning a J was Jared. 'For in his days the fallen angels descended upon the earth'. Jared was also the father of the great patriarch Enoch. Enoch became a King of Kings, where according to this Book of Jasher, all the Kings of the earth were afraid of him for his Godly aura and were obedient to him. So much of that Evil was kept in check whilst Enoch lived. Enoch was in a sense the 1st Warrior King. (The greatest Pre-Flood spiritual Warrior)

THE LETTER J HOWEVER DID NOT EXIST IN OLD HEBREW.

C.2 The letter J was invented by the Romans. However, it is *God who designs languages and letters*, and it is truly amazing that the tenth letter in the modern English language has such significance.

BIBLE NUMEROLOGY

C.3 The letter J is the 10th letter in the modern English Alphabet. The number 10 in Biblical numerology stands for leadership.

In the Bible, the number 10 is used 242 times. The designation "10th" is used 79 times. Ten is also *viewed as a complete and perfect number*, as is *3,* 7 and 12. It is made up of 4, the number of the physical creation, and 6, the number of man. As such, it signifies testimony, law, responsibility (leadership) and the completeness of order. <SOURCE: http://www.biblestudy.org/bibleref/mean-ing-of-numbers-in-bible/10.html>

THE FOLLOWING NAMES IN 'ENGLISH' ALL BEGIN WITH A J

C.4

JEHOVAH (Name of God)

JAWEH (Jewish Name of God)

JARED (Father of Enoch who was a King of Kings and a great Spiritual Warrior)

JACOB (Patriarch and Warrior)

JUDAH (Appointed to be leader over his brethren)

JEW (To lead people to the one true God)

JOSHUA (Warrior King)

JASHER (Book of Warrior Kings and leaders)

JUDGES (Book of Warrior leaders such as Samson)

JERUSALEM (Captured by 'WARRIOR KING' David)

JONATHAN (Prince, mighty warrior & close friend of King David)

JOSIAH (Good king of Judah)

JEHOSOPHAT (Good king of Judah)

JEREMIAH (Major prophet of Warning & JUDGEMENT)

JESUS (SAVIOUR & WARRIOR KING- JUSTICE-JUDGEMENT-JOY- for TRUE saved JEWS)

JOHN (BOOK OF REVELATIONS – Judgement & The 2nd Coming of Christ-New Heaven New Earth)

JERUSALEM (NEW) The Heavenly City.

IV Certainly, many serious scholars have concluded that this Book of Jasher is authentic. The well-known Hebraist and Rabbinic Scholar (and translator of the 1840 Book of Jasher) Moses Samuel wrote of Jasher: "...the book is, with the exception of some doubtful parts, a venerable monument of antiquity; and that, notwithstanding some few additions have been made to it in comparatively modern times, it still retains sufficient to prove it a copy of the book referred to in Joshua, Ch. x, and 2 Samuel, Ch. 1." - Moses Samuel - Hebraist and Rabbinic Scholar And my old friend and mentor, the late Dr Cyrus Gordon (who was the world's leading Semitist until his death) said: "There can be little doubt that the book of Jasher was a national epic... The time is ripe for a fresh investigation of such genuine sources of Scripture, particularly against the background of the Dead Sea Scrolls." - Dr Cyrus Gordon

SOURCE: http://nazarenespace.ning.com/group/bookofjasher

V THE BOOK OF JASHER

"The Book of Jasher," rendered in the LXX (Septuagint). "The Book of the *Upright One,*" by the Vulgate "The Book of Just Ones," was probably a kind of national sacred songbook, a collection of songs in praise of the heroes of Israel, a "Book of golden deeds," a national anthology. We have only two specimens from the book, (1) the words of Joshua which he spake to the Lord at the crisis of the battle of Beth-horon (Joshua 10:12 Joshua 10:13); and (2) "the Song of the Bow," that beautiful and touching mournful elegy which David composed on the occasion of the death of Saul and Jonathan (2 Samuel 1:18-27).

C.1 Author of 'Jasher Insights': I would like to add that the Book of Jasher is *not* mentioned in the Septuagint version of Joshua 10:12 &13. In 2 Samuel 1:18-27 of the Septuagint the Book of Jasher is also *not* mentioned but only a reference to the 'Book of Right'.

SOURCE: (https://www.biblestudytools.com/dictionary/jasher/)

VI LAND OF NOD:

DEFINITIONS: https://en.wikipedia.org/wiki/Land_of_Nod

HOLLOW EARTH: WAS THE LAND OF NOD HELL? OR THE BEGINNING OF IT?

http://www.echoesofenoch.com/a_hollow_earth.htm

NAZI RELATIVES? CAIN'S DESCENDANTS!

INNER EARTH: If Nod is east of Eden and Eden is inside the earth...that means Nod is inside the earth too? Gen 4:11-16, "And now art thou cursed *from* the earth, which hath opened up her mouth to receive thy brother's blood from thy hand. When thou till the ground, it shall not henceforth yield unto thee her strength; a fugitive and a vagabond shalt thou be 'In the earth'. And Cain said unto the Lord, my punishment is greater than I can bear. Behold, thou hast driven me this day from the face (surface) of the earth; and I shall be a fugitive and a vagabond in the earth; and it shall come to pass, that every one that finds me shall slay me. And the Lord said unto him, Therefore, whosoever slays Cain, vengeance shall be taken on him sevenfold, and the Lord set a mark upon Cain, lest any finding him should kill him. And Cain went out from the presence of the Lord, and dwelt in the land of Nod, East of Eden."

It is interesting to note that in the many translations of the Bible, only the older English versions the King James and the American Standard use the translation "in the earth". All of the more recent translations simply say, "on the earth". A big liberty of translation placed upon God's word because of the assumption that the earth is solid and therefore could not contain life inside. The only other translation I am aware of that agrees with the older versions is the Torah. This is the Old Testament translated into the English by the Jews themselves! Regardless of this compromise of interpretation, from prior scriptures the Bible clearly establishes that Eden or Paradise and Hell are two separate chambers inside the earth. With that firmly established, (at least according to the Bible itself) the only word that could be used in context is "*in*"!

CAIN WAS REMOVED FROM THE SURFACE OF THE EARTH INTO A SUBTERRANEAN REALM. He was given a " mark" that he would not be killed by others. This Hebrew word *owth* means an identifying mark in the sense of an agreement. When translated into the Greek, the word used is *semion,* in the sense of a supernatural sign of some type. When Cain killed Abel, it was in the "process of time" this actually means in the last days. This would be referring to a time just prior to the great flood. The soil not yielding her strength may not mean an agricultural problem, but rather a genetic defect of some type. Soil, seed land and fruit have always, in the

337

scriptures been used to refer to the literal geographical elements, spiritual conditions or physical bloodline. Cain's bloodline may be the seed of the serpent mentioned in Gen 3. Cain was a bad guy. The Bible says so.

I Jn 3:12 "Not as Cain, who was of that wicked one,"

In context here this statement about Cain can mean more than the fact he was of the wicked one because he committed murder. It might also imply he was actually from the wicked one. It was in his blood. This was the same lineage Goliath came from, he was a big white guy with a bad attitude! The word Giant has another meaning as a tyrant or bully and can mean much more than physical stature. The Physical stature although is clearly defined in the OT. Numbers 13:33, Deu2:11, 20, 3:11,13 Josh 12:4, 13:12,15:8,17:15 and18:16.

As strange as this all sounds the Bible stands true upon itself. The worldwide legends of "white" tribes and ascended "masters" may not be myth at all but the continual encounters with a race from within. The search by Hitler and the Nazi's for blood relations from an inner earth may have a thread of truth. If Hitler came to his own to proclaim Satan's seed, in the same but opposite pattern, it could mean that the modern-day Philistines may be the Germanic lineage. Now not to condemn anyone by their race or national bloodline, I must say I am a Caucasian of Germanic descent and I love the Lord! God has made a provision for salvation that is no longer based on anything but faith. In Isaiah 14 there is an end time prophecy that indicates a genetic tampering involving the Philistines and a tribe used to punish them continually, this would be the tribe of Dan. This genetic tampering started with Nazi Germany and is continued in America.

VII CAIN

Cain was also viewed as a type of 'utter perverseness', an 'offspring of Satan', "a son of wrath", 'a lawless rebel' who said, "There is neither a divine judgment nor a judge", whose words of repentance were insincere whose fleeing from God was a denial of His omnipresence (and all his generations must be exterminated "the desire of the spirit of sin" He is the first of those who have no share in the world to come

GENERATIONS OF CAIN

The seven generations of Cain, as the brood of Satan, are accordingly represented as types of rebels .While the pious men all descended from Seth, there sprang from Cain all the wicked ones who rebelled against God and whose perverseness and corruption brought on the flood: they committed all abominations and incestuous crimes in public without shame. The daughters of Cain were those "fair daughters of men" who by their lasciviousness caused the fall of the "sons of God"., but were attracted by the gay and sensuous mode of life in which the children of Cain indulged; the latter spending their days at the foot of the mountain, in wild orgies, accompanied by the music of instruments invented by Jubal, and by women, in gorgeous attire, seducing the men to commit the most abominable practises. Also speaks of the excessive wickedness of the posterity of Cain, which grew in vehemence with every generation; while the posterity of Seth remained virtuous during seven generations, after which the fall of the angels ensued who produced gigantic offspring in making love with the women on earth. The antidomestic pagan Gnostics declared Cain and other rebels or sinners to be their prototypes of evil and licentiousness.

Cain, Esau, Korah, the Sodomites, and even Judas Iscariot, were made by these Gnostics expounders of the "wisdom" of the serpent in rebellion against God. **SOURCE:** http://www.jewishencyclopedia.com/articles/3904-cain

CONCLUSION about THE CAINITE DOCTRINE

C.1 It would appear that, once God banished Cain, and sent him to the Land of Nod, (Nod means sleep or delusions), that there he sought to do everything in direct rebellion to God. For example, if God's law said one thing, then Cain sought to do the exact opposite, being an actual son of Satan himself. The Cainite women, or descendants of Cain, are the ones who attracted the Fallen Angels some centuries after Cain's 'Fall from Grace'.

C.2 CAINITE ORGIES: Cainites were known to have orgies with women in public, flaunting it. They were the origin of lustfulness and licentiousness. They would also pillage their neighbours bringing random disorder instead of order.

C.3 REBELLION: Every law of God, Cain and his descendants 'tore apart' and deliberately 'did the exact opposite', exactly as one would expect a demon or devil to do, which Cain was. In Cain's time him being a physical being he was not restricted. With the Judgement of the Great Flood more restrictions were put on both men and demons to limit total anarchy & random disorder. Even more restrictions were put on Satan and his Fallen angels after the destruction of the tower of Babel. After Babel we saw 6 empires of man that were much better organized and had less chaos. So, has it been since the Tower of Babel until now that there has been 'Law & Order' of some sort at least?

SATAN'S EMPIRES: 1) EGYPT 2) ASSYRIA 3) BABYLON 4) MEDIO-PERSIA 5) GREECE 6) ROME 7) COMING NEW WORLD ORDER-ANTI-CHRIST

C.4 Maybe God Himself prefers even the Devil himself ruling the planet earth for the time being through his governments and World Empires, rather than the Total Chaos that developed during the hundreds of years prior to the Great Flood. Total chaos and *unrest* will return in the time period known as the Last Days or during the last days of the Great Tribulation just before Christ Returns for the Rapture of all of the Saved on the planet.

339

CAIN - A FORE-RUNNER OF THE ANTI-CHRIST

C.5 Cain was literally an 'In the flesh Demon' as he was a son of Satan born through Eve. This is exactly how the coming infamous Anti-Christ will be. Just like Cain seeking to destroy all the laws of God and thus to abolish all religions with his eventual aim to cause all the inhabitants on earth to worship him - the Devil himself, in the flesh of the Anti-Christ.

VIII LUCIFER & THE FALLEN ANGELS

THE FALL OF SATAN & 1/3 OF THE ANGELS OF GOD.

C.1 Many of us have written about the Fallen angels and even Lucifer's Fall, but with this little essay, I would like to put certain things into perspective.

C.2 In studying ancient history at length and in particular Bible history from pre-Flood times until the time of Christ. Then moving on through the 20 centuries since… In fact, in examining the pre-Flood times, along with the immediate post-flood times and the tower of Babel. then moving on to the first world empire of mankind: the Egyptian dynasties & the Assyrian empire then the Babylonian empire - the Medio Persian empire - the Greek empire -the Roman empire - the last 2000 year - the coming world empire of the Anti-Christ - the following becomes apparent:

1) The forces of evil had more freedom before the Great Flood

2) God severely restricted the Forces of Evil after the Great Flood

3) After the Tower of Babel both Satan and his Fallen angels as well as mankind were all even more restricted as to what would now be permitted.

4) It is my conviction that right after the Tower of Babel, that God Himself called Satan onto the carpet before His throne and gave him a good tongue-lashing and stated to Satan: 'From now on I will not permit the *random*

chaos that you Lucifer and your roaming band of fallen angels have committed both on the earth and in the heavenlies (More on this later). From now on you must become a 'Law and Order' enforcer. This could also be when Satan became the *'Accuser of the Saints'* by twisting the law or at least trying to do so.

5) How have I come to this conclusion?

Well, look at the 6 World empires that followed the Towel of Babel. What was very different about their organization? Notice that the way the rulers went about doing things was somehow very different and much more organized and disciplined. Generally speaking, there was no longer the random chaos and the restless spirit that existed in pre-Flood times and that had even come back to some extent at the time of the Tower of Babel. Why? Because of the 'Return of the Nephilim'!

6) It is clear that Satan and his Powers have been somewhat held back and restricted to some degree ever since.

7) We do know that one day 'random chaos' will indeed return, but probably not until all light of God's Spirit has left the planet temporarily, at the very end of the Great Tribulation, and the Rapture of all of the saved.

8) The famous oriental prophet Avak stated that the original creation made by God was destroyed by Lucifer when he first rebelled. Then God re-created order out of the chaos that Lucifer had made. Some state that this is clearly shown in **Genesis 1.1** and **1.2**

GEN.1:1 In the beginning God created the heaven and the earth.

GEN.1:2 And the earth was without form, and void; and darkness was upon the face of the deep. And the Spirit of God moved upon the face of the waters.

9) What other writers have stated is that perhaps something happened between these two verses. Could that be? That first there was the Creation - then Chaos brought about by Satan - then Re-Creation by God Himself?

10) In spite of Satan's having tried relentlessly to defeat God's plan of Salvation by trying to insert Satan's Seed from the very beginning of Creation as in Cain and later in the seed of his Fallen Angels into humanity, & then for the millennia leading up to the coming of Jesus the Messiah – Satan failed miserably, although he got pretty close to destroying all of God's Creation when only Noah and his 3 sons and their wives were found righteous and survived the Great Flood judgement by God Himself.

11) SATAN IS THE ACCUSER. First, he tempted Fallen angels to Fall and then Adam and Eve and then the descendants of Cain and soon there was total chaos within a few hundred years of Enoch having been translated.

REV.12:9 And the great dragon was cast out, that old serpent, called the Devil, and Satan, which deceiveth the whole world: he was cast out into the earth, and his angels were cast out with him.

REV.12:10 And I heard a loud voice saying in heaven, Now is come salvation, and strength, and the kingdom of our God, and the power of his Christ: for the accuser of our brethren is cast down, which accused them before our God day and night.

C.3 SATAN IS SUCH A TWISTED TRICKSTER! First, he tempts people. Then when they do the wrong thing – he goes to the Courts of heaven acting as the Prosecuting Lawyer and accuses people before the throne of God. He then tells God that He must condemn mankind and judge them. We know from the Book of Job that God even uses the Devil himself to carry out some of His Judgements. At other times He uses His own angels to carry out Judgments:

JOB.1:6 Now there was a day when the sons of God came to present themselves before the LORD, and Satan came also among them.

JOB.1:7 And the LORD said unto Satan, Whence comest thou? Then Satan answered the LORD, and said, From going to and fro in the earth, and from walking up and down in it.

341

JOB.1:8 And the LORD said unto Satan, Hast thou considered my servant Job, that there is none like him in the earth, a perfect and an upright man, one that feareth God, and escheweth evil?

JOB.1:9 Then Satan answered the LORD, and said, Doth Job fear God for nought?

JOB.1:10 Hast not thou made an hedge about him, and about his house, and about all that he hath on every side? thou hast blessed the work of his hands, and his substance is increased in the land.

JOB.1:11 But put forth thine hand now, and touch all that he hath, and he will curse thee to thy face.

JOB.1:12 And the LORD said unto Satan, Behold, all that he hath is in thy power; only upon himself put not forth thine hand. So, Satan went forth from the presence of the LORD.

12) **THE BIGGER PICTURE**: There is a lot of evidence that at one time Lucifer and his marauding Fallen angels had access to far away galaxies and other planets and even other dimensions. There is however also evidence that Satan and his Rebellious Band of Fallen angels are currently being restricted more and more.

The picture is that eventually Satan and all of his Fallen angels and resultant many entities will all soon be locked-up in the Bottomless Pit. Eventually they will be cast into the Lake of Fire unless they repent.

12) **EVIDENCE of VISITATION TO OTHER PLANETS**: There are pyramids on Mars that are even bigger than the ones on earth and many claims that they are actually Stargates or dimensional Gateways. There is apparently even a massive Sphinx on Mars, which is over one mile wide – but now abandoned. There is evidence of very tall buildings on the far side of the moon. There are also structures on the moons of Saturn. So tall as to be seen from earth! Who built them? When were they built?

13) The Fallen Angels also apparently long to 'bring back' the so-called 'Golden Age' of the 'Times Before the Flood'- when '*They*' reigned supreme – at least 'over mankind'. Well it might have been the golden age of Atlantis, Lemuria, & the Kingdom of Mu, run by both Fallen angels and their sons the Giants and other hybrids. That is both chimeras and monsters, but the fact is that it was hell on earth for the human inhabitants who were made into slaves and sometimes literally devoured.

14) There is ample evidence that in the times just before the Great Flood that ancient civilizations-built cities under the ground in order to protect themselves from so many hybrid creatures and devouring monsters.

15) It has been noted that God originally only created the animals on earth to be *herbivores* and not *meat-eaters,* so where did the carnivore dinosaurs enter the picture? It has been mentioned on Steve Quayle's website, (and he being an expert in the field of the Giants), that possibly in Pre-Flood times, the Fallen angels, being in total rebellion against God, made the reptilian

dinosaurs, as ferocious meat-eaters in order to try and get rid of many of mankind as possible. Remember Satan's whole goal from the beginning of time has been to totally destroy all of God's Creation, including mankind.

THE GOOD NEWS IS THAT SATAN CANNOT DO ANYTHING TOO DE-STRUCTIVE WITHOUT PERMISSION FROM GOD.

16) The Forces of Evil are actually presently largely held back from their destructive purposes until it is the TIME of the END. There is so much evidence of this.

2TH.2:7 For the mystery of iniquity doth already work: only he (Angel of God) who now letteth (prevents) will let (prevent), until he be taken out of the way.

2TH.2:8 And then shall that Wicked be revealed,(Satan in the Flesh -The Anti-Christ along with his band of Fallen Angels), whom the Lord shall consume with the spirit of his mouth, and shall destroy with the brightness of his coming:

'NUCLEAR MISSILE SILOS' PREVENTED FROM FIRING 'HYGROGEN BOMB' MISSILES BY U.F.O's

The Militaries of both the USA and Russia tell us that when upon occasion they have been tempted to order the use of their nuclear big atomic and hydrogen bombs - that immediately UFO's showed up at the missile silos and prevented them for firing the missiles!

THE DEVIL HIMSELF CAN DO NOTHING REALLY TERRIBLE UNLESS HE IS PERMITTED TO DO SO BY GOD HIMSELF!

17) Contrary to what is pushed by Hellywood (Hollywood) and the Satanic agenda of the elite, Evil might appear at present to be winning and getting the upper hand, but it is only allowed by God himself to fulfil a much great purpose – To test those on earth.

REV.3:10 Because thou hast kept the word of my patience, I also will keep thee from the hour of temptation (The Great Tribulation), which shall come upon all the world, to try them that dwell upon the earth.

Those on Earth are being tested to see whom they will follow – the truth – Jesus – the Word of God or swallow the lies of Satan such as Evolution, Global Warming, and the 'dog eat dog' ways of materialism, modernism and unbelief as well as the great deception yet to come: Disclosure!

18) What is *Disclosure*? It is the idea that one day soon Aliens will appear in the heavens in UFO's to declare that 'They' 'seeded mankind' on the planet some millions of years ago, and have now come back to help us 'evolve into the next stage' - some crazy hybrids of aliens and humans. it sounds like more human abductions & alterations.

19) The truth of Disclosure is that it the same thing happening all over again: the return of the fallen angels & the Nephilim now masquerading as aliens

from distant stars. They will again try to rule over the earth as in the original golden age of Atlantis such as before the great flood. According to the Bible their leader the hybrid Anti-Christ will control all peoples on the face of the earth through commerce:

REV.13:11 and I beheld another beast (false prophet) coming up out of the earth; and he had two horns like a lamb, and he spake as a dragon (Satan or one of the fallen angels).

REV.13:12 And he exerciseth all the power of the first beast before him, and causeth the earth and them which dwell therein to worship the first beast (The Anti-Christ), whose deadly wound was healed.

REV.13:13 And he doeth great wonders, so that he maketh fire come down from heaven on the earth in the sight of men,

REV.13:14 And deceiveth them that dwell on the earth by the means of those miracles which he had power to do in the sight of the beast; saying to them that dwell on the earth, that they should make an image to the beast, which had the wound by a sword, and did live.

REV.13:15 And he had power to give life unto the image of the beast, that the image of the beast should both speak, and cause that as many as would not worship the image of the beast should be killed.

REV.13:16 And he causeth all, both small and great, rich and poor, free and bond, to receive a mark in their right hand, or in their foreheads:

REV.13:17 And that no man might buy or sell, save he that had the mark, or the name of the beast, or the number of his name.

REV.13:18 Here is wisdom. Let him that hath understanding count the number of the beast: for it is the number of a man (6); and his number is Six hundred threescore and six. 666 = [False Trinity of Man, The Anti-Christ & Satan]

IX THE FEMALE HOLY SPIRIT

MAT.12:31 Wherefore I say unto you, 'All manner of sin and blasphemy shall be forgiven unto men: but the blasphemy against the Holy Ghost shall not be forgiven unto men.'

MAR.3:29-30 But he that shall blaspheme against the Holy Ghost hath never forgiveness, but is in danger of eternal damnation; because they said, He hath an unclean spirit.

LUK.12:10 And whosoever shall speak a word against the Son of man, it shall be forgiven him: but unto him that blasphemes against the Holy Ghost it shall not be forgiven.

Comment: Why did Jesus make a distinction between Himself and the Holy Spirit here? If God and Jesus and the Holy Spirit were all masculine, which is how they are portrayed by most modern churches, then perhaps Jesus would not have made this distinction!

PROTECTION OF A WIFE COMES BEFORE THE PROTECTION OF A SON

A man who has a beautiful wife, whom he both loves and adores, and also has a strong son. If perchance another man comes and gives a blow to his son, it is conceivable that the father will make light of it and forgive the man. However, if the man hits his wife, I guarantee that he would neither forgive him or let him go unpunished. I do think that these above Bible verses prove one thing: The Holy Spirit has got to both feminine and God's wife. Nothing but wrath to those who would hurt and offend her!

GOD THE FATHER, JESUS THE SON & THE HOLY SPIRIT MOTHER.

If you would take all that the Catholics have seen, and heard, and envisioned of Mary, and conceived of her, her glorification as Queen of Heaven, including all the inspired art masterpieces of her etc., I think you would have a pretty good picture of the Holy Spirit as the spiritual mother of Jesus and therefore the wife of God and therefore the mother of the Holy Family, the Holy Trinity. It then all makes sense. In a way, like Jesus is a picture of God, Mary was in a way a picture of the Holy Spirit. That's literally what it means by the Word of God, it means the logo of God, the expression of God, the message of God. We studied that in Greek when I was in Bible college, what a deep meaning there was to the Greek word "logo" which is translated in John 1 as the "word". It was sort of like, the logo was a little bit of God himself, an expression of Him, a manifestation of Him in Jesus his Son.

SOURCE: http://www.peopleofthekeys.com/news/docs/library/Dream+Queen

THE FEMININE HOLY SPIRIT

1) http://www.pistissophia.org/The_Holy_Spirit/the_holy_spirit.html
2) http://www.hts.org.za/index.php/HTS/article/view/3225/html

X THE GIANTS – JOSEPHUS

QUOTES FROM JOSEPHUS CONCERNING GIANTS www.generationword.com

"This notion, that the fallen angels were, in some sense, the fathers of the old giants, was the constant opinion of antiquity, of gods accompanied with women, and begat sons that proved unjust, and despisers of all that was good, on account of the confidence they had in their own strength; for the tradition is, that these men did what resembled the acts of those whom the Grecians call giants."

"These kings had laid waste all Syria and overthrown the offspring of the giants. And when they were come over against Sodom. . ."

"They told them also, that they found at Hebron the posterity of the giants. Accordingly, these spies, who had seen the land of Canaan, when they perceived that all these difficulties were greater there than they had met with since they came out of Egypt, they were affrighted at them themselves, and endeavoured to affright the multitude also."

"For which reason they removed their camp to Hebron; and when they had taken it, they slew all the inhabitants. There were till then left the race of giants, who had bodies so large, and countenances so entirely different from other men, that they were surprising to the sight, and terrible to the hearing. The bones of these men are still shown to this very day, unlike to any credible relations of other men. Now they gave this city to the Levites as an extraordinary reward."

WHY KING DAVID'S MEN MADE DAVID RETIRE FROM BATTLE WHEN HE WAS OLD

"A little afterward the king made war against the Philistines; and when he had joined battle with them, and put them to flight, he was left alone, as he was in pursuit of them; and when he was quite tired down, he was seen by one of the enemy, his name was Achmon, the son of Araph, he was one of the sons of the giants. He had a spear, the handle of which weighed three hundred shekels, and a breastplate of chain-work, and a sword. He turned back and ran violently to slay King David their enemy's king, for he was quite tired out with labour; but Abishai, Joab's brother, appeared suddenly on the scene, and protected the king with his shield, as he lay down, and slew the enemy. Now the multitude were very uneasy at these dangers of the king, and that he was very near to be slain; and the rulers made him swear that he would no more go out with them to battle, lest he should come to some great misfortune by his courage and boldness, and thereby deprive the people of the benefits they now enjoyed by his means, and of those that they might hereafter enjoy by his living a long time among them."

"When the king heard that the Philistines were gathered together at the city Gazara, he sent an army against them, when Sibbechai the Hittite, one of David's most courageous men, behaved himself so as to deserve great commendation, for he slew many of those that bragged they were the posterity of the giants, and vaunted themselves highly on that account, and thereby was the occasion of victory to the Hebrews."

"They had a man who was *six cubits tall and had on each of his feet and hands one more toe and finger than men naturally have*. Now the person who was sent against them by David out of his army was Jonathan, the son of Shimea, who fought this man in a single combat, and slew him; and as he was the person who gave the turn to the battle, he gained the greatest reputation for courage therein. This man also vaunted himself to be of the sons of the giants. But after this fight the Philistines made war no more against the Israelites."

XI CHAPTER 6 DEMONOLOGY 101; GIANTS & GOD'S WRATH: https://youtu.be/F24OP2wjNGA?t=2393

MORE ABOUT THE GIANTS: http://www.outofthebottomlesspit.co.uk/411783108

ENORMOUS SKELETONS: http://www.outofthebottomlesspit.co.uk/411784132

XII WHAT DOES THE BIBLE SAY ABOUT CANNIBALISM WHICH WAS STARTED BY THE GIANTS?: https://www.quora.com/What-does-the-Bible-say-about-cannibalism

XIII KING JAMES BIBLE TIME CHART

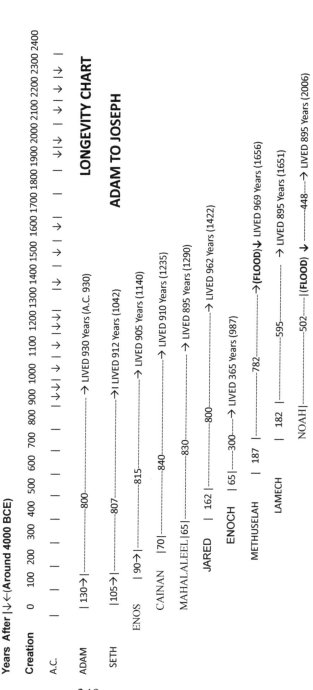

LONGEVITY CHART

ADAM TO JOSEPH

Years After | ↓ ←(Around 4000 BCE)

Creation 0 100 200 300 400 500 600 700 800 900 1000 1100 1200 1300 1400 1500 1600 1700 1800 1900 2000 2100 2200 2300 2400

A.C.

ADAM | 130→| --------800-------- → LIVED 930 Years (A.C. 930)

SETH |105→| --------807-------- →| LIVED 912 Years (1042)

ENOS | 90→| --------815-------- → LIVED 905 Years (1140)

CAINAN |70| --------840-------- → LIVED 910 Years (1235)

MAHALALEEL|65| --------830-------- → LIVED 895 Years (1290)

JARED | 162 | --------800-------- → LIVED 962 Years (1422)

ENOCH | 65 |----300---- → LIVED 365 Years (987)

METHUSELAH | 187 |--------782-------- →(FLOOD)↘ LIVED 969 Years (1656)

LAMECH | 182 |--------595-------- → LIVED 895 Years (1651)

NOAH|--------502--------|(FLOOD) ↓ --------448--------→ LIVED 895 Years (2006)

ARPHAXAD **(FLOOD)** ↓35| ————————403————→ LIVED 438 Years (2096)

SALAH |30| ————403———→ LIVED 433 Years (2126)

EBER |34| ————430——→ LIVED 464 Years (2187)

PELEG|30|209→ LIVED 239 Years (1996)

REU |32|207→ LIVED 239 Years (2026)

SERUG |30|200→ LIVED 230 Years (2049)

NAHOR |29|119→ LIVED 148 Years (1997)

TERAH |70|135→ LIVED 205 Years (2083)

ABRAHAM |100|75→ LIVED 175Years (2123)

ISAAC |60|120→ LIVED 180 Years (2228)

JACOB |91|56→ LIVED 147 Years (2255)

JOSEPH |110→ LIVED 110 Years (2309)

XIV The Book of Jasher – CONCLUSIONS

C.1 Having studied this Jewish Book of Jasher at length, I would state that much of it is inspired, but not all. Having cross-referenced it to both the K.J.V Bible of the O.T and the Septuagint version of the O.T, the strength of the Book of Jasher is in the amazing amount of Pre-Flood information especially about Enoch, as well as the immediate Post-Flood times with Noah, Nimrod and the Tower of Babel. The rest of the stories are very interesting as well, but it would seem that for whatever reason, someone has tampered with this book as to the genealogies. This is something that is mentioned in the New Testament and tells us to beware of:

1TI.1:4 Neither give heed to fables and endless genealogies, which minister questions, rather than godly edifying which is in faith.

MELCHISADEC IS JESUS CHRIST - THE SAVIOUR – THE MESSIAH

C.2 Unfortunately, it also appears that this Book of Jasher has altered the name Melkisadec to Adonizedec. This Book of Jasher even states that this Adonizedec is Shem. This is plain *incorrect* and is evidence that some-one didn't like the New Testament in the Book of Hebrews explaining that Melchisedec was in fact Jesus Christ who met Abraham at the time just after the 'slaughter of the kings.' Adonizedec is the name given to some of the kings of Jerusalem long before King David made Jerusalem his capital city.

HEB.6:20 Whither the forerunner is for us entered, even Jesus, made an high priest for ever after the order of Melchisedec.

HEB.7:1 For this Melchisedec, King of Salem, priest of the most high God, who met Abraham returning from the slaughter of the kings, and blessed him;

HEB.7:2 To whom also Abraham gave a tenth part of all; first being by interpretation King of righteousness, and after that also King of Salem, which is, King of peace;

HEB.7:3 Without father, without mother, without descent, having neither beginning of days, nor end of life; but made like unto the Son of God; abides a priest continually.

C.3 Some of the Jewish leaders didn't like the early Christians mentioning that it was Jesus in the form of Melchisedec who visited Abraham after his victory in the story of the 'slaughter if the kings'.

Sadly, some very influential people have gone to great trouble to both alter the original scriptures of both the Book of Jasher and the Old Testament part of the King James Bible.

C.4 According to the Septuagint, assembled in circa 300 B.C by 70 learned Hebrew Scholars, Abraham wasn't alive at the same time as Shem or Noah, so why does this Jewish Book of Jasher claim that it was Shem who Abraham met and who was Adonizedec (Melchisedec), if Abraham wasn't alive at the same time as Shem? This is clearly a deception!

C.5 The Leaders of the Jews didn't accept Jesus as their Messiah, and in their hatred of both Christ and Christianity, some of their forefathers had the power to both influence & to alter different passages of excellent original books such as the Book of Jasher and later they made sure that the Masoretic text was used in the Old Testament of the King James Bible instead of the much older and Original Hebrew text or even the Greek text of the Septuagint. Why? It was apparently all done to prove that Jesus was not Melchisedec who met Abraham as reported in the Book of Hebrews in the New Testament.

C.6 Unlike in the Masoretic translation of the Old testament which we have in our King James Bibles, I would like to add that the Book of Jasher is not even mentioned in the Septuagint version of **JOSHUA 10:12 &13,** or In **2 Samuel 1:18-27**, but only a reference to the **'Book of Right' in 2 Samuel**. Is it just possible that someone had the references to the Book of Jasher added to the Masoretic Text in order to endorse the Book of Jasher and in particular the story of Melchisedec being Shem?

C.7 In Conclusion: It is sad to see what would have been an excellent book in the form of the Book of Jasher has been corrupted. Why? Because of hatred and spite against both Christ and Christianity. The same goes for the Masoretic text used for the Old Testament in the Bible.

C.8 In order that people don't come to the wrong conclusions, it would be wiser for them to read the Septuagint version of the Old Testament which is more reliable than the Masoretic text, upon which the Old Testament in the K.J.V of the Bible is based.- with the exception of the altered TIME-LINE right after the Great Flood where someone has added 100 years to the lives of the Patriarchs. The question is why someone tampered with the otherwise excellent Septuagint. Read on to find out *why*?

XV BIBLICAL & SEPTUAGINT LXX LONGEVITY CHARTS

C.1 Which is correct? That we are living in circa the year 6000 according to the KJV of the Bible, or somewhere around the year 6700-7000 according to the Septuagint LXX version of the Old Testament?

THE OTHER SIDE OF THE STORy

AN ODD TWIST CONCERNING THE SEPTUAGINT

C.2 The 72 Jewish scholars were living in Alexandria in Egypt, when it was the Southern ¼th Segment of the Greek Empire, at the time that they translated the Septuagint from ancient Hebrew into Greek. The Pharaoh was apparently very proud of the amazing monolithic structures in Egypt including the pyramids and wanted to give Egypt the full credit for building them. But how could he do that?

C.3 What if those who put together the Septuagint LXX were asked to add 100 years to 6 of the Patriarchs from Arphaxad to Nahor? Why? In order to deliberately push back the biblical 'Time-Line' in favour of the Egyptians who claimed to have built the pyramids, but in fact it would seem that the *pyramids were actually built by a super-race prior to the Great Flood from all the evidence.*

C.4 'Is it just possible that 'The Pharaoh' who was apparently financing the writing of the Septuagint, simply asked the 72 men to do him *one favour* and that was to add 100 years to six of the Patriarchs thus *pushing back the annals of time itself,* so that it *would appear that the Pyramids had been built by the Egyptians* around 5000 years ago, which was actually 500 years before the Great Flood in circa 4500 years ago, as mentioned in the K.J.V of the Bible.' The above writing is the inspiration I received when I asked God: Who is right about the Longevity Chart: The Masoretic Text used in the King James, or the much older Septuagint?

C.5 The oldest books on earth are from India and dated as 5000 years old. They describe in great detail the gods and the demi-gods and their 'golden age' before the great Flood. This is when Atlantis and Lemuria and the land of Mu all existed. Cultures with very advanced technology, but technologies that were developed in different ways than our own of today. There are many things that these ancient cultures were capable of doing that even modern man still cannot yet do.

C.6 What I was inspired to receive, shocked me, that those who put the Septuagint together compromised, because of the wishes of Pharaoh, and the fact that the 72 Jewish scholars were guests in his court. Another strange difference in the Septuagint LXX is that it places an extra person called Cainan as the son of Arphaxad instead of Salah. In the Septuagint it states that Salah was the son of Cainan. However, in all the other translations ever found, Cainan is not mentioned? Why would the authors of the Septuagint seemingly deliberately add another person to the TIMELINE? One reason is it would push back the Time-line even further back: But what was the real motive? Why would 72 'Wise men' 'add in' an extra person such as Cainan, apart from to please Pharaoh? What if they actually knew back then that other 'wise men' coming later in time would quickly recognise that something was 'out of place' in the translation of the text? Maybe the 'wise men' who put together the Septuagint LXX were sending a message to future 'illuminated wise men'. Also, why add a person called Cainan after the Great Flood to the Timeline, when there was another Cainan before the Great Flood who was fourth generation from Adam? Sounds a bit out of place to say the least! Perhaps that is why some later translations altered the Septuagint's version on the Longevity Chart? Amazingly, the following confirms this inspiration that I received some 3 months ago:

C.7 'The oldest and most important translation of the Hebrew Old Testament (OT) is the Septuagint (LXX). It translated the Hebrew into Greek in the third century BC in Alexandria, Egypt. The Letter to Aristide tells the story how the Egyptian king Ptolemy II (285-247 BC) ordered his librarian, Demetrius to collect all the books of the world. Demetrius thought there should be a Greek translation of the Torah so 72 Jews, six from each tribe, were sent to translate the Torah into Greek which they did in 72 days *Larsson believes that the translators of the LXX tried to harmonize the Biblical chronology with the Egyptian chronology of Manetho by adding 100 years to the patri- archs ages to push back the time of the flood before the first Egyptian dynasty because there is no record of a great flood.* Early Christian chro- nologists emphasized the perfect agreement of Manetho with the LXX (Larsson, 403-4). It is interesting to see how they understood Genesis by the way they translated the text.'

SOURCE: https://www.bibleandscience.com/bible/books/genesis/gene-sisl1.htm

XVI MAPS OF ANCIENT ISRAEL & SURROUNDING KINGDOMS:

MAP OF ISRAEL'S JOURNEY FROM EGYPT TO THE PROMISED LAND: http://classic.scriptures.lds.org/en/biblemaps/2

MAP OF NATIONS SURROUNDING ANCIENT ISRAEL: Phoenicians, Assyrians, Egyptians, Chittim, Horites, Canaanites, Mesopotamia,Babylon Hittites, Midianites, Land Of Goshen: http://classic.scriptures.lds.org/en/biblemaps/9

MAP SHOWING LOCATION OF AMMONITIES, MOABITES & EDOMITIES: http://classic.scriptures.lds.org/en/biblemaps/1

XVII CONTINUED FROM CHAPTER 34

C.23 Why did God end up judging Israel so strongly In the Diaspora in 70 A.D? It is hardly surprising because they went and **killed their own Messiah Jesus Christ** and God's wrath came upon them in no uncertain terms. The Jews were driven away from Israel for almost 2000 years. That is some great judgement. Why did God judge Israel so severely as he obviously did? The answer is that they should have known better and not killed their own Messiah who had been prophesied by all of the Jewish prophets. So, they were really without an excuse.

C.24 Jesus the Messiah and the greatest of all warriors prophesied that Israel would be judged because they had rejected Him as their Messiah

MAT.23:29 Woe unto you, scribes and Pharisees, hypocrites! because ye build the tombs of the prophets, and garnish the sepulchres of the righteous,

MAT.23:30 And say, If we had been in the days of our fathers, we would not have been partakers with them in the blood of the prophets.

MAT.23:31 Wherefore ye be witnesses unto yourselves, that ye are the children of them which killed the prophets.

MAT.23:32 Fill ye up then the measure of your fathers.

MAT.23:33 Ye serpents, ye generation of vipers, how can ye escape the damnation of hell?

MAT.23:34 Wherefore, behold, I send unto you prophets, and wise men, and scribes: and some of them ye shall kill and crucify; and some of them shall ye scourge in your synagogues, and persecute them from city to city:

MAT.23:35 That upon you may come all the righteous blood shed upon the earth, from the blood of righteous Abel unto the blood of Zacharias son of Barachias, whom ye slew between the temple and the altar.

MAT.23:36 Verily I say unto you, All these things shall come upon this generation.

MAT.23:37 O Jerusalem, Jerusalem, thou that killest the prophets, and stonest them which are sent unto thee, how often would I have gathered thy children together, even as a hen gathereth her chickens under her wings, and ye would not!

MAT.23:38 Behold, your house is left unto you desolate.

MAT.23:39 For I say unto you, Ye shall not see me henceforth, till ye shall say, 'Blessed is he that cometh in the name of the Lord'.

C.25 The fact is exactly 40 years after Jesus prophesied these things to the Pharisee leaders of Israel, Israel was totally destroyed by the Romans as it was the time of the Wrath of God against Israel.

C.26 CONCLUSION: WHAT WAS GOD'S PURPOSE WITH 2000 YEARS OF JEWISH HISTORY FROM 2000 BCE UNTIL CHRIST?

God's purpose with the nation of Israel was to try to set an example and to teach other nations to follow God. Unfortunately, if we study the entire history of Israel up until the Messiah Jesus, we find that most of Israel's kings were classified by the Bible itself as evil. Very few of Israel's kings were dedicated to God. After 2000 years of its history Israel had become a very bad example to the nations and they topped their crimes by killing their own Messiah which has cost them dearly.

C.27 THE GREAT IMPORTANCE OF JESUS THE MESSIAH

JOH.1:17 For the law was given by Moses, but grace and truth came by Jesus Christ.

Moses and all those leading Israel up until the Messiah took the sword in hand and fought and slaughtered their enemies. When the Messiah came, He taught His disciples something completely different:

MAT.5:43 Ye have heard that it hath been said, Thou shalt love thy neighbour, and hate thine enemy.

MAT.5:44 But I say unto you, Love your enemies, bless them that curse you, do good to them that hate you, and pray for them which despitefully use you, and persecute you;

MAT.5:45 That ye may be the children of your Father which is in heaven: for he maketh his sun to rise on the evil and on the good, and sendeth rain on the just and on the unjust.

MAT.5:46 For if ye love them which love you, what reward have ye? do not even the publicans the same?

MAT.5:47 And if ye salute your brethren only, what do ye more than others? do not even the publicans so?

MAT.5:48 Be ye therefore perfect, even as your Father which is in heaven is perfect.

C.28 Of course all the early disciples of Christ and those who started the spread of Christianity were all Jewish and dedicated ones like Paul. It was difficult from them to unlearn the ways of Moses and the very strict laws such as 'an eye for an eye' 'a tooth for a tooth' etc. Through Jesus the Christians learned about God's forgiveness and mercy. They learnt that it is not by good works that we obtain righteousness and get to heaven. It is all by the Grace of God through his son the Messiah – Jesus Christ.

EPH.2:8 For by grace are ye saved through faith; and that not of yourselves: it is the gift of God:

EPH.2:9 Not of works, lest any man should boast.

2CO.5:17 Therefore if any man be in Christ, he is a new creature: old things are passed away; behold, all things are become new.

2CO.5:18 And all things are of God, who hath reconciled us to himself by Jesus Christ, and hath given to us the ministry of reconciliation;

2CO.5:19 To wit, that God was in Christ, reconciling the world unto himself, not imputing their trespasses unto them; and hath committed unto us the word of reconciliation.

2CO.5:20 Now then we are ambassadors for Christ, as though God did beseech you by us: we pray you in Christ's stead, be ye reconciled to God.

2CO.5:21 For he hath made him to be sin for us, who knew no sin; that we might be made the righteousness of God in him.

C.29 The job of all Christians is to preach the gospel about Jesus Christ and to also warn the world of its coming destruction for its wickedness

MAR.16:15 And he said unto them, Go ye into all the world, and preach the gospel to every creature.

MAR.16:16 He that believeth and is baptized shall be saved; but he that believeth not shall be damned.

C.30 Our job as Christians is also to warn the world of its coming Destruction for its wickedness

EZE.3:17 Son of man, I have made thee a watchman unto the house of Israel: therefore hear the word at my mouth and give them warning from me.

EZE.3:18 When I say unto the wicked, Thou shalt surely die; and thou givest him not warning, nor speakest to warn the wicked from his wicked way, to save his life; the same wicked man shall die in his iniquity; but his blood will I require at thine hand.

EZE.3:19 Yet if thou warn the wicked, and he turn not from his wickedness, nor from his wicked way, he shall die in his iniquity; but thou hast delivered thy soul.

XVII 'TOTAL TIME' OF ISRAEL IN CAPTIVITY:

Please read my other book '**JUBILEES INSIGHTS**' which has Charts and exact dates, which actually point out that the '430 years of the Jews being in Captivity' in Egypt, actually started with Abraham having a son called Ismael of an Egyptian woman who afflicted his biological son Isaac. The traditional **AGE OF THE EARTH** Timeframe Chart shows the '430 years of bondage of the Jews' starting when Jacob went down to Egypt. If we take this into consideration and take the date of Jacob entering into Egypt and compare it to the time of Abraham there is a discrepancy of 215 years!

XVIII FINAL CONCLUSION:

It would appear that the K J Version of the Bible is after all more accurate when it comes to the generations born after the Great Flood. After all, God did predict that He would cut man's years short to only 120 years and eventually that went down to 70. If these final conclusions are correct, then the earth is closer to 6000-years old than 7000. With what I hope is all the evidence in, you decide which you think is more likely to be correct concerning this one?

MY *FIVE BOOKS* IN ORDER OF PUBLICATION:

1) OUT OF THE BOTTOMLESS PIT: http://www.outofthebottomlesspit.co.uk/411702511

2) ENOCH INSIGHTS: http://www.outofthebottomlesspit.co.uk/418666481

3) EZDRAS INSIGHTS: http://www.outofthebottomlesspit.co.uk/420942154

4) JASHER INSIGHTS: http://www.outofthebottomlesspit.co.uk/421385649

5) JUBILEES INSIGHTS: http://www.outofthebottomlesspit.co.uk/413438217

USEFUL WEBSITE LINKS:

BIBLICAL CREATION: http://www.outofthebottomlesspit.co.uk/421607713

WORD WARRIORS: http://www.outofthebottomlesspit.co.uk/420555449

THE 4 HORSEMEN: http://www.outofthebottomlesspit.co.uk/412514886

HEAVEN: http://www.outofthebottomlesspit.co.uk/412320663

LIFE AFTER DEATH: http://www.outofthebottomlesspit.co.uk/412645521

BOOK OF DANIEL: http://www.outofthebottomlesspit.co.uk/420616689

BOOK OF REVELATION: http://www.outofthebottomlesspit.co.uk/421238965

MARK OF THE BEAST: http://www.outofthebottomlesspit.co.uk/412733219

SIGNS OF THE TIMES: http://www.outofthebottomlesspit.co.uk/413019004

SIGNS: http://www.outofthebottomlesspit.co.uk/418801558

BABYLON THE GREAT: http://www.outofthebottomlesspit.co.uk/412306605

ABOUT THE AUTHOR: http://www.outofthebottomlesspit.co.uk/413469553

AUTHOR AT AMAZON: www.amazon.com/author/777.7

FACE-BOOK: GROUP: ENOCH INSIGHTS: https://www.facebook.com/groups/323412114853716/

My website: www.outofthebottomlesspit.co.uk

E-mail: strangetruths@outofthebottomlesspit.co.uk